Bluegrass Cavalcade

UNIVERSITY OF KENTUCKY PRESS

Lexington   1956

Edited by THOMAS D. CLARK

Bluegrass
Cavalcade

Publication of this book is possible partly because of a grant
from the Margaret Voorhies Haggin Trust established in
memory of her husband James Ben Ali Haggin.

The University Press of Kentucky
Scholarly publisher for the Commonwealth,
serving Bellarmine University, Berea College, Centre
College of Kentucky, Eastern Kentucky University,
The Filson Historical Society, Georgetown College,
Kentucky Historical Society, Kentucky State University,
Morehead State University, Murray State University,
Northern Kentucky University, Transylvania University,
University of Kentucky, University of Louisville,
and Western Kentucky University.
All rights reserved.

Editorial and Sales Offices: The University Press of Kentucky
663 South Limestone Street, Lexington, Kentucky 40508-4008
www.kentuckypress.com

Cataloging-in-Publication Data is available from
the Library of Congress.

ISBN 978-0-8131-9275-8 (pbk: acid-free paper)

This book is printed on acid-free recycled paper meeting
the requirements of the American National Standard
for Permanence in Paper for Printed Library Materials.

Manufactured in the United States of America.

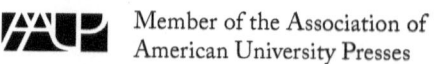 Member of the Association of
American University Presses

Dedicated to
J. WINSTON COLEMAN, JR.
Bluegrass Historian and Author

Table of Contents

Editor's Introduction

ONCE BLUEGRASS Kentucky was an Indian hunting ground. Here buffalo, elk, and deer flocked to its grassy meadows. In the latter half of the eighteenth century longhunters from the Carolinas and Virginia came seeking adventure in the country which both Indians and adventurers had described. Following them came settlers displaying energy never before seen in a new country. For almost fifty years after 1775, people climbed through Cumberland Gap and trudged up the Wilderness Road to the rich meadowland across the Kentucky River. Flatboats drifted homeseekers downriver from the northeast to spread over the Bluegrass. Here was a land where obvious opportunities prompted quick exploitation.

In this frontier vanguard imaginative authors were stirred to create a vigorous literature of pioneering. One was young Felix Walker, who helped Daniel Boone blaze the Wilderness Trail. He felt himself a missionary of empire building. His is a happy account of entering virgin country—happy, that is, until an arrow exposed Kentucky's treachery.

Kentucky was the first long rest on the path westward. It became a place of new beginnings. Land was fresh, and everything a man did made a mark. Felling a tree gapped the forest; a cabin in a clearing was a first house for miles around. A ripening field of grain was a first bread crop.

By their firesides, pioneer women wove the first Kentucky cloth, knit the first stockings, and rocked first-born babes. Kentucky was in fact a great loom on which a stout warp of pioneering was strung to be finished off with the brighter woof of civilized refinement. In early Kentucky, men boasted of their ability to tame the wilderness. They conceived being first to do things a particular accomplishment. Bluegrass literature is fairly sprinkled with "first" and "biggest" things. Achievements and possessions often became only comparatively important. A good horse, a beautiful daughter, a faithful wife, had only limited significance. Only the "best" was worth possessing, and the world has been a small place when Kentuckians have assessed their values.

A steep mountain range with its foothill barriers separated Kentucky from the older world. Love of that older world, however, was brought overland. Though George III and his crown officials embittered the pioneers with the encouragement of Indian raids, Bluegrass Kentuckians have always loved things English. In rolling vales they harmonized this ancient love of civilization with their new mode of life.

Pioneering in Kentucky was indeed a great experiment in national expansion. The country was a conditioning place where a backwoods democracy readied itself for greater conquests. Proud authors wrote of their pioneering. Scores of visitors saw the country firsthand and wrote home to encourage immigration. Geography placed it on the foreigner's "Grand Tour" of America, and most major travel accounts include a description of the Bluegrass, thus comprising a considerable volume of literature.

As sycamores grew tall along the Bluegrass streams, so grew some of the region's sons in popular estimation. But tallest of all Bluegrass sons was Henry Clay. This Virginia mill boy followed the pioneers up the Wilderness Trail to begin a meager law practice in Lexington. As bright young lawyer, eloquent campaigner, persuasive warhawk and statesman, he succeeded in the Bluegrass. In time he typified Kentucky personality. He became a subject of street-corner and country-lane conversation, and his name found its way into much Bluegrass literature. He became a Kentucky hero without benefit of military glory. In short, for almost a hundred and fifty years he has been one of the best biographical entries in the paddock for the main stake race of local history.

While Henry Clay became the Bluegrass' statesman, slavery became its great source of controversy. It was pleasant to drive down country lanes between rows of flowering locust, and across Bluegrass meadows pregnant with spring harvest. Hemp, corn, and broad-leaved tobacco crowded up to promise future wealth. These smiling fields captivated Stephen Collins Foster in his famous song. His song, however, had a second and less happy stanza. So did Bluegrass slavery. Men questioned whether this land which promised freedom so abundantly should also nourish slavery. Schoolboy Cassius M. Clay, home from Yale in the early thirties, was later to raise a voice of protest in his newspaper, the *True American*. Perhaps Bluegrass slaveowners would have tolerated this attack had their courage not been challenged by the dramatics of editor Clay's well-stocked arsenal. The *True American* was hauled out of Lexington, but the wild seeds of discontent over slavery were scattered too widely to be gathered by hotheads who did not comprehend the sacredness of freedom of the press.

Harriet Beecher Stowe's *Uncle Tom's Cabin* made an even louder accusation against slavery. Entrenched Bluegrass owners could neither haul away the book nor lay hands on its author. The book was far too widely dispersed to be loaded up like a newspaper press and sent away. Mrs. Stowe aimed a deadly blow at the Bluegrass master. She gave her first major character the great name of Shelby, and she described Kentucky slavery as a source for inhumane slave trading. This was a harsh indictment of Bluegrass slavery, and was a landmark in the long struggle to destroy the institution.

When war came Kentuckians were divided in sentiment. Boyish horsemen galloped away from the Bluegrass with Morgan to fight for the South, but less dramatic sons joined the Union army. The subsequent war made good copy. Such intense and fratricidal strife developed well-defined sides which were supported by their respective literary interpreters. In subsequent years there were those who wrote of the war as an emotional incident, plumbing the depths of human reactions to serve a chapter in Kentucky history.

War left turmoil behind it in the Bluegrass. Almost before the last soldier was home from battle, nostalgic authors were writing of ante bellum life. James Lane Allen impounded the ancient spirit of his Bluegrass neighbors in books which spoke reverently of earlier days. He sensed frustration in this new age, and his warnings were those of a sensitive man who thought he saw his generation running headlong into social change and confusion. For him there were few contemporary values in civilization. The pulpit had become the stand of bigotry and the merchant's counter a serving shelf for materialism. Even Lexington streets appeared inhospitable to leisurely men who once visited there with their neighbors.

The new Bluegrass was a place of growth. The region's social isolation was broken with the influx of mountaineers and southerners who, as new pioneers, came to improve their conditions of life. Where once slaves labored in the fields, free white men now sought a livelihood. With these changes newer horizons stood revealed. The world for Kentuckians grew larger. George D. Prentice lay in his grave, and Henry Watterson presided over the marriage bed of the *Courier* and *Journal*. Most old line Whigs and Democrats had joined Prentice, and Watterson spoke of a "new departure" in politics. A scattering of Republican editors bespoke their Yankee doctrine in the Bluegrass. In many ways the bottom rail was laid on top, but the Bluegrass gave in to outside influences only as it was forced to do so. Its people liked a settled routine of life. There was no fear of getting in a rut or becoming fossilized. Certain modes of life were regarded as constants, and if these changed with the seasons, then there was no human stability.

It is of this pattern of life that an army of authors has written of the Bluegrass. In selecting material for this volume an effort has been made to preserve a flavor which portrays the growth of a region where people have always been conscious of their individuality. Goodness of writing becomes merely a relative factor in these selections. A bit of writing is considered good because it gives a sense of the immediate present in a particular period in the Bluegrass story. Little writers, primitive writers, partisan authors, all find themselves in company with those who achieved wider recognition for their ability to write of the Bluegrass. It has been with genuine reluctance that many selections and the writings of many authors were bypassed. Other selections might be as effective in telling the Bluegrass story.

The writings of a region actually constitute its documentary history. Selections in this volume document more eloquently life of the Bluegrass than would formal official documents and deadly statistics. The reader is given a close insight into the minds and habits of writers and readers. Bluegrass pride and its misdoings are treated with equality. Hundreds of books and pamphlets embalm the Bluegrass story, but these are rare and scattered. The modern reader, even where he has a library available, has scarce access to many of these materials.

Bluegrass traditions are often warped and perverted by the distance between conveyor and source. Authors who have used the Bluegrass' history as grist to their mills have touched the subject with interest and care. Even in telling the hazards of their own lives or their shortcomings, they have not hesitated to be realistic. Kentucky history centers in the Bluegrass; this is not to say that the rest of Kentucky does not have a rich story, but chronologically the beginning was here. Too, Bluegrass history can scarcely be separated from the rest of the state. Boonesboro and Harrodsburg, Henry Clay and Elizabeth Madox Roberts are the cherished possessions of all Kentuckians. Jane Todd Crawford and Dr. Ephraim McDowell stood in for humanity. It is a great matter of local pride that they did so in Kentucky.

It is the hope of the editor that he has selected enough of the Bluegrass story to give his mature reader a taste of the rich regional flavor and to bring to the hands of the youthful reader an introduction to Kentucky history. Among the selections included in this volume is represented a small army of distinguished authors who have viewed Kentucky from various perspectives. This volume is meant to be a literary and historical reception where these writers are assembled to meet their readers.

BOOK ONE

The Promised Land

$\mathcal{T}$HOMAS WALKER saw in the woods of eastern Kentucky some hint of the promised land, though he failed to come within eyeshot of the Bluegrass. Boone went home from his lonely wanderings twenty years after Walker's visit to tell his North Carolina neighbors of the rich Eden which awaited their exploitation. In 1775 when Daniel led his trailblazing party to Boonesboro to begin settlement, he had as a companion young Felix Walker from Virginia. In language which portended the writings of James Lane Allen, young Walker gave a glowing account of the vaulted forest land.

Eden was to become a theme of the great Bluegrass plateau which produced grass and trees in abundance. This was a country where nature had been prodigal with its blessings: water, soil, climate, vegetation, and animal life. All a man had to do to make a living was to scratch the ground, drop some corn, and sit back and wait for the harvest. That at least is what the early promoters said.

As accounts of the rich land passed from mouth to mouth, the Bluegrass became more attractive than the Biblical promise of a delightful hereafter. The first pioneers kept diaries and

journals, and occasionally wrote letters back home to describe
the new lands of Kentucky, but it was their words that filled
the trails with immigrants. Revolutionary soldiers rushed west
to claim bounty lands. Church members came in traveling con-
gregations to make new beginnings in an atmosphere free of
stifling politics.

In 1784 John Filson set the pattern for thousands of Bluegrass boosters of the future. His little book, calling itself history, was a eulogy of the land and its famous citizen, Daniel
Boone. Gilbert Imlay took up where Filson left off. His work
differed from Filson's because he actually saw settlers evolve
into Bluegrass citizens. He saw their farms and towns organized, and the beginnings of a culture which matured rapidly.

Almost as soon as the first fire was built in the earliest Bluegrass cabin, visitors came to see the fabulous land of Boone
and Walker, of Henderson and Filson, and they were inspired
to record their impressions. The Bluegrass was a stop on what
became the "Grand Tour" of foreign travelers to America. In
a sense these charitable visitors became the early historians of
the Bluegrass. Their accounts take up the Eden theme in lock-
step with the natives, and their books had much to do with the
rapid growth of Bluegrass communities.

Ordinary adjectives were inadequate to describe the Bluegrass. There were no American lands with which the region
could be compared, only the remote Biblical paradise seemed
to equal this geographical wonderland of the frontier. "Gosh-
en," "Eden," and the "Promised Land" of Moses came nearer
describing this sprawling plateau of the West. Henry Clay,
Timothy Flint, James Lane Allen, Grant C. Knight, and Bernard Mayo have continued the tradition of beatification of the
region.

In less factual writings a perennial crop of authors fill the
promotional magazines and Sunday supplements with their
songs of praise. Promoters of all kind who eye the cash register
as well as the inviting scenery sing of the magic charms of their
Bluegrass Eden in terms of commercial crops, sporting, liquor,

and women. They have only surface concepts of the region; unlike the serious writers they have never cut into the heart of the subject to appraise its maturity or its history. They agree readily with Timothy Flint that the Bluegrass is "a heaven of a place."

JOHN FILSON

JOHN FILSON (1753-1788) came westward seeking opportunities as academy master and surveyor; he was even interested in land speculation. The Kentucky frontier captivated him, and he used his literary talents to write of the country and its great hero Daniel Boone. The Filson narrative, The Discovery, Settlement and Present State of Kentucke *(Wilmington, Del., 1784), is defective, of course, but the fact that it established the Boone legend so thoroughly in American history makes it significant. Filson was not so far away from the scenes of his subject that he could not talk with the actors, and he sensed firsthand the excitement of his times.*

With Joy and Wonder

THE FIRST white man we have certain accounts of, who discovered this province, was one James M'Bride, who, in company with some others, in the year 1754, passing down the Ohio in Canoes, landed at the mouth of Kentucke river, and there marked a tree, with the first letters of his name, and the date, which remain to this day. These men reconnoitred the country, and returned home with the pleasing news of their discovery of the best tract of land in North-America, and probably in the world. From this period it remained concealed till about the year 1767, when one John Finley, and some others, trading with the Indians, fortunately travelled over the fertile region, now called Kentucke, then but known to the Indians, by the name of the Dark and Bloody Ground, and sometimes the Middle Ground. This country greatly engaged Mr. Finley's attention. Some time after, disputes arising between the Indians and traders, he was obliged to decamp; and returned to his place of residence in North-Carolina, where he communicated his discovery to Col. Daniel Boon, and a few more, who conceiving it to be an interesting object, agreed in the year 1769 to undertake a journey in order to explore it. After a long fatiguing march, over a mountainous wilderness, in a westward direction, they at length arrived upon its borders; and from the top of an eminence, with joy and wonder, descried the beautiful landscape of Kentucke. Here they encamped, and some went to hunt provisions, which were readily procured, there being plenty of game, while Col. Boon and John Finley made a tour through the country, which they found far exceeding their expectations, and returning to camp, informed their companions of their discoveries: But in spite of this promising beginning, this company, meeting with nothing but hardships and adversity, grew exceedingly disheartened, and was plundered, dispersed, and killed by the Indians, except Col. Boon, who continued an inhabitant of the wilderness until the year 1771, when he returned home.

FELIX WALKER

YOUNG Felix Walker (1753-1828), lying wounded after the skirmish of Twetty's Defeat, was on the edge of the promised land. Indians and hunters had spread the fame of the region

*far and wide; here was to be the land of the pioneers. Who
cannot forgive this impressionable youth, full of gratitude for
the preservation of his life, for indulging in hyperbole!*

*Long before Walker enriched the vocabulary of politics by
"speaking for Buncombe" in Congress, he wrote a narrative of
his experiences with Boone in Kentucky in 1775. This account
was preserved by his son, who published it in* De Bow's Review
in 1854.

A New Sky and Strange Earth

ON LEAVING that [Rockcastle] river, we had to encounter and
cut our way through a country of about 20 miles, entirely covered with dead brush, which we found a difficult and laborious
task. At the end of which we arrived at the commencement of
a cane country, traveled about 30 miles through thick cane and
reed, and as the cane ceased, we began to discover the pleasing
and rapturous appearance of the plains of Kentucky. A new
sky and strange earth seemed to be presented to our view. So
rich a soil we had never seen before; covered with clover in
full bloom, the woods were abounding with wild game—turkeys so numerous that it might be said they appeared but one
flock, universally scattered in the woods. It appeared that nature, in the profusion of her bounty, had spread a feast for all
that lives, both for the animal and rational world. A sight so
delightful to our view and grateful to our feelings, almost inclined us, in imitation of Columbus, in transport to kiss the
soil of Kentucky, as he hailed and saluted the sand on his first
setting his foot on the shores of America. The appearance of
the country coming up to the full measure of our expectations,
and seemed to exceed the fruitful source of our imaginary
prospects.

We felt ourselves as passengers through a wilderness just ar-

rived at the fields of Elysium, or at a garden where was no
forbidden fruit. Nothing can furnish the contemplative mind
with more sublime reflections, than nature unbroken by art;
we can there trace the wisdom of the Great Architect in the
construction of his works in nature's simplicity, which, when
he had finished, he pronounced all good. But, alas! fond man!
the vision of a moment made dream of a dream, and shadow
of a shade! Man may appoint, but One greater than man can
disappoint. A sad reverse overtook us two days after, on our
way to Kentucky river. On the 25th March, 1775, we were
fired on by the Indians, in our camp asleep, about an hour
before day. Captain Twetty was shot in both knees, and died
the third day after. A black man, his body servant, killed dead;
myself badly wounded; our company dispersed. So fatal and
tragical an event cast a deep gloom of melancholy over all our
prospects, and high calculations of long life and happy days in
our newly-discovered country were prostrated; hope vanished
from the most of us, and left us suspended in the tumult of
uncertainty and conjecture. Col. Boon, and a few others, appeared to possess firmness and fortitude. In our calamitous
situation, a circumstance occurred one morning after our mis-
fortunes, that proved the courage and stability of our few remaining men (for some had gone back). One of our men,
who had run off at the fire of the Indians on our camp, was
discovered peeping from behind a tree, by a black woman belonging to Colonel Callaway, while gathering small wood. She
ran in, and gave the alarm of Indians. Colonel Boon instantly
caught his rifle, ordered the few men to form, take trees, and
give battle, and not to run till they saw him fall. They formed
agreeably to his directions, and I believe they would have
fought with equal bravery to any Spartan band ever brought
to the field of action, when the man behind the tree announced
his name, and came in. My situation was critical and dangerous, being then a youth, three hundred miles from white inhabitants. My friend and guardian, Captain Twetty, taken

dead from my side, my wounds pronounced by some to be mortal, produced very serious reflections. Yet withal I retained firmness to support me under the pressure of distress, and did not suffer me to languish in depression of mind.

But where shall I begin, or where can I end, in thanks and grateful acknowledgments to that benign and merciful Protector who spared and preserved me in the blaze of danger and in the midst of death! I trust I shall remember that singular and protecting event, with filial sensations of gratitude, while I retain my recollection. We remained at the same place twelve days; I could not be removed sooner without the danger of instant death. At length I was carried in a litter between two horses, twelve miles, to Kentucky river, where we made a station, and called it Boonsborough, situated in a plain on the south side of the river, wherein was a lick with two sulphur springs strongly impregnated. On entering the plain we were permitted to view a very interesting and romantic sight. A number of buffaloes, of all sizes, supposed to be between two and three hundred, made off from the lick in every direction; some running, some walking, others loping slowly and carelessly, with young calves playing, skipping, and bounding through the plain. Such a sight some of us never saw before, nor perhaps never may again. But to proceed, Colonel Richard Henderson, Colonel Luttrell, from North Carolina; Captain Wm. Cock, since the Honorable Judge Cock, of Tennessee, and Colonel Thomas Slaughter, of Virginia, arrived in the month of April with a company of about thirty men. Our military forces, when united, numbered about sixty or sixty-five men, expert riflemen. We lived plentifully on wild meat, buffalo, bear, deer, and turkey, without bread or salt, generally in good health, until the month of July, when I left the country.

Colonel Richard Henderson, being the chief proprietor in the purchase of the bloody ground (indeed so to us), acted as Governor, called an assembly, by election of members, out of our small numbers; organized a government, convened the assembly in May, 1775, consisting of eighteen members, exclusive of the speaker, passed several laws for the regulation of our little community, well adapted to the policy of an infant government.

This assembly was held under two shade trees, in the plains of Boonsborough. This was the first feature of civilization ever attempted in what is now called the Western Country.

This small beginning, that little germ of policy, by a few adventurers from North Carolina, has given birth to the now flourishing State of Kentucky. From that period the population increased with such rapidity, that in less than twenty years it became a State.

GILBERT IMLAY

GILBERT IMLAY'S A Topographical Description of the Western Territory of North America *(London, 1792) may well be regarded as one of the most interesting books about the early period in Kentucky history. Gilbert Imlay (1754-1828) came from New Jersey to Kentucky in 1784, and a year later he left the state. No doubt he was involved in some way in the various western conspiracies which brought many strange characters to Kentucky. Whether or not Imlay wrote his letters while actually in Kentucky has little or no bearing on their nature from the standpoint of interest. His powers of observation were well developed, and the information contained in his letters is full enough to bring early Kentucky life into sharp focus. As for Imlay himself, he lived to become a prominent figure in French society and politics, and his treatment of Mary Wollstonecraft became an international story of infidelity.*

This Delectable Region

In some of my first letters I gave you an account of the first settlement of this country. The perturbed state of that period, and the savage state of the country, which was one entire wilderness, made the object of the first emigrants that of security and sustenance, which produced the scheme of several families living together in what were called Stations. These stations were a kind of quadrangular, or sometimes oblong forts, formed by building log-houses connectedly only leaving openings for gate-ways to pass as they might have occasion. They were generally fixed in a favourable situation for water, and in a body of good land. Frequently the head of some party of connections who had a settlement and pre-emption right, seized upon these opportunities to have his land cleared, which was necessary for the support of the station; for, it was not only prudent to keep close in their forts at times, but it was also necessary to keep their horses and cows up, otherwise the Indians would carry off the horses, and shoot and destroy the cattle.

Under such circumstances, the first settlement of Kentucky was formed, which soon opened a considerable quantity of land in the county of Lincoln, which lies in the upper part of the state, and contiguous to the wilderness, which ends in this delectable region.

As the country gained strength, the stations began to break up in that part of the country, and their inhabitants to spread themselves, and settle upon their respective estates. But the embarrassment they were in for most of the conveniences of life, did not admit of their building any other houses but of logs, and of opening fields in the most expeditious way for planting the Indian corn; the only grain which was cultivated at that time.

A log-house is very soon erected, and in consequence of the friendly disposition which exists among those hospitable people, every neighbour flew to the assistance of each other upon occasions of emergency. Sometimes they were built of round logs entirely, covered with rived ash shingles, and the interstices stopped with clay, or lime and sand, to keep out the weather. The next object was to open the land for cultivation. There is very little under-wood in any part of this country, so that by cutting up the cane, and girdling the trees, you are sure of a crop of corn. The fertility of the soil amply repays the labourer for his toil; for if the large trees are not very numerous, and a large proportion of them the sugar maple, it is very likely from this imperfect cultivation, that the ground will yield from 50 to 60 bushels of corn to the acre. The second crop will be more ample; and as the shade is removed by cutting the timber away, great part of our land will produce from 70 to 100 bushels of corn from an acre. This extraordinary fertility enables the farmer who has but a small capital to increase his wealth in a most rapid manner (I mean by wealth the comforts of life). His cattle and hogs will find sufficient food in the woods, not only for them to subsist upon, but to fatten them. His horses want no provender the greatest part of the year except cane and wild clover; but he may afford to feed them with corn the second year. His garden, with little attention, produces him all the culinary roots and vegetables necessary for his table; and the prolific increase of his hogs and poultry, will furnish him the second year, without fearing to injure his stock, with a plenty of animal food; and in three or four years his flock of cattle and sheep will prove sufficient to supply him with both beef and mutton; and he may continue his plan at the same time of increasing his stock of those useful animals. By the fourth year, provided he is industrious, he may have his plantation in sufficient good order to build a better house, which he can do either of stone, brick, or a framed wooden building, the principal articles of which will cost him little more than the labour of himself and domestics; and he may readily barter or sell some part of the superfluous productions of his farm, which it will by this time afford, and procure such things as he may stand in need of for the completion of his building. Apples, peaches, pears, &c. &c. he ought to plant when he finds a soil or eligible situation to place them in, as that will not hinder, or in any degree divert, him from the object of his aggrandizement. I have taken no notice of the game he might kill, as it is more a sacrifice of time to an industrious man than any real advantage.

Such has been the progress of the settlement of this country, from dirty stations or forts, and smoaky huts, that it has expanded into fertile fields, blushing orchards, pleasant gardens, luxuriant sugar groves, neat and commodious houses, rising villages, and trading towns. Ten years have produced a difference in the population and comforts of this country, which to be pourtrayed in just colours would appear marvellous. To have implicit faith or belief that such things have happened, it is first necessary to be (as I have been) a spectator of such events.

Emigrations to this country were mostly from the back parts of Virginia, Maryland, Pennsylvania, and North Carolina, until 1784: in which year many officers who had served in the American army during the late war came out with their families; several families came also from England, Philadelphia, New Jersey, York, and the New England States. The country soon began to be chequered after that æra with genteel men, which operated both upon the minds and actions of back woods people, who constituted the first emigrants. A taste for the decorum and elegance of the table was soon cultivated; the pleasures of gardening were considered not only as useful but amusing. These improvements in the comforts of living and manners, awakened a sense of ambition to instruct their youth in useful and accomplished arts. Social pleasures were regarded as the most inestimable of human possessions—the genius of friendship appeared to foster the emanations of virtue, while the cordial regard, and sincere desire of pleasing produced the most harmonizing effects. Sympathy was regarded as the essence of the human soul, participating of celestial matter, and as a spark engendered to warm our benevolence and lead to the raptures of love and rational felicity.

With such sentiments our amusements flow from the interchange of civilities, and a reciprocal desire of pleasing. That sameness may not cloy, and make us dull, we vary the scene as the nature of circumstances will permit. The opening spring brings with it the prospect of our summer's labour, and the brilliant sun actively warms into life the vegetable world, which blooms and yields a profusion of aromatic odours. A creation of beauty is now a feast of joy, and to look for amusements beyond this genial torrent of sweets, would be a perversion of nature, and a sacrilege against heaven.

The season of sugar making occupies the women, whose mornings are cheered by the modulated buffoonery of the mocking bird, the tuneful song of the thrush, and the gaudy plumage of the parroquet.—Festive mirth crowns the evening.—The business of the day being over, the men join the women in the sugar groves where inchantment seems to dwell.—The lofty trees wave their spreading branches over a green turf, on whose soft down the mildness of the evening invites the neighbouring youth to sportive play; while our rural Nestors, with calculating minds, contemplate the boyish gambols of a growing progeny, they recount the exploits of their early age, and in their enthusiasm forget there are such things as decrepitude and misery. Perhaps a convivial song or a pleasant narration closes the scene.

BERNARD MAYO

HENRY CLAY (1777-1852) personified much that was the Kentucky of the first half of the nineteenth century. A politician extraordinary, he had behind him a vast amount of legal

*experience, and as a Bluegrass farmer he kept a close kinship
with the soil. In 1797 young Clay, a legal knight-errant, rode
across the mountains by way of the Wilderness Road from Virginia to Kentucky. The pull of the West was great. He came
searching for clients and modest fortune. The thriving town
of Lexington toward which he was headed was a place of excitement and high promise. It was the West's proudest metropolis.*

This selection from Henry Clay, Spokesman of the New West
*(Boston, 1937) is one of the choicest pieces of Kentucky descrip-
tion. Here Bernard Mayo (1902-   ) recaptured a spirit, cast a
fitting background, and paraded the proudest of Kentuckians
across the sprawling stage.*

Goshen of the Western World

IN HEARTY agreement were Henry and his father-in-law with
the preacher who, exhorting outside the state and finding
himself at a loss to describe the joys of the hereafter, thus
concluded his sermon: "In short, my brethren, to say it all
in a word, heaven is a Kentuck of a place." Kentucky was
the garden spot of the frontier, and Lexington, according to
fulsome accounts in the *Gazette,* was truly "the Goshen of this
Western World."

Henry's friends later recalled these flush times as a golden
age, when "every independent farmer's house was a house for
all, and a temple of jollity," when every young man with his
horse, gun, and violin had unparalleled pleasures at the "round
of frolics," fish-feasts, barbecues, "races, shooting-matches, squirrel hunts, and what were dearer than every other enjoyment,
the dancing parties." Perhaps memory's picture of halcyon
days, when man's "great business was to pass life off with as
little care as possible," was more roseate than truth warranted.

Yet an old Indian-fighter as early as 1802 found much fault
with the social season because there were only "three or four
balls in Lexington, and one play acted."

This Kentucky and this Goshen of the Western World, which
were moulding young Henry Clay into Harry of the West,
variously impressed visitors in the years following the eventful
Louisiana Purchase. They remarked upon Lexington's uncom-
monly wide, stone-paved streets with spacious footways guarded
by hitching-posts; the some "six hundred houses mostly brick,
which appear to have neatness, elegance, and convenience combined"; the stores, with their swinging signboards, filled with
varied merchandise; the clean and commodious inns with their
cherry or walnut furniture and panelling, and bells on the
roofs which summoned guests to an excellent and bounteous
table; and the many thriving industries in this "singularly neat
and pleasant town." Visitors from adjoining Western states
looked up to Lexington as "the seat of wealth and refinement
of the western country." Those from the East, however, were
often hypercritical: amid the din of exploitation they grudging-
ly discerned some elements of refinement but many more of
rawness and crudity.

Such a hypercritical observer was Mr. Alexander Wilson of
Philadelphia, the poet-naturalist, who arrived at Satterwhite's
Eagle Tavern one day weary and saddle-sore. At first he was
pleased to record that Lexington's "numerous shops piled high
with goods, and the many well-dressed females I passed in the
streets, the sounds of social industry, and the gay scenery of
'the busy haunts of men' had a most exhilirating effect on my
spirits after being so long immured in the forest." After dis-
posing of his luggage, pistol, and dirk, he set forth on an extended survey of the Athens of the West which, alas, failed to
confirm his first impressions.

"Restless, speculating set of mortals, here, full of lawsuits,
no great readers," he noted. "The sweet courtesies of life, the
innumerable civilities in deeds and conversation, which cost
one so little, are seldom found here. Every man you meet

with has either some land to buy or sell, some lawsuit, some coarse hemp or corn to dispose of; and if the conversation do not lead to any of these he will force it. Strangers receive less civilities than in any other place I have ever been in."

It was court day, recorded the splenetic Mr. Wilson, and there were "not less than one thousand horses in town, hitched to the sideposts—no food for them all day. Horses selling by auction. Negro women sold the same way: my reflections while standing by and hearing her cried: 'three hundred and twenty-five dollars for this woman and boy! Going !Going!' Woman and boy afterwards weep. Damned, damned slavery." The citizens were "rude and barbarous," sadly in need of razors, scissors, and soap. Fayette's new and expensive courthouse was a curious pile of bricks with "all the gloom of the Gothic, so much admired of late," wherein sat the judges "like spiders in a window corner, dimly discernible." In the unfinished brick Cheapside Markethouse one sank ankle-deep in mud and slime, and saw there displayed products which in quality and variety sharply belied the boasted reputation of this "metropolis of the fertile country of Kentucky."

These caustic comments on Lexington, and on the "savage ignorance, rudeness, and boorishness" of Henry Clay's fellow townsmen, were deeply resented. Given to boasting, to the breezy, highly colored, and uncritical optimism peculiar to a new country, Westerners (and Clay not the least) were un-usually sensitive to real or fancied jibes. Brash and callous as they might appear, the Children of America were remarkably thin-skinned. They fumed at the criticisms of Easterners and, especially, of Tory Britishers who seemed ever to delight in rancorous assaults upon "the National Character." Some of these "Munchausen gentry" had never crossed the Alleghenies, yet they portrayed "Jacobinic" Kentucky as a region inhabited by savage Yahoos or strange creatures half-man, half-ape; as a frontier alembic which made men narrowly intolerant politi-cally, intellectually, spiritually; as a refuge or dumping-ground for the lawless and incompetent of the seaboard and of Europe.

Under the circumstances the reply made to carping Mr. Wilson was in surprisingly good temper and good taste.

"Thirty years ago we had no right to expect that literature and science would so soon appear among us," wrote a Lexingtonian to the arch-Tory *Port Folio* of Philadelphia, which had published Wilson's critique. "We hardly dreamed, by this time, to have been exempted from the necessity of exciting our youth to savage warfare, by making an enemy's scalp the diploma of their merit." It was surprising, to say the least, to hear the Blue Grass described as "sequestered wilds." Perhaps the Fayette courthouse was "a heavy labour'd monument of shame," but never had there been exposed at Cheapside "skinned squirrels cut up into quarters." Mr. Wilson should heed Washington Irving's advice to English travellers: because one Jerseyman is fat all Jerseymen are not. Because some Kentuckians were in filthy guise it should not be assumed that to all Kentuckians soap was an article unknown.

In truth, the amenities of life had measurably increased since young Clay's arrival from Virginia in '97. His Goshen of the Western World had become "as handsome, as far as it extends, as [Mr. Wilson's] Philadelphia." His adopted state, especially the central Blue Grass region, was maturing socially: there had been a steady growth, a quickening development.

Kentucky, "the chicken hatched by Virginia," seemed to present more of a cross-section of the stratified seaboard society than the one-class society common to a frontier in its first stages of development. While it was a "mixing bowl" of divers peoples, domestic and foreign, and while it was frequently remarked that Kentuckians were like the Irish in their high independence, quick temper, and frank generosity, indeed, that Kentucky was "the Ireland of America," tribute was generally paid to "the considerable tone" which the many Virginia emigrants of education and property had given to "the happy and cultivated state of Kentucky," to the "genial atmosphere of our great western garden." John James Audubon, the naturalist, early fell under the romantic spell of the Kentuckian as he came to be typified nationally by Henry Clay, of "the free, single-hearted, Kentuckian, bold, erect, and proud of his Virginian descent." Neither Audubon nor Timothy Flint could praise too highly the "frank and cordial Virginian spirit of hospitality," which in the case of Flint was impressed "the more forcibly, for being unexpected" by one who in the Northeast had imbibed prejudices against the backwoodsmen of Republican Kentucky.

Strong was the Virginia influence, along with other factors racial and geographical. Yet even among those Kentuckians who like Clay had come from the Old Dominion, distinguishing traits had developed: the chicken hatched by Virginia had become a young Western rooster, lusty, loud-crowing, far more aggressive than the mother hen. When young Clay went back East, to Congress, there was a peculiar appositeness in the term, "The Cock of Kentucky," applied to him by John Randolph. In the same spirit Virginia cousins stated that their frontier relatives had "lost a portion of Virginia caste and assumed something of Kentucky esteem, an absence of reticence and a presence of presumptuousness."

There were distinguishing traits, in temperament as well as in politics, religion, economics. For it was not true, said Timothy Flint, that the Kentuckians as a whole were "too recent, and too various in their descent and manners, to have a distinct character as a people." Already there was "a distinct and striking moral physiognomy to this people; an enthusiasm, a vivacity, and ardour of character, courage, frankness, generosity, that have been developed with the peculiar circumstances under which they have been placed. These are the incitements to all that is noble in a people," said the Reverend Mr. Flint. "Happy for them, if they learn to temper and moderate their enthusiasm, by reflection and good sense."

In Clay's Blue Grass country, as in Virginia and in England, the term "Gentleman" had come to be associated with landed estates. Success at the bar or in trade was signalized by the purchase of a country seat. John Breckinridge had early removed from Lexington to Cabell's Dale, where, in 1806, he had 128 horses, 70 head of cattle, and Negroes so numerous that he hired them out to Peter January, John Nancarrow, and other merchant-manufacturers. General William Russell had his Mount Brilliant, Thomas Irwin his Mansfield, and General Levi Todd his Ellerslie—to mention a few of the estates which gave to Clay's section of the West a rustic opulence and made the beautiful country about Lexington a region of "finely cultivated fields, rich gardens, and elegant mansions."

Some of these Blue Grass plantations and stock-farms, it was said, resembled estates in Languedoc and Provence. Unique, however, was David Meade's Chaumière du Prairie near Lexington, in Jessamine County, a mansion composed of rustic cottages grouped together, with a drawing-room draped in silk brocades, flower gardens after those at Versailles, serpentine walks, and a lake presided over by a Greek temple and statuary. Colonel Meade, eccentric and charming, was an old-school Virginian who dressed in smallclothes and periwig, had the manners of a grandee, and delighted Clay and others with his hospitality. . . .

In the spring of 1806 Henry established himself upon his own country seat, which he called Ashland from its wood of native ash, situated on slightly rising ground about a mile and a half south of Lexington. From it he could see the spire of Christ Church and the cupola of Fayette courthouse. Quarters were simple when he and his family removed from town. It was not until a few years later that he built the spacious brick mansion, designed by Benjamin Latrobe, with its projecting ells, its wooded paths and shrubbery, which became associated with the name of Ashland. At intervals he purchased adjoining lands, including the estate of Mansfield, until he possessed some six hundred fertile acres. It pleased him always to be able to say that Ashland had been acquired by his own labors; that no part of it was hereditary except one slave, who would oblige him if he would accept his freedom.

Thus young Clay, the erstwhile "Mill Boy of the Slashes,"

had become the landed gentleman, a many-acred squire, with a country seat commanding flourishing fields and rolling blue-grass meadows where his blooded cattle and horses peacefully grazed. Before he was thirty Henry drank of this "brimming cup of felicity."

Like Jefferson and others who favored gradual emancipation, he farmed his estate with slave labor—and the slaves of Kentucky, said a visiting British Whig, were "better fed, better lodged, and better clothed, than many of the peasantry in Britain." Henry's slaves increased from six in 1805 to fourteen in 1808 and to eighteen in 1811; his horses from eight to forty and thence to sixty-five during the same years. He planted hemp and corn and rye, but he was mainly interested in stock-breeding. Shortly after he moved to Ashland, with Judge Thomas Todd and three other gentlemen he purchased "the Celebrated Imported Turf Horse Buzzard," at "the extraordinary price of 5500 Dollars." This splendid stallion, the pedigree of which commanded a full column in the *Gazette*, stood at Ashland, where it served the mares of the owners and of all those who wished to improve the stock of the Blue Grass.

It was a horse country, a sporting country, already in a fair way to surpass Virginia and South Carolina in blooded animals, high racing stakes, and colorful Jockey Club meetings. John Breckinridge in Washington was probably as much interested in the forty mares being served at Cabell's Dale by his stud, Speculator, and in the slanderous stories of Speculator's unsatisfactory performance, as he was in the Lexington Bank struggle. Wherever the young squire of Ashland and his friends congregated one heard horse talk—"the most astonishing animal of the age, sir," "no horse on the Continent stands higher in the public estimation," "of great size, fine bone, symmetry and action," "she easily distanced the field," "able to run with any horse in the world." All classes, even the slaves, had the "Kentucky mania"—indeed, wrote a citizen to the *Gazette*, it is said throughout the Union that "horse-jockeying and tippling is [our] chief employment."

To the contrary, there were now many polite diversions for a gay Blue Grass society that had its own musical clubs and theatre company, enjoyed travelling exhibitions, sojourned in summer at Olympian Springs, and accepted the fashionable dictum that "cold water and ice cream are extremely pernicious." Both Henry and Lucretia were fond of society; Henry passionately so. Many occasions demanded their presence—dancing assemblies and tea parties; the gala launching on the Kentucky of Mr. Jordan's two-hundred-ton brig, the *General Scott;* the marriage of gay and talkative Doctor Warfield to Maria Barr, that of Lucretia's dashing young brother, Nathaniel, to Ann Gist of Frankfort, and the wedding at Cabell's Dale of Alfred Grayson and Letitia Breckinridge.

When young people were "put into the same alphabet," Henry's good friend, Doctor Sam Brown, would doubtfully shake his head. Himself a most eligible bachelor, Sam Brown added much to the social tone by his attractive person and by his scientific dabblings—his pioneering in smallpox inoculation, his improvements in cleaning ginseng, his scheme to heat the whole town of Lexington by steam. Educated to Edinburgh and at Philadelphia, he was often irked by Western manners. Yet always when he returned from "the wilderness parts of the state," from those "comfortless regions" outside the Blue Grass, he rejoiced in the metropolitan civilities of Lexington.

As a pioneer on the frontiers of science, who contributed to the *Medical Repository* at New York, who made reports to the Philosophical Society at Philadelphia on Kentucky's fossils, Indian mounds, and limestone caverns, and who was interested in all aspects of the natural world, Professor Brown appreciated the unusual educational opportunity of 1805 when an "African Lion" was shown at Satterwhite's Tavern. At Travellers Hall, competing with this exciting exhibit, was Mr. Rennie, the magician, who promised Lexingtonians that he would cut off their fingers, slash their clothes, and smash their watches—and then restore all with his "Magic Cement." When a "Living Elephant" arrived in town the event was so unusual that Editor

William Worsley of the Lexington *Reporter* exhorted his readers to see the mammoth beast: "Perhaps the present generation
may never have the opportunity of seeing an Elephant again,
as this is the only one in the United States, and perhaps the
last visit to this place."

In the new dining and assembly room of Mr. Bradley's Travellers Hall—a fine hostelry which Clay in 1808 purchased, re-
named the Kentucky Hotel, and leased out—the Musical Society
gathered for "Songs, Glees, Rounds, Marches, etc." These con-
certs, with the liberal servings of spiced Sangaree punch, often
inspired poems which appeared in the *Gazette's* column titled
"Sacred to the Muses"—alongside debates on the morals of the
ancients, Baptist pleas for the education of the Indians on Mad
River, perhaps letters on monsters born from unnatural unions,
and robust, Rabelaisian anecdotes in the spirit of *Humphry
Clinker* or *Tom Jones*. At the taverns assembled the Bachelors
Club for the Promotion of Marriage and the debating societies.
It was here that the Amusing Club, the Tomahawks, the Frogs,
and the notorious Free and Easy Club "cut up didoes" and
planned escapades alarming to the night watchmen as they went
their rounds crying "in a shrill, unearthly tone, the time of
night, and the weather."

Sometimes the young bloods would take the town fathers to
task. "We have had Hog Laws, Dog Laws, Theatre Laws, and
Laws about the Hay Scale . . . Kitchen Slops, Soap Suds, the
Filth of every kind," read an open letter from the Frogs, "and
in no single instance have they been executed." Attempts to
regulate their whiskey aroused a manly opposition—"Ain't this
a free country? My father fought for liberty against the British,
and I'll get drunk whenever I please." What a dreary world
if a free-born son of Old Kentuc couldn't take his gum-tickler
(about a gill of spirits) of a morning or his phlegm-cutter (a
double dose) before breakfast; his anti-fogmatic (a similar
dram) before dinner; and a few gall-breakers (about a half
pint) during the day? A decent respect for society usually re-

strained them, however, when they frequented the public gardens which Captain John Fowler, on retiring from Congress in 1807, had opened. Or when at Monsieur Terasse's Vauxhall, where, in the grape arbor under the moon and the glow of variegated lanterns, they danced to the shrill fiddling of *Roy's Wife* and *Jefferson's March* or listened to the black fiddlers scrape away at *Just Like Love is Yonder Rose,* a sentimental piece much in demand among Lexington's belles, in their silks and muslins, and Lexington's gallants, spruced and essenced with pomatum.

Since Henry's arrival from Richmond Mr. Weber had built his "Warm and Cold Baths for Both Sexes," and lotteries—promising "600 DOLLARS FOR $5!!!"—had paved Main Street and erected the brick building of Sam Brown's Lexington Medical Society. There was now a Coffee House, a club for gentlemen only, where Henry could select his favorite newspaper or magazine from the file in the reading-room, play billiards, chess, or backgammon, and drink the best of wines and spirits. At their ease, after tedious saddle journeys to county court towns, he and his friends drank, exchanged snuff, smoked Spanish seegars, and swapped stories. They discussed Henry Fenk's alleged discovery of Perpetual Motion (which British agents, it was rumored, were attempting to steal), and congratulated Editor Dan Bradford on his pioneer Western magazine, *The Medley, or Monthly Miscellany.* Armed with *The Medley's* essays, poems, and moral tales, said Bradford, one was safe from embarrassment in any company—"such a company amongst whom you could easily discover the phiz of the profound sage, the learned divine, the deep philosopher, the well-read politician, the subtil casuist, the fluttering coxcomb, and the snarling critic—the pious matron, the prudent wife, the sprightly maid, and the gay coquette."

GRANT C. KNIGHT

THE AUTHOR who touched the tenderest chords of human emotions in the Bluegrass pastureland was James Lane Allen (1849-1925). For him the Bluegrass was more than a physical part of the political state of Kentucky; it was a way of life. When Grant C. Knight (1893-1956) came to write his biography, James Lane Allen and the Genteel Tradition (Chapel Hill, N. C., 1935), he, too, had to capture on paper the spirit of the region. Professor Knight savored the Bluegrass tradition as it merged into the brackish modern period between two world wars. It was with a distinct nostalgia of his own that he recreated in words the vanishing world of James Lane Allen.

God's Very Footstool

IN 1849 it would not have been much of an exaggeration to have said that all good Kentuckians hoped to go to the Bluegrass region of their native state when they died. That broad central plateau in Kentucky was to them literally, as it had been to their pioneer fathers, a promised land upon which their hearts were set with an affection that admitted no change. To be born anywhere in Kentucky was a privilege, but to be born in the Bluegrass was to be especially favored of providence, and though destiny might arrange one's birth in another section of the dark and bloody ground yet it could not prevent one from dreaming of the time when he might own acres of the chosen rich soil or retire to live amid the blessings of the Bluegrass capital, Lexington. Dwellers on this plateau believed their country was God's very footstool and said so in those exact words, nor could a traveler from abroad or a visitor from any other part of the state persuade them to any opinion which would deny that the Bluegrass was the most beautiful part of the whole world.

An outsider on his first entrance into this region might for a time have been at a loss to account for this unusual sectional pride, which has by no means vanished from the speech of the present generation of Kentuckians. The landscape offers no spectacular attractions. The mountain ranges which bestow loveliness and majesty upon the sister states of North Carolina, Tennessee, Virginia, and Maryland do not penetrate the Bluegrass; its average elevation is between nine hundred and a thousand feet, and it has no hills or waterfalls worthy of special mention. The Kentucky River, it is true, cuts its circuitous way through a gorge whose cliffs parade a pageant of beauty in spring and autumn, but the river was, with the exception of its appeal to hunting instincts, little in the mind of the Kentuckian of 1849. It was upon the rolling pastures that his eyes liked to rest; it was down the fine pikes, fragrant with honeysuckle, colorful with redbud, trumpet-vine, and dogwood, shaded by elms and locusts and oaks that he liked to ride at a slow canter, while his thoughts swelled with the realization that this was his own, his native land. For him it needed no peaks, no lakes, no valleys; he was content with its soft contours, its blue sky, its golden haze. The man of this section loved those swells and falls of land covered with luxuriant grass trampled by his sheep and cows and, above all, by his horses. Everything was quiet, serene, and plentiful so far as Mother Nature was concerned. The limestone soil nourished abundant crops as well as the grass which gave the country its name, and to the agricultural society it supported, want in its sharp sense was almost unknown.

This land of unbroken verdure, of forests, lawns, lanes, turnpikes, fields of grain and hemp, brooks and creeks and ponds, flocks and herds and paddocks, this land of natural repose, of material ease, of tranquil beauty, exerted a peculiar charm upon its inhabitants. Certainly their immediate ancestors had

been roving enough in character, but once settled in the Bluegrass the Anglo-Saxon stock put down tenacious roots and grew
from the soil like a plant. The characteristics of the landscape
came, in time, almost to dominate the characteristics of its population; its meadows and tilled fields were so English in detail
that the American seemed to revert to his English type, to cling
to English social customs, to revive that passion for the land
which was so marked a trait of the English country squire.
Kentucky, too, had its country gentry, living in Georgian
houses, entertaining with a hospitality sometimes too lavish,
devoted to sport, tory in politics but democratic in behavior,
fiercely assertive of individual rights, and covetous of privacy.
The Kentucky gentleman took life much more easily than did
his Yankee relative. Whereas New England or Pennsylvania
children had been taught for two centuries that idleness was
a vice, the Kentucky boy of family was instructed to live elegantly, to remember that a gentleman delegated as much work
as possible to subordinates; the girl was reminded that her
supreme virtues were goodness and beauty, and it was not in-
frequently the boast of a Kentucky belle before the Civil War
that she never walked outside her garden—there was always a
carriage with a slave to drive for her.

The man who owned little land may have looked with envy
upon the well-to-do landowner, but he did not allow that envy
to come too near the surface. Since the population of the Bluegrass in the forties and fifties was, as a whole, mid-western
rather than southern in its manners and in the matter of social
distinctions, the small landowner made it a point to hold his
head as high as that of his richer neighbor. And he could do
so, especially if he were allied to the ever-important "good
family." He did not, because of any need to do manual labor,
lose caste; he certainly lost the coveted leisure of the gentleman,
but in a section where the pioneer ideology was actual and the
genuinely southern feeling (that is, the feeling of a Virginian
or a Carolinian) was present mainly as a wish, he might still

think of himself as belonging to the aristocracy and as being only temporarily shut off from some of the higher privileges. Economics triumphed over any attempt to establish an artificial class system, so that manual labor was quite consistent with membership in one of the better families. Birth, not fortune, determined the extent of the aristocracy. To be sure, people who gave their minds to reflection upon gentility were not likely to overwork with hands and arms, even when there was good reason for their doing so. But they were a vital people, all the more so, perhaps, because of their refusal to develop a harsh competitive system of any kind, by their unwillingness to work themselves to death for someone else even if well-paid for so doing. Life was made an occasion for living. These people, rich or poor, were bent upon enjoyment of their earth, of all that they could put into it and get out of it, and not greatly troubled whether in doing so they went to Heaven or went to Hell. Religion was, to be sure, the cause of public debates, or bitter schisms, of baptisms in creeks and ponds, of decorous worship, but it did not greatly interfere with a free plunge into all the red-blooded pleasures within reach, pleasures most keen when shared with friends. Spring races (much slower in 1849 than today), summer barbecues, autumnal fairs, picnics in the greenwoods to the music of fiddles, venison suppers, court days, Christmas festivities when the entire land was blue with the smoke from smokehouses, duels, shootings, stabbings, frank drunkenness and frank profanity—these embroidered the texture of an agrarian society essentially romantic and peaceful but dangerous when aroused to combat, a society whose men were by actual measurement taller and broader than those of any other state save Tennessee and whose women have always been looked at admiringly.

The traditions of these people were chiefly those of provincial England of the eighteenth century, and in these traditions family prestige bulked large. To belong to one of the best families was to have a distinction that could arrive through no

other circumstance. Achievement counted for less than birth,
although achievement might lay the foundation for a good
family and certainly a good family might make a name for itself
in ways other than the social usages. As in England, the preferred career was that of service to the state; the ambitious
Kentucky gentleman read law, entered politics, and practised
oratory in the hope of going to Congress. Painting, literature,
science, music were neglected, almost scorned by the many.
The Waverley novels were read, it is true, and so was the poetry
of Byron, because they ministered to a taste for chivalry and
tempestuous expression respectively, but the Bluegrass youth
of ante-bellum days who attempted to write novels or verse
was likely to be discouraged if not shunned. The landowner
might name his daughter after one of Sir Walter's heroines or
send his architect abroad to copy the plan of Newstead Abbey,
but he turned his own urge for expression into the channel of
political speech-making and apprenticed his son to Blackstone.
Generally speaking, the art of the Bluegrass found its outlet
in the building of houses that fitted the scene; science was made
useful in stock-breeding and in farming; literature was converted into shelved books to be read occasionally; and music
was left to blacks who sang while they toiled and who danced
behind many a small log cabin after the sun had gone down.

The heart of the Bluegrass region was Lexington, called by
its citizens "the Athens of the West." It had some claim to that
appellation. Founded in 1775 and named for the Massachusetts
town in which minute-men had died, the Kentucky Lexington
had grown rapidly for thirty years after the Revolution; then
the development of steamboat traffic on the Ohio River had
carried commercial supremacy to Cincinnati; but the coming
of railroads in the middle of the nineteenth century had restored some of its lost prosperity. In 1849 its population was
about nine thousand, of which approximately one half were
Negroes. To its markets farmers brought horses, mules, cattle,
hogs, and sheep for sale or exchange, while the many fields of

hemp supported fifteen establishments in which that com-
modity was prepared for eastern factories. It was not in its
commercial activities, however, or in its eleven well-built
churches or in its two daily newspapers that Lexington took
the greatest satisfaction. It reflected most complacently about
its cultural past, the galaxy of notable men who had once
moved through its streets, its former leadership in the theatre
and in the appreciation of literature—literature always being
defined as something written by a Greek, a Roman, or an Englishman. It boasted of the fact that the fascinating Aaron Burr,
revolving schemes for a western empire of which Kentucky
might have been a province, had stopped at Postlethwaite's
Tavern; so had Lafayette during his visit in 1825. In Lexington Matthew Jouett, a pupil of Gilbert Stuart, had painted
portraits of local gentlefolk; Joel Hart had produced his sculp-
tures; Constantin Rafinesque had taught botany; Edward West
had navigated on the Town Branch the first steamboat. From
Lexington John Breckinridge had gone to Washington to be
Jefferson's attorney-general. Henry Clay, pride of American
Whiggism, lived just outside Lexington and often visited its
courthouse when Congress was not in session; now he was
brooding over his late defeat for the presidency of the United
States. In Lexington a newspaper had been published as early
as 1787; a magazine, in 1803; a college was founded in 1798;
a theater was built at the opening of the nineteenth century.
With its place in history thus assured and with proof of its
wealth apparent in handsome residences and well-dressed citizens, Lexington felt pretty well pleased with itself. Louisville
might surpass it in size and St. Louis in contemporary culture,
but they could not filch from the Bluegrass city its memory of
the time when it had been the metropolis of the West.

ANTHONY TROLLOPE

*K*ENTUCKIANS *came off rather well, compared to the rest of their fellow Americans, in a highly critical book by an English woman, Frances Trollope (1780-1863), who for three years was a resident of Cincinnati. Thirty years later, her son published an account of his travels in* North America *(New York, 1862). Anthony Trollope (1815-1882), a prolific producer of novels, visited the Bluegrass after the outbreak of the Civil War. His observations showed a sympathy with the peculiar position Kentuckians held in the internecine struggle, and his criticisms were gently worded. On the other hand, only once did he go beyond adjectives of faint praise to the superlatives which were usual in descriptions of the Bluegrass.*

A Very Pretty Place

I VISITED the little towns of Lexington and Frankfort, in Kentucky. At the former I found in the hotel to which I went seventy-five teamsters belonging to the army. They were hanging about the great hall when I entered, and clustering round the stove in the middle of the chamber;—a dirty, rough, quaint set of men, clothed in a wonderful variety of garbs, but not disorderly or loud. The landlord apologized for their presence, alleging that other accommodation could not be found for them in the town. He received, he said, a dollar a day for feeding them, and for supplying them with a place in which they could lie down. It did not pay him,—but what could he do? Such an apology from an American landlord was in itself a surprising fact. Such high functionaries are, as a rule, men inclined to tell a traveller that if he does not like the guests among whom he finds himself, he may go elsewhere. But this landlord had as yet filled the place for not more than two or three weeks, and was unused to the dignity of his position. While I was at supper, the seventy-five teamsters were summoned in to the common eating-room by a loud gong, and sat down to their meal at the public table. They were very dirty; I doubt whether I ever saw dirtier men; but they were orderly and well-behaved, and but for their extreme dirt might have passed as the ordinary occupants of a well-filled hotel in the West. Such men, in the States, are less clumsy with their knives and forks, less astray in an unused position, more intelligent in adapting themselves to a new life than are Englishmen of the same rank. It is always the same story. With us there is no level of society. Men stand on a long staircase, but the crowd congregates near the bottom, and the lower steps are very broad. In America men stand upon a common platform, but the platform is raised above the ground, though it does not approach in height the top of our staircase. If we take the average altitude in the two countries, we shall find that the American heads are the more elevated of the two. I conceived rather an affection for those dirty teamsters; they answered me civilly when I spoke to them, and sat in quietness, smoking their pipes, with a dull and dirty, but orderly demeanour.

The country about Lexington is called the Blue Grass Region, and boasts itself as of peculiar fecundity in the matter of pasturage. Why the grass is called blue, and or in what way or at what period it becomes blue, I did not learn; but the country is very lovely and very fertile. Between Lexington and Frankfort a large stock farm, extending over three thousand acres, is kept by a gentleman, who is very well known as a breeder of horses, cattle, and sheep. He has spent much money on it, and is making for himself a Kentucky elysium. He was kind enough to entertain me for a while, and showed me something of country life in Kentucky. A farm in that part of the State depends, and must depend, chiefly on slave-labour. The slaves are a material part of the estate, and as they are regarded by the law as real property—being actually adstricti glebæ—an inheritor of land has no alternative but to keep them. A gentleman in Kentucky does not sell his slaves. To do so is considered to be low and mean, and is opposed to the aristocratic traditions of the country. A man who does so willingly, puts himself beyond the pale of good-fellowship with his neighbours. A sale of slaves is regarded as a sign almost of bankruptcy. If a man cannot pay his debts, his creditors can step in and sell his slaves; but he does not himself make the sale. When a man owns more slaves than he needs, he hires them out by the year; and when he requires more than he owns, he takes them on hire by the year. Care is taken in such hirings not to remove a married man away from his home. The price paid for negro's labour at the time of my visit was about a hundred dollars, or twenty pounds, for the year; but this price was then extremely low in consequence of the war disturbances. The usual price had been about fifty or sixty per cent. above this. The man who takes the negro on hire feeds him, clothes him, provides him with a bed, and supplies him with medical attendance. I went into some of their cottages on the estate which I visited, and was not in the least surprised to find them preferable in size, furniture, and all material comforts to the dwellings of most of our own agricultural labourers. Any comparison between the material comfort of a Kentucky slave and an English ditcher and delver would be preposterous. The Kentucky slave never wants for clothing fitted to the weather. He eats meat twice a day, and has three good meals; he knows no limit but his own appetite; his work is light; he has many varieties of amusement; he has instant medical assistance at all periods of necessity for himself, his wife, and his children. Of course he pays no rent, fears no baker, and knows no hunger. I would not have it supposed that I conceive slavery with all these comforts to be equal to freedom without them; nor do I conceive that the negro can be made equal to the white man. But in discussing the condition of the negro, it is necessary that we should understand what are the advantages of which abolition would deprive him, and in what condition he has been placed by the daily receipt of such advantages. If a negro slave wants

new shoes, he asks for them, and receives them, with the un-
doubting simplicity of a child. Such a state of things has its
picturesquely patriarchal side; but what would be the state of
such a man if he were emancipated to-morrow?

The natural beauty of the place which I was visiting was
very great. The trees were fine and well-scattered over the
large, park-like pastures, and the ground was broken on every
side into hills. There was perhaps too much timber, but my
friend seemed to think that that fault would find a natural
remedy only too quickly. "I do not like to cut down trees if
I can help it," he said. After that I need not say that my host
was quite as much an Englishman as an American. To the
purely American farmer a tree is simply an enemy to be trod-
den under foot, and buried underground, or reduced to ashes
and thrown to the winds with what most economical despatch
may be possible. If water had been added to the landscape
here it would have been perfect, regarding it as ordinary English park-scenery. But the little rivers at this place have a dirty
trick of burying themselves under the ground. They go down
suddenly into holes, disappearing from the upper air, and then
come up again at the distance of perhaps half a mile. Unfortunately their periods of seclusion are more prolonged than
those of their upper-air distance. There were three or four
such ascents and descents about the place.

My host was a breeder of race-horses, and had imported sires
from England; of sheep also, and had imported famous rams;
of cattle too, and was great in bulls. He was very loud in praise
of Kentucky and its attractions, if only this war could be
brought to an end. But I could not obtain from him an assurance that the speculation in which he was engaged had been
profitable. Ornamental farming in England is a very pretty
amusement for a wealthy man, but I fancy,—without intending
any slight on Mr. Mechi,—that the amusement is expensive. I
believe that the same thing may be said of it in a slave State.

Frankfort is the capital of Kentucky, and is as quietly dull
a little town as I ever entered. It is on the river Kentucky, and

as the grounds about it on every side rise in wooded hills, it is a very pretty place. In January it was very pretty, but in summer it must be lovely. I was taken up to the cemetery there by a path along the river, and am inclined to say that it is the sweetest resting-place for the dead that I have ever visited. Daniel Boone lies there. He was the first white man who settled in Kentucky; or rather, perhaps, the first who entered Kentucky with a view to a white man's settlement. Such frontier men as was Daniel Boone never remained long contented with the spots they opened. As soon as he had left his mark in that territory he went again further west over the big rivers into Missouri, and there he died. But the men of Kentucky are proud of Daniel Boone, and so they have buried him in the loveliest spot they could select, immediately over the river. Frankfort is worth a visit, if only that this grave and graveyard may be seen. The legislature of the State was not sitting when I was there, and the grass was growing in the streets.

CHARLES DUDLEY WARNER

CHARLES DUDLEY WARNER (1829-1900), the peripatetic New England editor, was not unimpressed by the beauty of the Bluegrass, but he was more concerned with its "tone." Visiting Kentucky in the 1880's, he sensed that the distinction of the central part of the state was threatened by the new commercialization. The Puritan in Warner, perhaps, led him to stress the moral qualities of the Bluegrass, all the more fascinating to him because they existed in spite of an economy based on racehorses and whisky. In his Studies in the South and West *(New York, 1889), Warner remarked at some length on the "subtle difference" of central Kentucky.*

An Orthodox and a Moral Region

THIS INCOMING of the commercial spirit will change Kentucky for the better and for the worse, will change even the tone of the blue-grass country, and perhaps take away something of that charm about which so much has been written. So thoroughly has this region been set forth by the pen and the pencil and the lens that I am relieved of the necessity of describing it. But I must confess that all I had read of it, all the pictures I had seen, gave me an inadequate idea of its beauty and richness. So far as I know, there is nothing like it in the world. Comparison of it with England is often made in the use of the words "garden" and "park." The landscape is as unlike the finer parts of Old England as it is unlike the most carefully tended parts of New England. It has neither the intense green, the subdivisions in hedges, the bosky lanes, the picturesque cottages, the niceness of minute garden-culture, of England, nor the broken, mixed lawn gardening and neglected pastures and highways, with the sweet wild hills, of the Berkshire region. It is an open, elevated, rolling land, giving the traveller often the most extended views over wheat and clover, hemp and tobacco fields, forests and blue-grass pastures. One may drive for a hundred miles north and south over the splendid macadam turnpikes, behind blooded roadsters, at an easy ten-mile gait, and see always the same sight—a smiling agricultural paradise, with scarcely a foot, in fence corners, by the road-side, or in low grounds, of uncultivated, uncared-for land. The open country is more pleasing than the small villages, which have not the tidiness of the New England small villages; the houses are for the most part plain; here and there is a negro cabin, or a cluster of them, apt to be unsightly, but always in view somewhere is a plantation-house, more or less pretentious, generally old-fashioned and with the colonial charm. These are frequently off the main thoroughfare, approached by a private road winding through oaks and ash-trees, seated on some gentle knoll or slope, maybe with a small flower-garden, but probably with the old sentimental blooms that smell good and have reminiscences, in the midst of waving fields of grain, blue-grass pastures, and open forest glades watered by a clear stream. There seems to be infinite peace in a house so surrounded. The house may have pillars, probably a colonial porch and door-way with carving in bass-relief, a wide hall, large square rooms, low studded, and a general air of comfort. What is new in it in the way of art, furniture, or bric-à-brac may not be in the best taste, and may "swear" at the old furniture and the delightful old portraits. For almost always will be found some portraits of the post-Revolutionary period, having a traditional and family interest, by Copley or Jouett, perhaps a Stuart, maybe by some artist who evidently did not paint for fame, which carry the observer back to the colonial society in Virginia, Philadelphia, and New York. In a country house and in Lexington I saw portraits, life-size and miniature, of Rebecca Gratz, whose loveliness of person and character is still a tender recollection of persons living. She was a great beauty and toast in her day. It was at her house in Philadelphia, a centre of wit and gayety, that Washington Irving and Henry Brevoort and Gulian C. Verplanck often visited. She shone not less in New York society, and was the most intimate friend of Matilda Hoffman, who was betrothed to Irving; indeed, it was in her arms that Matilda died, fadeless always to us as she was to Irving, in the loveliness of her eighteenth year. The well-founded tradition is that Irving, on his first visit to Abbotsford, told Scott of his own loss, and made him acquainted with the beauty and grace of Rebecca Gratz, and that Scott, wanting at the moment to vindicate a race that was aspersed, used her as a model for Rebecca in "Ivanhoe."

One distinction of the blue-grass region is the forests, largely of gigantic oaks, free of all under-growth, carpeted with the close-set, luscious, nutritive blue-grass, which remains green all the season when it is cropped by feeding. The blue-grass thrives elsewhere, notably in the upper Shenandoah Valley, where somewhat similar limestone conditions prevail; but this is its natural habitat. On all this elevated rolling plateau the limestone is near the surface. This grass blooms towards the middle of June in a bluish, almost a peacock blue, blossom, which gives to the fields an exquisite hue. By the end of the month the seed ripens into a yellowish color, and while the grass is still green and lush underneath, the surface presents much the appearance of a high New England pasture in August. When it is ripe, the top is cut for the seed. The limestone and the blue-grass together determine the agricultural pre-eminence of the region, and account for the fine breeding of the horses, the excellence of the cattle, the stature of the men, and the beauty of the women; but they have social and moral influence also. It could not well be otherwise, considering the relation of the physical condition to disposition and character. We should be surprised if a rich agricultural region, healthful at the same time, where there is abundance of food, and wholesome cooking is the rule, did not affect the tone of social life. And I am almost prepared to go further, and think that blue-grass is a specific for physical beauty and a certain graciousness of life. I have been told that there is a natural relation between Presbyterianism and blue-grass, and am pointed to the Shenandoah and to Kentucky as evidence of it. Perhaps Presbyterians naturally seek a limestone country. But the relation, if it exists, is too subtle and the facts are too few to build a theory on. Still, I have no doubt there is a distinct variety of woman known as the blue-grass girl. A geologist told me that once when he was footing it over the State with a geologist from another State, as they approached the blue-grass region from the southward they were carefully examining the rock formation and studying the surface indications, which are usually marked on the border line, to determine exactly where the peculiar limestone formation began. Indications, however, were wanting. Suddenly my geologist looked up the road and exclaimed:

"We are in the blue-grass region now."

"How do you know?" asked the other.

"Why, there is a blue-grass girl."

There was no mistaking the neat dress, the style, the rounded contours, the gracious personage. A few steps farther on the geologists found the outcropping of the blue limestone.

Perhaps the people of this region are trying to live up to the thorough-bred. A pedigree is a necessity. The horse is of the first consideration, and either has or gives a sort of social distinction; first, the running horse, the thorough-bred, and now the trotting horse, which is beginning to have a recognizable descent, and is on the way to be a thorough-bred. Many of the finest plantations are horse farms; one might call them the feature of the country. Horse-raising is here a science, and as we drive from one estate to another, and note the careful tillage, the trim fences, the neat stables, the pretty paddocks, and the houses of the favorites, we see how everything is intended to contribute to the perfection in refinement of fibre, speed, and endurance of the noble animal. Even persons who are usually indifferent to horses cannot but admire these beautiful high-bred creatures, either the famous ones displayed at the stables, or the colts and fillies, which have yet their reputations to make, at play in the blue-grass pastures; and the pleasure one experiences is a refined one in harmony with the landscape. Usually horse-dealing carries with it a lowering of the moral tone, which we quite understand when we say of a man that he is "horsy." I suppose the truth is that man has degraded the idea of the horse by his own evil passions, using him to gamble and cheat with. Now, the visitor will find little of these degrading associations in the blue-grass region. It is an orthodox and a moral region. The best and most successful horse-breeders have nothing to do with racing or betting. The yearly product of their farms is sold at auction, without reserve or favor. The sole business is the production of the best animals that science and care can breed. Undeniably where the horse is of such importance he is much in the thought, and the use of "horsy" phrases in ordinary conversation shows his effect upon the vocabulary. The recital of pedigree at the stables, as horse after horse is led out, sounds a little like a chapter from the Book of Genesis, and naturally this Biblical formula gets into a conversation about people.

And after the horses there is whiskey. There are many distilleries in this part of the country, and a great deal of whiskey is made. I am not defending whiskey, at least any that is less than thirty years old and has attained a medicinal quality. But I want to express my opinion that this is as temperate as any region in the United States. There is a wide-spread strict temperance sentiment, and even prohibition prevails to a considerable degree. Whiskey is made and stored, and mostly shipped away; rightly or wrongly, it is regarded as a legitimate business, like wheat-raising, and is conducted by honorable men. I believe this to be the truth, and that drunkenness does not prevail in the neighborhood of the distilleries, nor did I see anywhere in the country evidence of a habit of dram drinking, of the traditional matter-of-course offering of whiskey as a hospitality. It is true that mint grows in Kentucky, and that there are persons who would win the respect of a tide-water Virginian in the concoction of a julep. And no doubt in the mind of the born Kentuckian there is a rooted belief that if a person needed a stimulant, the best he can take is old hand-made whiskey. Where the manufacture of whiskey is the source of so much revenue, and is carried on with decorum, of course the public sentiment about it differs from that of a community that makes its money in raising potatoes for starch. Where the horse is so beautiful, fleet, and profitable, of course there is intense interest in him, and the general public take a lively pleasure in the races; but if the reader has been accustomed to associate this part of Kentucky with horse-racing and drinking as prominent characteristics, he must revise his opinion.

Perhaps certain colonial habits lingered longer in Kentucky than elsewhere. Travellers have spoken about the habit of profanity and gambling, especially the game of poker. In the West generally profane swearing is not as bad form as it is in the East. But whatever distinction central Kentucky had in profanity or poker, it has evidently lost it. The duel lingered long, and prompt revenge for insults, especially to women. The blue-grass region has "histories"—beauty has been fought about; women have had careers; families have run out through dissipation. One may hear stories of this sort even in the Berkshire Hills, in any place where there have been long settlement, wealth, and time for the development of family and personal eccentricities. And there is still a flavor left in Kentucky; there is still a subtle difference in its social tone; the intelligent women are attractive in another way from the intelligent New England women—they have a charm of their own. May Heaven long postpone the day when, by the commercial spirit and trade and education, we shall all be alike in all parts of the Union! Yet it would be no disadvantage to anybody if the graciousness, the simplicity of manner, the refined hospitality, of the blue-grass region should spread beyond the blue limestone of the Lower Silurian.

J. SOULE SMITH

J. SOULE SMITH (1848-1904), Lexington lawyer and journalist, waxed eloquent on the subject of the Bluegrass. Considered in his time one of the best literary stylists, he wrote with a flow of words much too saccharine for modern tastes. His longest essay on his favorite subject accompanied a collection of photographs entitled Art Work of the Blue Grass Region of Kentucky *(Oshkosh, Wisconsin, 1898). Smith had no trouble filling his allotted space; indeed, he almost never quit. He was certain that the Bluegrass was God's favored creation; he doubted that Paradise was its equal; the only consolation was that*

death would unite his body with the beloved soil and that his
spirit would be able to contemplate eternally the glories of
central Kentucky.

Near to Heaven

THE BLUEGRASS region of Kentucky is a land famous in song
and story, and loved by its people with a proud affection beyond
what the stranger can conceive. It is a remarkable land; inhabited by a people who are as unique in their individuality
as the land itself is unlike any other. It is a poem in itself, and
its men and women have the distinct outlines of figures in a
Shakespearian drama. It is unlike any other land; its people
are unlike any other people. No matter how deeply the snow
lies upon the landscape, the Bluegrass is green beneath it; and
no matter how crisp and brown it may become in the parching
drought of summer, it responds at once to the falling rain, and,
in a day's time the emerald verdure smiles its gracious greeting
to the passing breeze. One who has not seen its purple waves
ripple on wind swept pastures, in the late spring, has missed a
more gorgeous spectacle than the Bay of Naples, painted by
the setting sun, or the Great Sound of Bermuda.

It is indeed an unique land; perhaps nowhere else on earth
can be found the same conditions of soil, of climate, of people,
and location. Geologically it is the oldest, and the highest,
formation of the Western Continent. Its old Silurian rocks
rise from the very foundations of the earth's crust, forced up
like the peak of a volcano, round the edges of whose crater
other strata are piled up to form a level surface. And the un-
derlying stone—a soft limestone, full of minute sea shells, and
easily disintegrating—seems as if it had been formed of heat
and water; at the bottom of the sea, and lifted bodily up to
the surface by the expansive gases of the underworld. The

grass roots draw their nourishment from this natural phosphate, and the tendrills of red clover pierce down to the solid rock itself, and carry with them the solvent of the falling rain. So the fruits of the soil—the grass, the clover, and the corn are rich with nourishment for bone, and brawn, and brain. It is a land where great men and good women draw strong bodies and active brains from the earth beneath them, and find inspiration in the balmy air, and poetry in the bending sky. It is near to Heaven and most blest of all the earth.

Almost exactly in the centre of Kentucky lies this land of dream and sunshine. Fayette County is the central point, and from its Court House the bluegrass region stretches in a circle. Jessamine County, Woodford, Scott, Bourbon, and Clark surround it. Parts of Madison, Garrard, Boyle, Mercer, Anderson, Franklin, Harrison and Montgomery share in its glories; through the best part of it winds the Kentucky river, which has cut its deep bed into the soft rocks three hundred feet below the surface, and presents its picturesque cliffs in many featured crags, as sentinels over the wimpling waves below. Crowned with scanty growth of cedar, scarred here and there by the lightning's stroke, and wreathed with reminiscent legend, these battlements of ancient days are glorious in their majesty. The mists of morning wreathe them with subtile suggestiveness, the noon day sun crowns them with glory, and the soft moonlight loves to play hide and seek with flitting shadows in their crevices. The whole land is an epic poem—hill and valley, crag and plain, sombre forest and clover scented meadow, all furnish their separate beauties to the harmonious whole. . . .

The natural beauties of this land can hardly be selected. Where all is lovely, what can be the best? Not time, nor space, permit a detail of the fairest phases of this strangely charming portion of God's earthly garden spot.

Sometimes, it seems to me that nothing can excel a woodland pasture in the fall. The grass is brown, not dead, but only sombre with reflection of the Summer days. The maples shiver at the touch of frosty winds, and turn their pale leaves shrinkingly toward a pallid sun. The sturdy oak still wrestles with the breeze, defiant of the coming snow. The beech tree reddens with a hectic flush, the walnut hides its olive colored fruit amid the withering masses of its laggard leaves, and, where the sturdy hickory stands, ripe nuts drop suddenly upon the earth which rustles as they fall. Some faint suggestions of a cloud are over all the sky like spirit sympathy upon an earthly grief—yes, like the vapor of a vanished tear upon another tear. The haze of Indian Summer casts a ghostlike veil upon the distant slopes, and in sympathetic silence only can be heard the tapping of woodpecker on some withered tree, or squirrels chattering as they frisk among the boughs. Far off, the plaintive dove coos farewell to his Summer mate, and from the fence row, Bobwhite whistles to himself. A sweet and sacred solitude is this, with which all sounds do harmonize.

The browsing cattle seek the sunny slopes, and, on the upland, weanling colts are frisking by their dams. There is a chill in all the air, like, sometimes, comes the thought of death across a pleasant retrospect. And yet the face of Nature is so sweetly calm, that one would think it smiled into the very eyes of Death. And so it does; for, to the Bluegrass Land, Death is a little time of restfulness wherein the virgin soil waits for the resurrection of spring.

The virgin soil waits, sleeping; but it dreams the blue grass while it sleeps. Beneath the snow, beneath the sleet, despite the blizzard from the wrathful West, the blue grass grows serene, and calm, and verdant all the year. With steaming breath the cattle blow the drifted snow away and paw it with impatient hoof to find the juicy blades beneath, and draw from Nature's heart sweet nourishment.

And winter has its charms, as well as summer days or autumn afternoons. The pale blue sheen of sleet upon the boughs, beneath a cloudless moon, when frost is keen and blades of grass like fairy bells give forth their tinkle to the touch; the snow that sparkles like a phosphorescent wake behind the speeding sleigh; the new ice on the waveless pond which sings a welcome to the skate, all these are jewels of the Winter's crown, and robes of royalty.

A snow storm in the cedar thickets on the cliff, when scurrying flakes fight viciously against the stubborn twigs, until, in weariness, they yield, and bed themselves upon the bended boughs, presents a picture weirdly beautiful, and one which memory could not wish to lose. Great icicles hang from the rocks, and snow is drifted in their crevices, while, here and there, some sheltered ledge affords a dry and cozy nook in which a man may curl himself unpinched by frost, and calmly look abroad upon the whirling storm. Unseen, unknown of other men, here may he sit within a hermit's cell and feel the kiss of Nature on his lips. The wind howls down below him in the gorge, the snow flakes whirl in a delirious dance, the cedars creak, and crack, and crash beneath their burden of the snow, the gray clouds sweep their ragged trains athwart the sky, the crow sails swiftly on the rushing blast, and hawks are hastening to their hidden homes within the scarred seams of the precipice—all earth, and air, and sky, are in a tumult of unrest, but he who looks upon this moving snow is as serene, as though he were a thought within the centre of a placid soul. He views the panorama, and is still.

Such are a few of Winter's pictured scenes. Fair to the sight are they, and fairer to the thought. Yet who does not find fuller impulse in the spring? There is no spring in other lands like that which comes to this supernal spot. Some lands are bloomy all the year, until the roses seem like red cheeked harlots of the soil. They throw their kisses to the sun, and fling their odors on the breeze so lavishly, that, heartsick at their brazen wantonness, the soul sighs for a crocus in the snow. And there are lands where Winter tears her fleecy furs off with impetuous haste, and yields herself to Summer's hot embrace before the banns of her bethothal have been read. But in the Bluegrass Land, Spring is the Vestal Priestess who unites the two. The sun woos first the ice-encumbered brook, and dallies with the cold coquettish snow. The still stream smiles in silent thought, then gurgles to a laugh. The snow escapes and hides within the earth. The brook breaks into song; it trills and warbles all the day, and through the night it croons a lullaby. The crocus and the jonquil come, and then the violet is seen in sunny spots from which the snow has fled. The hyacinth brings its dainty breath, and tulips robe themselves in oriental gorgeousness.

Still Winter hesitates; her heart is warm but she will not be cheaply won. The sun must give more precious gifts before the kingly Summer wins her for his bride. He sends the March winds as his ministers, but still she says him nay. The grass grows greener on the slope, and from the pine the dove coos coaxingly. Then all the trees are diamonded with drops, when April shakes her tresses in the air. The mossrose swells her bud and bursts its soft envelope with a blush. The pale green bravery of the maple comes, and darkens as the days go by. The other trees are fitted with wedding robes. White lilies come upon their stalks, and mushrooms dot the pasture lands. The pear rejoices in its clustered sprays, the grape vine loads the air with heaviness at night, the apple drifts its snowy blossoms on the sward, and peach trees are a mass of pink deliciousness. May scatters flowers far and wide, and, just before the mystic birth of June, the locust bloom flings on the air its sacred frankincense—so short, so sweet, so brief its life, that while the soul is yet intoxicated with its balm, death claims it, and until another year has passed it is a blessed memory.

This is the wedding of a Bluegrass Spring. The Winter yields himself reluctantly, and Spring has passed before her kiss has been absorbed entirely in the Summer's heart.

And now has summer come indeed. The grass has grown in luxury and purpled into seed. The lark has hatched her chirping brood, young squirrels frisk among the trees, and half grown rabbits hop about the hedge row, or bide within the spreading lettuce tops. The rye, the wheat, the barley and the oats are billowing softly with the rhythmic breeze. Tobacco fields are coming into flower, the hemp begins to whiten into bloom, the rustling corn stalks float their yellow pollen on the air and show the shimmering silk above the nascent ear. The winter of the blackberry flower has passed and from the sky the sun sends messages of hope to every growing fruit. The world is beautiful—beautiful as a great glad heart can be—the days are long, and dreamy in their sensuousness. Nature puts forth her fullest strength in gladful exercise—the clover is abloom.

Who ever saw a field of clover, in its pristine beauty in the Bluegrass Land, shall not forget its glories. The sun of June makes splendid all the day, and, in the night, the silver sickle of the crescent moon reaps hours of gentle joy. Deep dew rests on the blushing bloom, when, from his couch of crimson clouds, the radiant sun uprises, all his face aglow with smiles; and soon his kisses warm the crystal drops, and melt them to his passionate desires, and call them heavenward in clouds of incense, sweet and soft, and fragrant as the nard that burns in censers of the Orient. The humming-bird flits here and there, the lark springs from her hidden nest to greet the God of Day, the hare leaps like a laggard through the matted sward, the bee is everywhere, industrious in the honied heart of flowers that almost force their bursting wealth of sweetness on his appetite, and, drowsily, the bumblebee drones as the sunbeams wake him from his slumbers in the loamy soil.

The day comes on apace; the cattle, rising from their blue grass beds beneath the walnut trees, scent clover on the breeze, and low, expectant of the feast which shall not come to them; knee deep in the pebbly bottomed creek they stand, with moist tails sprinkling their heaving sides as though they should purge their flanks with hyssop and be clean. They cannot reach the clover yet, although in other fields the reaper clicks its sharp defiance to the golden headed wheat. Everywhere, about the border of the meadow land, is locust bloom sending its benediction on the whispering breeze to meet and mingle with the meadow's breath, until the lazy sun at noon lies lapped in languorous swoon, half drunken with the balm. The bumble bee has ceased his drone, the honey bee has sought his hive, the lark unto her nestlings has returned, the cattle chew their cud beneath the locust trees, the clover blooms are closed and sleep beneath the over-arching sky rocked gently by the dreamy breeze.

But, with the dying day, the earth awakes once more. Slowly the sun sinks to his Western bed of purple clouds, which quiver with his palpitating heart, and flame with crimson glory as he wraps their fleecy folds about his form. The white moon, in mid heaven, gleams graciously as twilight comes. The click of reapers and the clank of chains has ceased. The plaintive cow lows in the distance for her calf, and katydids begin to chirp. Crows wing themselves toward the roost, flapping the still air wearily. The gurgle of the spring branch through its nodding beds of mint is audible. But now the clover wakens from its sleep, and, as the first bright star peeps from the purple shadows of the East, the dews begin to fall upon the flowers and their bended heads arise to greet the gentle ministrations of the night. Above the meadow, like the benediction of a blessed ghost, the faint, blue, mist has come, more gentle than the dew of Hermon. Scarce palpable to human sense, the clover feels its presence and draws new life from baptism in its gracious flood. Under the moonlight the meadow wakens and its myriad blossoms send heavenward the incense of their prayers. While the world of animal life is still, and slumbering, the meadow worships underneath the stars; so that at no time is Heaven desolate.

This is a fruitful meadow in the Bluegrass Land in June, and each night brings its morning more precious than the last; each today is more beautiful than yesterday.

And now this pleasant task is done. My pen would linger on this lovely theme, but that the end must come. The end must come to all things in this world, where sin makes sorrow possible, and death a certainty. Men live, men die, and after-life comes sweetly to the good and true. The beautiful is but the harmony of what is best for all. Beyond the bondage of the flesh, the spirit stands, supreme, and smiling, as it views the grave of what was once its cerement. So does the spirit of this Bluegrass Land smile on the outer world. Embodied in the hills, it is the soul of all the hills; and, from its fertile heart, the incense of its morning dew is wafted up to God—a prayer more precious than the lips of any man can speak. The oldest land, the gentlest land, the sweetest land of all the earth, its breath is worship and its life perfume. Who loves it not has never known its sweet beneficence; who does not dream as it would make him dream, has not the element of poetry within his soul; who has been son of blue grass soil, and dares to sully blue grass fame is but an atom of iniquity. Its skies are blue, its sunshine soft, its maidens fair, its men fit sons of noble sires.

Here heather blooms among the hills, and cedars sigh upon the rocks; high in the air the eagle soars, undazzled by the sun; the falcon flits, the wild hawk breasts his way against the Western breeze, the blast comes, and the lightning gleams, yet the Bluegrass Land serenely smiles, all confident in its most gentle strength. For, when the storm shall pass, the wet trees glisten in the sun; the grass uplifts its head; the white clouds part their fleecy fringe of Heaven's tapestry to show a smiling sky. Each laughs its greeting back into the blue, and God is good, as all the atmosphere attests.

To leave a theme so subtle and so sweet; to lay the lingering pen aside, and bid the brain go gathering moss from other lands; to turn the thought from poetry to pelf; seems little less than sacrilege. The memories that haunt this gracious land take deep hold on the heart that finds its home among the blue grass slopes. The locust bloom; the pungent savour of the mint; the tuberose aroma, so like an angel's benediction on an infant's dream; the gurgle of the stream let loose from winter's grasp, and babbling to its mossy bank; the cry of crow, and strident chirp of katydid; the still, deep silences of summer nights when Nature draws herself into herself to grow more honey-hearted for the coming day; the speechless stars that look their love through mists of unformed dew; the odor of ripe grapes be-

neath September skies; the sheen of heat that quivers through
the August day; the white snow sparkling underneath a winter
moon and crinkling to the tread—these, and a thousand other
things, come knocking at the entrance to my soul, and bid me
give them courtesy.

Yet must I cease. In some poor fashion have I spoken of the
land I love. In some poor, homely, way the heart has testified.
In poorer fashion has the pen traced words upon the scroll.
God made the Bluegrass Land. His angels made the outer
world—how then shall feeble man describe the blessed land
which God made with a smile? Into its mornings the glorious
gleams of Heaven are wrought; its noonday is significant of
bliss ineffable; and its nights, like sacred sanctuaries, hold
dreams so real, so supremely sweet, that to awake in paradise
would almost be a sorrow. Here shall I quit the theme—the
land I will not, cannot, quit until an angel wing shall brush
me from the world. Then, in the heart of old Kentucky shall
my body lie at rest, the while my spirit broods upon the Bluegrass Land.

ULRIC BELL

*JOHN FILSON was but the first of a long line of Bluegrass
promoters. Among present-day publicists must be classed
Ulric Bell (1891-   ), who took time out from his job as Washington correspondent of the Louisville Courier-Journal to write
an article for the American Legion Monthly, enticing Legionnaires to the 1929 meeting of their organization at Louisville.
Like Warner, Bell toyed with the geological theory of the special charm of the Bluegrass. A frank piece of propaganda, the
article nevertheless is a fair sample of the continuing "promised
land" motif.*

That Particular "It"

IF WOMEN are the prettiest, horses the swiftest and liquor the fieriest in Kentucky, it must be because of the soil.

Providence gave to the very earth of this superlative old commonwealth a racy richness of quality not to be found elsewhere. It is this vitality that makes the bluegrass blue—and nutritious blue bluegrass encourages thoroughbreds to be swift. Out of the same soil is derived that difference which causes that nectar known as Bourbon whisky to stand out among the gifts of the gods. Surely it makes the weed called Burley as smooth as the Bourbon.

There must be in it also a magic that gives bloom to the cheek, grace to the form and sparkle to the eye. That, and a slight recourse to poetic license, explains the beauty of Kentucky womanhood, if a reason need be given for perfection.

And the whole explains that particular "it" which is Kentucky's lure. One may question the explanation, but one cannot long deny the appeal. One literary authority has said that every Kentuckian is born a poet. A Kentuckian cannot write or speak dispassionately of Kentucky.

"Kentucky's greatest natural resource is history," someone else has said. Assuredly it has history and a lot of it. It has a galaxy of statesmen, warriors and men and women of letters and the sciences that should be the envy of lesser commonwealths. It was the fifteenth State to enter the union, but it had been a going concern, mixing up in all the best wars and having some of its own, long before that. Grizzled old Simon Kenton, confounding the Indians with his copious pipe and teaching them the vice of nicotine, was as much of a statesman in his way and on his scale as Henry Clay. Even among the redskins there were some pretty slick politicians.

But history must be reasoned out. In this instance the soil

fits into a kind of scientific exposition of the secret of Kentucky's superlativeness.

A few millions of years ago the tract which later became known as Kentucky lay, with sundry other tracts, at the bottom of the sea. Over this bottom crawled all manner of creatures whose shells and other impedimenta contained the plant food called phosphate. The waters went away; that was too bad for all this animal life. The casualties helped to form a sediment which is now limestone. It is by far the most abundant thing in Kentucky, save possibly the salubrious air itself. At places—you can prove this for yourself—the limestone stratum is 25,000 feet thick. As it decays, it turns its phosphatic vitality loose—into the soil and the streams and mayhap into the veins of the people.

Anyhow, this soil has a chemical property all its own. To this property is attributed the peculiar authority of the Bourbon, distilled from limestone water diluting sour corn mash; the blueness and vigor of the bluegrass and the velvety flavor of the burley Bourbon whisky never has been made successfully elsewhere. Just try to raise a crop of burley in any other place under the sun! Or enumerate spots outside Kentucky where bluegrass beckons. Or compare—but it is perhaps best that Legionnaires do not emphasize this geological side when they invade the proud old state this autumn. Kentuckians prefer to look back to less prosaic beginnings. They rather like to think they derived their virtues and blessings and cussedness from more mysterious sources. They won't admit that the hell-fire and starshine are right there in the phosphate limestone.

For them, the poet explains:

> God spoke
> And out of the Chaos
> Rose the Ocean, Earth and Sky—
> Rivers, flowing in majestic beauty to the Sea,
> Lofty Mountains, crowned by Forests,
> Overlooking Plains and Valleys,

Rich in Flowers and Fruits for Man,
His latest handiwork.
And in the midst of each Hemisphere
He set a Garden—
Eden in the East—
Kentucky in the West.

A professor in the University of Kentucky, J. T. C. Noe, thus takes leave of any theory of geological evolution concerning this marvelous land. Why, even the compilers of encyclopedias succumb a little to sentiment when they dwell upon Kentucky. "A land of milk and honey, indeed!" one of these staid volumes exclaims. "The best place outside of Heaven the good Lord ever made" is the common summing up among Kentuckians. . . .

Billy Sunday puts it succinctly. He says: "It's an emotional knockout." Thus does this land of magic affect those who would see its mysteries.

BOOK TWO

The Land and Its Heroes

*T*HE ROLL of the great westward movement across Kentucky left a generous number of landmarks of pioneering. Bryan's Station, Harrodsburg, Boonesboro, Ruddle's Mill, Hinkston's Blockhouse, and scores of other places outline this path in America's expansion. Every pioneer was some sort of a hero, if to no one but himself. Boone, Kenton, Patterson, Todd, Trigg, Harrod, Calloway, Howard, Hart were colorful men in an age of color. Breaking into a new country was hard work, but the fertile land, the generous streams, and the hospitable climate soon enabled Bluegrass Kentuckians to slow their pace.

As the frontier rolled on, and the land atop the plateau yielded up its bountiful harvests, the pattern of society became more like that of England and Tidewater Virginia. Men who had been common settlers pushing forward with ax and rifle to hack and shoot out a modest claim in the western woods quickly became landed barons. John Bradford, Humphrey Marshall, Mann Butler, and James Lane Allen sensed the diverse elements which made up the population of the Bluegrass. Not all men were in fact heroes. There were those who lived by their wits and their evil intentions. There were the swindlers, the rascals, and the laggards.

Whether it be on the political stump, aboard a flatboat bound for New Orleans, or standing before a faro table, Bluegrass man had to use his wits to survive. Nowhere on the frontier did the eddying society present sharper contrasts than in Kentucky. Astride the crossroads of the West, every imaginable kind of adventurer came to the region. There was the tragic figure of John Robert Shaw the well-digger, who possessed sound motives but a fragile willpower. He wandered like some inept Ulysses about the land from one bout with the bottle to another, incurring the ill fortunes of insobriety in what now seems unjust proportions, while nearby at Mayslick and Cincinnati Daniel Drake turned a lifetime of sober scientific interest into a revered tradition of accomplishments.

Samuel Drake, Sol Smith, Noble Luke Usher, and N. M. Ludlow brought the culture of the stage to the region. Ludlow, almost as much reporter as actor, recorded a story of naivete which illustrates how much the Bluegrass walked with one foot on the frontier and the other in the gracious manor-house ballroom. There was wide contrast between the sophisticated gatherings at Colonel David Meade's board at Chaumière, and the unexplainable conduct of theater patrons in Paris.

As though Harriet Beecher Stowe were anticipating the change of sentiment in Stephen Collins Foster's revered song, she set the scene for her famous book in Colonel Shelby's living room. Hard times were knocking at the Colonel's door, and he, like the Bluegrass itself, grew restive in a moment of hard decision. Within a decade after Mrs. Stowe electrified a nation with her account of slavery, the old way of life in the South was being disrupted. The Bluegrass was not to escape. Raiders, native and outsider, galloped over the fair land to destroy peace of mind. The great roads southwestward were blocked, and the largess of the soil lay without purchasers. Although the era of gentility was not entirely destroyed, it was badly enough shakened to give validity to a sense of demarcation between the old days and the new.

The Bluegrass could hardly be robbed of its traditions and its mores in a single war. There was change, of course, where the brigadier and rascal alike played their parts. Like actors in some ante bellum farce the virtuous were pitted against the scoundrels. Somehow their lives became entangled in a net of common interests. On the one hand James Lane Allen's Colonel Romulus Fields was unable to adapt himself to changing times, while the more flexible Riley Grannan found the new age one of golden opportunity.

JAMES LANE ALLEN

*N*O OTHER *Kentuckian has achieved the reputation of universal scholarship as did Nathaniel Southgate Shaler (1841-1906). A native of Newport, he was sent to Cambridge to follow in his father's footsteps at Harvard. In that great center of learning he became converted to strong belief in the Darwinian theory of evolution. As head of the Kentucky geological survey from 1873 to 1880, Shaler had an opportunity to view as a mature student the population of his native state. In 1884 he published a rather good interpretative history of Kentucky, the first time that anyone had looked at Kentucky with so much intimate interest yet with so much objective competence.*

No doubt the nostalgic scientific scholar overdrew the racial qualities of his fellow Kentuckians, but certainly the Bluegrass people have never had a more flattering description from so dependable a source. In the introduction to The Blue-Grass Region of Kentucky and Other Kentucky Articles *(New York,*

1892), James Lane Allen (1849-1925) leaned heavily on the Harvard dean for scientific evidence that English blood accounted for the heroic and gentlemanly qualities of Bluegrass Kentuckians.

Bluegrass Kentuckians

"IN KENTUCKY," writes Professor Shaler, in his recent history, "we shall find nearly pure English blood. It is, moreover, the largest body of pure English folk that has, speaking generally, been separated from the mother-country for two hundred years." They, the blue-grass Kentuckians, are the descendants of those hardy, high-spirited, picked Englishmen, largely of the squire and yeoman class, whose absorbing passion was not religious disputation, nor the intellectual purpose of founding a State, but the ownership of land and the pursuits and pleasures of rural life, close to the rich soil, and full of its strength and sunlight. They have to this day, in a degree perhaps equalled by no others living, the race qualities of their English ancestry and the tastes and habitudes of their forefathers. If one knows the Saxon nature, and has been a close student of Kentucky life and character, stripped bare of the accidental circumstances of local environment, he may amuse himself with laying the two side by side and comparing the points of essential likeness. It is a question whether the Kentuckian is not more like his English ancestor than his New England contemporary. This is an old country, as things go in the West. The rock formation is very old; the soil is old; the race qualities here are old. In the Sagas, in the Edda, a man must be overbrave. "Let all who are not cowards follow me!" cried McGary, putting an end to prudent counsel on the eve of the battle of the Blue Licks. The Kentuckian winced under the implication then, and has done it in a thousand instances since. Overbravery! The idea runs through the pages of Kentucky history, drawing them back into

the centuries of his race. It is this quality of temper and conception of manhood that has operated to build up in the mind
of the world the figure of the typical Kentuckian. Hawthorne
conversed with an old man in England who told him that the
Kentuckians flayed Tecumseh where he fell, and converted his
skin into razor-strops. Collins, the Kentucky Froissart, speaking of Kentucky pioneers, relates of the father of one of them
that he knocked Washington down in a quarrel, and received
an apology from the Father of his Country on the following
day. I have mentioned this typical Hotspur figure because I
knew it would come foremost into the mind of the reader
whenever one began to speak with candor of Kentucky life and
character. It was never a true type: satire bit always into bur-
lesque along lines of coarseness and exaggeration. Much less
is it true now, except in so far as it describes a kind of human
being found the world over.

But I was saying that old race qualities are apparent here,
because this is a people of English blood with hereditary agricultural tastes, and because it has remained to this day largely
uncommingled with foreign strains. Here, for instance, is the
old race conservatism that expends itself reverentially on established ways and familiar customs. The building of the first
great turnpike in this country was opposed on the ground that
it would shut up way-side taverns, throw wagons and teams out
of employment, and destroy the market for chickens and oats.
Prior to that, immigration was discouraged because it would
make the already high prices of necessary articles so exorbitant
that the permanent prosperity of the State would receive a
fatal check. True, however, this opposition was not without
a certain philosophy; for in those days people went to some
distant lick for their salt, bought it warm from the kettle at
seven or eight cents a pound, and packed it home on horseback, so that a fourth dropped away in bitter water. Coming
back to the present, the huge yellowish-red stage-coach rolls
to-day over the marbled roads of the blue-grass country. Families may be found living exactly where their pioneer ancestors

effected a heroic settlement—a landed aristocracy, if there be such in America. Family names come down from generation to generation, just as a glance at the British peerage will show that they were long ago being transmitted in kindred families over the sea. One great honored name will do nearly as much in Kentucky as in England to keep a family in peculiar respect, after the reason for it has ceased. Here is that old invincible race ideal of personal liberty, and that old, unreckoning, truculent, animal rage at whatever infringes on it. The Kentuckians were among the very earliest to grant manhood suffrage. Nowhere in this country are the rights of property more inviolable, the violations of these more surely punished: neither counsel nor judge nor any power whatsoever can acquit a man who has taken fourpence of his neighbor's goods. Here is the old land-loving, land-holding, home-staying, home-defending disposition. This is not the lunching, tourist race that, to Mr. Ruskin's horror, leaves its crumbs and chicken-bones on the glaciers. The simple rural key-note of life is still the sweetest. Now, after the lapse of more than a century, the most populous town contains less than twenty thousand white souls. Along with the love of land has gone comparative content with the annual increase of flock and field. No man among them has ever got immense wealth. Here is the old sense of personal privacy and reserve which has for centuries intrenched the Englishman in the heart of his estate, and forced him to regard with inexpugnable discomfort his neighbor's boundaries. This would have been a densely peopled region, the farms would have been minutely subdivided, had sons asked and received permission to settle on parts of the ancestral estate. This filling in and too close personal contact would have satisfied neither father nor child, so that the one has generally kept his acres intact, and the other, impelled by the same land-hunger that brought his pioneer forefather hither, has gone hence into the younger West, where lie broader tracts and vaster spaces. Here is the old idea, somewhat current still in England, that the highest mark of the gentleman is not cultivation of the mind,

not intellect, not knowledge, but elegant living. Here is the
old hereditary devotion to the idea of the State. Write the
biographies of the Kentuckians who have been engaged in national or in local politics, and you have largely the history of
the State of Kentucky. Write the lives of all its scientists, ar-
tists, musicians, actors, poets, novelists, and you find many
weary mile-stones between the chapters.

Enter the blue-grass region from what point you choose—
and you may do this, so well traversed is it by railways—and
you become sensitive to its influence. If you come from the
North or the East, you say: "This is not modern America.
Here is something local and unique. For one thing, nothing
goes fast here." By-and-by you see a blue-grass race-horse, and
note an exception. But you do not also except the rider or
the driver. The speed is not his. He is a mere bunch of mistle-
toe to the horse. Detach him, and he is not worth timing.
Human speed for the most part lies fallow. Every man starts
for the goal of life at his own natural gait, and if he sees that
it is too far off for him to reach it in a lifetime, he does not
run the faster, but has the goal moved nearer him. The Kentuckians are not provincial. As Thoreau said, no people can
long remain provincial who have a propensity for politics,
whittling, and rapid travelling. They are not inaccessible to
modern ideas, but the shock of modern ideas has not electrified
them. They have walled themselves around with old race instincts and habitudes, and when the stream of tendency rushes
against this wall, it recoils upon itself instead of sweeping away
the barrier.

The typical Kentuckian regards himself an American of the
Americans, and thinks as little of being like the English as he
would of imitating the Jutes. In nothing is he more like his
transatlantic ancestry than in strong self-content. He sits on
his farm as though it were the pole of the heavens—a manly
man with a heart in him. Usually of the blond type, robust,
well formed, with clear, fair complexion, that grows ruddier
with age and stomachic development, full neck, and an open,

kind, untroubled countenance. He is frank, but not familiar; talkative, but not garrulous; full of the genial humor of local hits and allusions, but without a subtle nimbleness of wit; indulgent towards purely masculine vices, but intolerant of petty crimes; no reader of books nor master in religious debate, faith coming to him as naturally as his appetite, and growing with what it feeds upon; loving roast pig, but not caring particularly for Lamb's eulogy; loving his grass like a Greek, not because it is beautiful, but because it is fresh and green; a peaceful man with strong passions, and so to be heartily loved and respected or heartily hated and respected, but never despised or trifled with. An occasional barbecue in the woods, where the saddles of South Down mutton are roasted on spits over the coals of the mighty trench, and the steaming kettles of burgoo lend their savor to the nose of the hungry political orator, so that he becomes all the more impetuous in his invectives; the great agricultural fairs; the race-courses; the monthly county court day, when he meets his neighbors on the public square of the nearest town; the quiet Sunday mornings, when he meets them again for rather more clandestine talks at the front door of the neighborhood church—these and his own fireside are his characteristic and ample pleasures. You will never be under his roof without being touched by the mellowest of all the virtues of his race—simple, unsparing human kindness and hospitality.

The women of Kentucky have long had reputation for beauty. An average type is a refinement on the English blonde —greater delicacy of form, feature, and color. A beautiful Kentucky woman is apt to be exceedingly beautiful. Her voice is low and soft; her hands and feet delicately formed; her skin pure and beautiful in tint and shading; her eyes blue or brown, and hair nut brown or golden brown; to all which is added a certain unapproachable refinement. It must not for a moment be supposed, however, that there are not many genuinely ugly women in Kentucky.

JOHN BRADFORD

*O*NE OF *the ablest of the early Kentuckians was John Brad-*
ford (1749-1830), who founded the Kentucke Gazette *in 1787,*
the first newspaper in the state. Bradford was a man of uncom-
monly good judgment, his perspective was good, and his knowl-
edge of what had happened about him was sound. Atop the
editorial stool he was in a position to gather and record the
story of pioneering. He knew in person the men who broke
trail through Cumberland Gap. He had experienced their
anxieties of Indian fighting and had seen British raiders fail
in their attempts to destroy the settlements below the Ohio.

The Kentucky editor assumed the responsibility of recording
the state's pioneer history, first published as special articles in
his newspaper. Later a portion of these notes was collected
under the title, The Western Miscellany, or, Accounts Historical, Biographical, and Amusing *(Xenia, Ohio, 1827). In a quiet,*
matter-of-fact style Bradford wrote an account of how two
wounded Kentuckians won their battle for survival.

A Most Singular Circumstance

IN THE month of October 1779, as two keel boats were ascend-
ing the Ohio river some small distance above the mouth of
Licking, the men on board discovered Indians standing on a
sand bar on the South side of the river, & a canoe coming across
to meet them with three or four in it. Capt. Rodgers who commanded the boats ordered the men to land and make their
boats fast to the same shore near which they were, which was
immediately done, when the party, consisting of about seventy
marched through the woods up until opposite to the sand bar
where they had seen the Indians, with the expectation of killing

or taking the whole; or driving them into the river, believing they were undiscovered by the Indians, and that their number did not exceed twelve or fifteen. When Rodgers and his party turned towards the river, the Indians who were fully apprised of their motions and from which they judged of their intentions, had so secreted themselves in the bushes, that Rodgers' party were within a few paces of them before they discovered them, upon which the Indians to the amount of several hundred rose and poured on them a deadly fire. All who were not killed or disabled by this tremendous fire, made a precipitate retreat and aimed to get to their boats, but the Indians pressed them so close, that many of them were at the boats as soon as the whites, and several whites were tomahawked in the attempt to get on board. Before the Indians got so close as to prevent it, one of the boats with five men on board cut loose and pushed off into the river, and soon floated out of reach of the Indians, (who were busily engaged with the other,) and thereby escaped.—Rodgers was himself killed, and the whole of his party consisting of 60 or 70 either killed or taken, except seven. Among those taken prisoners were Col. John Campbell, and Major Abner Chaplin.

The following most singular circumstance attended this defeat. A man whose name was Robert Benham was wounded through the hips, in such manner as to render him unable to walk, he crawled into the brush of a fallen tree, taking his rifle with him, and so secreted himself that the Indians passed him unnoticed. He lay concealed two days without a mouthful of sustenance, when a Raccoon came near him, and he shot it: immediately after his gun fired he heard somebody call, but suspecting it was Indians, he reloaded his gun determined to sell his life dear; by the time his gun was charged he heard the voice again very near and calling in plain English, "Whoever you are I beg you will answer me, for I am in the utmost distress." Upon this Benham answered him, and immediately appeared John Watson one of his unfortunte companions with both his arms broken; mutual congratulations were exchanged, when Benham pointed to the Raccoon where it lay, and directed Watson to kick it to him with his feet which he accordingly did. Having good use of both his hands, Benham was able to skin and prepare the Raccoon for the spit, as well as to procure fire, whilst John Watson having the full use of his feet, could with them kick and drag pieces of broken wood to Benham who could make the fire and cook the meat. Before the Raccoon was eaten up, a flock of wild turkeys came in view; Benham directed John Watson to go round them and induce them to come near him which was done, by which means he killed a large turkey. Happily the weather was mild, and the man with the broken arms could wade into Licking river (near where they lay) so deep into the water as to stoop down and drink; but Benham unable to move from the spot where he lay was likely to die of thirst; when this project occurred to John Watson: he desired Benham to put his hat in his mouth in such manner as that the hollow part of the crown should be upwards which was done, and he went into the water and filled it by stooping down, and by that means furnished his friend with water. Benham dressed and splintered up the broken arms of John Watson, as well as dressed his own wounds; to enable him to do which he tore up both their shirts. They remained in this situation fifteen days whilst their wounds healed very fast, insomuch that with the use of a crutch Benham began to be able to move a little, during which time he killed plenty of game to support them, whilst John Watson was able to bring wood with his feet and water with the aid of the hat. About four weeks after they were wounded, Benham and his companion went to the Ohio river at the mouth of Licking, and about a mile from where they were wounded, and from whence they were taken by a boat descending the river, which they hailed, and were taken on board.

JOHN A. McCLUNG

DIME *novelists found the individualistic exploits of the Kentuckians a gold mine of materials. Anytime a man went into the woods alone, he was almost certain to meet with a challenge of wit and strength which sounded like a tall tale when he described it. Novelists were not bound by fact—all they wanted was a suggestion—but John A. McClung, historian (1804-1859), was supposed to tell the truth in his* Sketches of Western Adventure *(Maysville, 1832). McClung, a native of Maysville, was a Presbyterian minister in his early years. Later he turned to the practice of law and politics, and served in the Kentucky legislature for a term.*

Possibly the ministry, law, and politics all helped the author to adorn a tale. Certainly he never let an opportunity to tell a good adventure story go unobserved. Simon Kenton and Alexander McConnel owe a part of their fame to this imaginative author. As for Alexander McConnel (d. 1782?), McClung made him appear a veritable death scourge among the Indians.

After Anxious Reflection

EARLY in the spring of 1780, Mr. Alexander McConnel, of Lexington, Ky. went into the woods on foot, to hunt deer. He soon killed a large buck, and returned home for a horse, in order to bring it in. During his absence, a party of five Indians, on one of their usual skulking expeditions, accidentally stumbled on the body of the deer, and perceiving that it had been recently killed, they naturally supposed that the hunter would speedily return to secure the flesh. Three of them, therefore, took their stations within close rifle shot of the deer, while the other two followed the trail of the hunter, and waylaid the path by which he was expected to return. McConnel, expecting no danger, rode carelessly along the path, which the two scouts were watching, until he had come within view of the deer, when he was fired upon by the whole party, and his horse killed. While laboring to extricate himself from the dying animal, he was seized by his enemies, instantly overpowered, and borne off as a prisoner. His captors, however, seemed to be a merry, good natured set of fellows, and permitted him to accompany them unbound—and, what was rather extraordinary, allowed him to retain his gun and hunting accoutrements. He accompanied them with great apparent cheerfulness through the day, and displayed his dexterity in shooting deer for the use of the company, until they began to regard him with great partiality. Having travelled with them in this manner for several days, they at length reached the banks of the Ohio river. Heretofore, the Indians had taken the precaution to bind him at night, although not very securely; but on that evening, he remonstrated with them on the subject, and complained so strongly of the pain which the cords gave him, that they merely wrapped the buffalo tug loosely around his wrists, and having tied it in an easy knot, and attached the extremities of the rope to their own bodies, in order to prevent his moving without awakening them, they very composedly went to sleep, leaving the prisoner to follow their example or not, as he pleased.

McConnel determined to effect his escape that night, if possible, as on the following morning they would cross the river, which would render it much more difficult. He, therefore, lay quietly until near midnight, anxiously ruminating upon the best means of effecting his object. Accidentally casting his eyes in the direction of his feet, they fell upon the glittering blade of a knife, which had escaped its sheath, and was now lying near the feet of one of the Indians. To reach it with his hands, without disturbing the two Indians, to whom he was fastened, was impossible, and it was very hazardous to attempt to draw it up with his feet. This, however, he attempted. With much difficulty he grasped the blade between his toes, and after repeated and long continued efforts, succeeded at length in bringing it within reach of his hands. To cut his cords, was then but the work of a moment, and gradually and silently extricating his person from the arms of the Indians, he walked to the fire and sat down. He saw that his work was but half done. That if he should attempt to return home, without destroying his enemies, he would assuredly be pursued and probably overtaken, when his fate would be certain. On the other hand, it seemed almost impossible for a single man to succeed in a conflict with five Indians, even although unarmed and asleep. He could not hope to deal a blow with his knife so silently and fatally, as to destroy each one of his enemies in turn, without awakening the rest:—Their slumbers were proverbially light and restless—and if he failed with a single one, he must instantly be overpowered by the survivors. The knife, therefore, was out of the question. After anxious reflection for a few minutes, he formed his plan. The guns of the Indians were stacked near the fire—their knives and tomahawks were in sheaths by their sides. The latter he dared not touch for fear of awakening their owners—but the former he carefully removed, with the exception of two, and hid them in the woods, where he knew the Indians would not readily find them. He then returned to the spot where the Indians were still sleeping, perfectly ignorant of the fate prepared for them, and taking a gun in each hand, he rested the muzzels upon a log within six feet of his victims, and having taken deliberate aim at the head of one, and the heart of another, he pulled both triggers at the same moment. Both shots were fatal. At the report of their guns, the others sprung to their feet, and stared wildly around them. McConnel, who had run instantly to the spot where the other rifles were hid, hastily seized one of them and fired at two of his enemies, who happened to stand in a line with each other. The nearest fell dead, being shot through the centre of the body; the second fell also, bellowing loudly, but quickly recovering, limped off into the woods as fast as possible. The fifth, and only one who remained unhurt, darted off like a deer, with a yell which announced equal terror and astonishment. McConnel, not wishing to fight any more such battles, selected his own rifle from the stack, and made the best of his way to Lexington, where he arrived safely within two days.

THEODORE ROOSEVELT

THEODORE ROOSEVELT (1858-1919) wrote in the John A. McClung vein. Pioneering was a tremendously exciting, if vicarious, experience for this historian who became President of the United States. Organizing and commanding a company of frontier militiamen defied all formal military procedure. Every man was a law unto himself, and backwoods militia officers had little more than a tenuous control of their troops. Robert Patterson (1753-1827) was somewhat an exception. He possessed a natural capacity for leadership as well as a strict Presbyterian philosophy of life.

One of the founders of Lexington, Patterson experienced the excitement of defending the Kentucky country against both Indians and British. He was the kind of man who appealed to Theodore Roosevelt as a hardy soldier who asked no odds. Thus he received special attention in The Winning of the West *(4 vols., New York, 1889-1896).*

The Covenanting Spirit

FAYETTE lay between the Kentucky and the Ohio rivers, and was then the least populous and most exposed of the three counties into which the growing young commonwealth was divided. In 1782 it contained but five of the small stockaded towns in which all the early settlers were obliged to gather. The best defended and most central was Lexington, round which were grouped the other four—Bryan's (which was the largest), McGee's, McConnell's, and Boon's. Boon's Station, sometimes called Boon's new station, where the tranquil, resolute old pioneer at that time dwelt, must not be confounded with his former fort of Boonsborough, from which it was several miles distant, north of the Kentucky. Since the destruction of Martin's and Ruddle's stations on the Licking, Bryan's on the south bank [*sic*] of the Elkhorn was left as the northernmost outpost of the settlers. Its stout, loopholed palisades enclosed some forty cabins, there were strong block-houses at the corners, and it was garrisoned by fifty good riflemen.

These five stations were held by backwoodsmen of the usual Kentucky stamp, from the up-country of Pennsylvania, Virginia, and North Carolina. Generations of frontier life had made them with their fellows the most distinctive and typical Americans on the continent, utterly different from their old-world kinsfolk. Yet they still showed strong traces of the covenanting spirit, which they drew from the Irish-Presbyterian, the master strain in their mixed blood. For years they had not seen the inside of a church; nevertheless, mingled with men who were loose of tongue and life, there still remained many Sabbath-keepers and Bible-readers, who studied their catechisms on Sundays, and disliked almost equally profane language and debauchery.

An incident that occurred at this time illustrates well their feelings. In June a fourth of the active militia of the county was ordered on duty, to scout and patrol the country. Accordingly forty men turned out under Captain Robert Patterson. They were given ammunition, as well as two pack-horses, by the Commissary Department. Every man was entitled to pay for the time he was out. Whether he would ever get it was problematical; at the best it was certain to be given him in worthless paper-money. Their hunters kept them supplied with game, and each man carried a small quantity of parched corn.

The company was ordered to the mouth of the Kentucky to meet the armed row-boat, sent by Clark from the Falls. On the way Patterson was much annoyed by a "very profane, swearing man" from Bryan's Station, named Aaron Reynolds. Reynolds was a good-hearted, active young fellow, with a biting tongue, not only given to many oaths, but likewise skilled in the rough, coarse banter so popular with the backwoodsmen. After having borne with him four days Patterson made up his mind that he would have to reprove him, and, if no amendment took place, send him home. He waited until, at a halt, Reynolds got a crowd round him, and began to entertain them "with oaths and wicked expressions," whereupon he promptly stepped in "and observed to him that he was a very wicked and profane man," and that both the company as well as he, the Captain, would thank him to desist. On the next day, however, Reynolds began to swear again; this time Patterson not only reproved him severely, but also tried the effect of judicious gentleness, promising to give him a quart of spirits if he immediately "quit his profanity and swearing." Four days afterwards they reached the boat, and Aaron Reynolds demanded the quart of spirits. Patterson suggested a doubt as to whether he had kept his promise, whereupon he appealed to the company, then on parade, and they pronounced in his favor, saying that they had not heard him swear since he was reproved. Patterson, who himself records the incident, concludes with the remark: "The spirits were drank." Evidently the company, who had so impartially acted as judges between their fellow-soldier and their superior officer, viewed with the same equanimity the zeal of the latter and the mixed system of command, entreaty, and reward by which he carried his point.

DANIEL DRAKE

DANIEL DRAKE (1785-1852), a physician who founded the medical college of the University of Cincinnati, produced a frontier classic in his Pioneer Life in Kentucky (Cincinnati, 1870). He was well enough educated to appreciate the importance of giving a completeness of detail of frontier life to make his narrative meaningful. He likewise appreciated the fact that pioneering in Kentucky was an important part of the American frontier story. Dr. Drake described almost all phases of early conditions of life in Kentucky with a charm and comprehension that will continue to make his book one of the most reliable sources of early social history.

I Well Recollect

THE FIRST event I can remember . . . occurred in the autumn or beginning of the winter of 1788 when I had entered my 4th year. For the next 6 years my father continued to reside at the same place, in the same original log cabin, which in due course of time acquired a roof, a puncheon floor below and a clap board floor above, a small square window without glass, and a chimney, carried up with *cats & clay* to the height of the ridge pole. These *cats & clay* were pieces of small poles, well imbedded in mortar. The rifle, indispensable both for hunting & defense, lay on two pegs driven into one of the logs. The axe and a scythe (no Jerseyman emigrated without that implement) were kept at night under the bed as weapons of defense, in case the Indians should make an attack. On the morning the first duty was to ascend a ladder which always stood, leaning behind the door, to the loft and look through the cracks for Indians lest they might have planted themselves near the door, to rush in when the strong crossbar should be removed, and the heavy latch raised from its resting place. But no attack was ever made on his or any other of the five cabins which composed the station.

The first and greatest labour after father had thus domiciliated his little family, was to clear sufficient land for a crop the following year, which was, of course, to consist of corn and a few garden vegetables. In this labour I was too young to participate, and he was too poor to hire; consequently his own hands had to perform the whole. At that time, and afterwards for more than 20 years, he was dyspeptic and by no means well fitted for the heavy task which lay before him. It was two or three years before his fields grew to any great extent. The soil, however, was highly productive and the autumn of 1789 would have brought forth a sufficient abundance but that on the night of the last day of August there came so severe a frost as to kill the unripe corn, and almost break the hearts of those who had watched its growth from day to day in joyous anticipation.

From the time of their arrival in Ky. 14 months before, they had suffered from want of bread, and now found themselves doomed to the same deficiency for another year. There was no fear of famine, but they cloyed on animal food, and sometimes almost loathed it, though of excellent quality. Deer were numerous and wild turkies numberless. The latter were often so fat that in falling from the tree when shot their skins would burst. There was no longing for the "*flesh* pots" of native land, but their hearts yearned for its neat and abounding *wheat-bread* trays. In this craving it seems I played no unimportant part (though I do not remember it) for my parents often told me afterwards that I would cry & beg for bread when we were seated round the table till they would have to leave it & cry themselves.

During the first 3 or 4 years of our residence at Mayslick, when I was from 3 to 6 or 7 years of age, a few incidents occurred, the memory of which has not like most which transpired, vanished from my mind. But I can not arrange them chronologically, nor are they worth relating, except to children.

I well recollect that in the spring of 1790 when I was 4½ years old mother was sick and that, on a certain day, I wandered with my little sister Lizzy, to whom I was always tenderly attached, across "The Road" into the woods. We found a tuft of yellow flowers which made so strong an impression on me that, nearly 30 years afterwards, while studying our native botany, I recognized the same flower and it brought up a throng of early reminiscences. . . .

About the same period the Indians one night attacked a body of travelers, encamped a mile from our village on the road to Washington. They were sitting quietly around their camp fire, when the Indians shot among them, and killed a man whose remains I remember to have seen brought, the next day, into the village on a rude litter. The heroic presence of mind of a woman saved the party. She broke open a chest in one of the wagons with an axe, got at the ammunition, gave it to the men and called upon them to fight. This, with the extinction of their Camp fires, led the Indians to retreat.

That night made an unfading impression on my mind. We went, with Uncle Abraham Drake's family, I think, to Uncle Cornelius' for concentration and greater safety. Several of the men of the village went to the relief of the travelers and one of them, a young married man, ran into the village and left his wife behind him! The alarm of my mother and aunts communicated, of course, to all the children, was deep and the remembrance of the scene was long kept alive by talking it over & over.

Up to the victory of Wayne, in 1794, the danger from Indians still continued; that is, through a period of six years from the time of our arrival. I well remember that Indian wars, midnight butcheries, captivities and horse stealings, were the daily topics of conversation. Volunteering to pursue marauding parties occasionally took place and sometimes men were drafted. This happened once to father. . . . He hired an unmarried man as a substitute and did not go. At that time as at present, there were many young men who delighted in war much more than work and, therefore, preferred the tomahawk to the axe. I remember that when the substitute returned he had many wonderful tales to tell, but am unable to rehearse a single one. . . .

In or near the year 1791, my aunt Lydia Shotwell was married. A number of Father's acquaintances in and around Washington were invited. They came armed, and while assembled in the house, report was brought that the Indians, about 5 miles up the Road toward Lexington, had attacked a wagon. All the armed men mounted their horses & galloped off in a style so picturesque that I shall never forget it. The alarm proved to be false.

At that period, the Shawnees residing on the Scioto, & the Wyandots on the Sandusky, were our great enemies. The children were told at night, "lie still and go to sleep, or the Shawnees will catch you." When I was at the mouth of the Kansas river in 1844 among the same tribes, removed to that region and considerably civilized, the mothers, I was told, threatened their children at night with the wild Indians who lived beyond them.

Thro' the period of which I have been speaking & for several years afterwards, as I well recollect, nearly all my troubled or vivid dreams included either Indians or snakes—the copper colored man & the copper headed snake, then extremely common. Happily I never suffered from either (except in dread). My escape from the latter I ascribe to cowardice or, to express it more courteously, to a constitutional cautiousness beyond the existence of which my memory runneth not. This original principle of my nature, which throughout life has given me some trouble & *saved* me from some was, perhaps, augmented by two causes. 1st For a good while, I had no male companions. The sons of my uncles were too old to play with me. . . . My cousin Osee Drake, uncle Abraham's oldest daughter, afterwards Mrs. Robert Taylor, and cousin Polly Drake, uncle Cornelius's daughter, now Mrs. Chinn, both a little older than me, were, for 4 or 5 years, my chief companions. We agreed well for they were good children and while they contributed to soften my manners and quicken my taste for female companionship, they no doubt increased my natural timidity. 2d My mother was, by nature and religious education, a noncombatant and throughout the whole period of her tutelage, that is, till I went from home to study medicine, sought to impress on me not to fight. Father had, constitutionally, a great amount of caution but was personally brave and, as I can now recollect, did not concur in the counsels of my mother.

At the early period of which I am writing, my health was generally good. The first illness I remember (and the only one in those days) was indeed both severe and protracted. It arose from a fall on the ice (I think) and produced an inflammation with fever on the lower part of the spine. It terminated in an abscess and an ulcer that continued for a long time. I was attended by Dr. Goforth of W. and distinctly remember how anxious I used to feel for his visits, and at the same time, how much I dreaded his probe. On the voyage down the river, he and my father had become, as the saying is, sworn friends. Father thought him on many points a very weak man, and knew that he was intemperate, but believed him a great physician. Already when 5 years old, I had been promised to him as a student and among the remembrances of that period is my being called Dr. Drake! No wonder then, as nearly 60 years have rolled away, that I sometimes have a difficulty in passing myself off for the old & primary Dr. Drake.

Soon after the settlement of Mayslick, all the people being either professors of religion in, or adherents to, the Baptist Church, a log meeting house was built about a quarter of a mile up The Road to the South and parson Wood of Washington frequently came out to preach. He was often at my father's and used to take me between his knees and talk to me on religious subjects. At length he brought with him a catechism and when I was about 6 years old and could read a little, I was put to its study. It opened with the doctrines of the Trinity which so perplexed me that I retain a prejudice against all catechisms to this hour. This parson Wood was the father of Mrs. Doctor Goforth, and I afterwards lived 4 years and half in her family. She is now alive in Cincinnati. I often feel sorrowful that many disagreeable qualities repel me from befriending her in her old age of poverty and desolation. In her manners, she was always pleasant enough but her lack of moral principle, her ingratitude and her disposition to slander (the latter especially if indeed they can be separated) were revolting. As a wife she was extravagant and sometimes ran in debt, to a most ruinous degree. Originally, she must have had many charms, for Dr. G. on the very night of his arrival at Washington, in supping at her father's table, fell in love with her, and was not long in making it known. But I must turn back. . . .

Soon after Father settled in Mayslick, that is within a couple of years, . . . a Mr. Lawson came to the same place and settled on a corner of Father's *estate!* The terms were (such as then prevailed) to build a cabin and clear as much ground as he pleased and cultivate it for five years, from the time of building, rent free. This Mr. Lawson had a son, Tom, about my own age and we were often together, a companionship which at length involved me in serious difficulty. I do not recollect my age but it was six or seven. When his father and mother were from home, he and I went into the "truck patch" and pulled off all the young cucumbers. The next day Tom's father made complaint to mine of the trespass, and I was brought under "dealings." I remember that father called it stealing—said it was very wicked—and that there was danger of my being taken off to W. and put in jail, a strong, dark house where I would be all alone. The salutary impression was so strong & durable, that I never committed another act of the kind till after I commenced the study of medicine. (I think it was in the summer of 1801) I was tempted early one morning, . . . on going to feed and curry [my preceptor's] horse, to clamber over the fence & get 5 or 6 peaches which grew [in the adjoining yard]. . . .

I remember another calamitous event of those days. When

about six years old, I was sent to borrow a little salt of one of the neighbors. Salt at that time was worth about $3 a bushel, or 12 times as much as at present. It was a small quantity, tied up in a paper, and when I had gotten about half way home, the paper tore, and most of the precious grains rolled out on the ground. As I write, the anguish I felt at the sight seems almost to be revived. I had not then learned that spilling of salt is portentous, but felt that it was a great present affliction, and apprehended that I should be blamed and scolded. Mother had, moreover, taught me to consider the waste of bread or anything that was scarce and could be used for food, as sinful. In this instance she thought, I believe, that the paper had not been properly tied. When I recur to this and other incidents, which I can not definitely relate, I discover that it was an original trait of character with me, to aim at a faithful execution of whatever was confided to me and feel unhappy if, through neglect or misfortune, I made a failure. To this hour I am more solicitous about that which is intrusted to me than that which is entirely my own. Hence I have given a great deal of time to public affairs (on a small scale to be sure) but often at the expense of my private interests. "But never mind."

Another affliction becomes a matter of indistinct recollection but I had no hand in producing it. Near the same period, my father had hired a horse of a man by the name of Haines. The animal died and his owner sued father, for what sum I can not say, but one sufficient to constitute a serious calamity to the family if it had been recovered. The trial was at the county court in Washington, and gave father a great deal of trouble— mother and myself, meanwhile, at home *speculating* on the result and its consequences. Haines employed Tom Marshall . . . as his lawyer and father, if I recollect correctly, employed Frank Taylor. . . . It is quite impossible that I should ever lose the remembrance of the joy in which I participated when Father returned victorious, and told mother that the jury did not leave their box (an expression which, of course, *I* did not understand) and that Marshall said that Haines was the damnest rascal that had ever employed him. In looking back to this incident, which occurred, I think, when I was about six years old, I find that I had a very early sympathy with my parents, and experienced sympathetic joy and grief before I could distinctly comprehend the causes of their emotions—a quality of constitution which has remained with me since I mingled in the world, and sometimes procured for me the credit of being tender hearted & benevolent from *sentiment* towards others, when I was governed by mere instinct, or "couldn't help it."

The first money I ever had, as far as I can recollect, came to me in the following manner. A man (I know not who—some acquaintance of father's) had lodged all night with us, and the next morning lost a silver knee-buckle (at that time an indispensable article) in the snow, near the door of our cabin. I was set to hunt for it, and father at length came to my assistance with a rake. I do not remember which found it, but I got the reward—a piece of cut money, at that time the circulating medium of Virginia & Kentucky. My joy was unbounded; and ever since I have had it reproduced by the receipt of money. Then, it was the mere *possession* that threw me into rapture. Since I grew up, it was the idea of appropriating it to the payment of some debt that gave me pleasure. That happiness I shall, perhaps, not enjoy hereafter as much as I enjoyed it from 1806 to 1843—through more than half my life; but I may probably find a substitute for it in some other mode of appropriation.

My first school master had the Scotch name of McQuitty, but whether he was from the "land o' cakes," I can not tell. He taught in a very small log cabin in sight of father's, up the creek which flows through Mayslick; and a beautiful stream it was when it had any water running in it. My dim recollections suggest that I was about 5 years old when I was his pupil for a short time. Of my progress I can say nothing. His successor was master Wallace, whose name again suggests a Scottish origin. Under his tuition I presume I made some progress, for

in 1792 and 3, I was a pretty good reader, and maintained my
place respectably when we stood up to spell, before school was
"let out" in the evening. My teacher then was Hiram Miram
Curry, who, I think, had been a Baptist preacher & made us,
I remember, "get by heart" the catechism. He taught at first
in the village, south of the brook, and then up the Road beyond
the meeting house, where hickory switches were abundant. I
think I went to him as late as 1794, and had begun to write
before I left him.

Although the country was so newly settled, at the period
under review, our locality presented strange people, and novel
and curious sights, almost every day. The emigration into Ky.
was, at that period, immense and nearly the whole passed
through Mayslick. Great quantities of merchandise, moreover,
were hauled into the interior. My Uncle Abraham, who lived
only across the Road from father's, kept both a store and tavern,
at which many persons stopped. I saw aspects of things and
people, which I should not have seen had we lived off the Road,
and the sight of which was no doubt intellectually beneficial.
It was during this period that I first tasted wine. Some travelers
from Virginia had brought it out, and the taste seems still to
dwell upon my tongue. Many of the travelers were wealthy;
and as the Road did not well admit of carriages, they journeyed
on horseback. Thus I often saw ladies and gentlemen riding
side by side, and remember I thought the latter must be the
happiest persons on earth; an estimate which nearly 60 years
has not entirely overruled. . . .

From the reminiscence which I have just recorded, I find
that an admiration for the sex was among the earliest sentiments developed in my moral nature. It has swayed me through
life, and will, I suppose, continue to govern me to its close.
When that solemn event shall come, I hope to see female faces
round my bed,

> And wish a woman's hand to close
> My lids in death, and say—*Repose!*

As years rolled on, Father began to conclude (very justly) that he should aim at a larger farm, seeing that the cultivation of the soil was his destiny, and that he had two sons and two daughters. Uncle Abraham Drake, moreover, was anxious to own the little tract on which father resided, as it so immediately adjoined his own. He had purchased 200 acres of one Shannon, lying about a mile directly West of Mayslick, and offered to exchange it for the place on which father resided. A bargain was at length concluded, and the deed is now in my possession. It is dated, I think, in the summer of 1794, when I was in my 9th year, and your uncle Benjamin (I believe, though perhaps incorrectly) an infant at the breast.

This was a new era in my life. The land acquired was covered with an unbroken forest, which must be cleared away, and a new cabin erected. Father was still too poor to hire a labourer for steady work, and was, himself, far from being a robust and vigorous man. My health was good and my spirit willing—I might, therefore, render some assistance in his new enterprise; and accordingly master Curry's hickory and myself parted, never to meet again. I was provided with a small axe—father had a larger, and a mattock for grubbing. Thus equipped, with some bread & meat wrapped in a towel, we charged upon the beautiful blue ash and buckeye grove, in the midst of which he proposed to erect his cabin.

Many days, however, did not pass away before each received a wound! Of the two, father's was the most honorable. Getting his mattock fast under the roots of a grub, and making an effort to disengage it, in which he stooped far forward, it suddenly came out, and he brought, by a jerk, the axe extremity of the implement against his forehead, making a gash through to the bone. Mine, which did not happen on the same day, was made by a jack knife, which passed more rapidly through a crust of bread than I expected, and made a deep wound across the ball of my left hand, the scar from which remained till it was obliterated by my great burn, 34 years afterwards. The loss of blood was not sufficient in either case to arrest the march of improvement and, day by day, we made new conquests over all that stood in our way. Shrubs and bushes were grubbed up; trees under a foot were cut down, and those of a larger diameter "girdled," except such as would make good logs for the projected cabin, or could be easily mauled into rails. It was father's business, of course, to do the "heavy chopping"; mine, to "hack" down saplings, and cut off the limbs of trees and pile them into brush heaps. The forest consisted chiefly of blue ash—tall, straight, soft while green, easily hewed & easily split into rails and puncheons; of sugar trees—generally preserved; of several kinds of hickory and walnut, and of Buckeye. The last was so soft that it soon became my favourite, and to the readiness with which it yielded to my axe I may ascribe the affection which I have ever since cherished for it. I loved it in proportion to the facility with which I could destroy it. But its obliging temper was not limited to *my* demands. It had a parasite, which sought the air and light of heaven by climbing to its limbs, and weaving those of many adjoining trees into a broad and tangled canopy. That parasite was the winter grapevine.

The brush was of course burnt up as fast as it was cut, and of all the labours in the forest, I consider that of dragging and burning the limbs of trees the most delightful. To me it made toil a pleasure. The rapid disappearance of what was thrown upon the fire gave the feeling of progress—the flame was cheering—the crackling sound imparted animation—the columns of smoke wound their way upwards, in graceful curves, among the tall green trees left standing; and the limbs & twigs of the hickory sent forth a balmy and aromatic odor, which did not smell of the school house.

In due time a "log rolling" frolic was gotten up, when the buckeye showed that, if pressed too far, it could resist; for its consumption by fire was affected with more difficulty than that of any other tree. The ground being prepared, and the logs collected and hewed on one side, the new cabin, a considerable improvement on the old, was "raised" and brought to some degree of finish; though glass could not be afforded, and a kitchen could not be put up till a stable had been first built. At length the day for removal arrived, and we left the village and public roadside, with its cavalcade of travelers, for the loneliness of the woods; a solitude which very soon was deeply felt by us all, but most of all, I think, by mother.

JOHN ROBERT SHAW

*J*OHN ROBERT SHAW (1761-?) was a Yorkshireman whom ill fortune of war had thrust upon the American shore. He fought with Howe in New York, went with Sir Henry Clinton to Charleston, and wintered with Cornwallis in Winnsboro, South Carolina. When the war ended, he wandered northward to Pennsylvania. Later he joined the American army under the command of General Arthur St. Clair and came west. Like so many hundreds of frontier immigrants, the peripatetic Yorkshireman found his way to Lexington, where fortune, but not fame, avoided him.

Shaw was a man who found solace in a bottle. He likewise found torture and horror. Well digger, turnpike worker, dam builder, and faithless husband, he lived out his turbulent life in and near Lexington. A hero not even to himself, John Robert Shaw recorded the facts of his life with humility, but it is doubtful that his frank book, A Narrative of the Life & Travels of John Robert Shaw, the Well-Digger (Lexington, 1807), saved many souls or graced many parlor tables.

Bottle Fever

AFTER recovering from my indisposition I commenced digging a well for John Boswell, four miles from Mr. Scott's ferry; a storm coming on prevented me from progressing, therefore turned to my old trade of frolicing, the result as usual, (the bottle-fever). Afflicted with it, I was one night lying in the tavern before the fire, when I was disturbed by a parcel of ruffians, consisting of major Mastin Clay, lieutenant Spence, a Mr. Moss and Sow. They entered the house and had not been long there, before making inquiry of the landlord who I was? Answered "old Shaw the well-digger, who is very sick." Damn him, observed Clay, let us have a little fun with him. With that he laid a chunk of fire on my leg which burnt me severely. I jumped to my feet requesting of them to let me alone, saying I was then sick and no person to take my part, but even so, I would try the best of them singly: this exasperating them, and Clay being the greatest scoundrel among them, urged the rest to lay hold of me, which they did, compelling a negro who was in the house to butt me with his head and gouge me severely. I observed to Clay, that if ever an opportunity offered I should pay him off in equal coin, which I fortunately did; for shortly after meeting him at Taylor's tavern in Lexington, I demanded satisfaction for the brutal treatment I had received from him; however by the intercession of some friends, and his making ample concessions, we compromised the matter amicably.

I started from Jessamine in the spring of 1793, and proceeded on to Clear creek, where I worked for Mr. Ephraim, James January, Joseph Wood, James Dunn and William and Joseph Hughes, by all of whom I was well treated. Leaving Clear creek I went to Lexington, where I engaged with one Trainer (a sort of a tavern-keeper) to quarry stone for him at two shillings per day—low wages, but he still wanted me for less, and strove by every means in his power to take advantage of me. His foreman, one Johnson, informed me that three blasts a day, from ten to twelve inches deep was a good day's work for a man. I observed to him, that such a man was not fit to work in a quarry, and bet him a wager of a bottle of whiskey, that I would blow three blasts before breakfast, which I won. After which Mr. Trainer offered me a share in the quarry, which I refused, observing at the same time, that I had not seen a man in Kentucky that I would join in that line of business with.

Shortly after I commenced digging a well for one Samuel Lamb on Clear creek, who generously supplied me with money to buy tools; he likewise furnished me with a horse to ride to Lexington in order to purchase them, which I did, and on my return fell off the horse, and had a very narrow escape for my life. The well I finished for Mr. Lamb, for which I was honourably paid. It was about this time that I dreamed a singular dream, which was that I thought I heard a voice calling to me saying, "Shaw! Shaw! repent or you will be damned;" and in the course of a few weeks after I dreamed another, in which I thought I heard the same voice saying, "Shaw! Shaw! repent and you shall be saved." This last dream alarmed me so much that I awoke the family and communicated my dream to them. There was in the house at the time a certain Andrew Ward, supposed to be a pious man, who exhorted me seriously to reform from the mode of life which I was in the habit of pursuing, and pointed out to me what must be the inevitable result of my perseverance therein, which I took extremely kind.

Leaving Mr. Lamb's I came to Black's station; and so on to Lexington, where I again commenced my mad career; falling in company with one Prothroe, who assiduously assisted in distributing my money.

My money being expended and having no place to stay, I requested liberty of this Prothroe to lie in a corner of his shop, (he being a cabinet maker) until I got better (being at the time of course afflicted with my old complaint the bottle fever). This he refused, observing I had no money, and therefore wished to have nothing to do with me, but immediately observing that if I would sign my name to a piece of blank paper, he would give me a dram, thinking no harm, I accordingly did, after which he insisted on my leaving his house, which I did in a very distressed situation, and went out to Maxwell's spring; there I drank a quantity of water, which occasioned me to vomit a quantity of blood. Night coming on I walked along intending to take up my quarters that night in a friends house, but growing weary and sick, I lay down in the woods, and shortly fell asleep, continuing so until midnight, when being awoke by a noise which I could not account for, I jumped up rather amazed, and within nine or ten feet of me saw a ball of fire, apparently as large as a bushel, and at the same time heard a voice over my head, crying Shaw! Shaw! will not you speak to me?

A thousand conjectures now began to float in my head; I began to reflect on my former dreams—I rose and began to pray fervently, in which posture I did not long continue before those gloomy visions totally vanished. I then proceeded farther into the woods, but did not continue long there, before I heard the voice and saw the fire as plain as before; however, day appearing, I felt relieved, and proceeded on the road, where I had not long continued before I observed a man walking along side of me, on a close view of him, I found it to be the exact likeness of Prothroe, immagining within myself that he was killed, and that this my companion must be his ghost. I then observed to him that I never did him any harm, therefore requested of him in God's name to leave me; at the name of God he immediately disappeared, and I continued my journey, hoping the worst was over; but shocking to relate, I did not go far before he met me full in the face, in quite a different dress, when again using my former arguments he again disappeared, and I proceeded on to the five mile cabin, where lo! again appeared my visitant dressed in black. Being determined to ascertain whether or not it was substance, I made a grasp at him, and wonderful to relate! it vanished like an airy vision, but again appeared behind some logs, which lay convenient, beckoning me to come to him; I did and followed him from log to log until he vanished and left me extremely exhausted. I then proceeded to the five mile cabin, got the man of the house to accompany me part of the road towards Lexington, passing by a house, the woman gave me some breakfast, after which observing some drovers going by, with whom I travelled on to Lexington, my visiting ghost appearing to me in different shapes, forms, attitudes and dresses, still beckoning me to approach him, which I now dreaded as he frequently appeared besmeared with blood; however, I found the name of God was my only safeguard, which I continually kept repeating to him, and he as continually disappearing until I arrived in Lexington.

When I arrived in Lexington I immediately went to the house of Prothroe, and told him what I had seen, exhorting him to reform and strive to live a better life, observing to him that I feared something extraordinary would shortly happen from the omens that were portending. He answered saying, "I am determined to live a more regular and christian life; for indeed I had shocking dreams latterly, which induces me to take up the resolution of becoming a better man." I left the house and proceeded up the hill, and meeting with Mr. Patterson and Ellison, who earnestly entreated me to quit the company of Prothroe, and to endeavour to lead a better and more uniform life.

NOAH M. LUDLOW

ALMOST before the forts were emptied in Kentucky, traveling actors appeared in the Bluegrass. One of these was Noah M. Ludlow (1795-1886), who came west to give the natives a generous helping of drama. Ludlow had a keen understanding of humanity and was able to take his experiences as they came with a keen sense of humor. Kentucky was filled with rich characters, and many of these are described in his book, Dramatic Life as I Found It *(St. Louis, 1880).*

From the beginning, Yankees and Kentuckians were dubious of each other. Moreover, in 1815-1820 not all native sons were ready for high drama, and Ludlow experienced many incidents to demonstrate this fact. For one thing, theatrical companies could never predict the reactions of their audiences to either tragedy or comedy. Literal-minded men sometimes viewed action on the stage as an actual fact of life.

Actors Were Funny People

AFTER landing at Limestone, I was requested by Mr. Drake to go up into the village and endeavor to procure a large wagon, that might be engaged to transport our trunks and other things to Frankfort; the distance I do not recollect, but think it less than a hundred miles. As soon as I had reached the level ground at the top of the slope leading to the river, I beheld a four-horse team attached to a covered wagon standing in front of a store. As I approached the wagon, I observed a stout, rough-looking man coming towards me. When he had come near me, I said to him: "Do you belong to this wagon?" "No," said he, "this wagon belongs to me." Oho! thinks I, a specimen of Kentucky wit. One must "speak by the card" here. "Well, sir," said I, "I wish to employ some one to haul a load to Frankfort." After asking how much of a load I had, and what it consisted of, he hesitated a few minutes and then said, "Well, stranger, I think I can haul your 'plunder' for you." Now, thought I, 'tis my turn to be critical. So I said, "Damnation, sir! what do you mean? Do you take me for a highway robber or a house-breaker? Plunder! what do you mean by that?"

"Mean?" said he, "I mean I can take your 'truck' for you."
"Look you, my friend," said I, "just be so good as to explain
what you mean by 'plunder' and 'truck?' I do not understand
your outlandish jargon." "Jargon?" said he, and squaring himself up and looking me full in the face, "Look here, my young
hoss, thar's no use for you to begin *rar-ing* and pitching here,
because you can't make nuthen off o' me in that way." I
thought from his looks he meant "something," and as I wished
to obtain his services, I thought it best to "soothe the animal."
After a few minutes' more talk, he consented to go down to
the boat with me, when he and our manager soon came to
terms for the transportation of our "plunder." . . .

As in about two weeks we should be required in Lexington
to reopen the theatre for the fall, we concluded to occupy that
time in the town of Paris, a small place, about twenty miles
from Lexington. Here, as before, we procured a ball-room in
the hotel, and opened with a good comedy and farce, the titles
of which I do not remember. On the second night we acted
the pathetic tragedy of the "Gamester," a play that seldom, if
ever, fails to move the audience to tears, no matter wherever
or by whomsoever performed. But on this occasion it failed
to produce that effect, certainly on one individual. This was
a jolly, round-faced, "huge fat man," whom I noticed seated
midway of the front bench, near the foot-lights. He appeared
to be about forty years of age, and was well dressed. I first
noticed him in the third scene of the third act, between *Beverly*
(Mr. Vaughan) and *Stukely* (Samuel Drake), where *Beverly*
rushes from the gambling-room, frantic with having lost all
his wealth. The characters were very respectably performed
by those two gentlemen; but this fat man burst out into a
most immoderate fit of laughter, that drew the eyes of the
actors and the audience upon him; yet he seemed not conscious
of it, and continued laughing and shaking his fat sides as though
he enjoyed it as much as he could have done had it been a most
laughable farce. Mr. Vaughan seemed very much annoyed,
and I thought at one time was about to speak to him; but

Drake said something to Mr. Vaughan in an undertone, and they went on with the scene, the man still enjoying it hugely, in his way.

In the fourth act I had a scene, as *Lewson,* with *Stukely;* the man still continued laughing at intervals, and at the point where *Lewson* puts himself on guard, expecting *Stukely's* assault with his sword, the fat man threw himself back and fairly roared. I must confess I felt exceedingly vexed, and was on the point of speaking to him, when Drake said, "Don't mind him; go on!" His laughing caused others, that were as silly as himself, to laugh. Before the fifth act commenced, we sent to the landlord a request that he or some one else would speak to the man, and inform him he was annoying the performers and disturbing the audience, and that he must either desist from his peculiar demonstrations or withdraw; and to tender him his price of admission, should he prefer the latter course. The man remained, and did certainly restrain his mirth to a considerable extent; but in the last scene of all, where Beverly is in the agonies of death, and the audience and actors were shedding tears, I looked at him to discover what effect the scene had upon him, and I beheld the villain holding his fat sides and laughing internally, his face being red with his efforts to restrain an outbreak; and as the curtain dropped he gave vent to a regular *explosion of mirth!* We were at a loss to account for his strange conduct, but the matter had arrived at that time to the point of the absolutely ridiculous, and we could not help laughing in our turn. Aleck Drake, who was not in the tragedy, had been highly amused with the man's strange behavior, and when he came behind the scenes to dress for the farce, said, "Well, I shall have one good laugher in front to help me on with the farce." But, to his horror, and the astonishment of us all the man sat out the whole of one of the most comic and truly laughable farces we performed, and never even smiled once. He was watched by most of the company, and while the audience were convulsed with laughter he sat as immovable as a statue, and to all appearance as insensible. We

were greatly puzzled what to make of the man; he appeared to
us a perfect *lusus naturæ*. We questioned our landlord, who
knew him, and who told us he was sure he did not act in that
way for the purpose of insulting us; that he was an honest,
civil, and simple-minded man; and to questions put to him by
persons after the performance, expressed himself as highly
pleased with the night's entertainment. The landlord suggested, what we thought probable, that the only way of accounting
for the conduct of this man was, that he had never witnessed a
dramatic performance before; that he had heard "actors were
funny people;" that he had come prepared to laugh, and as
the actions of the performers were strange to him, he did laugh,
without regard to or feeling any interest in what was said by
them. But then, why not laugh when the farce was performed?
The landlord supposed "by that time he had laughed his laugh
out," and had exhausted himself in the effort, or was too tired
to laugh any more.

HORACE HOLLEY

*D*AVID MEADE *(1744-1838) arrived in Kentucky in 1796
from Tidewater Virginia. He brought with him a considerable
household and the social philosophy of an anglicized Virginia
gentleman. On his rolling Bluegrass acres he erected a sprawling house of many materials and designs, and gave it the romantic name "Chaumière du Prairie." The grounds of Chaumière were planned after those of an English estate, and to
Bluegrass Kentuckians it was a wonder. Colonel Meade was
not interested in growing great rolling fields of hemp and
wheat, or in driving herds of cattle away to market every year.
He wanted to gather around him a congenial company and live*

*as gently as the soft breezes which stirred the branches of his
magnificent blue ash trees.*

*Chaumière became a port of call for every visiting dignitary
to the Bluegrass. The Meade carriage was hustled into Lexington to fetch an army of foreign travelers, visiting statesmen,
and local gentry to Colonel Meade's bountiful board. President
Horace Holley (1781-1827) and the professors of Transylvania
were often on hand to give intellectual stimulus to conversation
at Chaumière. Coming to the Bluegrass fresh from the austeri-
ties of New England society, Horace Holley vividly described
Colonel Meade's hospitality in a letter to his wife which was
later published in* A Discourse on the Genius and Character of
the Rev. Horace Holley LL.D. *(Boston, 1828), by Charles Cald-
well (1772-1853), whom President Holley had brought to Transylvania as professor of materia medica.*

Nothing for Profit

I WENT with a party of ladies and gentlemen, nine miles into
the country to the seat of Colonel Mead, where we dined and
passed the day. This gentleman, who is near seventy, is a Virginian of the old school. He has been a good deal in England,
in his youth, and brought home with him English notions of
a country seat, though he is a great republican in politics. He
and his wife dress in the costume of the olden time. He has
the square coat and great cuffs, the vest of the court, short
breeches, and white stockings, at all times. Mrs. Mead has the
long waist, the white apron, the stays, the ruffles about the
elbows, and the cap of half a century ago. She is very mild and
ladylike, and though between sixty and seventy, plays upon
the piano-forte with the facility and cheerfulness of a young
lady. Her husband resembles Colonel [Timothy] Pickering in
the face, and the shape of the head. He is entirely a man of

leisure, never having followed any business, and never using his fortune but in adorning his place and entertaining his friends and strangers. No word is ever sent to him that company is coming. To do so offends him. But a dinner—he dines at the hour of four—is always ready for visiters; and servants are always in waiting. Twenty of us went out today, without warning, and were entertained luxuriously on the viands of the country. Our drink consisted of beer, toddy, and water. Wine, being imported and expensive, he never gives; nor does he allow cigars to be smoked in his presence. His house consists of a cluster of rustic cottages, in front of which spreads a beautiful, sloping lawn, as smooth as velvet. From this diverge, in various directions, and forming vistas terminated by picturesque objects, groves and walks extending over some acres. Seats, Chinese temples, verdant banks, and alcoves are interspersed at convenient distances. The lake, over which presides a Grecian temple, that you may imagine to be the residence of the water nymphs, has in it a small island, which communicates with the shore by a white bridge of one arch. The whole is surrounded by a low rustic fence of stone, surmounted and almost hidden by honeysuckle and roses, now in full flower, and which we gathered in abundance to adorn the ladies. Everything is laid out for walking and pleasure. His farm he rents, and does nothing for profit. The whole is in rustic taste. You enter from the road, through a gate between rude and massive columns, a field without pretension, wind a considerable distance through a noble park to an inner gate, the capitals to whose pillars are unique, being formed of the roots of trees, carved by nature. Then the rich scene of cultivation, of verdure and flower-capped hedges, bursts upon you. There is no establishment like this in our country. Instead of a description, I might have given you its name, *"Chaumière du Prairies."*

HARRIET BEECHER STOWE

HARRIET BEECHER STOWE (1811-1896), the wife of a professor of Biblical literature in Lane Seminary in Cincinnati, saw slavery firsthand in Kentucky. She wrote her stories of Uncle Tom first for the National Era, *a Washington, D. C., abolitionist newspaper; then they were published in two volumes under the title,* Uncle Tom's Cabin, or Life Among the Lowly *(Boston, 1852).*

Two of the major scenes of the book were set in Kentucky. In fact, one of the most famous footraces in American history was the mad dash of Liza from Garrard County to Ripley, Ohio, crossing the Ohio River on blocks of ice. Mrs. Stowe was able to strike the slaveholding South a hard backhanded blow by using first-family names for several of her characters. Shelby was a name of great honor in the Bluegrass.

The Appearance of a Gentleman

LATE IN the afternoon of a chilly day in February, two gentlemen were sitting alone over their wine, in a well-furnished dining parlor, in the town of P——, in Kentucky. There were no servants present, and the gentlemen, with chairs closely approaching, seemed to be discussing some subject with great earnestness.

For convenience sake, we have said, hitherto, two *gentlemen*. One of the parties, however, when critically examined, did not seem, strictly speaking, to come under the species. He was a short, thick-set man, with coarse, commonplace features, and that swaggering air of pretension which marks a low man who is trying to elbow his way upward in the world. He was much over-dressed, in a gaudy vest of many colors, a blue neckerchief, bedropped gayly with yellow spots, and arranged with a flaunting tie, quite in keeping with the general air of the man. His hands, large and coarse, were plentifully bedecked with rings; and he wore a heavy gold watch-chain, with a bundle of seals of portentous size, and a great variety of colors, attached to it,— which, in the ardor of conversation, he was in the habit of flourishing and jingling with evident satisfaction. His conversation was in free and easy defiance of Murray's Grammar, and was garnished at convenient intervals with various profane expressions, which not even the desire to be graphic in our account shall induce us to transcribe.

His companion, Mr. Shelby, had the appearance of a gentleman; and the arrangements of the house, and the general air of the housekeeping, indicated easy, and even opulent circumstances. As we before stated, the two were in the midst of an earnest conversation.

"That is the way I should arrange the matter," said Mr. Shelby.

"I can't make trade that way—I positively can't, Mr. Shelby," said the other, holding up a glass of wine between his eye and the light.

"Why, the fact is, Haley, Tom is an uncommon fellow; he is certainly worth that sum anywhere,—steady, honest, capable, manages my whole farm like a clock."

"You mean honest, as niggers go," said Haley, helping himself to a glass of brandy.

"No; I mean, really, Tom is a good, steady, sensible, pious fellow. He got religion at a camp-meeting, four years ago; and I believe he really *did* get it. I've trusted him since then, with everything I have,—money, house, horses,—and let him come and go round the country; and I always found him true and square in everything."

"Some folks don't believe there is pious niggers, Shelby," said Haley, with a candid flourish of his hand, "but I *do*. I had a fellow, now, in this yer last lot I took to Orleans—'t was as good as a meetin', now, really, to hear that critter pray; and he was quite gentle and quiet like. He fetched me a good sum, too, for I bought him cheap of a man that was 'bliged to sell out; so I realized six hundred on him. Yes, I consider religion a valeyable thing in a nigger, when it's the genuine article, and no mistake."

"Well, Tom's got the real article, if ever a fellow had," rejoined the other. "Why, last fall, I let him go to Cincinnati alone, to do business for me, and bring home five hundred dollars. 'Tom,' says I to him, 'I trust you, because I think you're a Christian—I know you wouldn't cheat.' Tom comes back, sure enough; I knew he would. Some low fellows, they say, said to him—'Tom, why don't you make tracks for Canada?' 'Ah, master trusted me, and I couldn't,'—they told me about it. I am sorry to part with Tom, I must say. You ought to let him cover the whole balance of the debt; and you would, Haley, if you had any conscience."

"Well, I've got just as much conscience as any man in business can afford to keep,—just a little, you know, to swear by, as 't were," said the trader, jocularly; "and, then, I'm ready to do anything in reason to 'blige friends; but this yer, you see, is a leetle too hard on a fellow—a leetle too hard." The trader sighed contemplatively, and poured out some more brandy.

"Well, then, Haley, how will you trade?" said Mr. Shelby, after an uneasy interval of silence.

"Well, have n't you a boy or gal that you could throw in with Tom?"

"Hum!—none that I could well spare; to tell the truth, it's only hard necessity makes me willing to sell at all. I don't like parting with any of my hands, that's a fact."

Here the door opened, and a small quadroon boy, between four and five years of age, entered the room. There was something in his appearance remarkably beautiful and engaging. His black hair, fine as floss silk, hung in glossy curls about his round, dimpled face, while a pair of large dark eyes, full of fire and softness, looked out from beneath the rich, long lashes, as he peered curiously into the apartment. A gay robe of scarlet and yellow plaid, carefully made and neatly fitted, set off to advantage the dark and rich style of his beauty; and a certain comic air of assurance, blended with bashfulness, showed that he had been not unused to being petted and noticed by his master.

"Hulloa, Jim Crow!" said Mr. Shelby, whistling, and snapping a bunch of raisins towards him, "pick that up, now!"

The child scampered, with all his little strength, after the prize, while his master laughed.

"Come here, Jim Crow," said he. The child came up, and the master patted the curly head, and chucked him under the chin.

"Now, Jim, show this gentleman how you can dance and sing." The boy commenced one of those wild, grotesque songs common among the negroes, in a rich, clear voice, accompanying his singing with many comic evolutions of the hands, feet, and whole body, all in perfect time to the music.

"Bravo!" said Haley, throwing him a quarter of an orange.

"Now, Jim, walk like old Uncle Cudjoe, when he has the rheumatism," said his master.

Instantly the flexible limbs of the child assumed the appearance of deformity and distortion, as, with his back humped up, and his master's stick in his hand, he hobbled about the room, his childish face drawn into a doleful pucker, and spitting from right to left, in imitation of an old man. Both gentlemen laughed uproariously.

"Now, Jim," said his master, "show us how old Elder Robbins leads the psalm." The boy drew his chubby face down to a formidable length, and commenced toning a psalm tune through his nose, with imperturbable gravity.

"Hurrah! bravo! what a young 'un!" said Haley; "that chap's a case, I'll promise. Tell you what," said he, suddenly clapping his hand on Mr. Shelby's shoulder, "fling in that chap, and I'll settle the business—I will. Come, now, if that ain't doing the thing up about the rightest!"

At this moment, the door was pushed gently open, and a young quadroon woman, apparently about twenty-five, entered the room.

There needed only a glance from the child to her, to identify her as its mother. There was the same rich, full, dark eye, with its long lashes; the same ripples of silky black hair. The brown of her complexion gave way on the cheek to a perceptible flush, which deepened as she saw the gaze of the strange man fixed upon her in bold and undisguised admiration. Her dress was of the neatest possible fit, and set off to advantage her finely moulded shape;—a delicately formed hand and a trim foot and ankle were items of appearance that did not escape the quick eye of the trader, well used to run up at a glance the points of a fine female article.

"Well, Eliza?" said her master, as she stopped and looked hesitatingly at him.

"I was looking for Harry, please, sir;" and the boy bounded toward her, showing his spoils, which he had gathered in the skirt of his robe.

"Well, take him away, then," said Mr. Shelby; and hastily she withdrew, carrying the child on her arm.

"By Jupiter," said the trader, turning to him in admiration, "there's an article, now! You might make your fortune on that ar gal in Orleans, any day. I've seen over a thousand, in my day, paid down for gals not a bit handsomer."

"I don't want to make my fortune on her," said Mr. Shelby, dryly; and, seeking to turn the conversation, he uncorked a bottle of fresh wine, and asked his companion's opinion of it.

"Capital, sir,—first chop!" said the trader; then turning, and slapping his hand familiarly on Shelby's shoulder, he added—

"Come, how will you trade about the gal?—what shall I say for her—what'll you take?"

"Mr. Haley, she is not to be sold," said Shelby. "My wife would not part with her for her weight in gold."

"Ay, ay! women always say such things, cause they ha'nt no

sort of calculation. Just show 'em how many watches, feathers, and trinkets, one's weight in gold would buy, and that alters the case, *I* reckon."

"I tell you, Haley, this must not be spoken of; I say no, and I mean no," said Shelby, decidedly.

"Well, you'll let me have the boy, though," said the trader; "you must own I've come down pretty handsomely for him."

"What on earth can you want with the child?" said Shelby.

"Why, I've got a friend that's going into this yer branch of the business—wants to buy up handsome boys to raise for the market. Fancy articles entirely—sell for waiters, and so on, to rich 'uns, that can pay for handsome 'uns. It sets off one of yer great places—a real handsome boy to open door, wait, and tend. They fetch a good sum; and this little devil is such a comical, musical concern, he's just the article."

"I would rather not sell him," said Mr. Shelby, thoughtfully; "the fact is, sir, I'm a humane man, and I hate to take the boy from his mother, sir." . . .

"S'pose not; you Kentucky folks spile your niggers. You mean well by 'em, but 'tan't no real kindness, arter all. Now, a nigger, you see, what's got to be hacked and tumbled round the world, and sold to Tom, and Dick, and the Lord knows who, 'tan't no kindness to be givin' on him notions and ex-pectations, and bringin' on him up too well, for the rough and tumble comes all the harder on him arter. Now, I venture to say, your niggers would be quite chop-fallen in a place where some of your plantation niggers would be singing and whoop-ing like all possessed. Every man, you know, Mr. Shelby, nat-urally thinks well of his own ways; and I think I treat niggers just about as well as it's ever worth while to treat 'em."

"It's a happy thing to be satisfied," said Mr. Shelby, with a slight shrug, and some perceptible feelings of a disagreeable nature.

"Well," said Haley, after they had both silently picked their nuts for a season, "what do you say?"

"I'll think the matter over, and talk with my wife," said Mr.

Shelby. "Meantime, Haley, if you want the matter carried on in the quiet way you speak of, you'd best not let your business in this neighborhood be known. It will get out among my boys, and it will not be a particularly quiet business getting away any of my fellows, if they know it, I'll promise you."

"O! certainly, by all means, mum! of course. But I'll tell you, I'm in a devil of a hurry, and shall want to know, as soon as possible, what I may depend on," said he, rising and putting on his overcoat.

"Well, call up this evening, between six and seven, and you shall have my answer," said Mr. Shelby, and the trader bowed himself out of the apartment.

"I'd like to have been able to kick the fellow down the steps," said he to himself, as he saw the door fairly closed, "with his impudent assurance; but he knows how much he has me at advantage. If anybody had ever said to me that I should sell Tom down south to one of those rascally traders, I should have said, 'Is thy servant a dog, that he should do this thing?' And now it must come, for aught I see. And Eliza's child, too! I know that I shall have some fuss with wife about that; and, for that matter, about Tom, too. So much for being in debt,—heigho! The fellow sees his advantage, and means to push it."

Perhaps the mildest form of the system of slavery is to be seen in the State of Kentucky. The general prevalence of agricultural pursuits of a quiet and gradual nature, not requiring those periodic seasons of hurry and pressure that are called for in the business of more southern districts, makes the task of the negro a more healthful and reasonable one; while the master, content with a more gradual style of acquisition, has not those temptations to hardheartedness which always overcome frail human nature when the prospect of sudden and rapid gain is weighed in the balance, with no heavier counterpoise than the interests of the helpless and unprotected.

Whoever visits some estates there, and witnesses the good-humored indulgence of some masters and mistresses, and the affectionate loyalty of some slaves, might be tempted to dream the oft-fabled poetic legend of a patriarchal institution, and all that; but over and above the scene there broods a portentous shadow—the shadow of *law*. So long as the law considers all these human beings, with beating hearts and living affections, only as so many *things* belonging to a master,—so long as the failure, or misfortune, or imprudence, or death of the kindest owner, may cause them any day to exchange a life of kind protection and indulgence for one of hopeless misery and toil,—so long it is impossible to make anything beautiful or desirable in the best regulated administration of slavery.

Mr. Shelby was a fair average kind of man, good-natured and kindly, and disposed to easy indulgence of those around him, and there had never been a lack of anything which might contribute to the physical comfort of the negroes on his estate. He had, however, speculated largely and quite loosely; had involved himself deeply, and his notes to a large amount had come into the hands of Haley; and this small piece of information is the key to the preceding conversation. . . .

Mrs. Shelby was a woman of a high class, both intellectually and morally. To that natural magnanimity and generosity of mind which one often marks as characteristic of the women of Kentucky, she added high moral and religious sensibility and principle, carried out with great energy and ability into practical results. Her husband, who made no professions to any particular religious character, nevertheless reverenced and respected the consistency of hers, and stood, perhaps, a little in awe of her opinion. Certain it was that he gave her unlimited scope in all her benevolent efforts for the comfort, instruction, and improvement of her servants, though he never took any decided part in them himself. In fact, if not exactly a believer in the doctrine of the efficiency of the extra good works of saints, he really seemed somehow or other to fancy that his wife had piety and benevolence enough for two—to indulge a shadowy expectation of getting into heaven through her superabundance of qualities to which he made no particular pretension.

The heaviest load on his mind, after his conversation with the trader, lay in the foreseen necessity of breaking to his wife the arrangement contemplated,—meeting the importunities and opposition which he knew he should have reason to encounter.

BASIL DUKE

*K*ENTUCKY *boys who rushed away so gayly with John Hunt Morgan (1825-1864) to join the Confederate cavalry were most happy in 1863 to be heading back home, even if it was on a wild raid beyond the Ohio. Basil Duke (1838-1916), Morgan's brother-in-law and a colonel in his regiment, in his* History of Morgan's Cavalry *(Cincinnati, 1867) quotes an unnamed author who sensed the joy of Morgan's men as they prepared to rush across the Kentucky border from upper middle Tennessee on December 22, 1863. "Did you ever see Morgan on horseback?" Here is a heroic picture of a swashbuckling gentleman, riding triumphantly back to his Bluegrass home, with a cheering army at his heels.*

The Bearing of a Soldier

THE REGIMENTS had been carefully inspected by the Surgeons and Inspectors, and every sick soldier and disabled horse had been taken from their regiments, and the stout men and serviceable horses only were permitted to accompany the expedition. The men were never in higher spirits or more joyous humor; well armed, well mounted, in good discipline, with perfect confidence in their commander, and with hearts longing for the hills and valleys, the blue-grass and woods of dear old Kentucky; they made the air vocal with their cheers and laughter and songs and sallies of wit. The division had never operated together before the brigades had first been organized, therefore every regiment was filled with the spirit of emulation, and every man was determined to make his the crack regiment of Morgan's cavalry. It was a magnificent body of men—the pick of the youth of Kentucky. No commander ever led a nobler corps—no corps was ever more nobly led. It was splendidly officered by gallant, dashing, skillful men in the flush of early manhood; for of the seven Colonels who commanded those seven regiments, five became brigade commanders—the other two gave their lives to the cause—Colonel Bennett dying early in January, 1863, of a disease contracted while in the army, and Colonel Chenault being killed on July 4, 1863, gallantly leading his men in a fruitless charge upon breastworks at Green river bridge. This December morning was a mild, beautiful fall day; clear, cloudless sky; bright sun; the camps in cedar evergreens, where the birds chirped and twittered; it felt and looked like spring. The reveille sounded before day-break; the horses were fed, breakfast gotten. Very early came the orders from General Morgan announcing the organization of the brigades, intimating the objects of the expedition, and ordering the column to move at nine o'clock. Duke in advance. As the order was read to a regiment the utmost deathless silence of disciplined soldiers standing at attention was broken only by the clear voice of the Adjutant reading the precise but stirring words of the beloved hero-chieftain; then came the sharp word of command dismissing the parade; and the woods trembled with the wild hurrahs of the half crazy men, and regiment answered regiment, cheer re-echoed cheer, over the wide encampment. Soon came Duke, and his staff, and his column— his own old gallant regiment at the head—and slowly regiment after regiment filed out of the woods into the road, lengthening the long column.

After some two hours march, a cheer began in the extreme

rear and rapidly came forward, increasing in volume and enthusiasm, and soon General Morgan dashed by, with his hat in his hand, bowing and smiling his thanks for these flattering cheers, followed by a large and well mounted staff. Did you ever see Morgan on horseback? If not, you missed one of the most impressive figures of the war. Perhaps no General in either army surpassed him in the striking proportion and grace of his person, and the ease and grace of his horsemanship. Over six feet in height, straight as an Indian, exquisitely proportioned, with the air and manner of a cultivated and polished gentleman, and the bearing of a soldier, always handsomely and tastefully dressed, and elegantly mounted, he was the picture of the superb cavalry officer. Just now he was in the height of his fame and happiness; married only ten days before to an accomplished lady, made Brigadier justly but very tardily; in command of the finest cavalry division in the Southern army; beloved almost to idolatry by his men, and returning their devotion by an extravagant confidence in their valor and prowess; conscious of his own great powers, yet wearing his honors with the most admirable modesty, and just starting upon a carefully conceived but daring expedition, he was perhaps in the zenith of his fame.

JAMES LANE ALLEN

THE LUDICROUS figure of Romulus Fields to readers of today may seem a caricature of species Kentucky Colonel. James Lane Allen (1849-1925) undoubtedly did not intend his portrayal to arouse anything but sympathy for the Bluegrass gentleman unable to make the adjustment to the new life after the Civil War. With his faithful servant and former slave Peter

Cotton, Colonel Rom made a brave attempt to find a place in the new society, but old habits would not conform to the changed ways.

Allen's novelette, Two Gentlemen of Kentucky, *was published in* Flute and Violin and Other Kentucky Tales *(New York, 1891).*

Belated, Fruitless Efflorescence

ABOUT TWO years after the close of the war, therefore, the colonel and Peter were to be found in Lexington, ready to turn over a new leaf in the volumes of their lives, which already had an old-fashioned binding, a somewhat musty odor, and but few unwritten leaves remaining.

After a long, dry summer you may have seen two gnarled old apple-trees, that stood with interlocked arms on the western slope of some quiet hill-side, make a melancholy show of blooming out again in the autumn of the year and dallying with the idle buds that mock their sapless branches. Much the same was the belated, fruitless efflorescence of the colonel and Peter.

The colonel had no business habits, no political ambition, no wish to grow richer. He was too old for society, and without near family ties. For some time he wandered through the streets like one lost—sick with yearning for the fields and woods, for his cattle, for familiar faces. He haunted Cheapside and the court-house square, where the farmers always assembled when they came to town; and if his eye lighted on one, he would button-hole him on the street-corner and lead him into a grocery and sit down for a quiet chat. Sometimes he would meet an aimless, melancholy wanderer like himself, and the two would go off and discuss over and over again their departed days; and several times he came unexpectedly upon some of his old servants who had fallen into bitter want, and who more than repaid him for the help he gave by contrasting the hardships of a life of freedom with the ease of their shackled years.

In the course of time, he could but observe that human life in the town was reshaping itself slowly and painfully, but with resolute energy. The colossal structure of slavery had fallen, scattering its ruins far and wide over the State; but out of the very débris was being taken the material to lay the deeper foundations of the new social edifice. Men and women as old as he were beginning life over, and trying to fit themselves for it by changing the whole attitude and habit of their minds—by taking on a new heart and spirit. But when a great building falls, there is always some rubbish, and the colonel and others like him were part of this. Henceforth they possessed only an antiquarian sort of interest, like the stamped bricks of Nebuchadnezzar.

Nevertheless he made a show of doing something, and in a year or two opened on Cheapside a store for the sale of hardware and agricultural implements. He knew more about the latter than anything else; and, furthermore, he secretly felt that a business of this kind would enable him to establish in town a kind of headquarters for the farmers. His account-books were to be kept on a system of twelve months' credit; and he resolved that if one of his customers couldn't pay then, it would make no difference.

Business began slowly. The farmers dropped in and found a good lounging-place. On county-court days, which were great market-days for the sale of sheep, horses, mules, and cattle in front of the colonel's door, they swarmed in from the hot sun and sat around on the counter and the ploughs and machines till the entrance was blocked to other customers.

When a customer did come in, the colonel, who was probably talking with some old acquaintance, would tell him just to look around and pick out what he wanted and the price would be all right. If one of those acquaintances asked for a pound of nails, the colonel would scoop up some ten pounds and say,

"I reckon that's about a pound, Tom." He had never seen a pound of nails in his life; and if one had been weighed on his scales, he would have said the scales were wrong.

He had no great idea of commercial despatch. One morning a lady came in for some carpet-tacks, an article that he had forgotten to lay in. But he at once sent off an order for enough to have tacked a carpet pretty well all over Kentucky; and when they came, two weeks later, he told Peter to take her up a dozen papers with his compliments. He had laid in, however, an ample and especially fine assortment of pocket-knives, for that instrument had always been to him one of gracious and very winning qualities. Then when a friend dropped in he would say, "General, don't you need a new pocket-knife?" and, taking one out, would open all the blades and commend the metal and the handle. The "general" would inquire the price, and the colonel, having shut the blades, would hand it to him, saying in a careless, fond way, "I reckon I won't charge you anything for that." His mind could not come down to the low level of such ignoble barter, and he gave away the whole case of knives.

These were the pleasanter aspects of his business life, which did not lack as well its tedium and crosses. Thus there were many dark stormy days when no one he cared to see came in; and he then became rather a pathetic figure, wandering absently around amid the symbols of his past activity, and stroking the ploughs, like dumb companions. Or he would stand at the door and look across at the old court-house, where he had seen many a slave sold and had listened to the great Kentucky orators.

But what hurt him most was the talk of the new farming and the abuse of the old which he was forced to hear; and he generally refused to handle the improved implements and mechanical devices by which labor and waste were to be saved.

Altogether he grew tired of "the thing," and sold out at the end of the year with a loss of over a thousand dollars, though he insisted he had done a good business.

As he was then seen much on the streets again and several times heard to make remarks in regard to the sidewalks, gutters, and crossings, when they happened to be in bad condition, the *Daily Press* one morning published a card stating that if Colonel Romulus Fields would consent to make the race for mayor he would receive the support of many Democrats, adding a tribute to his virtues and his influential past. It touched the colonel, and he walked down-town with a rather commanding figure the next morning. But it pained him to see how many of his acquaintances returned his salutations very coldly; and just as he was passing the Northern Bank he met the young opposition candidate—a little red-haired fellow, walking between two ladies, with a rose-bud in his button-hole—who refused to speak at all, but made the ladies laugh by some remark he uttered as the colonel passed. The card had been inserted humorously, but he took it seriously; and when his friends found this out, they rallied round him. The day of election drew near. They told him he must buy votes. He said he wouldn't buy a vote to be mayor of the New Jerusalem. They told him he must "mix" and "treat." He refused. Foreseeing he had no chance, they besought him to withdraw. He said he would not. They told him he wouldn't poll twenty votes. He replied that *one* would satisfy him, provided it was neither begged nor bought. When his defeat was announced, he accepted it as another evidence that he had no part in the present—no chance of redeeming his idleness.

A sense of this weighed heavily on him at times; but it is not likely that he realized how pitifully he was undergoing a moral shrinkage in consequence of mere disuse. Actually, extinction had set in with him long prior to dissolution, and he was dead years before his heart ceased beating. The very basic virtues on which had rested his once spacious and stately character were now but the mouldy corner-stones of a crumbling ruin.

It was a subtle evidence of deterioration in manliness that he had taken to dress. When he had lived in the country, he had never dressed up unless he came to town. When he had moved to town, he thought he must remain dressed up all the time; and this fact first fixed his attention on a matter which afterwards began to be loved for its own sake. Usually he wore a Derby hat, a black diagonal coat, gray trousers, and a white necktie. But the article of attire in which he took chief pleasure was hose; and the better to show the gay colors of these, he wore low-cut shoes of the finest calf-skin, turned up at the toes. Thus his feet kept pace with the present, however far his head may have lagged in the past; and it may be that this stream of fresh fashions, flowing perennially over his lower extremities like water about the roots of a tree, kept him from drying up altogether.

Peter always polished his shoes with too much blacking, perhaps thinking that the more the blacking, the greater the proof of love. He wore his clothes about a season and a half—having several suits—and then passed them on to Peter, who, foreseeing the joy of such an inheritance, bought no new ones. In the act of transferring them the colonel made no comment until he came to the hose, from which he seemed unable to part without a final tribute of esteem, as: "These are fine, Peter;" or, "Peter, these are nearly as good as new." Thus Peter, too, was dragged through the whims of fashion. To have seen the colonel walking about his grounds and garden followed by Peter, just a year and a half behind in dress and a yard and a half behind in space, one might well have taken the rear figure for the colonel's double, slightly the worse for wear, somewhat shrunken, and cast into a heavy shadow.

Time hung so heavily on his hands at night that with a happy inspiration he added a dress-suit to his wardrobe, and accepted the first invitation to an evening party.

He grew excited as the hour approached, and dressed in a great fidget for fear he should be too late.

"How do I look, Peter?" he inquired at length, surprised at his own appearance.

"Splendid, Marse Rom," replied Peter, bringing in the shoes with more blacking on them than ever before.

"I think," said the colonel, apologetically—"I think I'd look better if I'd put a little powder on. I don't know what makes me so red in the face."

But his heart began to sink before he reached his hostess's, and he had a fearful sense of being the observed of all observers as he slipped through the hall and passed rapidly up to the gentlemen's room. He stayed there after the others had gone down, bewildered and lonely, dreading to go down himself. By-and-by the musicians struck up a waltz, and with a little cracked laugh at his own performance he cut a few shines of an unremembered pattern; but his ankles snapped audibly, and he suddenly stopped with the thought of what Peter would say if he should catch him at these antics. Then he boldly went down-stairs.

He touched the new human life around him at various points: as he now stretched out his arms toward its society, for the first time he completely realized how far removed it was from him. Here he saw a younger generation—the flowers of the new social order—sprung from the very soil of fraternal battle-fields, but blooming together as the emblems of oblivious peace. He saw fathers who had fought madly on opposite sides talking quietly in corners as they watched their children dancing, or heard them toasting their old generals and their campaigns over their champagne in the supper-room. He was glad of it; but it made him feel, at the same time, that instead of treading the velvety floors, he ought to step up and take his place among the canvases of old-time portraits that looked down from the walls.

The dancing he had done had been not under the blinding glare of gas-light, but by the glimmer of tallow-dips and star-candles and the ruddy glow of cavernous firesides—not to the accompaniment of an orchestra of wind-instruments and strings, but to a chorus of girls' sweet voices, as they trod simpler measures, or to the maddening sway of a gray-haired negro fiddler standing on a chair in the chimney-corner. Still, it is significant to note that his saddest thought, long after leaving, was that his shirt-bosom had not lain down smooth, but stuck out like a huge cracked egg-shell; and that when, in imitation of the others, he had laid his white silk handkerchief across his bosom inside his vest, it had slipped out during the evening, and had been found by him, on confronting a mirror, flapping over his stomach like a little white masonic apron.

"Did you have a nice time, Marse Rom?" inquired Peter, as they drove home through the darkness.

"Splendid time, Peter, splendid time," replied the colonel, nervously.

"Did you dance any, Marse Rom?"

"I didn't *dance*. Oh, I *could* have danced if I'd *wanted* to; but I didn't."

Peter helped the colonel out of the carriage with pitying gentleness when they reached home. It was the first and only party.

GEORGE B. LEACH

THE LIKES of Colonel Rom undoubtedly were shocked that such a lowbred person as Henry Price McGrath (1814-1881) should be able to parlay his gambling success into a Bluegrass estate which produced Aristides, the first winner of the Kentucky Derby. Charles (Riley) Grannan (1868-1908), like Mc-Grath a professional gambler, was more congenial to a later generation of Kentucky aristocracy, for he had the grace to die penniless and so uphold the public mores.

George B. Leach, then sports editor of the Lexington Leader, recalled the colorful careers of McGrath and Grannan for the readers of the souvenir magazine commemorating the opening of the Keeneland track at Lexington in 1936.

Something Never Forgotten

OF THE people connected with the old Lexington track none seemed to come up to Price McGrath and Riley Grannan for color. Both were Kentuckians born in counties adjoining Fayette; both were gamblers. While McGrath was a great plunger he never measured up to Grannan in that respect. It is doubtful that anyone ever did. McGrath also was a breeder of note. He was born of poor parentage in Woodford county, and the first dime he ever made he gave to a wealthy landowner going into Versailles with the request that he purchase him a blue-back spelling book. All day McGrath sat on the fence waiting for the landowner to return. At sundown he saw the buggy in the distance and ran forward to meet it. The man returned his dime with the remark that "the books cost twelve and one-half cents." McGrath gave up his longing for learning and in later years told his friends, "For two and one-half cents I was denied an education."

Lack of an education, however, did not stop him. He went west in '49, later went to New York where he opened a gambling house on 42nd or 45th street. Princeton students from Kentucky often visited his New York place. He never allowed them to enter the gambling rooms, but welcomed them in his restaurant. His decision to return to Kentucky and enter the horse business followed his exceptional winnings in a three-handed game of Boston. During a single evening McGrath won $105,000, which he pocketed and started for the Blue Grass.

He was the first man to sell a pool in the city of Lexington and sold it in front of the Phoenix Hotel entrance. Throughout his life he gambled freely. He purchased McGrathiana Stud (now Charles Shaffer's Coldstream Stud) and began breeding horses. Never, however, did he drive a horse. Instead he drove one or two mules to a Jersey wagon. On the eve of Aristides' race with Ten Broeck he pulled up in front of the office of one young Kentucky lawyer who had attended Princeton and told him to go to the bank and get all his money to bet on Aristides. The following day McGrath put up thousands on his horse, but never made a note of any wager. One friend made the statement he ought to keep books on the race. To that McGrath replied, "The little brown horse is keeping books today."

The parties at McGrathiana on Sundays prior to the races at Lexington were something never forgotten by those who attended. The public was invited—and went. An aged Negro, "Old Pete," was in charge of the drinks that were served the entire length of the veranda across the front of his home. Beeves, whole pigs and mutton that had been cooked over wood fires were served during the all-day party. After McGrath's death in 1881, his place was purchased by Colonel Milton Young, who became one of America's foremost breeders.

Colorful as was McGrath's life it hardly matched that of Grannan, who was born in Bourbon county. Grannan led one of the most spectacular lives connected with the Turf. He won and lost on many races more money than the average man hopes to accumulate in a lifetime. He was at the top as often as he was at the bottom. He was broke one day and immensely wealthy the next. An incident that occurred in New York in 1896 was typical of his life. The races had broken him and as he started plans to regain his finances he got out a spring suit to have it cleaned. In a pocket he found a fifty-dollar bill left there when the suit was put away for the winter. The following afternoon he ran that note into $20,000 at the race track. Such incidents occurred many times during his life.

He was a regular figure on the Lexington track and in 1894 opened the Navarre Cafe on Main street in Lexington, naming it for the great race horse, Henry of Navarre. For his patrons he imported the finest liqueurs from every continent. He brought sea foods from the coast. All sorts of fowls could be had for the asking. Grannan often boasted that anything available in New York's finest restaurant could also be had in the Navarre Cafe. But Grannan also lamented, "Lexington people never want anything but a half-dozen fried or a half-dozen raw." Nevertheless, he thought he would make a success of the cafe. During the racing season, however, was the only time he could make the place pay. It was finally closed by creditors. The story is told that Grannan knew his restaurant was to be closed and that he and his associates planned an elaborate party as one final splurge. Silverware, furniture, china and other items were sent over by the Phoenix Hotel for this great party. It was in full swing when at one minute past midnight the sheriff stepped in and attached everything in the restaurant. The Phoenix lost approximately $7,000 worth of equipment, so the story goes.

Grannan went broke for the last time in California, where he went to attend the races. From there he went to a mining camp in Nevada in an effort to recoup his losses. He died at Rawhide and his funeral was even more extraordinary than his life. His body was placed in a rough coffin and the services were conducted in a variety theater in the rear of a saloon. Only a mining camp could produce the people that attended his funeral. Rough miners, women in their silk kimonos of the dance hall, gamblers, business men, bartenders, and bankers assembled for his last rites. Jack Hines, of Alaska mining fame, and a woman who had been a noted actress provided the solos. A former preacher was roused from his slumbers at the gambling tables for the services. His sermon, treasured by those who have been fortunate in procuring a copy, was as follows:

"I feel it incumbent upon me to state that I now occupy no ministerial or prelatic position. I am only a prospector. I make no claim to moral merit whatever or to religious authority, except it be the religion of the brotherhood of man. I wish to be only as a man among men, feeling that I can shake hands and style as my brother the most humble of you all. If there may come from me a word of moral admonition, it springs not from a sense of moral superiority, only from the depths of my experience.

"Riley Grannan was born in Paris, Kentucky, about forty years ago. He cherished all the dreams of childhood. Those dreams found their fruition in phenomenal success financially. I am told from the position of bell boy in a hotel he rose to be a celebrity of world wide fame. Riley Grannan was one of the greatest plungers the continent has produced. He died day before yesterday at Rawhide.

"That is a brief statement. We have his birth and the day of his demise. Who can fill the interim? Not I. Who can tell his hopes and fears? Who knows the misery of his quiet hours? Not I.

"Riley Grannan was born in the sunny southland of Kentucky. He died at Rawhide. That is the beginning. That is the end. Is there in this a picture of what Ingersoll said at the grave of his brother? 'Whether it be near the shore or in mid-ocean, or among the breakers at the last, a wreck must mark the end of one and all.'

"Born where the brooks and rivers run musically through prolific soil; where magnolia goldiflora—like white stars—glow in a firmament of green; where lakes dot the greensward and the softest summer breezes dimple the wavelets; where the air is resonant with the melody of a thousand sweet-voiced birds, and redolent of the perfume of blooming flowers—that was the beginning. Riley Grannan died in Rawhide, where in winter the tops of the mountains are clothed in garments of ice, and where in summer the blistering rays of the sun beat down upon the skeleton of the desert.

"Is there a picture in this of universal life? Sometimes when I look upon the circumstances of life, there comes to my lips a curse. I relate to you only my views. If these run counter to yours, believe what I say is sincere. When I see the ambitions of man defeated, I see his aim and purpose frustrated only by a combination of circumstances over which he can exert no

control. I see his outstretched hand, about to grasp the flag
of victory, seize instead the emblem of defeat.

"I ask, What is life? What is life? Dreams, awakening death.
Life is a pendulum betwixt a smile and a tear. Life is but
a momentary halt with the waste and then the nothing we set
out from. Life is a shadow; a poor player who struts and frets
his hour upon the stage and then is heard no more. Life is a
child-blown bubble that reflects the shadow of its environment
and is gone—a mockery, a sham, a lie, a fool's vision, its happiness but Dead Sea apples, its pain the crunching of a tyrant's
heel.

"If I have gauged Grannan's character correctly, he accepted
circumstances surrounding him as the mystic officials to whom
the universe had delegated its whole office concerning him. He
took defeat and victory with equal equanimity. He was a man
of placid exterior. His meteoric past shows him invincible in
spirit, and it is not irreverently that I proclaim him a dead
game sport. When I use that phrase, I do so filling it as full
of practical human philosophy as it will hold.

"There are those who will condemn him. They believe that
today he is reaping the benefits of a misspent life. There are
those who are dominated by medieval creeds. These I am not
addressing. They are ruled by the skeleton hand of the past.
They fail to see the moral side of a character lived outside their
puritanical ideas. Riley's goodness was not of a type that
reached its highest manifestations in ceremonious piety. It
found its expression in the handclasp of friendship. It found
its voice in the word of cheer to a discouraged brother. His
were deeds of quiet charity. His were acts of manhood.

"Riley Grannan lived in a world of sport. My words are not
minced, because I am telling what I believe to be true. It was
a world of sport, sometimes hilarity, sometimes worse. He left
the impress of his character upon us all, and through the medium of his financial power he was able with his money to
brighten the lives of all who knew him.

"He wasted his money, so the world says; but did it ever

occur to you that the men and women and the class upon whom he wasted it were yet men and women? A little happiness brought into their minds means as much to them as happiness carried into the lives of the straight and good. If you can take one ray of sunshine into the night life and thereby carry a single hour of happiness, you are a benefactor. Riley Grannan did this.

"God confined not his sunbeams to the nourishing of potatoes and corn. His scattering of sunshine was prodigal. Contemplate—He flings the auroral beauties 'round the cold shoulders of the North. He hangs quivering pictures of the mirage above the palpitating heart of the desert. He scatters the sunbeams like scattered gold upon the bosom of a myriad of lakes that gem the robe of nature. He spangles the canopy of night with star jewels and silvers the world with the reflected beams from on high. He hangs the gorgeous curtain on the Occident across the sleeping room of the sun.

"God wakes the coy maid of the morning to step timidly from her boudoir of darkness to climb the steep of the Orient, to fling wide the gates of morning and trip over the landscape, kissing the flowers in her flight. She arouses the world to herald with its music the coming of her king, who floods the world with effulgent gold.

"These are wasted sunbeams, are they? I say to you that men and women who by the use of money or power are able to smooth one wrinkle from the brow of human care, to change one man's sob into song, or to wipe away a tear and place in its stead a jewel of joy, are public benefactors. Such was Riley Grannan.

"The time has come to say goodbye. For the friends and loved ones not here to say the word let me say 'goodbye, old man.' We will try to exemplify the spirit you left as we bear the grief at our parting. Words fail me here. Let those flowers, Riley, with their petaled lips and perfumed breath, speak in beauty and fragrance those sentiments too tender for words. Goodbye!"

CLEMENT EATON

THE MODERN Bluegrass gentleman is a far cry from David Meade or Romulus Fields, Clement Eaton (1898-   ) found when he visited J. Winston Coleman, Jr. (1898-   ) in 1941. But there is a similarity too, the college professor from Pennsylvania noted—a common philosophy of enjoying life. The Bluegrass must have had its attractions for the North-Carolina-born historian, for a few years later he made Lexington his home. Eaton recorded his impressions of the owner of Winburn Farm in an article, "Kentucky Colonel—New Vintage," for the Southern Literary Messenger.

This Appreciation of Leisure

ON A RECENT trip to Kentucky I had an opportunity to observe the 1940-41 style of Kentucky Colonels. Driving south from Cincinnati, I approached the fertile limestone basin of Lexington and was immediately conscious of being in a "fency" country, with white rails to confine the spirited race horses and quaint stone fences that were unlike those of New England. As I approached the home of the squire, I was reminded of the childhood story of "The Little Colonel" who rode on her pony, "Tar Baby," down a long avenue of locust trees.

The squire of Winburn Farm was proud to announce that he was a "dirt farmer." There was nothing about him to suggest the stage version of the old Kentucky Colonel, with Van Dyke beard, frock coat, and gold-headed cane. Rather, he was a robust gentleman of early middle age, with a frank, suntanned countenance, and a hearty voice. His coat was off, his belt was loose, and his shirt was open at the throat. He made his living by growing tobacco and raising hay and corn to feed the race horses in his vicinity. He informed me that before the Roosevelt agricultural policies were adopted, he had cultivated thirty-two acres of tobacco, but since the Government had curtailed production of "the sovereign weed," his quota had been fixed at sixteen acres. The machine age has reached the Kentucky farms. The squire uses tractors instead of horses to plough his land, and he plants his tobacco crops with an ingenious machine. He communicates with his tenants by a private telephone system, and he rides into Lexington for his luxuries in a Pontiac car. In olden days the Kentucky Colonels had obtained their ice for their juleps from domestic ice houses sunk in the ground, with conical shaped roofs. Such relics of the past may still be seen in the rear of "Ashland," Henry Clay's home. But the modern Colonel has a General Electric refrigerator that provides him with ice cubes. His food is cooked on an electric stove and a washing machine lightens domestic service. In fact, the rural life of the well-to-do in the South has been revolutionized by electricity and gasoline.

Around his farm are the luxurious estates where the Kentucky thoroughbred horses and their long-legged colts graze. This Lexington limestone basin is not a country for the yeoman farmer. Land is too expensive. The squire told me that the proprietor of a neighboring farm had been offered seven hundred and fifty dollars an acre for his farm. Many of these lordly estates are owned by Northern capitalists, such as "Dixiana," and "Faraway Farm," the home of Man o' War. They are the playthings of the rich absentee owners. The Colonel does not attempt to breed race horses, for he says it is the quickest way "to break" a gentleman of moderate means. Nevertheless, he delights in horseflesh and is proud of the Kentucky racers. He escorts his guests to these "show places" and jokes with the old Negroes who display the retired heroes of the turf. Old Will [Harbut], who should be called the major-domo to his majesty, Man o' War, has a tremendous sense of his importance in caring for the famed racer, "that super-hoss," who was defeated but once in his career of racing, and the jockey who rode him on that occasion, Will significantly remarks, received his walking papers. . . .

The squire has attained a happy and tranquil philosophy of life on his blue grass farm, which has been owned by the family since 1810. In his earlier years he was a business man, but the worries and uncertainties of that mode of life caused him to abandon it and return to the soil. Now he enjoys the independence and peace of mind of a country gentleman. No Southerner could be more hospitable than the Colonel. The food that he serves his guests is grown largely on his farm, the bread and pancakes are made from his own grain, the sausages and hams from his own hogs, the chickens and eggs are furnished by his tenants, the cream and strawberries are home products, and the flowers that adorn his table are gathered from his garden. When he makes a mint julep, he steps outside his door and pulls a sprig of mint from the bank of the stream by the spring house. He serves his delicious concoction from coin silver julep cups that his grandfather drank from, and he gleefully shows you how worn are the edges of the spoon with which his "grandpappy" stirred his juleps. . . .

The focal room in the house of Winburn Farm is the library. Its shelves are filled with books on Kentuckiana, for the squire is one of the nonprofessional historians of the South. Many of the dollars that were earned from the sale of tobacco and livestock have gone into buying rare books on Southern history. The Colonel has written books on the romance of stage-coaching days and of the old taverns of Kentucky, such as Postlethwait's in Lexington. His *magnum opus*, however, is a mellow study of slavery times in Kentucky. On the walls of his library hang the photographs of many eminent Southern writers who have visited his home. They indicate that the proprietor has a gift for friendship and has carried on the old Southern virtue of hospitality. . . .

But one of the most appealing facets of his personality is his philosophy of enjoying life. He thoroughly believes in leisure. Hence he does most of his farming by telephone. Especially does he believe that every person should have a hobby. He is fond of contrasting his carefree and pleasant mode of existence with the prosaic life of some other farmers who work hard, fret, and fume, and have little fun out of life. It is this appreciation of leisure, to use for culture and the enjoyment of good companionship, that forms the connecting link between this splendid specimen of the Kentucky Colonel of 1941 and his prototype, the old Colonel with the Van Dyke beard and the gold-headed cane.

JOE H. PALMER

ABSENTEE ownership is the rule for the Bluegrass horse farms today, a rule proved by a number of notable exceptions. The operations of the local landowners, however, are usually consistent with the gentlemanly tradition of gracious, leisurely living, with no material profit. The Parrish family of Midway, Woodford County, had been the chief benefactors of the small town since its founding, and James Ware Parrish (1862-1940) was not one to shirk his responsibility.

Joe H. Palmer (1904-1952), a Bluegrass boy who made good in the city, met another Midway horse breeder at Miami's Hialeah track; out of this chance encounter came the story of Jim Parrish's philanthropies and material for Palmer's racing column in the New York Herald Tribune, *later reprinted in* This Was Racing *(New York, 1953).*

The Finger of Providence

DURING the closing days of the Hialeah meeting, this department was prowling the grounds looking for tapped wires and transmitting stations, when a familiar face appeared in the picture. There is a certain nicety of complexion which can be produced only by fried chicken, country ham and corn muffins, and when I see it I know someone has dropped in from the horse country.

Since Circus Clown had just won a race and both he and the face are owned by W. Julian Walden, it seemed the thing to do to say congratulations and how were things in Midway, Ky. If your geography has been neglected, Midway is between Payne's Depot and Nugent's Crossroad. It turned out that Walden, being averse to the slings and arrows of outrageous weather, was spending the winter fishing for fish in Naples and for money at Hialeah, and was doing quite well in both departments. So the news from Midway was a little stale.

"Tell you what, though," he said. "I brought my mother to the races. She's seventy-five, and this was the first time she ever saw a horse race. As a minister's wife, she's always been opposed to racing."

A slip once every seventy-five years ought to be permitted anyone. But now that Mrs. Walden had seen the devil's children at play among the flamingoes and the morning line, what had she thought of it?

"Well," said Walden, "she waved Circus Clown in with a program and a pair of white gloves. Then after the numbers were up she turned around to me and said, 'You know, I don't see anything bad about this.' "

It was already known that there is little wrong with anyone around a racetrack that a winner won't cure, and apparently this included religious scruples about racing.

"That I wouldn't know," said the owner. "But I can tell you that it makes all the difference in the world about the length of the drive back to Naples."

The ministerial attitude, a lengthy acquaintance with Walden suggested, had skipped a generation. But with this sort of background, how had he got into racing in the first place?

"Father was very much opposed to racing," Circus Clown's owner remarked, "and he used to preach against it. Then he came to Midway, and he found out pretty soon that Uncle Jim Parrish had put up most of the money to build the church, and most of the money to keep it going. So father had sense enough to keep his mouth shut."

The reference was to the late J. W. Parrish, who enjoyed unusual success in breeding and racing horses. He seldom went beyond his own stock, rarely availed himself of outside stallions, and never had a pretentious stable. But he won a lot of races, and he bred a good many stakes horses. When he got to naming them, he was sometimes a hard man to follow. Once, for instance, he named a horse Pameiob. It was some time before he explained that the name came from the initial letters of "putting all my eggs in one basket," which was a popular song of the time.

Several years after the Rev. Walden arrived in Midway, the more responsible members of the congregation decided that the church should have a pipe organ, and various schemes for raising the necessary money were discussed.

Parrish listened for a while, and then put in an idea of his own. "Let's put this off until next week," he said. "Rolled Stocking's running in a stake at Latonia Saturday. If he wins it, go ahead and put the organ in."

I do not remember how Rolled Stocking was backed at Latonia, but he had the undivided support of the Midway Christian Church. Whether for this reason or another he came home rolling, and Sunday morning in Midway began to be tinctured with the sound of organ music.

There was another incident a few years later, showing how

the finger of Providence moves in small matters. This time the church needed painting outside, and redecorating in, and the lowest estimate that could be got was $2,000. Parrish was shipping a horse to Chicago, not altogether to amuse the Chicagoans. "If this horse wins," he said, "get started on the painting."

As you will have surmised, this one won too, and the result was no more than official when the first paintbrush was dipped in Midway. Parrish had other business in Chicago, and it was nearly a month before he returned. The refurbishing had been completed, and on the first Sunday after his return he went with pleasant anticipation to church.

He was, it developed, highly pleased with the result, but as he sat and looked about him, he began to smile with an amusement which did not seem wholly to fit the situation. It was some time later that it was discovered that the committee on decorations had, apparently inadvertently, painted the inside of the church in the Parrish racing colors—terra cotta and straw.

"Well," concluded Walden, "I suppose the example was too strong. The family didn't want me to get into racing, but I got in. What do you do when you grow up in a church decorated in racing colors?"

Last year Walden came down to Florida with a filly he had bred out of a $50 mare. He won about $20,000 with her, sold her for $30,000. The filly was Fighting Fan, and she represented $50 parlayed into $50,000. This year he's won two races with Circus Clown.

The wages of sin, as nearly as I can make it out, are Naples and Hialeah.

BOOK THREE

A Joy to Man

$\mathcal{F}$ROM THAT far-off day when Rebekah and Jemima Boone ended their lonely wilderness journey on the south bank of the Kentucky River, woman has played a central role in Bluegrass history. Kentucky woman has been no shrinking violet who like a Hindu matron sat concealed behind a screen while her husband entertained visitors; she has sat in honored position at the family board, expressed political views, and made her menfolks come to time. She helped to clear the trees away from the land, raised the cabin, tended the sheep, spun and wove the family clothing. She bore the children, wiped the fevered brow, dressed the corpses, and suffered the grief of death and disappointment. It was she who was often victimized by the violent Indian raids; she was a prize sought by bronze warriors who sneaked up to Bluegrass cabin doors at the least expected moments.

On the face of pioneer Kentucky woman was scrawled the hard cipher of planting a civilization in a new country. The marble monument at Harrodsburg honors her, and modest stones in the nearby cemetery extend her story. In time, Kentuckians canonized those hardy pioneer souls who mothered a rugged generation of men and who endured so much with so little complaint.

Elizabeth Madox Roberts, herself a gentlewoman, wrote of these early mothers with a tenderness possible only in an author who could respect profoundly the price of human sacrifice. The women of her *Great Meadow* knew the price of the new land in terms of human anxieties; they knew that the departures of their menfolk into the woods ever portended the disruption of their primitive homes. The lowing of the nervous family cow was the alarm of destiny, and the crack of the rifle was the bursting of doom.

The story of Leah and Rachael was repeated many times in the Bluegrass. Hard labor used up female pioneers before it was their chronological time to go, and sometimes Pioneer Jacobs married through a whole family of sisters. There were more heroines, however, than those who loaded the rifles for their menfolks and stood guard by cabin doors with uplifted axes. Jane Todd Crawford, a humble woman of Greensburg, carried the burden of death in her feverish womb. Thousands of women before her had sunk into a painful grave with her common female ailment. Medical science had stood helplessly outside the pale of the human abdomen; doctors had guessed correctly the cause of these deaths, but they had not courage to cross the threshold of life itself to do battle with the ovarian tumor. Jane Todd Crawford's courage and physical endurance and Dr. Ephraim McDowell's nerve and skill form inseparable parts of a great American medical saga. Dr. James T. Flexner's account of this triumphant moment in medical pioneering is a song of praise for Kentucky womanhood.

Cassius Marcellus Clay and Jefferson J. Polk dealt with the other side of woman's place in Kentucky. Love and its triumphs and frustrations was their theme. Dr. Polk's experience was that of a shamefully naive adolescent who was hoisted on the petard of quackery, while Cassius Clay's story involved the very foundations of the Bluegrass marital code.

While Clay and Polk stroked the lute of love with clumsy

fingers, Sally Ward played another game with her throng of admirers and suitors. Few Kentucky women could captivate a multitude of men as did Sally. Draped in the flag of the United States, she sent a weeping regiment of Salt River Tigers away to fight the war with Mexico. In her time the flirtatious Sally marched to the altar often enough to know her way without the usual landmarks set up for such occasions. Four husbands extended her name, satisfied her vanity, and then dropped their mortal coils at convenient enough intervals.

It would be a mistake to assume that all Bluegrass women were rugged pioneer mothers swinging ax and shuttle alike with equal dexterity, or that they were Jane Todd Crawfords enduring the bare surgeon's knife with the fortitude of stone, or Sally Wards sending masculine hearts a-wandering. There were those meeker souls who defended the code of regional honor for sake of purity and the love of a sacred cause. How many Miss Tessie Tates have worn away their fragile lives in the Bluegrass is not a matter of crass statistical record. But the Miss Tessies have left their mark. The state's and region's honor have been their charges. Where other women were worn and spent with the cares of husbands and children, the Miss Tessies have labored for causes. These gentle souls owe a profound debt to Irvin Cobb, who viewed their labors with non-malicious humor; it was he who inscribed their deeds in rollicking words upon the scroll of Bluegrass honor.

ELIZABETH MADOX ROBERTS

*O*NE OF Kentucky's most brilliant novelists cut her literary teeth on the subject of the frontier. With a woman's intuition, Elizabeth Madox Roberts (1885-1941) described the important role of women in the settlement of Kentucky. The Great

Meadow *(New York, 1930) shows a keen sensitiveness of the hardships and frustration which the new land brought the settlers. Living in stockade and cabin was a hard ordeal, and in this short selection the author packs in a full story of a pioneer woman's approach to Kentucky.*

Buckskin Petticoat

THE CLOTHING of those who had been in the fort for a year or more was falling into rags and there was nothing out of which to sew more garments for winter wear. The women took continual thought of how they would find clothing to save them from the cold and of how they would clothe their children. The nettle cloth was not sufficient.

"The men can wear buckskin. A man-person, seems, can make out with a buckskin suit," they said, one or another speaking the thought. "But I couldn't content myself to wear a buckskin petticoat."

There were no sheep to cut for wool. The women talked of this when they gathered in a cabin or at the vat where the skins were prepared. Diony would send a swift thought out over imagined pastures where sheep grazed, her hands knowing the whole process from shearing to weaving, her hands longing for their weaving knowledge to have a place. Then Anne Pogue began to try a quantity of buffalo wool to see what could be made of it, and she drew it into a silky yarn, the other women telling of what she did with wonder and half-belief. She made a black yarn of a fine brittle texture, and presently she wove a bit of it on a warp of the nettle. All day Diony heard the beating of her loom as the slay pounded the buffalo wool into cloth.

The great scar Berk had made lay green across the front of the door post. He continued away and her hate went with his hate. Anger sank more deeply into her mind and worked quietly there when she remembered Elvira lying on the floor of the hut, when she saw this picture clearly. It would fade to a dimness as she went about her daily labors, but it would return when she sat quiet to give Tom his drink from her breast or when she lay down to sleep. She would recall the cool security of the inside of the hut, the warm sun outside, herself sitting lax and secure, on the cool earth floor; then the coming of the savages and their hushed war-cries, her terrified knowledge that her end had come, that life would now be cut off from her and she would be left alone with whatever . . . then Elvira pushing a way into the hut. Herself not dead then, but continuing.

She marked the days as they passed, making a sign for each one on the door of her cabin. When Berk had been gone twenty days by the count, Muir walked into the fort one day when evening was falling. Bringing her cow through the gate, Diony met him there, and a patter of quick questioning fell from her lips. He had come back from the north with a wound in his hand.

Diony tore strips of nettle cloth to bind up his hurt after she had washed it clean. It was a bad wound, a week old now. Between his groanings while she tended it he told of all that had happened in the north. With Lawrence as guide, Berk and his men had made a stealthy foray into the Shawnee land, into the river jungle where Blackfox habitually went.

"And on the next day, what?" she would ask. "And then?"

It was a story of encampments on the river bank high up in the Ohio Valley, of swift forays and stealthy flights. Berk rested now on the bank of the river, Muir said, but he would make another sally. He had sent Diony three trophies, three tokens, Muir said, and with one sound hand he stirred about among the pile of things he had dropped beside the door. Three dark scalps were the gift. They had been stretched on a frame of bent withe and they were dry now, three long black scalp-locks of a coarse hairy substance, each like the tail of a horse.

"He got this on a Tuesday," Muir said. He told an incident that made the Tuesday scalp stand apart from the Thursday ones. He went away to the corner house where he slept. Diony hung the tokens over the fireboard, above the place where Berk's gun and powder horn rested when they were put by.

Scalps hung in other cabins and thus hers were no wonder to see, but those who came to ask after Berk would sit for a short while under the fireboard recounting.

"I dreamed last night three witches walked across the hill toward Logan's Fort," Molly Anne said, "and I took it in head, even in my dream, that they went for no good, that they went to carry bad omens. When I waked I looked to see was the moon set, and for a fact it was well towards low and red like blood."

"When you hear the dogs howl without cause you can look to hear a report of war," another voice. "Last week the dogs howled all the fore part of a night and next day the ravens croaked until the day broke away fair, towards noon."

"You wouldn't have to wait for ravens to bring you word. You'd know hit. There's war, ravens or not."

"Some men gather war around themselves, but some, it seems, gather peace."

"But the war, it's there, whe'r you gather it or not. Some men leave it be."

"Some men is natured to leave hit be. Seems."

"You can't leave it be."

These shapes, crooning of war, went from under the fireboard, and Diony blew out the candle and lay in her bed to rest. All about the fort, over the whole caneland, the high pitch of summer had come. The stars of summer were in the sky. There was no money in the belt now. She thought of Berk's corn in the field at Deer Creek and she began to contrive ways to have it plowed, thinking that she might trade some trinket, as the empty money belt perhaps, to Harmon for a plowing.

The gourds were flowering on the stockade wall. Five-petaled white clouds were flung out on the hewn fence, each petal of a crumpled texture, an indetermined mist, as soft as fine linen that had been beautified by use. Some of the flowers were withering and some were passing into the fruit, passing daintiness by to become of a great hearty sort.

"Hit takes a fool to grow gourds, was always said." Molly Anne made a joke of the fine growth of Diony's gourd vines.

The cabin was as Berk had left, but for the scalps, nothing being added. She had one pewter spoon and two wooden spoons which she had cut out for herself. In the iron pot she boiled the meat, if there was game to be had, but the pot was often idle now that Berk was away. There were three wooden platters from which food was eaten. Berk had carried away the sharpest knife in his belt, but there was another that served her needs. Her tools and the bed on which she slept, her fire beyond the hearth—she knew all their ways as one would know the people of his house.

"Hit takes a fool to grow gourds, I've always heard said," Molly Anne called out to see Diony's pride in her fine noggin crop.

"There's a heap of gourds in the world, no matter," Diony called in answer. "Fort Harrod is full of gourds, some in every cabin, and it's a wonder how they got here, if it takes a fool to grow the gourd-kind."

She was a tall strong woman and a child clung to her breast. She passed her tools from hand to hand, lightly, knowing each one lightly, each one intimately sensed at the ends of her fingers and in the lifting parts of her arms and shoulders. For drink she had three pewter cups or flagons, two of them from Elvira's goods. She longed for a sieve through which to pass the meal to strain it of the husks, and she thought of the smooth fine loaf that was eaten in Albemarle. She helped Anne Pogue to make cloth of the buffalo wool or to make a thin cloth of the wild nettle fiber, or she tended her child to keep him free of the vermin. Remembering some phrase from a book which was now more than half forgotten she had a sudden sense of herself as eternal, as if all that she did now were of a kind older than kings, older than beliefs and governments.

Although the year was at July her bread-food was still the old grain of the previous season pounded to hominy or to meal. About her the children of the fort watched eagerly for the growth of the corn, measuring daily the height of the stalk, for they wanted soft new food. The corn increased each day, watched and measured by the eye, the mind following it into the wet of the rain and the heat of the sun or into the dark of the night when it rested from growth. The blades swung lightly in the wind and the field was a field of great grass, allied to their flesh by the needs of hunger until it became their flesh held in abeyance by the slow processes of growth. They waited upon the corn. The tassel came first of the flowering, came as an infinitely tender stem folded into the upper sheath but marked with delicate carvings which increased in size and became small buds, as yet sterile of power, holding only the matrix of the pollen, the mother of the male principle, the green sappy stem of the corn. Diony looked now for Berk's coming, herself appeased of hate. He had killed enough. She wanted him with her in the cabin.

Having no skins out of which to make moccasins and her old ones being worn away, she left her feet continually bare. Her skirt was made of the buffalo wool woven on a warp of the nettle and her jacket was of the cloth of the nettle, these garments woven on Anne Pogue's loom and bought with her labor. She tended Muir's wound with a medicinal salve of slippery-elm bark pounded to a fine meal, and when the angry flesh began to cool and to form a scar she soothed it with bear grease. One day while she leaned over his hand to lay on the elm poultice he told her that he had planted a field of flax.

"Against spring comes you'll have flax to spin," he said. "It's a field of blue flowers now."

Elvira's wheel hung from the rafters, but hearing of Muir's field of flax she saw the distant spring and saw herself drawing a firm filament, a hair-like thread, from the distaff, making ready for weaving. It was a momentary desire, her first need reappearing to overthrow it, Berk being yet away. Carrying little Tom in her arms she went with the boys and girls to the field near the fort to see the progress of the corn. There were delicate shoots at the side of the stalk growing out of the sappy stem, the female element having come now, taking form on the surface of the everlasting mother, the corn itself. Within the sheath were the delicate beginnings of husks, as yet pale and green and tender, scarcely unlike the buds prepared to hold the pollen above on the top of the strand. Within the pale, tender, female husks would flow the fine white milk of the corn which would congeal to be their food.

There was dancing in one of the cabins. A fiddler, back from his wars, had been unwilling to go with Clark into the Northwest. The people of the fort shifted and new faces continually appeared, and thus a new fiddler played, one who had no knowledge of Betsy Dodd, but he played the same tunes that were played formerly, and the forms and figures of the dance were the same. The half-grown girls danced first, and their ragged little half-length skirts hung limply over their quick little thin legs. Then Molly Anne would join, the first of the women to take a part, and others would follow, the men and the women stepping carelessly into the reels.

"There's no varmints in the woods today. Might as well dance on't."

A man stood on the high ladder against the wall to look out on the open spaces. There would be dancing, a set flinging at a bit of a reel, but all would stop then to listen or look upward to see that the man at the loop-hole made no sign. Diony knew what troubled the fort. No news had come from Boonesborough now for many days and the summer was at an end. Scouts had been sent to discover what caused the silence of the other fort.

Molly Anne always knew the news of the stockade; news gathered to her and was by her dispersed again. She was a ubiquitous woman, and there were three children in her cabin who had inherited ubiquity from their mother. News and opinions of her floated about in turn. It was said of her while she danced that if Alex Harmon were killed in a battle she would grieve heartily for a week and then brighten up to catch Muir.

"Molly Anne, she married in too big a hurry. She might better 'a' looked around a spell longer."

"Hit wasn't known to her what a fine-set-up widow-man had come down the Trace, when she tied up along with Harmon, she and Harmon already known to each other back east where they did live. And Muir, nobody a-knowen he was widowed . . ."

"She keeps her eye on Muir though, you notice."

"But not more'n she ought, I hope."

Comments thus accompanied the music of the fiddle and counter-opinions were passed about to touch the stillness that came out of Boone's Fort and make surmises of it, or flow back to Molly Anne's intentions or desires.

The morning brought business about the inner quadrangle and business about the spring. Toward noon the scouts appeared before the gates and there was running hither and thither and Molly Anne was calling Diony from the door. Men gathered to the gates that were flung open, and by the time Diony arrived with Molly Anne to stand at the edge of the crowd and listen, the scouts were well into their story and were answering the questions and oaths of comment. Boonesborough had endured a heavy siege that had lasted nine days. They were a garrison of but sixty men and only forty of these were fit to carry arms. Three hundred had come from the north, Shawnees under Blackfish with white men from the

King's army as officers. Twelve days they had camped around
the fort, but three days were spent in parleying before the fire
began. . . .

Here Diony ceased to listen, giving heed now to her own
inner query. For if all the Shawnees had come under their
Blackfish, had marched down from Ohio with guns in plenty,
where then was Berk? How had he kept out of their way? She
made no spoken comment, but these questions took form within her and changed the shape and aspect, the whole color and
kind, of all the land as seen over the fort wall, of all the day
as it shone out of a blue sky. The scouts were speaking, going
forward with their telling, retelling now with more detail.

"Surrender was what they wanted, to carry off the whole of
Boonesborough to sell in Detroit." The comments flew about
and the story doubled back. "The Indians dug a mine, tried
to dig a way under the fort wall, but the fort made a mine
that threatened to meet it halfway. . . . Picked up, after it was
all over, the Indians gone, a hundred and twenty-five pounds'
weight of bullets near the fort . . . as many more bedded in
the logs . . . Two killed and four hurt right bad, a fearful
time . . . Three hundred outside, ranged around in full sight
south of the fort, to cut off retreat this way . . . Only forty inside to hold guns . . . First-place Blackfish calls a parley with
Boone, to meet outside the fort wall."

Boone had come back from captivity in the north, had escaped from his captors in the middle of the summer when he
saw that they were preparing to invade the forts in the cane.
Of the three forts, Harrod's alone had passed the summer without a siege. Diony loved Harrod's then with a rush of thank-
fulness, loving the security of the inner court, loving the women
who came to pound at the mortar and to dip their vessels into
the spring. Out of this passion of security for herself and Tom
rushed her continual query: Where had Berk gone and where
were Tandy and Gowdy? Why was there no news of them?
An army had come down from the north, walking over the

way Berk had gone. War stood back for a brief interval, giving place to questioning and giving place again to safety and kindness in the fort. The women who met at the spring spoke kindly together, giving way to her with acts of gentleness. Boone had come back; where then was Berk?

Walking back from the spring a new query entered her mind. The women had been kind to her because they knew that an army of Shawnees had walked over Berk's track, because they had made an answer to the query. "Berk Jarvis never is lost neither," she said. Boone had come back whole. The questions and answers leaped up in her thought and lay down in the middle of her confused anxiety. In the cabin she took the scalps from their place above the fireboard and set them in the heart of a great flame that burned in the fireplace, having no longer any pride in them.

JAMES T. FLEXNER

THERE may be an open question as to whether Dr. Ephraim McDowell (1771-1830) or Jane Todd Crawford (1762-1841) was the braver in 1809 when Dr. McDowell removed an ovarian tumor from Mrs. Crawford's abdomen. In the country town of Danville both of these persons made medical history: Dr. McDowell by his skill, and Mrs. Crawford by her physical courage and stamina. James T. Flexner (1907-   ) wrote dramatically of this landmark in American medical history in his Doctors on Horseback *(New York, 1937).*

A Heroic Choice

AT THE sound of hoofs the door flew open, disgorging a flood of people. A huddled crowd in a forest clearing, they stared over the hill. Behind them a cabin smoked, its black walls varied by white stripes where the logs were chinked with lime. The crowd waited silently while the hoofbeats grew louder on the frozen earth, and then a rider appeared over the crest of the slope. He was so tall that his legs almost touched the ground. As he approached, the knot of people moved forward to meet him, and a dozen hands reached out to hold his mount.

"You're Dr. McDowell?"

The newcomer nodded. In the gap between his coonskin cap and his fur collar nothing was visible but tiny, brilliant eyes and a huge nose blue with cold. After he had dismounted with the slow movements of fatigue, he painstakingly distinguished the people before him. Then he stepped aside with the two local doctors.

They treated him deferentially, for this man of thirty-eight had during the ten years since 1799 been the leading surgeon of the Kentucky frontier. Ephraim McDowell's name was known in every forest settlement where the language spoken was English, not the guttural accents of Algonquin tribes. Whenever a pioneer required an operation that was beyond the skill of the rural doctors, word was sent to Danville by pony express, by courier, or by some traveler going that way, and McDowell hastily crammed his instruments and drugs into worn saddle bags. The sixty-mile trip he had taken through the wilderness to treat Mrs. Thomas Crawford was a routine matter; often he rode a hundred.

Reconstructing what occurred after McDowell reached her cabin is like the task of an archæologist who must piece together scattered fragments into the statue they once formed.

McDowell left three separate brief accounts of the events that were to make him immortal. By combining them with facts we know about the frontier and statements by McDowell's contemporaries, we can rebuild an image which, even if occasionally inexact, will resemble the truth more closely than the uncombined fragments could ever do.

The two local doctors told McDowell that Mrs. Crawford was pregnant; she knew the symptoms well for she was already the mother of five children. Although the ninth and tenth months brought the most terrible labor pains, there were no signs of a birth. By the time the doctors were consulted, she was so big they were convinced she would have twins. When all their skill failed to bring on a delivery, they had called McDowell.

He preceded his colleagues into the cabin. A short, tremendous woman who lay in a box bed filled with willow boughs attempted a smile of greeting, but a spasm of pain pulled her mouth tight. McDowell sat down beside her, asked a few questions, and then launched forth, as was his custom, into a discussion of politics, repeating the news so precious in isolated settlements. While he talked, he began his examination, his hands moving with extreme gentleness over her tortured frame. Suddenly the words died on his lips. He walked to one side with his colleagues and, after a hurried exposition, asked to be left alone with Mrs. Crawford. When all had filed out, he told her that he brought her bad news. She was not with child; she had a tumor of the ovaries. But perhaps there was some hope.

As dusk faded into night beyond the window of oiled paper, the surgeon and his pain-racked patient held a dialogue that will be famous as long as medical history is written. The little room that housed a whole family was lighted by one candle and an open fire over which heavy iron kettles simmered. The flames became brighter in the growing dimness, the flickering more distinct, while the tall doctor, overflowing a home-made chair, told Mrs. Crawford the truth and gave her a heroic choice.

McDowell has left a short account of their conversation. He explained that he had studied in Edinburgh with some of the world's greatest surgeons, who had taught him that women with ovarian tumors must invariably die; they could promise a patient nothing but two years of gradually increasing misery unless God worked a miracle. However, beneath the pessimism of the professors, there was an undertone of self-communion; they wondered whether ovarian tumors might not be cured by cutting out the diseased part. The operation would be similar to spaying, and animals recovered from being spayed. But no sooner was this suggestion made in the halls of the medical great than it was taken back again, McDowell told Mrs. Crawford. Surgery, as he supposed she knew, was practically limited to dressing wounds and amputating limbs; operators did not dare invade the great cavities of the body. He explained that "John Bell, Hunter, Hey, A. Wood, four of the first and most eminent surgeons in England and Scotland, had uniformly declared in their lectures that such was the danger of peritoneal inflammation that opening the abdomen to extract the tumor was inevitable death." They believed that once the inner wall of the abdomen was exposed to the atmosphere, nothing could protect it from infection.

During the hundred years in which excising tumors had been discussed, no surgeon had ever dared hazard an operation. And so the patients had always died in long-drawn-out agony. McDowell could not understand, he said, why no one had ever made the test. He believed that a patient would be likely to recover even as animals did, but supposing it was a fifty-to-one chance—was not even that desperate gamble better than no chance at all? Perhaps the doctors were thinking more of themselves than of their patients, of how their reputations would be destroyed by a failure.

McDowell knew that if he operated and if Mrs. Crawford

died, as all medical authority said she must, no doctor would disagree with a coroner's jury that found him guilty of murder. And even should he escape criminal prosecution, the practice he had built up over many years would be wiped out at one blow; who would dare trust again to a surgeon so reckless and mad?

"If you think you are prepared to die," he none the less told his patient, "I will take the lump from you if you will come to Danville."

A woman like Mrs. Crawford could never look heroic. Short, her naturally heavy body distorted by a tremendous tumor, her face marred by features too large and a long mouth too firmly set, she was a figure of pity, not romance. Yet there must have been a strange look in her gray eyes as she spoke quietly.

"I will go with you."

It seemed a mad scheme to make Mrs. Crawford ride sixty miles through the wilderness in mid-winter, but McDowell's examination had shown that she was strong enough, and there was nothing else to do. Only in his own home, where his drugs, instruments, and trained assistants were at hand, could he give her the care that would be essential to the success of an operation so hazardous that no one had ever tried it before.

The next day Mrs. Crawford was helped from bed and onto the quietest horse that could be borrowed; her huge tumor pressed against the pommel of the saddle, but that was unavoidable. Mrs. Baker, a neighboring housewife, accompanied her, since her husband had to care for the farm. He stood in the doorway of his log cabin surrounded by his sniveling children and watched the little cavalcade move slowly away. It took them minutes to arrive at the crest of the rise, and then they were gone. He gathered the children together and returned to the cabin, certain he would never see his wife again.

When the three riders passed through the near-by village, the faces of the settlers who crowded to the doors showed pity for Mrs. Crawford, but only hostility for the tall doctor who was sacrificing her to his foolishness and pride. The instant the houses were left behind, the forest locked over their heads, a braided canopy of glass, for every branch was sheathed with ice. They rode through gleaming vistas of silence, and although they moved continually, they did not seem to advance, so unchanging was the wilderness. Only the increasing agony of the tumor, which, as McDowell tells us, chafed against the pommel, testified to miles traversed. At night they sought lodgings in some cluster of log cabins that appeared beside the trail. Always the settlers received Mrs. Crawford with sympathy and her doctor with suppressed indignation. Long before he reached Danville, McDowell must have begun to expect trouble from the mob.

At last the sixty miles were behind them. They rode down the main street of a hamlet boasting less than a hundred houses and stopped before one of the finest. Standing at the doorway under the fanlight was the doctor's wife, a tall, graceful woman who received Mrs. Crawford with the expert kindness of long usage, and put her to bed.

When the surgeon's nephew and partner, Dr. James McDowell, heard what his uncle intended to do, he was horrified. Well educated in Philadelphia, he knew that Mrs. Crawford would certainly die, dragging their reputations and their practice to oblivion with her. He argued with his uncle. He washed his hands of such madness several times a day, only to return to the attack a few hours later.

The proposed operation soon became the only topic of conversation in the tiny community of Danville, which had for a long time known no such excitement. Naturally, McDowell's less successful medical rivals did not fail to point out that the butchery he planned was contrary to all medical canons and certain to end fatally. At first the popular murmur ran on the note of gossip, but soon the pitch heightened, the voices became emotional, and men began to say that McDowell must be stopped, either by the law or by the people if need be.

He had decided to operate on Christmas Day, when the prayers of all the world, rising up to God, would create a propitious atmosphere. In the meantime, he engaged in intensive preparation. Anxious to have Mrs. Crawford as strong as possible, he saw to her every comfort and fed her on a planned diet. He studied the plates of the abdomen in his medical books and tried to re-enact in his mind every dissection he had ever made. Since James McDowell had refused to take part in the experiment, he was forced to rely for assistance entirely on his apprentice, Charles McKinny. Each day he rehearsed the youngster, going over and over the operation in pantomime to be sure there would be no slip.

Christmas Day dawned with a ringing of bells. No sooner had Dr. McDowell arisen than his nephew came to him, his face tight with determination. He had struggled with himself all night, he said, and decided at last that, since a life was at stake, it was his duty to help if he could. McDowell must have gone about his preparations with a lighter heart; such trained assistance might make a vast difference.

As Mrs. Crawford walked into the operating-room, the streets were quiet, for everyone was at church. One of the ministers, an exhorter famous for snatching brands from the mouth of hell, chose the operation as the subject of his sermon. He told his congregation of pioneers, who were used to being a law unto themselves, that, although only God had a right to deal out life and death, Dr. McDowell was preparing to destroy one of God's creatures.

The chamber where Mrs. Crawford found herself had no resemblance to the operating-theater of a modern hospital. It was a room like any other in the house, bare except for a plain wooden table onto which Mrs. Crawford was strapped. Since ether had not yet been discovered, she could be given no stronger anæsthetic than a few opium pills; naturally she had to be fastened down. Devoid of white uniforms and gauze masks, the surgeons waited in their ordinary clothes, their coats off and their sleeves rolled up to avoid the blood. The instruments did not repose in steam sterilizers, for antiseptic methods lay far in the future. The knives and forceps had been washed like table silver and laid on an ordinary linen cover.

McDowell tells us that he bared the patient's swollen abdomen, marked with a pen the course of the incision, and handed the knife to his nephew; if James were to share the possible danger, he must share the possible credit too. Seeing the gleaming blade poised over her body, Mrs. Crawford closed her eyes and started to sing a hymn. When the knife bit deep, her voice quavered but the tune continued to fill the little room.

After his nephew had completed the incision, McDowell started on the serious part of the operation. His hand never shook, but his face burned red and he sweated at every pore in the icy chamber. Whenever Mrs. Crawford's voice, attempting hymn after hymn, shook with unusual agony, he whispered tender and soothing words, as he might to a frightened child.

Suddenly the silence of the street gave way to a confused murmur; church was out. More than a hundred people gathered in front of the house, some curious, some sympathetic, but the most vocal screaming with righteous indignation. In the room where Mrs. Crawford lay, her anguished hymns were drowned out by loud shouts of male voices calling for the operation to stop. James McDowell's inwards must have rocked queasily to think what might happen if Mrs. Crawford died. He searched her prostrate body for some symptoms of approaching death, but the suffering woman, her knuckles white where they clenched the table, sang bravely on.

According to McDowell's daughter, the mob swung a rope over a tree so that they might not lose any time in hanging the surgeon when Mrs. Crawford died. As the long minutes passed with no news from the silent house at which all eyes stared, the ringleaders could control their excitement no longer; they dashed for the door and tried to smash it in. But the sheriff, assisted by the more sober citizens, intervened; for a moment there was a struggle outside the surgeon's house. If McDowell heard the uproar, he gave no sign as he proceeded with the operation he later described as follows:

"I made an incision about three inches from the musculus rectus abdominis, on the left side, continuing the same nine inches in length, parallel with the fibers of the above-named muscle, extending into the cavity of the abdomen, the parietes [walls] of which were a good deal contused, which we ascribed to the resting of the tumor on the horn of the saddle during her journey. The tumor then appeared in full view, but was so large that we could not take it away entire. We put a strong ligature around the Fallopian tube near the uterus, and then cut open the tumor, which was the ovarium and fimbrious part of the Fallopian tube very much enlarged. We took out fifteen pounds of dirty, gelatinous-looking substance, after which we cut through the Fallopian tube and extracted the sac, which weighed seven pounds and one-half. As soon as the external opening was made the intestines rushed out upon the table, and so completely was the abdomen filled by the tumor that they could not be replaced during the operation, which was terminated in about twenty-five minutes. We then turned her upon her left side, so as to permit the blood to escape, after which we closed the external opening with the interrupted suture [a series of stitches placed a short distance apart], leaving out, at the lower end of the incision, the ligature which surrounded the Fallopian tube. Between every two stitches we put a strip of adhesive plaster, which, by keeping the parts in contact, hastened the healing of the incision. We then applied the usual dressings. . . ."

The sound of hymns, which had been getting weaker and weaker, stopped at last. Ephraim and his assistants carried the half-unconscious patient to her bed. When the mob learnt that the operation was over and that Mrs. Crawford lived, there was silence for a moment, and then the air was riven by a cheer.

Actually the real danger was yet to come; would Mrs. Crawford develop peritonitis, that deadly infection of the abdominal wall? Dr. McDowell put her on the depleting diet then thought essential for combating fevers, and waited. When he came into her room five days later, he was horrified to see her standing up and making her bed. At his grave reproof, she laughingly replied that she had never been able to lie still. By means of persuasions, dire warnings, and threats he induced her to remain an invalid for twenty-five days, but at the end of that time she insisted on riding back to the neglected household tasks that had been worrying her more and more. With renewed energy she threw herself into the active life of a pioneer, moving on a short time later to a frontier outpost in Indiana, where there was new land to conquer from the forest. She remained in excellent health until her death at the age of seventy-nine.

JEFFERSON J. POLK

KENTUCKIANS before the Civil War seemed to have placed a great deal of faith in potions. In Danville, Dr. Jefferson J. Polk (1802-1881) recalled his callow days when he became involved in a near-disastrous affair with a love potion. With good humor he told of his youthful embarrassment in the Autobiography of Dr. J. J. Polk (Louisville, 1867). Dr. Polk succeeded only in ringing the wedding bells for another.

Love Entered into Me

IT IS NOT perhaps known to one in a hundred of the youth of the present time (1867) that this wonder-working medicine was ever used by the fathers at the first of the present century. It was discovered by a poor mechanic of G——, a native Kentuckian. Notwithstanding he enjoined great secrecy on those who purchased and used it, yet his fame and the utility of his medicine got abroad, and he had many customers.

I was so fortunate as to be indentured as an apprentice in the very town in which he lived. I was a well-grown boy, about seventeen years of age, and it was my habit to visit my aged mother once a fortnight, who lived four miles in the country. About half-way between the village and my mother's house there lived rather a wealthy farmer, Mr. C——, who had two beautiful daughters, Mary and Rebekah. Mary was the eldest, and very lovely in form and feature. Rebekah was her junior by about two years. The family record, into which I got a sly glance months afterward, made her twenty-four years old, although she called herself eighteen. She had an exquisite form, auburn hair, hazel eyes, a delicate hand, small foot, the neck of a swan, her mouth handsomely chiseled, and her teeth rivaling pearls. To see her was to love her.

> "Love drew her image on my heart of hearts,
> And memory preserves it beautiful."

One day, as I was passing to the country, I ventured to call at the gate and ask for a drink of water. Miss Rebekah came to the door and invited me into the house. I declined, telling her it was late and I must get on. She then asked me if I would have a glass of sweet cider. I thanked her, and she brought it out. I drank it, bade her good evening, and passed on. That night, you may be sure, my mind was troubled; for, after the *cider,* love entered into me. I rolled and tossed upon my bed until midnight, occasionally uttering a half-suppressed groan. My mother, who was very infirm, and consequently a wakeful person, called to me to know if I was sick. I answered, *"Not much."* I then heard her say, "Poor boy, he labors so hard, the walk home is too much for his feeble frame." Ah! dear fathers and mothers, you little know what it is that most troubles the hearts of youths, unless you remember your own youthful ailments forty years ago.

In the morning my purpose was fixed—I would marry Miss Rebekah, that I would. I immediately thought of *Dr. B——'s love powders.* Perhaps *they* might greatly assist me. After breakfast I hurried off to town to consult the doctor. He told me he had none of the powders on hand, but on the next Saturday he would have a package ready, and give me directions how to administer them. That was an anxious and tedious period of my life—minutes seemed lengthened into hours, and hours into days. The auspicious day at last arrived. It was not my usual time to go to see my mother, but I ventured to ask the foreman to grant me the privilege. He at first refused, but immediately said, "If you will catch and saddle my horse, and black my boots, you may go." Jacob did not perform his task for Leah and Rachel with greater alacrity and delight than I did for the foreman. My servitude for the day was ended. I put on my best "Sundays," washed and powdered my skin, stuck a small vial of bergamot drops in my pocket, and then stood before the glass for a few moments adjusting my *stand-collar* and combing my hair. I then went straight to the doctor's office. He had the *love powders* prepared, wrapped up neatly in a piece of white paper, labeled *"Dr. B——'s magic love powders,* warranted to cure where the directions are strictly followed." The doctor then delivered his prescription verbally. It ran as follows: "You must prepare yourself with some stick-candy, candy-kisses, and some raisins—figs will do. Roll the whole in the powder. Visit the lady at her father's house. The first dose must be stick-candy; then draw your chair a little closer, and incline your head toward her, if her parents are not in sight; then take her by the hand, gently pressing it; then administer the other two doses—the candy-kisses first, and the raisins or figs last. The two last need no manifestation; the work is accomplished, and you have nothing to do but to consult the old people."

I paid my half-dollar for the package and departed, the happiest of men. I started straight for the country. It was sundown when I arrived at Mr. C——'s house. Miss Rebekah was

at home: she received me graciously. After the common salutations, I began to tell Miss Rebekah of the many pretty girls
I had made the acquaintance of in town. I was fond of their
company, but did not think I could ever love any of them. I
did not think they were calculated to make their husbands
happy—to all of which Miss Rebekah assented with a smile.
I offered her a stick of candy. She took it in her delicate fingers
and looked at it as much as to say, "What does this dust on
the candy mean?" For a few moments I feared that the cheat
was found out, but my fears were removed when she ate it,
asking no questions. I then leaned toward her and attempted
take her hand; she declined, and I made no further advances.
She then informed me that she had an engagement to attend a
party that evening. I asked her if she would accept of my company. With a gracious smile she accepted. It was in the month
of October; there had been a long drought; the leaves were
beginning to fall. She soon prepared herself—putting her shoes,
and then her hose, knit by her own delicate fingers, and a coarse
towel, into her reticule—and we departed for the place of fun
and frolic. When we had traveled about half the journey I
gave forth the candy-kisses. She ate them, and put the *love
verses* they contained in her bosom. Now I was a happy man.
I was sure the *love powders had begun to work*. We went on,
and soon reached the point of destination. Before we entered,
she sat down and wiped the dust off her feet with the coarse
towel. She then drew on her hose and shoes. I modestly turned
my head aside while she thus prepared herself, but I could not
help casting a *sly glance* at her beautifully-tapered ankle and
delicate foot.

We entered. The youngsters were in the midst of a play—
"*tired of my company.*" As we changed and whirled about, I
thought I noticed that Miss Rebekah was never "*tired of her
company*" when I was by her side, and I am sure I could have
sat there forever. Before she was compelled to leave my side
I administered the last dose, the raisins. Next was introduced,

"paying pawns." This was my favorite play—there was so much kissing in it. The first article was held over Miss Jones's head, and the question asked, "What must he do that owns this?" Answer, "He must kiss Miss Rebekah C——." That was too good, for it was my own red bandana. You may depend upon it our lips soon met, but not in silence, for it was an *old-fashioned Kentucky buss,* which threw the whole house into a titter. After some other amusements the company broke up. It had rained very hard while the frolic was going on.

Miss Rebekah and I started for her father's house. Before she left the yard she shed off her hose and shoes, and placed them again in her reticule. I would have given a kingdom, had I possessed it, to have been permitted to carry the precious treasure, but she kept it in her own hands. We had not gone far when we came to a small creek; its waters had been greatly swollen by the rain. Thinks I, what a blessing! fortune certainly favors me. I proposed to bear Miss Rebekah safe and dry across the stream. She assented, and in a moment I landed her safely on the shore nearest her home. I now thought it a favorable time to make full proof of her love for me, and the effect of the *love powders.* As I sat her down upon the ground, I drew her gently toward me and attempted to kiss her. She repelled me, and said: "Young man, you are too familiar; something has certainly crazed your brain." I, however, ventured to put the *pointed question.* She answered, "My heart has been given to another; next Thursday is the *wedding-day."* Blood and thunder! All was over—I was lost—I was a used-up man. We reached her father's house. I lodged there all night, and on Sunday morning returned to G——, pondering over my bad luck. I saw the doctor daily on the streets, but he never asked after my health, and of course I said nothing to him. This was my first and last experience with *love powders.*

Young friends, I now advise you to avoid quack doctors and their *love powders.*

CASSIUS MARCELLUS CLAY

CASSIUS MARCELLUS CLAY (1810-1903) may not have been either the Bluegrass' most prominent author or statesman, but he was one of its most colorful figures. Born into a proud pioneer family and the landed gentry, he was in a position to develop a rugged personality. In his schooldays at Transylvania and Yale, the handsome lad from Madison County was exposed to the world of ideas. At Yale he fell under the spell of William Lloyd Garrison, who gave him a contrary perspective on slavery from that held south of the Ohio. He came home fresh from the rarefied environment of the classroom to tackle the "peculiar institution" with the same vigor which had made his father a frontier military hero.

Coming home from New Haven, young Clay found more than slavery to attract his interest. He renewed his acquaintance with the beautiful eighteen-year-old Mary Jane Warfield (1815-?). Mary Jane was the daughter of the famous horseman Elisha Warfield, who had made his Meadows Stud one of the best known in the Bluegrass. Clay's courting of Mary Jane was as vigorous as were all his other acts. He attacked his rivals with the same violence that was to mark his future career, even fighting one of them in a duel the day before his wedding.

The marriage of Cassius M. Clay and Mary Jane Warfield was marked with many rifts, and when Mrs. Clay left the General's bed and board, he rushed to the public with their troubles. Clay's autobiography is a curious piece of personal writing; it is direct and frank, and is often unfair to his family. But despite its rich frankness, the Life of Cassius Marcellus Clay *(Cincinnati, 1886) is a colorful document.*

A Moment of Supreme Bliss

MARY JANE had not yet reached her eighteenth year, and was still going to school in Lexington. Her house was already open to her young friends. Her elder sister, Anne, about this time had returned from an Eastern school, and made her entrance into society. She imported all the follies and habitudes of such academies; and aspired to lead the elegant society for which Lexington has ever been noted. She was dark-skinned, slightly freckled, with thin hair and person, and "jimber-jawed." So that, in early life, "her nose and chin did threaten 'ither!" She had what was then, in cant phrase, called the "Grecian bend," an inclination of the body forward, after the manner of some of the classic Venuses. This indecent attitude of self-consciousness, well enough in the sensual pagan idea of womanhood, was avoided by my friend, Joel T. Hart, in his "Woman Triumphant." Whilst following nature in the course of time, he impersonates the modern woman of purity, and the flexibility of features which comes of mental and moral culture. Whilst some women are said to gush with sympathy or affection, Anne reversed that artistic operation. She gushed with an affectation of contempt or hatred. She would throw up both hands, roll her eyes as if all was over with her, and then, opening wide her mouth, she would break out in an indescribable guffaw. She seemed at daggers'-points with herself and all the world, which was ominous of all the ills of her future life! As a scandal-monger, she terrorized all Lexington. Never, therefore, had woman so magnificent a foil to set off her charms, as the younger sister had in the elder Warfield.

The guests would sit in some constraint, talking to each other, or the family, till Mary Jane returned from school. She would come at times bolting in, with hair uncombed, leaving her sun-bonnet and satchel of books in the ante-room; or, throwing them down in a chair, dressed in plain but loose-cut school-girl's attire, and, entering at once into general conversation, she soon had the whole attention of the visitors. Was this simplicity or the highest art? The morning and the evening hours of reception were thus so occupied, that I had no opportunity of saying a word of love to her. I saw that she was as much attracted by me as I was by her. So she said quietly to me, that she was going on a certain day hickory-nut-hunting with a few girls, at the house of John Allen, Esq.—with his daughter—in Fayette County. She never asked me to go; yet I was there when the party arrived.

Now, in Kentucky, hickory-nut-hunting has been one of the diversions of the young folks, rich and poor, from the beginning; and continues so to this day, being one of the most agreeable of picnics.

John Allen was a typical Kentuckian of those days. He had married my blood-relative through the Paynes—the mother of Madison C. Johnson, (my brother-in-law, who had allied himself with my sister, Anne, after the tragic death of her first husband, Edmund Irvine, Esq., of Madison County,) and of George W. Johnson, who was made Confederate Governor of Kentucky, and was killed in battle during the Rebellion. Allen had, also, by his first wife, a fine looking and genial daughter, Eliza, and several handsome sons. So we "girls and boys" all went a hickory-nut-hunting.

There are no finer forests in the world than the natural parks of the "Blue-grass region" of Kentucky. The sugar-maple, tulip, coffee-bean, hickory-nut, and other trees, were just touched with an October frost, so as to cause the nuts to fall. The leaves wore that celebrated many-colored foliage which comes of the maturity of the sap, which is seen to such perfection in no other portion of the world. The long blue-grass, which turns the forests into parks, was yet green as in midsummer; the subdued rays of the October sun, falling with shimmering light through the half-nude boughs of the trees, warmed the genial air, and dispelled the moisture from the soil. Some birds yet ventured into fragmentary songs, ere taking their flight of migration further South, to winter; whilst the grey squirrels, with their long bushy tails turned over their backs, like an ostrich-feather over a military hat, barked with vivacity at the intruders upon their quiet retreats.

Mary Jane, by all the standards of personal description, was of medium size. Her grandfather, Barr, was a native Irishman; and the Warfields were a Maryland family of fair standing. When I visited Baltimore, on my way to college, a Miss Warfield was a leading belle in polite society. The Barrs were fair, but the Warfields had dark skins and hair. She had the complexion of her Irish ancestors—a fair smooth skin, at times touched with rose-color; a face and head not classical, with rather broad jaws, large mouth, flexible lips, rather thin and determined, but with outline well cut, and an irregular nose. Her hair was of a light auburn or nut-color, long and luxuriant. Her eyes were a light greyish-blue, large and far apart, with that flexibility of the iris which gives always great variety and intensity of expression. She was the best amateur-singer I ever heard; and, as I have been familiar with the voices of Jenny Lind, Lucca, Patti, and all the most celebrated singers of my day, I venture to say that hers was, in compass and tone, unsurpassed. In disposition, she was *apparently* the most amiable of women; and basking, as the sex rarely does, in the light of universal admiration, she might be said to be the impersonation, like Calypso's isle, of "eternal springtime."

One of the calamities of civilization is the deterioration of the five senses—the sight, the touch, the smell, the hearing, and the taste. But, of all these, the faculty of distinguishing odors is thus the most impaired. Every one of the fauna and flora, and many of the mineral kingdom have a distinct smell. The odor of the horse is very disagreeable; but who has not read in poetry (if not familiar in fact,) of the sweet breath of the ruminating kine? Who has failed to observe how the dog recognizes the master more by the smell than the sight? For by the sight is recognition, whilst the smell is that and more—a source of pleasure. So the well-cultivated dog hates the tramp, not for his rough dress, but for his offensive odor. How he pushes his nose, at every opportunity, upon the garments, face, and hands, of his beloved master, and touches him fondly with his tongue! So bees like one and hate another, no doubt for the same reason. Now, never having dulled my senses with tobacco, tea or coffee, whiskey or opium, and living much in the open air, they have ever remained acute. Of all odors, which city folks know so little, those of the wild grape-vine, crab-apple, and the fresh hickory-nuts are the most delicious.

I sat down under the trees on the long grass; and, with two small stones, easily picked up in this limestone region, I was hulling the nuts, whilst the others, with hands and handkerchiefs, were picking them up, and in groups also cracking them, carrying and emptying them into a pile near me. Mary Jane, usually so careless in her dress, I noticed now wore more costly material, prepared with more care, but all in admirable taste. Her hair, the bonnet off, with exercise having fallen down, she had hastily and loosely adjusted. She came to me when the others were farthest off, and busily engaged in talk, and, picking up the nuts, emptied her handkerchief on the pile. I said: "Come and help me." She replied, with some tremor in her voice: "I have no seat." Putting my feet closer together, as they were stretched out on the ground, I said: "You may sit down here, if you will be mine." She hesitated a moment (she was standing near me, with her face in the same direction), and then—down she came! brushing my cheek with her disordered hair, with the aroma, sweeter than orange-blossoms, of the hickory-nuts. She just touched me with the skirts of her dress, and said: "I am yours." Then she hurried off to mingle with her companions again. Thus she attacked nearly all my senses at once! Was it simplicity, or the highest art? This, at all events, was a moment of supreme bliss, which comes but once in life, when the soul has not felt the degrading union of the earthy with the immortal, by which come sin and woe and death into the world!

J. WINSTON COLEMAN, JR.

DRIVING a stagecoach in nineteenth-century Kentucky involved a man in many human situations. Obstetrics was not the least of the calls made upon the ingenious Jehus, as Thomas Irvine (1810-1892) learned on his run from Maysville to Lexington. The names of both woman and child, in this instance, remain unknown to this generation, but J. Winston Coleman, Jr. (1898-   ), has given them a deserved place in Kentucky history in his Stage-Coach Days in the Bluegrass *(Louisville, 1935).*

Emergency

ONE EARLY autumn afternoon in the ante-bellum days, the veteran stage driver, Thomas H. Irvine, drove his horses at a brisk gallop along the winding highway from Lexington to Maysville. Black, ominous clouds were piling up over the horizon north of the Licking River. Three passengers sat inside the dusty, swaying vehicle, a man, an elderly woman, and her daughter. About nightfall, near the Blue Licks, the storm broke with a deluge of rain, heavy gusts of wind, and terrific thunder and lightning.

For several hours Irvine's drenched horses plodded wearily along the rutted road, steadily losing time, utterly heedless of the shouts, muttered curses, and soggy whip with which he attempted to urge them forward. Suddenly a blinding bolt of lightning crashed through the inky darkness, and a large tree standing near the roadside reeled like a stricken giant and fell in two sections across the pike a short distance ahead. Irvine stopped the stage-coach immediately, dismounted from the box, and, with the man passenger, groped his way to the obstruction, visible only by the intermittent flashes of lightning.

Suddenly a call came from the stage, and when Irvine returned to the vehicle the elderly woman informed him that her daughter's child was about to be born. Both women were almost frantic at this emergency, under the existing circumstances. No doctor, no light, none of the bare necessities which such an occasion required, and the storm was still raging.

But the old stage driver, a man of courage and action, was undaunted even in the presence of a situation never before encountered in all the years of his varied experience. In a moment he had produced from under one of the seats a battered, soot-stained lantern. The passenger's small leather-covered trunk was hastily removed from the rear boot of the coach and made available. Then Irvine mounted bareback one of the best horses in his team and dashed off in the darkness. About a mile down the road he halted at the farm house of an experienced pioneer woman whom he knew. In a short time he was splashing back over the rain-swept road, carrying a steaming cedar piggin, with the woman clinging on behind him. Her husband followed with some candles and a blanket wrapped in old newspapers to keep it dry.

Then, while the three men worked on the fallen tree, the "granny" woman, wise in the lore of her sex, with her crude obstetrical equipment, brought a new life into the world. Several hours later the sun shone brightly over the muddy Ohio, as the jaded stage horses slowly trotted down the hill to Maysville, carrying the United States mail, safely, but late, and an additional passenger for which the way-bill signed at Lexington did not provide.

THOMAS D. CLARK

OF ALL the products which the proud little Elkhorn Valley sent away to market, none was finer than Sally Ward (1827-1896). Sally loved the men, and they reciprocated in full measure. Before she came to her end in the old gas-lit Gault House she had led four of them to the altar and had extended the proud name of Ward to Lawrence-Hunt-Armstrong-Downs. She had bowed the heads of proud Boston and Bluegrass families alike. A scion of the religious Hunt family expressed his determination to marry the divorcee in what must have been male sentiment in general. He wrote his family on his wedding day that "he would far rather go to hell with Sally Ward than to heaven without her." Sally's energy held out to the end though her beauty failed her, and she left behind an indelible memory of feminine charm which will ever captivate Kentuckians, including the editor of this book, who devoted a full chapter to Sally Ward in The Kentucky (New York, 1942).

Belle of the Elkhorn

IT WAS on the North Elkhorn that Sally Ward's father and mother settled when their families pushed through the mountains from the Huguenot settlements in low-country South Carolina and from Virginia. Robert Ward became an influential planter, then he moved away to Louisville to become a lawyer, capitalist, and politician.

Colonel Ward was a successful man. He grew wealthy and tremendously influential. It seems that he was entirely too influential never to have been more outstanding in the state's services than he was. Perhaps he could have wielded almost

as much power in Kentucky as Clay, Breckinridge, or Crittenden. He was far wealthier than any one of these men. His
wealth was a matter of table talk in the state. When his famous
cook placed an order for culinary supplies, it was no measly
package affair. Two stout Negro slaves shoved wheelbarrows
before them to the markets each morning and returned panting
under heavy loads of choice vegetables, fruits, and meats. The
Ward table was always loaded with the rarest food to be had
in Kentucky, a state where good food has ever been a religion.
Colonel Robert had to dig up $50,000 a year to keep his famous
family living on a "respectable" plane; a sum which to most
Louisville people was a tidy fortune.

This is the environment in which young Sally grew to womanhood. An admiring neighbor commented defensively upon
this famous southern belle by philosophizing that "genius comprehends all the loveliness of woman, and to be a famous belle
one must be a genius." I would like to know—and our obliging
"neighbor" does not exactly answer the question—was Sally
Ward so overpowering in her beauty? Again, the good "neighbor" observes that her "beauty was not as great as that of many
other women of her time." Then he begins to ask the rambling
rhetorical question: "Her wit was often overmatched. What
was it then that brought her homage of all men she met, and
most of the women?"

One, of course, can never hope to stare at a rigid steel engraving and be much charmed by the lady whose impression
is before one. But even in all its stereotyped rigidity, a steel
engraving can impart some reasonable conception of feminine
proportions. An oil painting is an even better source of information. There hangs in the Speed Museum in Louisville an
excellent oil painting, and I hope an accurate likeness, of this
famous woman who received "homage from all men." Yet it
is difficult to reconcile her feminine attractions in life with her
chubbiness in print and on canvas. Her face, if her portrayers
were capable and truthful men, was that of a well-nourished
cherub, and her figure was like those used to illustrate chastity

in the romantic magazines of the fifties. The great painter, Healy, so it is said, thought that "she was the most exquisite woman that he had ever painted." Sally had what the simpering Mrs. Ellet called "aristocratically" small hands and feet. Her hair was auburn, and her blue eyes were shaded by delicately penciled brows. Her features were set in an exceedingly fair face.

Sally Ward seems to have been a contradiction in feminine history. Since time immemorial those women who have had men standing around them in humble supplication were willowy maidens. Earlier in female history Delilah and Cleopatra were sinuous charmers, and so it goes through the ages. Perhaps it was in the plushy forties and fifties, when family albums with heavily stuffed lids were popular, that plump women came into their own. Of Sally Ward's charm there can be no doubt. Chubby or not, perhaps no other southern belle attracted as much attention as she did.

At Graham's Springs Sally was the high light of the gay assemblies. At the huge dining table it was a three-cornered race among the famous belle, her witty neighbor, George D. Prentice of the Louisville *Journal,* and gracious old Dr. Christopher Columbus Graham. No one else dared interrupt when Sally and George were exchanging thrusts with their flashing wits. On the dance floor, Sally Ward was the leading belle. The idolizing Mrs. Elizabeth Fries Ellet, who put very sweet little stories of the famous American belles in a book, goes much into detail about the manner in which she dressed. Sally was never content with a single gown for a ball; with her it was a continuous rushing out to change a gown and rushing in to show the new one off. It was she who set the trend which the fancy balls were to take.

A fine example of the extravagance in dress indulged in by Robert Ward's oldest daughter was the fancy ball given by her relative, Lillie Ward, in Cincinnati for Alice Carneal, the famous Ohio belle. It was a matter of keen rivalry between Sally and Alice to see which could outdo the other in dazzling dress.

The auburn-haired Kentucky belle appeared in light-blue antique moire set off with diamonds of "wonderful size and brilliancy." She had about her shapely neck a necklace of thirty-two costly solitaires, and over her shoulders was draped a delicately woven point-lace shawl. When she walked into the room she glittered like a drunken conquistador's dream of El Dorado.

Not to be outdone by the Bluegrass beauty, Alice Carneal appeared as a Polish princess at the Russian court. She wore a "heavy dress of white silk, the shirt trimmed with ermine, and four rows of wide scarlet bands embroidered with gold. The corsage was high, and striped across the front with scarlet satin bands and gold lace. A hussar jacket of scarlet lace, embroidered with gold and trimmed with ermine, hung from her left shoulder, fastened with a gold cord and tassel. A jaunty cap of scarlet satin, with a band of ermine and the emblematic Polish feather, fastened with opals and diamonds, completed the costume." Never had the Queen City of the Ohio valley seen such a gaudy display of femininity and feminine wearing apparel. Rivalry between the two famous belles grew fierce, and there is a tradition that a dispute broke out between them, when it was said that the blue antique moire dress which Sally wore was copied from that of another, and a lesser belle. This was indeed a mean thrust at so sensitive a woman, and only by adept counseling was a hair pulling averted in high society.

Young Miss Ward was a highheaded girl. She was so full of spirit and daring that it was hard to tell what she would do next. In personality she was both a wily practical joker, and a good psychologist. Kentuckians have not yet ceased telling the story of her wild and mischievous gallop through the Louisville market house. She was out riding with one of her army of beaux who, it seems, was willing to follow every move the impetuous girl made. Perhaps it was the devil in her or an impulse to test the mettle of her escort which caused her to rein her spirited horse into the market house doorway and dare her patronizing riding companion to gallop through with her. It was with a great deal of hesitancy that the gallant swain followed, but the pair loped down the long rows of vegetables, sending baskets of earthy cabbages, onions, beans, cucumbers, and potatoes sprawling. Scurrying market attendants fell back in fright, afraid, no doubt, that General Santa Anna's bloodthirsty Mexican raiders were bearing down upon them. Of course, when it was discovered that it was the high-spirited belle who was breaking the tedium of an afternoon's riding with a boring companion, all was forgiven.

ELIZABETH MADOX ROBERTS

ELIZABETH MADOX ROBERTS (1885-1941) was one of Kentucky's most significant novelists. Her writings showed the influence of Robert Hardy upon her thought processes. Though she left the calm of her home community of Springfield to complete her education in Chicago, she returned to it to write her poems and novels. Miss Roberts' affinity for the simple people who were her characters, and for the land on which they lived, is a remarkable thing. Nellie, Henry, Mrs. Donahue, and the others still exist in prototype in Washington County.

In The Time of Man *(New York, 1926), the Knob Country burgeons with life, new life transformed into something sacred and tender with the Hardy-like touch of a gentle, sensitive author. The harsh realities of the Washington County hills fade into the azure softness of a poetic eventide of eloquent words in which situations of man, woman, and land within themselves become a plot for a story.*

Morning Star

ONE EVENING late in May Henry failed to come home from the field. Nellie fretted over the uneaten supper and Ellen worked among the stock. When he had not come at nightfall, Nellie and Ellen went across the farm, calling with uneasy voices, and after a search through the lower field they heard his groan coming weakly from the direction of the quarry. They found him in one of the stone pits, fallen among the stones, and when they lifted him one of his legs fell limp from the thigh. Ellen went to Mrs. Donahue's house for help and Pius was soon hurrying to St. Lucy to telephone for a doctor. When Pius returned he brought the Carriers who remained all night. Bill and Pius helped the doctor set the bone and bind in the boards, and Bell sat near the bed for many hours, happy and kind, fervid because she knew someone who had broken a limb. Her blank face turned from the bed to Nellie and back again, but she was apart from the pain, feeling no twinge of it.

"It just seemed like the ground rose up in the air and hit me," Henry said. "I worked out till nigh dark and I was on my way in when all of a sudden the ground just rose up outen the earth and hit me a terrible lick. That's just how it seemed. The ground hit me one awful lick and then I found myself in the bottom of that-there hole and no idea how I got there. Like that, it was."

The doctor went through the small house gathering up the things he needed, or he would ask Ellen, and his assurance and his speed filled the house. When he had set the bone in place and bound on the splints, the limb lay very large and white and wooden and still on the bed, and Henry came sickly out from the sleep of the chloroform. He would have to lie in bed many days, the doctor said, and Ellen brought water in a basin and bathed away the dust of the fields, a new kindness in her mind. To be bathing her father who lay white and still under her hands, yielding easily to her gentle demands, she passed with quietness and dignity through the room, the world grown simpler and less significant.

Henry lay in his bed for two weeks and after that he learned to sit in a chair with his injured leg stretched out heavily upon some support, hobbling back to bed on the crutches the doctor loaned him. Ellen finished setting the tobacco without help when the rainy season came, the land having been prepared many weeks before. She went slowly along the rows, carrying the plants from the bed at the foot of the hill. The season lay before her as a vast unweighed burden, and all the stooping and dragging and hauling, felt in anticipation, rested on her shoulders, on her arms, on her thighs, on her mind. She wondered who would plow the corn, the next labor after the tobacco setting, and after that would be the cutting of the hay, and there would be the garden to hoe and the little wheat crop to reap. Half of everything would go to the man who owned the land, ten hills for the man who owned the soil and then ten for them, ten shocks for Orkeys before their ten. She came in from the field too tired to care for the garden. She ate her food too weary to listen to Henry's story of twingeing bones and Nellie's report of the sow's litter and the disasters among the hens. She would eat her supper silently when Nellie piled it onto her plate and nod in her chair while the dishes were being cleared. But after she had set the tobacco, just when the need of the plowing grew actual, the man from Wingate's farm came offering to plow. "I'll put it in between my own and never miss the time," he said.

The next day Ellen saw a plow going up and down their rows and heard a voice speaking sharply to guide the horse. Jasper Kent had come to plow their fields. She could hear him gee and haw at the horse all morning, his voice speaking suddenly out of the hill, now and then hurling out an angry threat, oaths and threats and sharp commands a part of the business of getting the horse turned squarely in the furrow. She would stop her hoe in the garden to listen; she had long since ceased to heed Henry's more feeble plowing voice. In the later afternoon Kent stopped at the yard door to talk a little with Henry who sat there in a chair, to tell how the crops did and to offer help, and many afternoons later he would come. "I'll try to see my way to plow that-there patch out for you-all this week," he would say. As she went up and down the yard to feed the stock Ellen would catch the meanings of their voices. Sometimes both men talked at once, each trying to convince the other, but Henry was grateful and he would concede in the end, bought by his gratitude.

"Nohow I always taken notice if you plant potatoes in the dark moon of March you get a better crop," Kent said.

"Light moon," Henry said. "I always thought light moon."

"No, dark. Dark moon. That's science. Cabbage, now, in the light moon. Beans, corn, peas, all light. Beets, now, they go in in the dark of the moon. There's a science to that-there. You ought to set a post in the dark of the moon, did you ever hear? If you don't it'll rot under ground sure."

Passing down the yard with the feed for the hogs Ellen would catch the wonder of their talk. "I taken a look at the almanac and I see Venus was the morning star and forthwith I . . ." she would pass beyond the reach of their words. She never joined them at the kitchen door for Kent was felt to be Henry's friend. The thought that there should be a morning star, given to the morning, would haunt her sense of the pigs as she poured out their mash, and the beauty of the words lingered with her as she said them over and over. The morning star; she had never said these words before. The thought that men knew the morning star and had it in mind, calling it by name, other names—this reared a new wonder. Once as she returned to the house Kent arose suddenly and stood before her.

"Lock this-here away somewheres along with the other, will you, Ellen? I got no safe place to keep a trifle." He put some bills into her hand. "Sold the calves today and this-here is my share. Could you put it by for me for a spell?"

Albert Wingate came back from town any night, he said, and tormented his mother until she gave him whatever money she had by her. When he came there were dark ways in the house, he and his mother quarreling all night and calling names. Sometimes he brought a band of revelers with him and there was a great noise with random pistol shots. When he was gone all the boxes and cupboards were turned out onto the floor, for he was never done searching the house for money and even robbed his mother if she slept.

"She lets him take all she's got and when he's gone she pukes up a pile of hard words after him for a spell. A Tuesday he drove off a heifer that was half mine. I let that go for the time, and whilst I'm a peaceful man I don't aim to let no low-trash like Albert run over me, and if he comes again and takes off the property he'll maybe see trouble and a lavish of it too."

Ellen put the money, twenty dollars, in the trunk and thought of it no more. The pressure of the planting was past and whenever the need for the plow became immediate Kent found a few spare hours to give. Ellen cut the hay, driving their old mare hitched to the cutting implement, and afterwards she raked the hay by hand and built it into stacks. J. B. Tarbell would pass along the road every day, going and coming from his work; he was painting for Squire Stigall. He would stop for a drink at the spring by the roadside and in the sigh that followed his deep draught he would say:

"That-there's the best water anywheres this side of Muldraugh's Hill and I've tasted about all the wells in thirty mile around. That-there is rich cold water, I say."

Often he would sit all afternoon to chat. He would talk about tasty fruits and juicy mouth-watery berries until his own mouth dripped with its imagined sweet, or he would tell of clear springs and long ways to go, of the many times he had passed up and down. Often the Carriers came, and on Sunday afternoon Susie and Pius and Regina, and sometimes the Stigall youth would linger for a little about the door, or Kent would stop as he passed. J. B. Tarbell would have candy that was wrapped in bits of colored paper on which, folded inside, were lines of verse which expressed admiration and affection. He would pass the candy about with his own hand, taking the pieces out of the sack and presenting each with a bow, scraping his foot. He would hold back some choice bit, the largest piece or the piece wrapped in fringed paper, choosing another for Nellie, another for Bell or Regina, but when he came to Ellen he would kiss the chosen piece and give it to her with a deep bow, or he would say, "Here's a sweet for Sweetnen."

"I'm due over beyond the Ridge long afore now," he said. "I know they-all are a-wonderen why I don't show up. Well, they'll be powerful glad to see me walk in some day." He told long stories while all sat listening. "As soon as they seen it was J. B. Tarbell they called the dogs off. . . . They offered me a big salary to stay and work all year but I'd a heap rather be footloose and my own boss. There's only one man ever a-goen to boss old J. B. and that man is a woman. And so I says I'd a heap rather be my own boss, but no offence meant. That was when I followed picture-taken." His little string tie would sprangle under its faint blackness, always tied in a neat bow. Sometimes he would sing a song,

> Oh, my poor Nellie Gray
> They have taken her away,

or he would play a mouth harp. Often as he passed along the road he would leave a paper of the sweets for Ellen who would be in the field. Bell's hens were in a setting mood and she often came to sit with Henry to share in the taffy. Sometimes Ellen would pile her hair in its soft rolls and fasten a small blue ribbon at her throat, and then, if Tarbell came, she would sit apart smiling a little at the unveiled wooing, or she would laugh outright when she unrolled the bit of paper from the sweet drop he had kissed, and smile again as she passed into her hard white room and turned about from the clock shelf to the wooden chest. Jasper Kent's money lay on the bottom of the chest underneath her blue dress of thin muslin, the cloth for which Nellie had bought from the peddler. Ellen had taken the cloth quietly and had tried on the garment quietly when Nellie had sewed the seams, but her eyes liked to linger on the blue folds that were sweet scented and crisp to touch. She had persuaded Nellie to buy herself a piece of bright cloth for a dress, and Nellie had chosen a gray with some small purple flower hanging in the mesh. They talked softly about the sewing of the seams and of whether there should be a bit of lace or a bow, for Ellen could not give delight or glee to a muslin or a frill now, her mind one with the wants of the fields, with the beasts and the plowed trenches. In the fields she wore the faded dresses of the summer before, and there, seen distantly, her figure blended evenly with the turned soil or sank into the corn rows, now waist high or more. In the dark blue dress, now turned to gray by the sun and the wind and the rain, she moved almost unseen through the windrows of the hay or came down the steep path among the stones beside the quarry. In the pale washed-out dress she drifted all morning up and down the lines of the tobacco, the tobacco flower come before its season, as the pale flower of the tobacco come to tend its young.

But the near way of the clods, as she knew them, as she leaned over them, were a strength to destroy her strength. There, present, the heaviness of the clods pulled at her arms and the field seemed to reach very far before it stopped at the pool by the quarry. The struggling grass, matted into the soil, clung about the plants here and there and scarcely yielded to the two or three blows of the tool. She felt the weight of the grass as she tore it away, and now and then a blow so sharp that it made her flanks ache was needed to turn the soil. The field had been neglected for the summer rains had lasted overlong. She ceased to think of any day before this day or of any task before this. Each plant freed of weeds was something liberated, but another stood trammeled, the same endlessly snared, the same, until she tramped a treadmill and her thought was clodded with earth. The sun was warm on her aching shoulders and her strong knees quivered with the strain. As she plied the hoe a quick image of a year, a season, from planting to cutting and stripping, stood forth as if it were in the soil, a design, all finished and set apart. The design of the grass roots matted with the soil lay under her eyes, complete forever, varying in every detail but forever the same. The hoe came down over and over, no two blows exactly alike but no varying in the form. The year stood plainly designed, one with the grass and the dust, a certain year, formed with beginning and end, planting and cutting, gay laughing and places to go. She had said happy things and they had seemed to have meanings, and people had said things back to her, things she had kept in mind to smile at afterward. All now lay in the form of the year. A little nick in the bright edge of the hoe twinkled in and out of the brown of the earth. The hoe cut in half its depth or it cut in more, and the grains of earth fell airily against the dull upper part. The year began to turn, a form moving lightly upon itself, but she minded nothing of the year, for her body had changed, and the hoe and the soil now cut each other sharply, visible and near. "Jonas," she said, over and over. It was a name, that was all, a name for something that was gone.

Her feet were uncomfortable in Henry's old shoes, but her own were nearly out. The loose old plow shoes dragged heavily under her feet and rubbed at her bare ankles. She could say the word over and over, "Jonas, Jonas, Jonas." It was nothing but a word, gone out of her body, as gone as last year's breath. Clods had fallen into one of the shoes and she stopped an instant to shake the brogue free, then back to the hoe again. She felt the stride of her limbs as she moved to the next plant and her shoulders knew the power of the grass. "Jonas," she said, "Jonas." It was a word, less than a being, a bit of a design lost in a turning year. "Jonas," a flat sound without meaning. Suddenly a wave of pity and grief swept over her. She had played too long with the name and it had taken life. Lonely flesh beside her lonely flesh. She was standing by MacMurtrie's gate in the moonlight and the hounds were running down the field. She was sitting half the night seeing the logs burn low and renew. The year broke and fell out of its design, becoming real, becoming a stored-up part of herself, and emotion rolled over her to drown her. The dust was enlarged and the sharp edge of the hoe wavered, for tears were washing over her eyes.

But the dust was dust again and her vision was clear, the edge of the hoe standing straight and flashing keenly into the soil. "Not him," she said, "not him." She went endlessly down the row, plant after plant, the same, no thought of how long she would endure or of the end. Her body and mind were of the earth, clodded with the clods; the strength of her arms and her back and her thighs arose out of the soil, the clods turned upon themselves to work back into their own substance endlessly. The bell at St. Lucy rang for the mid-morning but its tones beat upon the outside of the dust. A little while the bell flowed onto the outer faces of the clods but it could not pierce the inner part and it fell away, scarcely missed when it went. She turned the row-end without thought, without liberation, treading a mill. Then she heard an echo of her blade falling, or a repetition of it, nearer than St. Lucy's bell and more resonant of the inner way of the soil, but she went steadily on. The echo became another hoe at work, drawing nearer, and then a shadow began to creep toward her down the row and she saw that Jasper Kent had come to the field. He worked toward her steadily and she stopped at the labor, aware now of the day and of the farm, and she rubbed her aching arms and smiled across the tobacco plants, aware now of the quarry. When he came up to her he stopped and looked at her and laughed a little, as if he knew that the conveyance of his arrival there had been the hoe.

"You could do some easy work if you'd rather," he said. "I can finish this in no time." Then he took some bills from his pocket and handed them to her, saying, "Another piece of money I wish you'd put away for me. Sold a little truck. Go do some easy work whilst I finish this-here."

She took the roll of bills from his hand and felt the coins wrapped inside it. Then she saw him move swiftly across the row, moving toward the end of the field with swift strokes of the hoe, three or four blows to each plant and it was finished. She went slowly away, startled and unprepared, hearing the withdrawing thud of the hoe as she went. Then she sat on the stile beside the garden patch under a thin ash tree and shelled the peas for the dinner. She began to think of Susie Whelen and of how her mouth was full and wide and her eyes soft and blue, her dark hair in a roll over her forehead. If Jasper or if Tarbell should look at Susie Whelen it would be seen that she was pretty and they would want her in their arms, all the more if they should look at her mouth when she smiled. She was soft and warm and full of laughter, or sullen and short, easy with her curses. To look at her was to see how full she was with her woman-ness, and Tarbell would surely see. Beyond the fields rose the wall of the quarry and above this the crest of the high pasture ran in a rugged line against the sky, all faint now in the heat of the mid-morning. It would have taken her two days to finish the field, she reflected, but now it would be done that day. He had smiled when he had said "some easy work" and his eyes had been on her face and on her eyes. She thought that she might get another ribbon or a fan on a long chain of beads, and she could feel the fan softly opening in her hand. Perhaps Jasper would take it into his hand or touch it against his face as he talked, but Susie Whelen came as a menace to the edge of her vision of the fan against Jasper's face, or Tarbell's, her mouth breaking easily into a smile, careless of its smile or of its oath. Her curses broke on her smooth lips and her bright large teeth, and one could kiss her damp mouth with a deep kiss, pushing in on her lips, eating her oath back to its core and living on its life, knowing her soft bosom and her shoulders.

Now she dropped the peas into the basket and felt Jasper's

money in the pocket of her skirt, lying against her thigh, and she remembered the words. She would hate Susie Whelen and she would watch her and she would not trust her warm body and the warm breath of her laugh. After the sugar and coffee were bought she would have something for herself, and she reckoned the price of eggs against the number in the basket under Nellie's bed to test out the sum. The hens had fallen away from their laying with the mid-season and eggs were hard to find. The huckster refused any that were thin-shelled and old and often laid aside half she carried out to him. She remembered the huckster's drooping eyes and his serious mouth drawn in a little when he counted the eggs, his ways all intent upon his business. "Twelve cents," he would say, driving a hard bargain with Nellie, "I say twelve. If I let you women run my business I'll land in the poor farm." But for her his way was gentler, giving little kindnesses, reckoning the sum in her favor and giving her the odd unreckoned cents if she bought a ribbon or a pin, and he would let her try all the pins to see which looked best on her bosom. All this for her because she was young and because she had clear straight eyes, but he listened less to Regina because her looks were slow and her step plodding, her skin sewed crookedly onto her cheeks. But he laughed with Susie Whelen and let her have her time to choose a pin or a lace, easy and happy with her, walking briskly about the wagon, because she made him feel young himself.

There was something crooked about Jasper's skin as it was set to the contour of his face, but he was in no way like Regina. When he came up out of the pasture and out of the curve of the road she would see his face and its heavy skin, unevenly traced and deeply seamed, darkly stained with years of sun and wind, heavy with work. As he came bending toward her she would see his face, but after he came she would no longer see; his serious talk of plowing and seasons, of cures and signs and selling prices, and his suspicions and hates would surround him. She herself was a woman now, that she knew. She had seen her

mouth that morning in the kitchen glass and again in the pool
that lay at the foot of the quarry. Under his heavy skin with
its uneven sewing and rugged marks of sun and wind, under
his bent shoulders, he had been quietly bold, taking the field
away from her with a few words and a smile, his hands strong
on the hoe, the sinews working flat and strong, drawing directly, fast to their purpose. Some day Tarbell would look at
Susie Whelen and he would see that her eyes were blue and
bold and that she took the world easily, and that is what a man
wants. Then he would give her the printed verses with the
choicest sweets. Space between one and Susie Whelen melted
down and away and she reached out all ways, her dark hair
rolled up from her forehead. Jasper would be bound to look
at Susie some time and then he would want her in his arms
with her easy-going laugh and her careless curses. She herself,
then, would hate Susie and she would watch her, and she
would not trust the days or the accidents of the summer. She
hated the house Susie lived in, back a little from the road with
a few flowers struggling to bloom when the drouth had eased.
A ragged shagbark tree grew across the road, in Susie's sight
day after day, and the pigs in the pen beside the barn walked
in and out of the sun, the gate tied up with a string, a rosebush
over against the garden; she would hate all of it.

Jasper was visible as a distant spot on the even green of the
field. His hoe would be tearing away the weeds to make the
soil fresh and light, and his lips would hang loose as he worked,
relaxed to the toil, his back bent deeply to the straight of the
hoe, the sweat running into the furrows of his uneven face.
He was twenty-six years old. He gave her his money to hide
away for him because she was near at hand and because he
could trust her to be careful, but he would like Susie Whelen's
carelessness and her easy mouth. He knew the wonder of the
light moon and how it drew the herbs and grains, and how the
dark moon settled things back into the earth, and he knew the
name of the morning star. She gathered the shelled peas into

her apron and carried the hulls to the pen for the pigs, her mouth shut upon its determination and anxiety. She would take more care. She would watch for the huckster when he came and buy the best he had, a fan on a long chain, perhaps. The land was hard and rough and she must take what she could out of the bitter soil, and she bent to lift the heavy pig trough, a hollowed log, to turn it over and set it to rights, ready for the mash she would bring after a little. The pigs ate the pods hurriedly and when the last one was gone there was not one green thing left in the brown trampled dirt of the pen. When they had eaten the pods the swine went back to lie in the shade of the barn, lying long and narrow side by side on the dried wallow.

IRVIN S. COBB

*B*ORN *and raised in Paducah, Irvin S. Cobb (1876-1944) knew first hand the attitudes toward the Lost Cause. He enjoyed the tales of old soldiers, and appreciated the stresses and strains which arose locally in efforts to keep the memory of the war alive. Miss Tessie Tate of his delightful story, "At the Feet of the Enemy,"* Harper's Bazaar, *February, 1929, might well have been Cobb's neighbor. She was an active member of the United Daughters of the Confederacy and had been diligent in molding that organization to her concepts of the great intersectional struggle. Outspoken and caustic, she made her feelings known to all within long earshot. Lincoln was a beast, and the Union was of doubtful validity. In Miss Tessie's doings Cobb had the material which gave him an opportunity to tell a fine leisurely story with a fast-exploding twist at the end.*

Unreconstructed Rebel

SOMEHOW the figure of Lincoln, when done in bronze or even in marble, seems to take on a majesty and a splendor which is denied to others among our great men—contemporaries of Lincoln—who in their day and time surely were regarded as being infinitely more comely than the Rail Splitter was. Perhaps it is his tall shape, gaunt but, so they claim, not ungainly which, with its huge, powerful hands and its heavy, angular feet, lends itself so well to the sculptor's art. Not even the hideous garments of the period—the bee-gum hat, the square-toed boots and all—altogether can hide the strength of it. Or perhaps it is the long tired face in which those of his generation saw only an utter homeliness, but in which we of this generation think we see a compassion, a sweetness that makes it very glorious and very beautiful to look upon.

Still, it was so easy for the modeler in his straining after realism to exaggerate that shape and the contours of the face and the head, that one marvels not that there should be so many bad statues of Lincoln scattered about over the country, but that there should be so few of them. Now, in the particular case of the bronze statue which was done for our new State House, many of the critics agreed that the artist, whoever he was, had shown a commendable restraint. He may have emphasized his subject's features, but he had not distorted them.

Certainly it looked fine and imposing when set up on its dark pedestal at the end of the right wing of the new Capitol with the light falling from above upon it and the stone stairways flanking it. It was a gift to the State from a wealthy descendent of one of our distinguished families—a family whose members had been Unionists in the Civil War, and one of whom occupied a high place in Lincoln's political household and in Lincoln's private regard. It was, so people said, the first large statue of Lincoln to be erected south of the Ohio River. This circumstance was supposed to give the dedication a special significance. Prominent ex-Confederates served on the committee which had the ceremony in hand. If memory serves me right, the governor who accepted it on behalf of the Commonwealth and as a gift to the Commonwealth was himself an ex-Confederate. And the speakers chosen for the formal unveiling in their orations said that this gracious act symbolized the wiping out of the last vestige of sectional bitterness among us and marked the dawning of a newer and a better day, would be a lesson to posterity and all that sort of customary thing, whereupon the assembled audience applauded generously.

Nearly all the State officials were assembled on the notable occasion and a majority of the Capitol employees as well, on down to the ground-keepers and the janitors and the black door-keepers. But little Miss Tessie Tate, the assistant librarian, was not there—not she. All through the day, in a state of tremulous and simmering indignation, she stayed at home in her little brown cottage overlooking the river. She hadn't seen the Lincoln statue yet. Nor did she mean to see it, ever. Miss Tessie was what you Northerners would call an unreconstructed Rebel, meaning by that, one remaining unreconciled to what happened one April morning so long ago at Appomattox Court House, Virginia. There are not nearly so many such as there used to be in the South. Still, at that, you now and then will run across one of them or a group of them. Nowadays they nearly always are women—elderly women, for the most part. To them the Lost Cause is not a dead cause, or if it is, they mean to be the last of the mourners to join in burying it.

Miss Tessie was one who had never abated of her principles nor hid her feelings under a bushel. She was an outspoken, quick-stepping, high-headed little body, still pretty in a faded and weather-beaten sort of way, and still full of the quality of spunk. She was the leading spirit in the local chapter of the U. D. C.; indeed, she was its ruling spirit. She had helped to organize it and she had been its president ever since it was organized. She read papers at its meetings dealing with the character of Alexander Stephens; and with the life and achievements of Morgan or Forrest or Stonewall Jackson or Judah P. Benjamin; and with the need for the caring for the graves of those whom invariably she called either "our heroic Confederate dead," or "our gallant immortals—the Wearers of the Gray." On Memorial Day, which is in nowise to be confused with Decoration Day, she was aquiver with patriotic sentiments. The Confederate monument upon Cemetery Hill was, in a way of speaking, her own handiwork. Largely through her efforts the funds to provide it had been raised. And the largest of the "floral offerings" which annually were deposited at its foot was sure to be Miss Tessie's. Her brother's name was carved on that monument.

To her, Lincoln was not Lincoln the Martyr, not yet Lincoln the Saviour of the Union; she believed profoundly that the Union as constituted in 1861 should not have been saved. To her he was the Yankee Clodhopper, the Leader of the Black Radicals, the Illinois Nigger-Lover, the Mudsill President. In short, this small, spry, peppery partisan of a Miss Tessie was as old-fashioned in her prejudices as she was in her way of doing her mop of curly, lovely white hair, which is to say very old-fashioned indeed.

On the day following the dedication and with her close friend and ally, Mrs. Jasper Gayle, for a witness to it, she made what amounted to a very solemn and very sacred declaration.

"My dear," she said, "never to my dying day do I intend to set foot in the place where that statue stands. My office is in that end of the building, but going and coming, I shall walk all the way around to the farther side. I can not conceive why the governor, and he a gallant Southron, ever consented to accept it." (Miss Tessie was the kind who would say "Southron" instead of "Southerner.")

Mrs. Gayle said: "I absolutely agree with you, Miss Tessie—

absolutely. But still, you know after all, Old Abe Lincoln was a native-born of this State and perhaps he—they—felt that—"

"Was not our own persecuted and beloved Jefferson Davis a Kentuckian, too? And has anyone given a figure of him to stand in the new Capitol? No! When there is a statue of our War President in the other wing, then it may be time for me to countenance the presence of a statue to their War President under the same roof—but not before!"

Mrs. Gayle said: "There, you've put your finger on it! And I think you're exactly right, Miss Tessie. Your sentiments are exactly what my sentiments are."

Mrs. Gayle felt that it behooved her on all occasions to prove the loyalty that was in her. Because it was a shameful fact that Mrs. Gayle's family, like so many prominent families in this border country, had been divided on the issue of Secession. A misguided uncle of hers had actually served with the Northern armies. Of him, though, Mrs. Gayle never spoke. With her it was as though he had not existed. Another uncle was the one whose memory she extolled. For this uncle had been a major in the Orphan Brigade, and wounded at Shiloh and promoted after Stone's River and honorably mentioned in dispatches to Richmond during the Retreat from Atlanta or, as they put it at chapter meetings, the Withdrawal from Atlanta.

But Miss Tessie had no such inky blotch on her ancestral escutcheon. Her U. D. C. membership was based upon the splendid record of a brother, the late John William Tate, who, enlisting as a private, had volunteered for secret service and, being captured within the enemy's lines, had been condemned to death by hanging as a spy, but while awaiting execution had managed to escape from a military prison at Washington and, with his health undermined by earlier privations and by the rigors of his confinement, had died, still in age a mere boy, as he tried to make his way back home. The place where his wasted body found burial was unknown; and since he died before he reached his comrades, even the manner of his escape remained a mystery. All his people knew about it was that he managed to get out of his captivity and that he fell, alone and exhausted and spent and dying, somewhere along the dreary way in the territory occupied by the Federals up in West Virginia. It made a pathetic, moving story as Miss Tessie told it—the agony in the stricken household when first word came that he had been taken and then, quick on that, the word that he'd had a summary trial and had been sentenced to die a shameful death, and then the suspense of the waiting and then finally, by delayed and roundabout sources, the news that having gotten clear of prison and off and away for freedom, he had dropped on a mountain roadside, and as one of the minor, unconsidered tragedies of the war, had been shoveled underground by strange hands.

She, who was only a child then, away back in '63, had idolized this somewhat older brother of hers. She grew up worshipping the image of his remembered youth. She counted him—and rightly so, as you'll agree—as great a hero as any who took a mortal wound in battle. She never married. In her heart this brother's memory took for her the place of a husband, the places of the children she might have borne. So, at seventy-odd, she hated all that was Northern. She hated it because of the cruel, ruthless machinery set in motion to speed Private John William Tate to the gallows and because no answer, no acknowledgment even, had been made to the frantic, hurried appeals for mercy sent to Lincoln at the White House through former friends of her family who, being faithful to the Union, were said to have influence in that quarter; and most of all she hated because hating had come to be a very part of her warp and fiber.

Last year, as you may remember, Lincoln's birthday fell on a Sunday and was celebrated—in the sections where they do celebrate Lincoln's birthday—on Monday. On that Monday, February 13, Mrs. Gayle had occasion to call on Miss Tessie upon patriotic business connected with an impending meeting of the Daughters. In the librarian's office they told her that

Miss Tessie wasn't there, hadn't been there at all this morning, hadn't telephoned either—possibly she was sick or something. Mrs. Gayle was turning away when one of the old negro attendants of the Capitol force who had entered in time to hear the latter end of these remarks, spoke up:

"Nome, I reckon she ain't sick—leastwise I jest now seen her downstairs on de main floor. I jedge mebbe you'll find her down dere."

"Whereabouts downstairs, Uncle?" asked Mrs. Gayle.

"Right down below yere in de righthand rotunder wuz whar I seen her."

"Oh, you must be mistaken," stated Mrs. Gayle. "She never comes in that way. She never would, no matter how big a hurry she might be in."

"Mebbe not, heretofo', lady, but not five minutes ago I seen her comin' in the front do' jes ez I waz startin' up the stairsteps myse'f. I ain't mistooken, lady. Ain't but one Miss Tessie 'round dis yere State House, nome."

So the puzzled Mrs. Gayle went to find her friend. She descended the curving stone treads and, descending, saw how the winter sun, filtering through the skylight in the roof above, made a sort of golden nimbus about the head of the statue and she saw a skimpy little garland of bronzed oak leaves which early that day the surviving members of the local G. A. R.—two feeble old white men and one feeble old black man—had placed at its foot and then, almost touching the oak leaves where with drooped head she clung against the pedestal in a posture which, oddly, might betoken devotion, Mrs. Gayle saw the shape of Miss Tessie.

Had Miss Tessie gone suddenly mad? That was the question which framed itself in Mrs. Gayle's mind as she quickened her pace to a bird-like little scamper.

Filled with distress and bewilderment, she reached the level and skittered across the marble floor.

"Why Miss Tessie!" she cried, drawing near. "Why, Miss Tessie, what in the world!"

Miss Tessie raised her white head and Mrs. Gayle saw that while the face of her friend was swollen from weeping it was a face transfigured and glorified by some tremendously uplifting emotion.

She said nothing, though. She handed to Mrs. Gayle a scrap of paper crumpled by close pressure of her hands, and in amazement Mrs. Gayle unfolded it and flattened it out. It was a half page torn from one of yesterday's big city papers—part, evidently, of a Sunday "feature article."

Mrs. Gayle's agile eye caught the page-wide heading: "A New Light on Lincoln's Life for Lincoln's Birthday." Then swiftly she skimmed through the florid introductory paragraphs, sensing that the story dealt with discoveries of interesting and, so it was alleged, previously unpublished documents belonging to a collector of rare manuscripts in the North, and so on, skipping along until at the top of the second column she came to a reproduction in facsimile of a letter, or note. She read it and it read as follows: "Dear Stanton: There is a young Rebel named Johnnie Tate under sentence of hanging for being a spy. Don't hang him. Speed brought me a letter today from his old mother down in Kentucky. I understand this boy is mighty sick. If he were turned loose he couldn't do any more damage to the Union and, anyhow, Speed promises me he'd go home, should he live to get there, and behave himself from now on. So since you've been fussing at me for letting so many spies off with their necks unbroken, and some of the newspapers have been jumping on me for being what they call too softhearted, I wish, as a personal confidential favor to the writer, you'd keep this particular case out of the official records and instruct somebody whom you can trust with the secret, just to leave the door of this youngster's cell unlocked and the gate ajar the next dark night. I know this is irregular, but everything seems to be irregular these times and if there is any trouble over it, I'll take the responsibility on my own shoulders. Much obliged. (Signed) A. Lincoln."

"Oh!" exclaimed Mrs. Gayle understanding. "Oh, Miss Tessie!"

Miss Tessie appeared not to hear her. Miss Tessie was on tiptoe flat against the pedestal, stretching her two arms upwards as though seeking to reach the hem of The Emancipator's garment. She couldn't make it, though. She just could manage to touch with her reverent lips the tip of one huge, ugly, box-toed bronze boot.

BOOK FOUR

The Sports of Gentlemen

CONQUERING a wilderness empire was a challenge to the Kentucky pioneers. Had they taken the task as seriously as Moses did in leading the Children of Israel across the great Wilderness, it might not have been accomplished so easily. Every advance made into the Kentucky backwoods had the flavor of adventure, and every incident was another experience. With ax, rifle, and horse the storied pioneers crossed the Appalachians and laid the mudsill for a new society and a new state.

The ax was effective in bringing the forest low, while the rifle stood off the Indian and fetched home meat enough to sustain the people. Neither of these instruments of settlement, however, proved so durable as the horse. Long after the ax was stacked away with the antiques and the long rifle had become a collector's item, the horse enjoyed popularity. He pulled the plow and the carriage with equal grace, and he raced down main street and around hillside tracks to prove his own worth and to sustain his master's pride.

As a sporting animal the horse sometimes got entangled in local politics. As the number of people increased, he was de-

nied use of main street as a race path, and when formal tracks
were organized, politicians at Frankfort and on the hustings
took notice. There were few better places to find a readymade
assembly of men who were willing to do political bidding than
at a militia muster and a race meet. Fired by the excitement
of a close race and the generous libations of bourbon, men were
highly susceptible to oratory.

The sports of horseracing and politics have produced their
share of stories. About the courthouses the little fellows have
poured forth their streams of flowery oratory in which they
praised God, home, and mother with sententious reverence.
They have ever made protestations of stern personal virtue and
good intentions, and have declared their opponents knaves and
cutthroats who, except for a humane people, would be hanged.
The issues they discussed were seldom vital, and almost never
pertinent, but the political orator had an amusement function
in Kentucky history. Above the noise of the rabble who fed
a stream of abuse, humor, and buffoonery, there came the clear
notes of the "tall timbers" of Kentucky politics. Henry Clay
could take so vital a question as a prospective American System
and analyze a nation's economic problems. He could elucidate
the intricacies of domestic and international trade, and at the
same time send opponents away from the hustings confounded
and confused.

Lanky John Jordan Crittenden of the deep-set eyes and soft
voice could discuss the issues of compromise hoping to stave
off a fratricidal war, or cut a bumptious opponent with a wit-
ticism almost in the same breath. Throughout Kentucky history, problems real and imaginary have been lifted to the levels
of great sacredness. A tender memory, a cherished tradition, a
benevolent sin, or an unkept promise could be couched in the
language of beauty and fidelity. Possibly this is the one public
nest which politicians have never befouled beyond engaging in
personal abuse and attack. When the interest of the people,
the traditions of the state, and the aspirations for the future
have been grist to the politicians' mills, they have ground gent-

ly. Eating, drinking, sporting, and speaking have been revered components of politics. Who could falter greatly with a full stomach, a bourbon-inspired imagination, and within the sound of golden oratory?

At the polls the song has not always been so gentle and virtuous. Voting sometimes has involved irregularities that called forth brute strength. The protection of democracy's unchecked roster at the precinct level could be a horrendous matter. Kentucky was born of great physical exertion, and at times a part of its political system has survived by the same force. Anything was fair in an Indian fight and an election. Often voters paid for their indiscretions at the polls with hide and hair, and the state's honor suffered the same kind of hiding. Some visitors to early Kentucky were horrified by the muscular process of electing officials. They seldom appreciated the sporting aspects of the affairs, and they were unable to reconcile the soft oratory of the campaign with the physical realities of vote casting.

Whether it be a gathering of voters to hear a political speech, or a group of neighboring farmers come together to settle the burning issue of who had the best horse, Kentuckians have been gregarious people. There are few better genre stories in American literature than that describing a quarter race in Kentucky. Two nags of uncertain ancestry and speed, a cross-eyed judge, and a naive outsider were the elements of this story. Of more refined qualities were those reports of the growing interest in the turf of the Bluegrass. William Porter in his *Spirit of the Times* and the editor of the *Turf Register,* to say nothing of the local press, recorded a vivid history of racing in Kentucky. The racehorse Lexington set a record of speed which will ever remain a pleasant overtone in Bluegrass history. Morgan's men added luster to the horse's story in the region, even if they did establish a part of it by what General Basil Duke called "horse pressing." The thundering hoofs of the Morgan command combined the sounds of Bluegrass sporting glory with the rattle of destructive war.

WILLIAM LITTELL

WILLIAM LITTELL (1768-1824) was an outstanding legal scholar in early Kentucky; his codification of the laws of the state from 1792 to 1819 represented an invaluable service. In his relaxed moments he wrote political satire, which marked him as the first humorist in the state. The "Petition of Gregory Woodcock," included in Littell's Festoons of Fancy *(Louisville, 1814), bitingly criticized the prevailing method of electioneering.*

Too Much Spirit

TO THEIR MAJESTIES THE SOVEREIGN PEOPLE OF KENTUCKY

The Petition of *Gregory Woodcock* most humbly sheweth—

That your petitioner hath grown grey and poor, and become an idler and a drunkard, in attempting to serve his country in the capacity of a legislator. He has been six times a candidate for a seat in the Assembly, and twice for one in the Senate, but never had the good fortune to be elected: He would now willingly live a private life, if he had any thing to live on—but his fortune, which was at the first but small, has been entirely swallowed up in prosecuting ways and means to obtain your majesties favour; and your petitioner moreover contracted a disrelish for all ordinary industry, and such a relish for strong drink, that it is utterly impracticable for him ever to retrieve his circumstances, or even to procure a livelihood for the remainder of his days.

Under these circumstances, he thinks he may with profound submission to your majesties, request a reimbursement of all expenses to which he has put himself in order to obtain your favour, and the more especially as your majesties did actually receive and consume his living, notwithstanding you withheld your favour. Your petitioner will further remark, that he makes no charge of loss of time, for one half of the first four years, and the whole of the last four, which he spent in riding about from house to house, in going to raisings and log-rollings and in frequenting taverns, tippling houses, gambling tables, dram shops, and every other hole and corner where your majesties were to be met with, in order to accommodate himself to your majesties humour: He likewise lays out of his account, the great danger of damnation to which he has subjected himself, by the manifold falsehoods and calumnies and slanders, which he has invented and circulated from time to time, to the disparagement of his competitors—and only charges your majesties with what he has actually expended.

Annexed hereto is a statement exhibiting his expenditures on the above moderate scheme of calculation;—and your petitioner humbly prays, that you will give special instruction to your representatives the next session, to direct it to be paid out of the public treasury: And your petitioner as in duty bound, shall pray.

GREGORY WOODCOCK

STATEMENT

THE SOVEREIGN PEOPLE OF KENTUCKY,
TO GREGORY WOODCOCK, DR.

To the expenses of the election of 1799.—To 225 half pints of whiskey at different times and places, as introductory to declaring myself a candidate, $28 12 5

To 100 do. purchased during the summer, merely for the purpose of shewing that I was attached to diets and drinks of domestic growth and manufacture, and was disposed to encourage them,   12 66

To ten bottles of wine at different times among merchants, for the purpose of shewing that I was a gentleman and fond of the importation of foreign luxuries,   20

Whiskey drank at my house, 41 gallons,   20 50
Expenses of election days in whole,   80 00

To the expenses of the election of 1800.—For introducing
myself as a candidate, 100 half pints of whiskey,   12 66
Treating those who had voted for me last year, 200 half
pints,   25 33
Drank with farmers, 120 half pints,   15
Drank with lawyers five bottles of wine, they promised to
vote for me if I would raise their fees, which I told them I
would,   10
This year my fellow citizen, Timothy Twisty, was likely to
be put in gaol, he had voted for me last year and promised that
he would again, I went his bail, but before the election he ran
away, so I lost his vote and had the debt to pay,   107 50
Expenses of the election days,   90 00

To the expenses of the election of 1801.—As soon as I announced myself a candidate this year, Tom Bluster insulted me,
and I, to shew myself a man of spirit challenged him to a fist
fight, in which he whipped me severely; this made so much
noise that I had no occasion to announce myself by half pints
of whiskey; but in the fight he bit off a piece of my ear, chewed
one of my fingers all to jelly, and gouged one of my eyes—for
curing these wounds the Doctor's bill was   50 00
But as I was a long time confined at home, and utterly forbid
to drink anything myself, my other electioneering expenses
amounted only to,   15 00
Expenses of the election days,   85 00

Expenses of the election of 1802.—At the commencement of
this year's election I had a fight about politics with Sam Slink,
and whipped him most unmercifully, he brought suit against
me and recovered $60 with costs, which with what I gave to my
own lawyers, amounted to   80 00

I came within one vote of being elected this year, and should have succeeded far ahead if I had not foolishly commenced suit against Tom Bluster for whipping me last year; this I did not do 'till Sam Slink sued me, and then only for the purpose of setting off my damages against Slink's; but as soon as I commenced suit there was an outcry against me as acting unworthy of a man of spirit—I dismissed it at my own costs, but it would not do—　　　　　　　　　　　　　　　　　　　　　　7 50

Expenses in drinking and treating before the election,　50 00
Expenses at the election,　　　　　　　　　　　　　　100 00

Expenses of the election of 1803.—This year I was a candidate for the Senate, and I had by this time become so habituated to idleness and drinking that I was seldom at home, and kept no regular accounts; but I suppose what I drank and what I gave away would at least amount to half a pint a day for 200 days,　　　　　　　　　　　　　　　　　　　　　　　　25 33

Being a candidate for a higher dignity, I thought it incumbent on me to treat several times to wine and brandy toddy; all my bills on that score amount to　　　　　　　　　　62 50

Runagate Rattle offered to ride about and support my election if I would lend him my best horse, which I did, having great hopes in his talents and attachment to me; however, he paid little attention to my business, and what he did operated to my prejudice; but he rode helter skelter all over the country wherever his folly or caprice led him, until he killed a horse for me worth $150—he was not willing to pay for him, nor was he able—so I took it all in good part,　　　　　　　　150 00

Expenses of the election of 1804.—My success the last year was not flattering, nor was it discouraging, and I offered for the Senate again. I had unfortunately read that a great man of the name of Whelks or Whilks, or some such name, had secured several elections by caressing the wives of the voters. I was a little afraid to try the experiment; but as I had tried every thing else, I ventured: The lady I had selected for the first trial was about thirty, of a pleasing inviting countenance, and very familiar—her husband was a man of influence, and consequence; but, alas! she disliked me, or thought I was too forward or not forward enough, or I know not what, but she resisted me like a Tiger, raved and stormed, and called me every thing that was base and detestable: I fled from her presence, determined to abandon that mode of electioneering for ever. But this was only the beginning of sorrows: three days afterwards, her husband, a robust determined man, met with me and gave me a severe cowhiding in spite of all the resistance I could make. In order to deprecate his wrath as much as possible, I protested that I never had any love for his wife, and that it was only an electioneering scheme. This made him despise me as much as he hated me—he made no secret of my concessions—and my character was blasted completely. I resolved however, not to give up: I found it necessary in order to keep myself in countenance, to drink two half pints of whiskey upon an average each day; this with what I gave away to every one who would drink with me, amounted to 400 half pints,   50 00

My expenses on the election days were now but trifling, as few were willing to drink in my name—$15 paid all my treats in both counties,   15 00

Expenses for the election of 1805.—This year I was put into prison bounds for debt, staid there 20 days and came out because I could not pay my prison fees, and my creditor would not pay them. I now offered myself a candidate for the lower house, merely to shew that I did not under-value myself. This year I drank at the rate of three half pints of whiskey a day, when I could get it, which was not often, say 100 half pints,   12 66

But my face had become red, interspersed with purple spots, and it was generally said I was stupefied with hard drink. My expenses at the election were nothing, for no tavern keeper would credit me, and I had no money; but I got 12 votes.

The year 1806.—I had not intended to be a candidate this year, but I had declared myself so when drunk, and had too much spirit to retract it when sober: However I was at no expense now for I had nothing to expend, being dependent on a relation for victuals and clothes, and on any company which I could fall into for drink. At the election for this year, my old enemies Tom Bluster and Sam Slink made me very drunk, which was an easy thing done, and then took me to the court house and persuaded me to vote for myself, which was the only vote I had.—When I became sober, I concluded that it was now time to abandon politics forever—and set myself about unlearning all my idle and evil practices; Without entering into detail of my efforts, I will just assure you, that I find a reform to answer any purpose in this world utterly impossible.

The sum total of the expenses which I think the people bound in duty to indemnify me for, is $1166 01

HENRY CLAY

*H*ENRY CLAY *(1777-1852), probably the most outstanding of Bluegrass politicians, made hundreds of speeches, but none of them so important perhaps as his "American System" speech before Congress on March 31, 1824. He restated the Hamiltonian philosophy of American economy and government, and brought it up to date. Clay used all of his powers of persuasion to convince his fellow lawmakers of the wisdom of his plan for a self-contained America. Possibly the great Kentucky orator made some of his most intensive preparation for this speech. Whatever may be the faults with its reasoning and data, there is no flaw in its sincerity.*

Like most major political speeches of this period, the American System oration was long, and even dull; the full version of

it in the Annals of Congress *is tedious reading. Regardless of a
lack of entertainment qualities in this famous speech, it is a
major one in the history of congressional oratory and a landmark in American philosophical political history. It expresses
afresh one of the fundamental views of the first quarter of the
nineteenth century.*

A Genuine American Policy

IN CASTING our eyes around us, the most prominent circumstance which fixes our attention, and challenges our deepest
regret, is, the general distress which pervades the whole country. It is forced upon us by numerous facts of the most incon-
testable character. It is indicated by the diminished exports
of native produce; by the depressed and reduced state of our
foreign navigation; by our diminished commerce; by successive
unthreshed crops of grain, perishing in our barns and barn-
yards for the want of a market; by the alarming diminution of
the circulating medium; by the numerous bankruptcies, not
limited to the trading classes, but extending to all orders of
society; by an universal complaint of the want of employment,
and a consequent reduction of the wages of labor; by the rav-
enous pursuit after public situations, not for the sake of their
honors, and the performance of their public duties, but as a
means of private subsistence; by the reluctant resort to the
perilous use of paper money; by the intervention of legislation
in the delicate relation between debtor and creditor; and,
above all, by the low and depressed state of the value of almost
every description of the whole mass of the property of the
nation, which has, on an average, sunk not less than about
fifty per cent. within a few years. This distress pervades every
part of the Union, every class of society; all feel it, though it
may be felt, at different places, in different degrees. It is like
the atmosphere which surrounds us—all must inhale it, and

none can escape it. In some places, it has burst upon our people without a single mitigating circumstance to temper its severity. In others, more fortunate, slight alleviations have been experienced, in the expenditure of the public revenue, and in other favoring causes. . . . And it is the duty of the statesman, no less than that of the physician, to survey, with a penetrating, steady, and undismayed eye, the actual condition of the subject on which he would operate; to probe to the bottom the diseases of the body politic, if he would apply efficacious remedies. We have not, thank God, suffered in any great degree for food. . . .

What, again I would ask, is the cause of the unhappy condition of our country, which I have faintly depicted? It is to be found in the fact that, during almost the whole existence of this Government, we have shaped our industry, our navigation, and our commerce, in reference to an extraordinary war in Europe, and to foreign markets, which no longer exist; in the fact that we have depended too much upon foreign sources of supply, and excited too little the native; in the fact that, whilst we have cultivated, with assiduous care, our foreign resources, we have suffered those at home to wither, in a state of neglect and abandonment. The consequence of the termination of the war of Europe has been the resumption of European commerce, European navigation, and the extension of European agriculture and European industry, in all its branches. Europe, therefore, has no longer occasion to any thing like the same extent as that which she had during her wars, for American commerce, American navigation, the produce of American industry. . . .

The greatest want of civilized society is a market for the sale and exchange of the surplus of the produce of the labor of its members. This market may exist at home or abroad, or both, but it must exist somewhere, if society prospers; and wherever it does exist, it should be competent to the absorption of the entire surplus of production. It is most desirable that there should be both a home and a foreign market. But, with respect to their relative superiority, I cannot entertain a doubt. The home market is first in order, and paramount in importance. The object of the bill under consideration is to create this home market, and to lay the foundations of a genuine American policy. It is opposed; and it is incumbent upon the partisans of the foreign policy (terms which I shall use without any invidious intent) to demonstrate that the foreign market is an adequate vent for the surplus produce of our labor. . . .

The policy of all Europe is adverse to the reception of our agricultural produce, so far as it comes into collision with its own; and, under that limitation, we are absolutely forbid to enter their ports, except under circumstances which deprive them of all value as a steady market. The policy of all Europe rejects those great staples of our country, which consist of objects of human subsistence. The policy of all Europe refuses to receive from us any thing but those raw materials of smaller value, essential to their manufactures, to which they can give a higher value, with the exception of tobacco and rice, which they cannot produce. Even Great Britain, to which we are its best customer, and from which we receive nearly one half in value of our whole imports, will not take from us articles of subsistence produced in our country cheaper than can be produced in Great Britain. In adopting this exclusive policy, the States of Europe do not inquire what is best for us, but what suits themselves, respectively; they do not take jurisdiction of the question of our interests, but limit the object of their legislation to that of the conservation of their own peculiar interests, leaving us free to prosecute ours as we please. They do not guide themselves by that romantic philanthropy, which we see displayed here, and which invokes us to continue to purchase the produce of foreign industry, without regard to the state or prosperity of our own, that foreigners may be pleased to purchase the few remaining articles of ours which their restrictive policy has not yet absolutely excluded from their consumption. What sort of a figure would a member of the British Parliament have made—what sort of reception would his opposition have obtained, if he had remonstrated against the passage of the corn law, by which British consumption is limited to the breadstuffs of British production, to the entire exclusion of American, and stated that America could not, and would not, buy British manufactures, if Britain did not buy American flour? . . .

Is this foreign market, so incompetent at present, and which, limited as its demands are, operates so unequally upon the productive labor of our country, likely to improve in the future? If I am correct in the views which I have presented to the Committee, it must become worse and worse. What can improve it? Europe will not abandon her own agriculture to foster ours. We may even anticipate that she will more and more enter into competition with us in the supply of the West India market. That of South America, for articles of subsistence, will probably soon vanish. The value of our exports, for the future, may remain at about what it was last year. But if we do not create some new market; if we persevere in the existing pursuits of agriculture; the inevitable consequence must be to augment greatly the quantity of our produce, and to lessen its value in the foreign market. Can there be a doubt on this point? Take the article of cotton, for example, which is almost the only article that now remunerates labor and capital. A certain description of labor is powerfully attracted towards the cotton-growing country. The cultivation will be greatly extended; the aggregate amount annually produced will be vastly augmented. The price will fall. The more unfavorable soils will then be gradually abandoned. And I have no doubt that, in a few years, it will cease to be profitably produced any where north of the thirty-fourth degree latitude. But, in the mean time, large numbers of the cotton growers will suffer the greatest distress. And whilst this distress is brought upon our own country, foreign industry will be stimulated by the very cause which occasions our distress. For, by surcharging the markets abroad, the price of the raw material being reduced, the manufacturer will be able to supply cotton fabrics cheaper, and the consumption in his own country, and in foreign nations, other than ours, (where the value of the import must be limited to the value of the export, which I have supposed to remain the same,) being proportionately extended, there will be consequently an increased demand for the produce of his industry.

Our agricultural is our greatest interest. It ought ever to be predominant. All others should bend to it. And, in considering what is for its advantage, we should contemplate it in all its varieties, of planting, farming, and grazing. Can we do nothing to invigorate it? nothing to correct the errors of the past, and to brighten the still more unpromising prospects which lie before us? We have seen, I think, the causes of the distresses of the country. We have seen that an exclusive dependence upon the foreign market must lead to still severer distress, to impoverishment, to ruin. We must then change somewhat our course. We must give a new direction to some portion of our industry. We must speedily adopt a genuine American policy. Still cherishing a foreign market, let us create a home market, to give further scope to the consumption of the produce of American industry. . . .

The creation of a home market is not only necessary to procure for our agriculture a just reward of its labors, but it is indispensable to obtain a supply of our necessary wants. If we cannot sell, we cannot buy. That portion of our population (and we have seen that it is not less than four-fifths) which makes comparatively nothing that foreigners will buy, has nothing to make purchases with from foreigners. It is in vain that we are told of the amount of our exports, supplied by the planting interest. They may enable the planting interest to supply all its wants; but they bring no ability to the interests not planting, unless, which cannot be pretended, the planting interest was an adequate vent for the surplus produce of the labor of all other interests. It is in vain to tantalize us with the greater cheapness of foreign fabrics. There must be an ability to purchase, if an article be obtained, whatever may be the price, high or low, at which it was sold. And a cheap article is as much beyond the grasp of him who has no means to buy, as a high one. Even if it were true that the American manufacturer would supply consumption at dearer rates, it is better to have his fabrics than the unattainable foreign fabrics; for it is better to be ill supplied than not at all. A coarse coat, which will communicate warmth and cover nakedness, is better than no coat. . . .

Our Confederacy comprehends within its vast limits great diversity of interests—agricultural, planting, farming, commercial, navigating, fishing, manufacturing. No one of these interests is felt in the same degree, and cherished with the same solicitude, through all parts of the Union. Some of them are peculiar to particular sections of our common country. But all these great interests are confided to the protection of one Government—to the fate of one ship; and a most gallant ship it is, with a noble crew. If we prosper, and are happy, protection must be extended to all—it is due to all. It is the great principle on which obedience is demanded from all. If our essential interests cannot find protection from our own Government against the policy of foreign Powers, where are they to get it? We did not unite for sacrifice, but for preservation. The inquiry should be, in reference to the great interests of every section of the Union, (I speak not of minute subdivisions,) What would be done for those interests if that section stood alone and separated from the residue of the Republic? If the promotion of those interests would not injuriously affect any other section, then every thing should be done for them which would be done if it formed a distinct Government. If they come into absolute collision with the interests of another section, a reconciliation, if possible, should be attempted, by mutual concession, so as to avoid a sacrifice of the prosperity of either to that of the other. In such a case, all should not be done for one, which would be done if it were separated and independent, but something; and, in devising the measure, the good of each part and of the whole should be carefully consulted. This is the only mode by which we can preserve, in full vigor, the harmony of the whole Union. The South entertains one opinion, and imagines that a modification of the existing policy of the country, for the protection of American industry, involves the ruin of the South. The North, the East, the West, hold the opposite opinion, and feel, and contemplate, in a longer adherence to the foreign policy, as it now exists, their utter destruction. Is it true that the interests of these great sections of our country are irreconcilable with each other? Are we reduced to the sad and afflicting dilemma of determining which shall fall a victim to the prosperity of the other? Happily, I think, there is no such distressing alternative. If the North, the West, and the East, formed an independent State, unassociated with the South, can there be a doubt that the restrictive system would be carried to the point of prohibition of every foreign fabric of which they produce the raw material, and which they could manufacture? Such would be their policy, if they stood alone; but they are, fortunately, connected with the South, which believes its interest to require a free admission of foreign manufactures. Here, then, is a case for mutual concession, for fair compromise. The bill under consideration presents this compromise. It is a medium between the absolute exclusion and the unrestricted admission of the produce of foreign industry. It sacrifices the interest of neither section to that of the other; neither, it is true, gets all that it wants, nor is subject to all that it fears. But it has been said that the South obtains nothing in this compromise. Does it lose any thing? is the first question. I have endeavored to prove that it does not, by showing that a mere transfer is effected in the source of the supply of its consumption from Europe to America; and that the loss, whatever it may be, of the sale of its great staple in Europe, is compensated by the new market created in America. But does the South really gain nothing in this compromise? The consumption of the other sections, though somewhat restricted, is still left open, by this bill, to foreign fabrics purchased by Southern staples. So far its operation is beneficial to the South, and prejudicial to the industry of the other sections, and that is the point of mutual concession. The South will also gain by the extended consumption of its great staple, produced by an increased capacity to consume it, in consequence of the establishment of the home market. But the South cannot exert its industry and enterprise in the business of manufactures. Why not? The difficulties, if not exaggerated, are artificial, and may, therefore, be surmounted. But can the other section embark in the planting occupation of the South? The obstructions which forbid them are natural, created by the immutable laws of God, and therefore unconquerable. . . .

At the commencement of our Constitution, almost the whole population of the United States was confined between the Alleghany Mountains and the Atlantic Ocean. Since that epoch, the western part of New York, of Pennsylvania, of Virginia, all the western States and territories, have been principally peopled. Prior to that period we had scarcely any interior. An interior has sprung up, as it were, by enchantment, and along with it new interests and new relations, requiring the parental protection of Government. Our policy should be modified accordingly, so as to comprehend all, and sacrifice none. And are we not encouraged by the success of past experience, in respect to the only article which has been adequately protected? Already have the predictions of the friends of the American system, in even a shorter time than their most sanguine hopes could have anticipated, been completely realized in regard to that article; and the consumption is now better and cheaper supplied with coarse cottons, than it was under the prevalence of the foreign system.

Even if the benefit of the policy were limited to certain sections of our country, would it not be satisfactory to behold American industry, wherever situated, active, animated, and thrifty, rather than persevere in a course which renders us subservient to foreign industry? But these benefits are two-fold, direct, and collateral, and in the one shape or the other, they will diffuse themselves throughout the Union. All parts of the

Union will participate, more or less, in both. As to the direct benefit, it is probable that the North and the East will enjoy the largest share. But the West and the South will also participate in them. Philadelphia, Baltimore, and Richmond, will divide with the Northern capitalists the business of manufacturing. The latter city unites more advantages for its successful prosecution than any other place I know, Zanesville, in Ohio, only excepted. And where the direct benefit does not accrue, that will be enjoyed of supplying the raw material and provisions for the consumption of artisans. Is it not more desirable to put at rest and prevent the annual recurrence of this unpleasant subject, so well fitted, by the various interests to which it appeals, to excite irritation and to produce discontent? Can that be effected by its rejection? Behold the mass of petitions which lie on our table, earnestly and anxiously entreating the protecting interposition of Congress against the ruinous policy which we are pursuing. Will these petitioners, comprehending all orders of society, entire States and communities, public companies, and private individuals, spontaneously assembling, cease in their humble prayers by your lending a deaf ear? Can you expect that these petitioners, and others, in countless numbers, that will, if you delay the passage of this bill, supplicate your mercy, should contemplate their substance gradually withdrawn to foreign countries, their ruin slow, but certain, and as inevitable as death itself, without one expiring effort? You think the measure injurious to you; we believe our preservation depends upon its adoption. Our convictions, mutually honest, are equally strong. What is to be done? I invoke that saving spirit of mutual concession under which our blessed Constitution was formed, and under which alone it can be happily administered. I appeal to the South—to the high-minded, generous, and patriotic South—with which I have so often co-operated, in attempting to sustain the honor and to vindicate the rights of our country. Should it not offer, upon the altar of the public good, some sacrifice of its peculiar opinions? Of what does it complain? A possible temporary enhancement in the objects of consumption. Of what do we complain? A total incapacity, produced by the foreign policy, to purchase at any price, necessary foreign objects of consumption. In such an alternative, inconvenient only to it, ruinous to us, can we expect too much from Southern magnanimity? The just and confident expectation of the passage of this bill has flooded the country with recent importations of foreign fabrics. If it should not pass, they will complete the work of destruction of our domestic industry. If it should pass, they will prevent any considerable rise in the price of foreign commodities, until our own industry shall be able to supply competent substitutes.

THOMAS N. ALLEN

*P*OLITICAL *oratory was the order of the day for Fourth of July celebrations in central Kentucky, and if the candidates in an impending election could be induced to debate, so much the better. Thomas N. Allen (1839-?) recalled in his fiction-alized reminiscences,* Chronicles of Oldfields *(Seattle, 1909), such an occasion when the throng assembled heard a Bluegrass gentleman go down to defeat before a mountain boy who had overcome the handicap of his heritage and environment. The issue was trivial, but interest was kept high with burgoo and toddy.*

The 4th of July

THE YEAR after the memorable contest between Henry Clay and Andrew Jackson, Bill Bassett and Randolph Jones ran for the legislature. Bill is a Whig and Randolph is a Democrat.

The hot fires of the presidential election had simmered down but still retained live coals in abundance, and the campaign waxed warm.

The candidates stumped the county, making speeches in every precinct. A big barbecue took place on the 4th of July in Doc Humes' woods pasture. Hand-bills on gate posts and barn-doors throughout the county giving notice of public speaking arrested the attention of the passers-by; and by the time the race was fairly on every man, woman and child had taken sides, many of the men passionately advocating the election of the candidate they preferred, and neglecting their business to talk politics. The barbecue was the great event of the campaign. It was held, as I have mentioned, in a woods pasture of Doc Humes', near town. The day was an ideal summer day; not one of those days when the sky has no clouds and the sun beats down on you with a fierce heat; but one when between a lot of clouds of fantastic shapes patches of deep blue could be seen. To make a droll description, it was like looking through a sort of woolly lattice-work far away into immeasurable space where God lives. A gentle wind rustled the foliage of the sugar trees and the black walnuts, making a soft murmur up among the leaves as if they were whispering to one another. How beautiful the world is on such a day! How its loveliness and its serenity permeates my soul and makes me glad to be alive!

Under Obe Crews' supervision, for Obe is a master hand at a barbecue, a long trench was dug, the full length of which was now a bed of live coals, and across this trench poles were placed at intervals, some to support great iron kettles and others the divers kinds of meats to be roasted—muttons and shoats and beeves. In the kettles, green corn, tomatoes, potatoes, red peppers, chickens and squirrels bobbed up and down in the bubbling water, intermingling their rich juices, the hot vapors filling the air, and sending off a sweet savor that made my mouth water. This was the burgoo, the most delicious soup in the world. Talk about your French soups, la!

A dozen negroes, hatless, bare-armed and grinning from ear

to ear, turned and basted the roasts, and stirred the burgoo.
Negro women under the directions of my old Dinah, spread
cotton cloths on the rude tables, and distributed along the
whole length of them loaves of bread, cakes, pies, pickles, and
jellies. In addition to all this generous spread of eatables, there
was a great hogshead of whiskey toddy, with numberless bright,
new tin cups which did double duty as goblets for the liquor
and as soup plates for the burgoo.

I was on the ground early for I dearly love, on such occasions,
to be among the first so that I can see and hear all that's said
and done from start to finish; the busy stir of preparing everything, the people flocking in from every direction and by every
means, afoot, horseback, in wagons, buggies, carriages; the old
folks with their little children; the young men and the rosy-
cheeked damsels, all in their Sunday-go-to-meeting clothes,
ribbons and furbelows, and gayly colored parasols, smiling,
laughing, chatting; here and there an old maid, prim and
demure; bachelors of matured age, whose sweethearts were now
the mothers of children who called them "Uncle," and negroes
of every age and sex, the whites of their eyes and their white
teeth contrasting with the dusky browns or sable blacks of their
skins. Then the fife and drum corps, playing like mad, the
old fifer, McDonald, blowing his very soul away through the
instrument, which he says is the only one in the world that can
make real music; a six-foot negro beating the big drum, and
Sim Drake rattling away on the little drum at such a rate you
could hardly see his drum-sticks.

The crowd was prodigious. And the noise! The talking, the
hallooing, the quips and the quirks, the neighing of the horses,
and over all the rustling leaves of the trees, the summer clouds
and the glimpses of blue sky far away.

First the burgoo and the various roasts and eatables, with
liberal potations from the hogshead of toddy, and then came
the speeches. And this brings me naturally to the two candidates, the orators of the day, Bill Bassett and Randolph Jones.
I must essay a pen picture, so to speak, of these.

Randolph is a man somewhere in the forties, a handsome, well-dressed fellow always, brown-haired, blue-eyed, and a thorough aristocrat from top to toe. On his two thousand acres of blue grass land he lives like a lord. His house, his fine cattle, his Grey Eagle race horses, his fox hounds and pointer dogs, his everything that abundant wealth can supply, his college education in this country, and abroad,—nothing is lacking, one would say, to make him the very darling of fortune. Nothing except the good will of his fellow men. Randolph is not a popular man and he never tried to be. Why he came out as a candidate for the legislature is more than I know, unless, having everything else heart could wish, he concluded he would have a seat in the Capitol of the State, also and make laws for the rest of us. He prides himself on his blue blood, being closely connected on both sides with the best families in the State, and his father before him having been a man of some distinction. 'Pon my word, I think he is the most stuck-up man I ever saw in my life. I never hear his name mentioned that I do not recall some lines of poetry I stumbled on in one of Disraeli's books,—Disraeli, Senior:—

> "He was so proud, if he should meet
> The twelve Apostles in the street
> He'd turn his nose up at them all,
> And Christ himself must take the wall."

Randolph is a man of fine manners in fine company, and of no manners at all with those he considers his social inferiors. He nods in a patronizing way when he meets Squire Buckley or Doc Humes—I hear that he says the Squire "is nothing but a quill-driver" and the Doc is an "old mid-wife." He gives me a sort of a peck of his head when he looks my way, and as to poor old Obe, "he looks clean through me and beyond," says Obe, "as if my belly was a window pane."

To think of such a man attempting to be elected to the legislature, or to anything else, for that matter, in this country!

He ought to be a lord and live in England, where, as I hear (and believe), the bulk of the people take off their hats and stand bareheaded in the big road when a man of rank passes by, and they would rather lick his shoes than go to a horse race.

I hear that his mother, a sensible woman, told him he was a fool to go into politics, and that if he didn't change his ways and let out his pride several buckle holes he wouldn't get a vote in the county. The result showed—but I'll not anticipate.

Bill Bassett is as much unlike Randolph in every particular as it is possible for one man to differ from another. Both belong to the human race, both are white and both are of the male gender, but that's as far as the similarity goes. Bill was born and raised on a little farm up near the head waters of Lulbegrud, where the people are so poor they go hunting in the morning before they can have breakfast, and so lean and angular "their bones make eye-holes in their skin." But Bill was an exception to the general worthlessness and shiftlessness of his neighbors. He was energetic and smart, and before he had reached middle age he got out of that country and managed to lay up enough money to buy a fine piece of land out on Stoner. That was ten years ago, and now he was, as the Yankees say, one of the forehandedest men in the county. Very thrifty, Bill is, in spite of his passion for politics. My observation tells me that, taking the matter by and large, a man can't mix politics with honest work. No matter what the work is, farming, merchandising, doctoring, even practising law, if that comes under the head of honest work, you must attend to it and let politics alone, or you must attend to the politics and let your work go by the board, in which case, nine times out of ten, you'll eat your heart out and die in the poorhouse. But, as I say, Bill Bassett is an exception. He goes around through the county buying up calves, and he never gives more than they are worth, and at the same time he tells jokes to the "boys," flatters the women and kisses the babies. There isn't a more popular man in all the county. A hearty, frank, straightforward fellow, honest as the days are long, with a sharp eye to business, and fonder of talking politics than any man I ever saw in my life.

He is a large man with a jolly face, and he always dresses in common blue jean clothes.

To get back now, to the barbecue, and to the speaking: 'Twas agreed that the candidates should have an hour each, and Randolph and Bill threw up "wet or dry" to decide who should have the closing speech. Bill won. And so Randolph took the stand—a rude platform constructed for the occasion— and opened up. The burning issue in our county that year was whether Four Mile Creek should be declared by law to be a navigable stream. Some of the farmers on Four Mile were in favor of the bill and some were against it. Those for it had timber on their lands which they could sell in case boats were permitted to pass up and down the creek, or if they could put a boom at the mouth of the creek and collect their logs there ready when there was a rise, to be floated down the Kentucky River. Those opposed to the bill had no timber to speak of on their lands, they contended that such use of the stream would injure them, and that so long as it remained a non- navigable creek their lines ran to the middle of it, or clean across it if they owned both banks, and they could protect their property by law.

Well, it was a matter that concerned, in reality, only the Four-milers—not more than a dozen men in all—but that was enough for an "issue." There must be *something* to differ about or what would be the use of having politics at all, and to have no politics . . .

Surely in Kentucky you might as well say we'll have no re- ligion.

Randolph was in favor of enacting a law making Four Mile a navigable stream. Bill Bassett was agin it. The former led off with a speech that didn't touch the issue with a ten-foot pole, as the saying is. Instead of arguing the right of the thing, the fact that it would not injure anybody, but, on the contrary would benefit every land holder on the creek and more or less directly, every citizen of the county, which I opine was the fact, he told the people how old his family was, what a great man his father had been, and that the soil of Kentucky was honored as the resting place of the bones of his ancestors. He pictured Washington at Valley Forge and General Jackson at New Orleans and continued to tell us that his great-grand-mother was a cousin of the Father of his Country, and that an uncle had married a relation of Old Hickory. 'Pon my word, I never saw a man make such an ass of himself in my life!

When Randolph had finished his speech Sim Drake threw his hat up into the air and shouted "Hurra for Jones!" But Sim, by this time, was so full of liquor he didn't know whether he was a Whig or a Democrat, and didn't care, and would have hurrahed for one man or one sentiment just as readily as for another. There were shouts from a few old hide-bound Demo-crats but they didn't hold out long.

Then came Bill Bassett, pushing his way through the crowd amidst a perfect storm of hurras, and ascended the platform.

I wish I could give Bill's speech verbatim et literatim and ipso factum, as Greenbury Crupples would say. First, with a solemn face, he told the crowd how it would just about ruin a lot of people on Four Mile if the creek was declared to be a navigable stream; that it was a mean, selfish project on the part of certain persons who proposed to put money into their pockets at the expense of their neighbors; that when he was a boy a law was passed making Lulbegrud a navigable stream and what was the result? Why, fellow citizens, it started a feud in them parts which still raged and had cost the lives of forty men; that even when black suckers were running on the riffles a man couldn't go spearing for them, except at the risk of his life; that to run boats up a small stream like Four Mile would shove the water out of its banks and flood the adjacent lands, besides scaring all the fish away, and the boom that would be built at the mouth of the creek would prevent them from coming back; that if the law was passed a number of his con-

stituents out there intended to abandon their farms and move
to Missouri. Then he pitched into Randolph Jones' speech,
and 'pon my word, I never heard a speech so belittled and
ridiculed in my life. "Four fathers!" said Bill, "Mr. Jones
tells us he has four fathers. Why, fellow citizens, wouldn't you
say one was enough, and to spare? Mr. Jones is a Democrat
and voted for James K. Polk against Henry Clay, the greatest
man that ever trod dirt. Where was Polk when Henry Clay
was thundering in the Senate of the United States with such
power and eloquence as to astonish the world? I'll tell you
where he was: He was running errands for his master, Andrew Jackson, down yonder in Tennessee, or combing burrs
out of the tail of Jackson's horse. Mr. Jones thinks he is better
than the ordinary run of mankind. He thinks that when you
and me are humbly seated in a little bunch up in heaven
a-playin' on our jews-harps, he will be a sittin' alongside of
God tellin' him about his four fathers and his ancestors' bones."

There was no end to such droll nonsense. The crowd was
with Bill, and applauded and laughed at everything he said.
And I may add right here, that when the election came off Bill
was elected by a large majority. Every Whig voted for him,
of course, while the Democrats gave Randolph such feeble support he swore in his wrath that he would never again give the
county a chance to send him to Frankfort.

Of course from the early morning all through the day the
hogshead of whiskey toddy was paid devoted attention, the
liquor receding, so to speak, all the time, and along towards
the shank of the evening getting so low that only a long-legged
and long-armed man could reach it with his cup. Sim Drake,
between waking and sleeping, had been drunk and partly sober
several times; hundreds of men lay around on the grass too
full to get up but still able to shout, "Hurra for Bill Bassett."
The big drum was hopelessly floored, and old McDonald's fife,
while he sat propped up against a sugar tree, asleep, had been
stuffed with grass, and let him blow ever so hard when he
awoke, he couldn't produce a note. A number of fist-fights

took place on the grounds, the Sheriff slipping away not caring to make any arrests. Constable Scraggs, under the eye of his stern superior, Greenbury Crupples, indiscreetly attempted to stop a fight between two of the Four Mile boys, whereupon they ceased to pummel each other and turned on the Constable and put him to flight. Sim Drake lost his balance trying to dip up another cup of toddy, from the hogshead, and fell in, and when I left for town McDonald was on the platform swearing he could whip the man who put grass in his fife.

ANONYMOUS

THIS story has gone the rounds. Attributed to a half-dozen famous Bluegrass politicians, it appeared in the Spirit of the Times *in 1857. From the earliest pioneer days there has been a difference in political attitudes and approaches between the Bluegrass and the mountains. To this day of modern communications systems, the wit, antics, and personalities of politicians have outweighed intelligent discussions of issues. Both voters and candidates accept the fact that campaigns are little short of being bamboozling contests.*

Left-Hand Doin's

INSURE me a brass band and I'll insure your election. And so widely during the last election was music called in to aid oratory that this answer serves as a good endorsement to the poet's note that "Music hath charms to soothe the savage breast," and attractions to "go to the polls and Vote Early."

The forty horsepower music on elections being thus settled

by common consent, leads us to believe that "too much credit cannot be awarded" to the Kentuckian who faced his political opponent's music as follows:

Both were candidates for the office of Governor of Kentucky, and "stumped" the state together quite harmoniously until they reached one of the counties in the "hill country." Here it was necessary to make a decided demonstration, and accordingly the two candidates fairly spread themselves to catch all the votes possible—scaring up the American Eagle, and calling down the shade of Washington; pitching out profuse promises, and pitching into each other's party politics, in a manner decidedly refreshing to the hearers. On the first day's canvass, victory hung suspended by the tail feathers over the rival forces, but the second day fell slap into the lap of the shortest and stoutest candidate, leaving his long and lean opponent "no kind of a show." In vain the long man pumped up the waters of drink. But round the short man elbowed and crowded a mass of thirsty voters, drinking in his tones with delight. Why this attraction? Had he a barrel of old bourbon? No; he had a fiddle! Getting the start of Long Man he had addressed the voters in a short speech, and then, for the first time, bringing out a fiddle, retired a short distance from the speakers' stand, in order to let his opponent reply, playing, however, such lively airs, that he soon drew the entire assemblage away, and left the other side of the question unattended to, unheard.

For three days in succession Short Man and the fiddle carried the day, in three successive mass meetings, in as many towns in the hill country, and Long Man's chances for a single vote in those parts grew remarkably slim. In vain a long consultation was held by the latter with his political friends.

"Get the start of him at the next meeting and speak first," advised one.

"Raise a fiddle and play them choones!" said another.

"Yell him down," shouted a third.

The Long Man followed the advise of the first counsellor,

and got the start in voice, but the noise of the fiddle run him neck and neck; he would have listened to his second monitor, and raised a fiddle, only he knew it would fall through, as he couldn't scrape a note; and as for his third adviser, he told him that "yelling down" Short Man was simply ridiculous.

Affairs grew desperate with Long Man, when, on the third meeting, he saw, as usual, the entire crowd of voters sweeping off after Short Man and his fiddle, leaving only one hearer, and he a lame one, who was just about to hobble after the others.

"Can it be possible that freemen—citizens of this great and glorious country—neglecting the vital interests of their land, will run like wild men after cat-gut strings? Can it be possible, I say?" And the lame man, to whom Long Man was thus eloquently discoursing, answered, as he too cleared out:

"Well, it can, old hoss!"

Despair encamped in the Long Man's face, as he watched Short Man, at a distance, playing away for dear life and the Gubernatorial chair on that "blasted" old fiddle; but suddenly a ray of hope beamed over his "rueful visage," then another and another ray, till it shone like the sun at midday.

"Got him now, sure!" fairly shouted the Long Man, as he threw up his arms, jumped from the stand, and started for the tavern, where he at once called a meeting of his political friends, consisting of the landlord and one other, then and there unfolding a plan which was to drive his rival "nowheres in no time."

The fourth meeting was held. Short Man addressed the crowd with warmth, eloquence and bluntly vacating the stand for his adversary, and striking up a lively air on the violin, in order to quash his proceedings; but, though as usual, he carried the audience away, he noticed that they were as critical as numerous. One six-footer, in homespun, walnut-dyed clothes, with wild-looking eyes and a 'coonskin cap, eyed every movement of the fiddle-bow, with intense disgust, finding utterance at last, in:

"Why don't you fiddle with that t'other hand o' yourn?"

"T'other hand!" shouted a chorus of voices. "Fire up with that t'other hand!" Faster played the Short Man, but louder and louder shouted the crowd, "T'other hand, t'other hand!"

"Gentlemen, I assure you—"

"No more honey, old hoss. We ain't b'ars!" shouted the man with the 'coonskin cap.

"T'other hand, t'other hand!" yelled the crowd; while even from the distant stand where the Long Man was holding forth "to next to nobody" for some listeners, seemed to come a faint echo, "T'other hand, t'other hand!"

Short Man began to be elbowed, crowded, pushed; in vain he tried to draw the bow; at one time his bow-arm was sent up to the shoulder over the bridge, at another, down went the fiddle, until he shouted out:

"Gentlemen, what can I do but assure you that—"

"T'other hand!" roared 'coonskin, shouldering his way face up to the Short Man, "we've heard about you! You fiddle down thar in that d—n Bluegrass country, 'mong rich folks, with your right hand and think when you git up in the hills 'mong pore folks, *left-hand fiddlin's* good enuf for them; you've cussedly missed it! Left-hand doin's wont run up hyar; tote out your right, stranger, or look out for the squalls!"

The Short Man looked out for squalls, threw down the fiddle and the bow, oh! oh—jumped on his horse and put a straight horse tail between him and his enraged "fellow citizens."

"It's a fact," says the Long Man, "my opponent's being left-handed rather told against him up in the hill-country and whoever circulated the story, up there, that he always fiddled with his right hand down in the Bluegrass country, *headed off his music* for that campaign."

A. B. GUTHRIE, JR.

*M*ID-*DECEMBER, 1935, A. B. Guthrie, Jr. (1901-   ),
city editor for the Lexington* Leader, *rode back from Frankfort
after the inauguration of Albert Benjamin Chandler (1898-   )
as governor of Kentucky. Chandler had startled the old-hand
Kentucky politicians by beating the administration's hand-
picked candidate in a second primary and then defeating the
Republican nominee in the November election.*

*Chandler had been a free-swinging campaigner. He sang
"Sonny Boy" from the Big Sandy to Mill's Point, and had
shaken hands with every Kentuckian in reach. The reporter
summed up in his story for the* Leader *readers this sudden
change in Kentucky campaigning and the impact of this new
face in the governor's office. He drew a rich human contrast
between the bubbling Chandler coming into office and his sad-
eyed predecessor shambling out of Frankfort.*

Sonny Boy

KENTUCKY had a new governor today, a smiling, somewhat
florid 37-year-old who won his first political campaign by singing "Sonny Boy" in the country school houses of Woodford,
Scott and Jessamine counties.

In the Albert Benjamin Chandler who squeezed through a
packed inaugural stand Tuesday afternoon to take the oath of
office there were still some signs of the old "Happy" Chandler,
the youthful state senator who delighted rural school marms
and their juvenile charges by crooning in the corridors of the
capitol, who took the floor too often for a first-termer, who
was so hail-fellow-well-met that more restrained associates
looked upon him with an indulgent condescension.

There were still his open-handed friendliness, his wide smile and his ready flow of words.

But it was an older and more thoughtful, a maturer and more decisive "Happy" who Tuesday became the governor of 2,600,000 people.

Back in 1930, fellow senators would have howled had you predicted that within five years this well-meaning upstart play-boy would be sitting in the executive chair. Why, with his obliging readiness to sing a syrupy song, his thoughtless presumption in debate with more seasoned men and his boisterous back-slapping, he was becoming a joke who detracted from the dignity of the senate. Chief executive? Rather, one-termer in the upper house, then back to private life.

Even when he was nominated and elected lieutenant-governor, the wiseacres of the hustings looked upon his further success as a rather sour political joke, brought about through the powerful backing of the aged and eccentric Ben Johnson.

It was as lieutenant-governor that Chandler began that development that was to carry him eventually to the executive mansion. None were more astonished than the colleagues who had tolerated him good-naturedly in 1930 when the one-time "Sonny Boy" began to show that he was capable of convictions and determination. Behind that smiling face and beyond that geniality of nature, they found to their amazement, there lay stout opinions and there lay courage.

Gradually but steadily, he assumed leadership. Johnson kept with him always. The late Allie Young swung in. Dan Talbott saw his possibilities. Another young political leader, John Young Brown, helped him along. A group of senators, Democrats and Republicans, organized to stand behind him.

And as he made friends, so he made enemies. A foe of the sales tax, he incurred the antagonism of the administration and its supporters. They fought him tooth and nail. They tried to wean away his retainers. And finally they stripped him of a lieutenant-governor's authority; they made him a figurehead.

Throughout it all, Chandler remained good-natured and stout of heart. He maintained friendly personal relations with his most determined opponents, who were learning to respect the resources behind his youthful joviality.

Defeated on the sales-tax issue, Chandler made his boldest and most astute stroke when Gov. Laffoon left for Washington last winter. Faced with the fact that the administration expected to railroad through a convention its candidate for nominee as governor, Chandler called a special session of the legislature to enact a compulsory primary law. The call was declared valid by the courts, and at the ensuing session a primary bill was passed.

Waiting until former Gov. J. C. W. Beckham had definitely decided not to make the race, Chandler then announced his candidacy. His chances of success, one would have said, were about 20 to 1. But the long shot came home.

And so the one-time crooner, the "Sonny Boy" of derision, the former senatorial nuisance was inaugurated Tuesday as governor of Kentucky. There was something youthful and exultant and shining in his countenance as he pressed through the crowd shaking hands right and left. But there was nothing of eager hope in the face of the retiring governor, to whom not more than a dozen hands were extended as he crowded forward on the inaugural stand. His face was old and drawn, and his eyes were weary.

And later, when Happy came in to the capitol, pushed and shoved and mauled by a crowd of boisterous backers, he was still good-natured and smiling. A half-dozen of his faithful saw Gov. Laffoon into the building. Making his last visit to his one-time offices, he looked even older and more melancholy. Seeing that lined and sorrowful face, one couldn't avoid a pang of sympathy, however opposed to the record that he had just brought to a close.

PATRICK O'DONOVAN

IN 1955, A. B. Chandler (1898-   ) again made a successful race for governor of Kentucky. Given no chance whatever by political experts, he soundly defeated the incumbent Democratic machine and went on to win the November election handily. In their post mortems, the experts conceded that once again they had overlooked the vote-gaining power of the flamboyant showmanship displayed by the Versailles lawyer. To Patrick O'Donovan, Washington correspondent of The Observer *of London, England, Happy's wide-open campaign was a marked contrast to the quiet methods used by British politicians. O'Donovan accompanied the Bluegrass candidate into western Kentucky, where, as he recorded in "A Britisher's Reminiscence of a Kentucky Campaign," published in* The Reporter *for January 12, 1956, he found that Chandler's personal touch extended even to nonvoters.*

Let the Folks See You

A FOREIGN correspondent in Washington is continually assaulted with a cliché whose variations are known in every capital in the world. You must get out of Washington, they say, and see the country, or you will never understand America. So I went to Kentucky, and in a way they were perfectly right. At the time there was much talk of an election for governor, and of how the local Democratic Party had torn itself apart in the process.

In a British election, if you followed, say, Clement Attlee, you had first to find him in a maze of deserted back streets. Caught coming out of a school, he would smile unhappily, murmur a word of optimism through his teeth, and hurry into his small coffee-colored car. His wife would be at the wheel and crouched at the back would be a police officer and an election agent. You could obtain a grudging permission to follow the lonely car if you didn't get in the way as it hurried from meeting to meeting.

It was no more rewarding with Sir Winston. His cavalcade, even in election time, tended to have a dauntingly official look, and no one in Britain likes to join processions uninvited.

The result is that in Britain I, at least, approach political stories with an anxiety not over whether I shall be able to write the truth but whether I shall find anything to write at all.

In Louisville, things were different, Democratic headquarters were in a hotel. I was shown without question into a room full of people sitting around the edge. A cheerful man introduced himself. Adherents in heavy overcoats and non-removable hats kept coming in for a few words. Conversation became disjointed. The cheerful man said, "You're from England; I'll send for a cup of tea." I explained my business. I wanted to see Happy Chandler in action. Yes, I had a car. No, I couldn't wait a week.

And then everything was fixed. I had only to drive that evening from Louisville to Paducah (farther than from London to York) and be at a town on the bank of the Ohio River at nine in the morning. The men in the hotel had maps out. They marked them. A state senator said he would be there and would fix everything. (I never saw him again.) Telephones rang and rooms were reserved. Mr. Chandler was starting on a two-day motorcade the next day.

More than an hour early, I was in the little red-and-white town. Children rioted past and disappeared into school. The sun shone through the trees.

The Ohio River, disproportionately and marvelously wide for so intimate and disciplined a landscape, flowed noiselessly along at the end of the street. The sidewalks were almost empty. The courthouse was deserted. Inside, it was worn and gently decayed. The doors sagged but they wore padlocks. It felt like Sunday morning with everyone else at church. My anxieties came back reinforced.

Ten minutes before the scheduled time, things began to happen. A man started hanging little posters on the trees. Dozens of cars carefully blocked off the streets. Forty or fifty men were standing ankle deep in the fallen leaves outside the courthouse. A few well-dressed women, who in England would have been wives of candidate, agent, and more important supporters, arrived and went upstairs. Nothing unfamiliar here.

Then the loudspeaker called out "Happy's here! Give him a hand!" And a stout, determined man, with a tremendous smile and that air of being bigger and more elaborately made that marks the successful politician, with a rasping, public voice and a camel-hair coat, was surging, hat in hand, through the groups of quiet men.

He shook every hand he could reach. He turned back from the door to cross the road and shake the hand of an aged Negro who stood apart and looked embarrassed. He led the men, clattering up the boot-worn stairs, into the courtroom.

This was a quiet meeting. No questions or heckling. But they had come to hear and to see in a way that no longer happens in England. The farmers sat pressed together with their hats on their knees and listened intently. They were all Democrats.

But I was worrying about what came next—the motorcade. I explained my uncertainties to a keen young man who took my ignition key and said "Relax." When we got outside, my car was No. 5 in a line of at least a hundred.

So we set off. The sheriff of Graves County led in a formidable sedan, then the loudspeaker car playing over and over "Happy Days Are Here Again," then Mr. Chandler, then state senators and supporters, then the local press and then me.

We poured out into the countryside, past the white wood houses, through the brief fury of color that is autumn. We drove faster than I have ever driven through defiles and past farms. When we came to a village, all the horns sounded, but nobody came out to watch or perhaps they hadn't time. Sometimes you could hear "Happy Days Are Here Again" being played at seventy miles an hour to the hills. I had fallen to sixteenth place by the time we reached Marion, where a high-school band was playing "My Old Kentucky Home."

The keen young man took my car again and I went up into the courthouse. I was seated under the battered rostrum. A great iron stove shook with heat in the center. The roof was of pressed tin, and there were bees bumping themselves against it. Mr. Chandler began. The eyes of the world are on Kentucky, he said. It seemed a safe opening. The room was filled with prosperous, unworried, contented people—people who smiled while they waited. That's the truth, said Mr. Chandler. He is a rare natural speaker. He could have been a pastor in Wales. His sentences were short and they balanced like a chant. They were full of images and you wondered what was coming next. That's true, he said; what you decide next week will be heard in Moscow. He told them that yesterday there'd been a fine young man from Norway come to report their election. Today, he said, there's another from abroad. He's been sent all the way from England to report what we're doing. Stand up, Boy, he said, and let the folks see you.

In England, I suspect, his audience would have frozen into resentful silence. Instead they clapped for quite a long time. I understand now why the British have a reputation here for being stiff. I never felt stiffer. Mr. Chandler talked a little about the Queen and expressed his sympathy for Princess Margaret. There was really no need to be embarrassed. He talked of old troubles between our countries—all over now. And he waved the wars aside. Come a bit closer, Boy, and he clapped me on the shoulder. But, he said, you're lucky. You've come to the real country and to the best part of it. And then he launched into a torrent of well-organized and moving speech—praise of the state, jibes at his opponents, praise of his own record. And I edged back to my seat, my part in the American political scene ended. When he was finished, Mr. Chandler came up and held out his hand and said, "My name is Happy Chandler."

The motorcade moved on, and now I avoided the keen young man and sat at the back of meetings. Indeed, I soon started back for Louisville (not quite as far as from London to Penzance).

When I was in Washington again, nobody was interested. It was not a typical election. When I insisted that it had been the sort of introduction to politics that compels an affectionate admiration, I was assured that I still had not seen the real thing.

JAMES LANE ALLEN

COUNTY court day was an institution back in Virginia. Under the magisterial system of local colonial government, people flocked to the county seats to be present at the meeting of the court because they had interest in cases that were to be tried, in tax adjustments, and in seeking public jobs, while others came to see and be seen. Court day came to be a market day also. Farm produce and animals were brought for sale. Horses were traded, mortgages and breaking-up sales were held, and great piles of implements and household goods were offered country buyers.

In Kentucky, court day embodied all that it had in colonial Virginia. It was a social and sporting occasion. No self-respecting county seat was without its jockey grounds. Lexington had its famous Cheapside, named after a similar trading ground in London. The modern Lexingtonian, however, has to be most imaginative to conjure up the scene about the Fayette County courthouse described by James Lane Allen (1849-1925).

This early "local color story," one of Allen's best short essays,
was first published in The Blue-Grass Region of Kentucky and
Other Kentucky Articles *(New York, 1892).*

County Court Day

THE INSTITUTIONS of the Kentuckian have deep root in his
rich social nature. He loves the swarm. The very motto of the
State is a declaration of good-fellowship, and the seal of the
commonwealth the act of shaking hands. Divided, he falls.
The Kentuckian must be one of many; must assert himself,
not through the solitary exercise of his intellect, but the senses;
must see men about him who are fat, grip his friend, hear cordial, hearty conversation, realize the play of his emotions. Society is the multiple of himself.

Hence his fondness for large gatherings: open-air assemblies
of the democratic sort—great agricultural fairs, race-courses,
political meetings, barbecues and burgoos in the woods—where
no one is pushed to the wall, or reduced to a seat and to silence,
where all may move about at will, seek and be sought, make
and receive impressions. Quiet masses of people in-doors ab-
sorb him less. He is not fond of lectures, does not build splendid theatres or expend lavishly for opera, is almost of Puritan
excellence in the virtue of church-going, which in the country
is attended with neighborly reunions.

This large social disposition underlies the history of the most
social of all his days—a day that has long had its observance em-
bedded in the structure of his law, is invested with the authority and charm of old-time usage and reminiscence, and
still enables him to commingle business and pleasure in a way
of his own. Hardly more characteristic of the Athenian was
the agora, or the forum of the Roman, than is county court
day characteristic of the Kentuckian. In the open square
around the court-house of the county-seat he has had the centre

of his public social life, the arena of his passions and amusements, the rallying-point of his political discussions, the market-
place of his business transactions, the civil unit of his institutional history.

It may be that some stranger has sojourned long enough in
Kentucky to have grown familiar with the wonted aspects of
a county town. He has remarked the easy swing of its daily
life: amicable groups of men sitting around the front entrances
of the hotels; the few purchasers and promenaders on the uneven brick pavements; the few vehicles of draught and carriage
scattered along the level white thoroughfares. All day the subdued murmur of patient local traffic has scarcely drowned the
twittering of English sparrows in the maples. Then comes a
Monday morning when the whole scene changes. The world
has not been dead, but only sleeping. Whence this sudden
surging crowd of rural folk—these lowing herds in the streets?
Is it some animated pastoral come to town? some joyful public
anniversary? some survival in altered guise of the English
country fair of mellower times? or a vision of what the little
place will be a century hence, when American life shall be
packed and agitated and tense all over the land? What a world
of homogeneous, good-looking, substantial, reposeful people
with honest front and amiable meaning! What bargaining and
buying and selling by ever-forming, ever-dissolving groups, with
quiet laughter and familiar talk and endless interchange of
domestic interrogatories! You descend into the street to study
the doings and spectacles from a nearer approach, and stop to
ask the meaning of it. Ah! it is county court day in Kentucky;
it is the Kentuckians in the market-place.

II

They have been assembling here now for nearly a hundred
years. One of the first demands of the young commonwealth
in the woods was that its vigorous, passionate life should be
regulated by the usages of civil law. Its monthly county courts,

with justices of the peace, were derived from the Virginia system of jurisprudence, where they formed the aristocratic feature of the government. Virginia itself owed these models to England; and thus the influence of the courts and of the decent and orderly yeomanry of both lands passed, as was singularly fitting, over into the ideals of justice erected by the pure-blooded colony. As the town-meeting of Boston town perpetuated the folkmote of the Anglo-Saxon free state, and the Dutch village communities on the shores of the Hudson revived the older ones on the banks of the Rhine, so in Kentucky, through Virginia, there were transplanted by the people, themselves of clean stock and with strong conservative ancestral traits, the influences and elements of English law in relation to the county, the court, and the justice of the peace.

Through all the old time of Kentucky State life there towers up the figure of the justice of the peace. Commissioned by the Governor to hold monthly court, he had not always a courthouse wherein to sit, but must buy land in the midst of a settlement or town whereon to build one, and build also the contiguous necessity of civilization—a jail. In the rude courtroom he had a long platform erected, usually running its whole width; on this platform he had a ruder wooden bench placed, likewise extending all the way across; and on this bench, having ridden into town, it may be, in dun-colored leggings, broadcloth pantaloons, a pigeon-tailed coat, a shingle-caped overcoat, and a twelve-dollar high fur hat, he sat gravely and sturdily down amid his peers; looking out upon the bar, ranged along a wooden bench beneath, and prepared to consider the legal needs of his assembled neighbors. Among them all the very best was he; chosen for age, wisdom, means, weight and probity of character; as a rule, not profoundly versed in the law, perhaps knowing nothing of it—being a Revolutionary soldier, a pioneer, or a farmer—but endowed with a sure, robust, common-sense and rectitude of spirit that enabled him to divine what the law was; shaking himself fiercely loose from the grip of mere technicalities, and deciding by the natural justice of the case; giving decisions of equal authority with the highest court, an appeal being rarely taken; perpetuating his own authority by appointing his own associates: with all his shortcomings and weaknesses a notable, historic figure, high-minded, fearless, and incorruptible, dignified, patient, and strong, and making the county court days of Kentucky for wellnigh half a century memorable to those who have lived to see justice less economically and less honorably administered.

But besides the legal character and intent of the day which was thus its first and dominant feature, divers things drew the folk together. Even the justice himself may have had quite other than magisterial reasons for coming to town; certainly the people had. They must interchange opinions about local and national politics, observe the workings of their own laws, pay and contract debts, acquire and transfer property, discuss all questions relative to the welfare of the community—holding, in fact, a county court day much like one in Virginia in the middle of the seventeenth century.

III

But after business was over, time hung idly on their hands; and being vigorous men, hardened by work in forest and field, trained in foot and limb to fleetness and endurance, and fired with admiration of physical prowess, like riotous school-boys out on a half-holiday, they fell to playing. All through the first quarter of the century, and for a longer time, county court day in Kentucky was, at least in many parts of the State, the occasion for holding athletic games. The men, young or in the sinewy manhood of more than middle age, assembled once a month at the county-seats to witness and take part in the feats of muscle and courage. They wrestled, threw the sledge, heaved the bar, divided and played at fives, had foot-races for themselves, and quarter-races for their horses. By-and-by, as these contests became a more prominent feature of the day, they would pit against each other the champions of different neighborhoods. It would become widely known beforehand that next county court day "the bully" in one end of the county would whip "the bully" in the other end; so when court day came, and the justices came, and the bullies came, what was the county to do but come also? The crowd repaired to the common, a ring was formed, the little men on the outside who couldn't see, Zaccheus-like, took to the convenient trees, and there was to be seen a fair and square set-to, in which the fist was the battering-ram and the biceps a catapult. What better, more time-honored proof could those backwoods Kentuckians have furnished of the humors in their English blood and of their English pugnacity? But, after all, this was only play, and play never is perfectly satisfying to a man who would rather fight; so from playing they fell to harder work, and throughout this period county court day was the monthly Monday on which the Kentuckian regularly did his fighting. He availed himself liberally of election day, it is true, and of regimental muster in the spring and battalion muster in the fall—great gala occasions; but county court day was by all odds the preferred and highly prized season. It was periodical, and could be relied upon, being written in the law, noted in the almanac, and registered in the heavens.

A capital day, a most admirable and serene day for fighting. Fights grew like a fresh-water polype—by being broken in two: each part produced a progeny. So conventional did the recreation become that difficulties occurring out in the country between times regularly had their settlements postponed until the belligerents could convene with the justices. The men met and fought openly in the streets, the friends of each standing by to see fair play and whet their appetites.

Thus the justices sat quietly on the bench inside, and the people fought quietly in the streets outside, and the day of the month set apart for the conservation of the peace became the approved day for individual war. There is no evidence to be had that either the justices or the constables ever interfered.

These pugilistic encounters had a certain law of beauty: they were affairs of equal combat and of courage. The fight over, animosity was gone, the feud ended. The men must shake hands, go and drink together, become friends. We are touching here upon a grave and curious fact of local history. The fighting habit must be judged by a wholly unique standard. It was the direct outcome of racial traits powerfully developed by social conditions.

IV

Another noticeable recreation of the day was the drinking. Indeed, the two pleasures went marvellously well together. The drinking led up to the fighting, and the fighting led up to the drinking; and this amiable co-operation might be prolonged at will. The merchants kept barrels of whiskey in their cellars for their customers. Bottles of it sat openly on the counter, half-way between the pocket of the buyer and the shelf of merchandise. There were no saloons separate from the taverns. At these whiskey was sold and drunk without screens or scruples. It was not usually bought by the drink, but by the tickler. The tickler was a bottle of narrow shape, holding a half-pint—just enough to tickle. On a county court day wellnigh a whole town would be tickled. In some parts of the State tables were placed out on the sidewalks, and around these the men sat drinking mint-juleps and playing draw poker and "old sledge."

Meantime the day was not wholly given over to ·playing and fighting and drinking. More and more it was becoming the great public day of the month, and mirroring the life and spirit of the times—on occasion a day of fearful, momentous gravity, as in the midst of war, financial distress, high party feeling; more and more the people gathered together for discussion and the origination of measures determining the events of their history. Gradually new features incrusted it. The politician, observing the crowd, availed himself of it to announce his own candidacy or to wage a friendly campaign, sure, whether popular or unpopular, of a courteous hearing; for this is a virtue of the Kentuckian, to be polite to a public speaker, however little liked his cause. In the spring, there being no fairs, it was the occasion for exhibiting the fine stock of the country, which was led out to some suburban pasture, where the owners made speeches over it. In the winter, at the close of the old or the beginning of the new year, negro slaves were regularly hired out on this day for the ensuing twelvemonth, and sometimes put upon the block before the courthouse door and sold for life.

But it was not until near the half of the second quarter of the century that an auctioneer originated stock sales on the open square, and thus gave to the day the characteristic it has since retained of being the great market-day of the month. Thenceforth its influence was to be more widely felt, to be extended into other counties and even States; thenceforth it was to become more distinctively a local institution without counterpart.

To describe minutely the scenes of a county court day in Kentucky, say at the end of the half-century, would be to write a curious page in the history of the times; for they were possible only through the unique social conditions they portrayed. It was near the most prosperous period of State life under the old regime. The institution of slavery was about to culminate and decline. Agriculture had about as nearly perfected itself as it was ever destined to do under the system of bondage. The war cloud in the sky of the future could be covered with the hand, or at most with the country gentleman's broad-brimmed straw-hat. The whole atmosphere of the times was heavy with ease, and the people, living in perpetual contemplation of their superabundant natural wealth, bore the quality of the land in their manners and dispositions.

When the well-to-do Kentucky farmer got up in the morning, walked out into the porch, stretched himself, and looked at the sun, he knew that he could summon a sleek, kindly negro

to execute every wish and whim—one to search for his mis-
placed hat, a second to bring him a dipper of ice-water, a third
to black his shoes, a fourth to saddle his horse and hitch it at
the stile, a fifth to cook his breakfast, a sixth to wait on him at
the table, a seventh to stand on one side and keep off the flies.
Breakfast over, he mounted his horse and rode out where "the
hands" were at work. The chance was his overseer or negro
foreman was there before him: his presence was unnecessary.
What a gentleman he was! This was called earning one's bread
by the sweat of his brow. *Whose* brow? He yawned. What
should he do? One thing he knew he *would* do—take a good
nap before dinner. Perhaps he had better ride over to the
blacksmith-shop. However, there was nobody there. It was
county court day. The sky was blue, the sun golden, the air
delightful, the road broad and smooth, the gait of his horse
the very poetry of motion. He would go to county court himself. There was really nothing else before him. His wife would
want to go, too, and the children.

So away they go, he on horseback or in the family carriage,
with black Pompey driving in front and yellow Cæsar riding
behind. The turnpike reached, the progress of the family carriage is interrupted or quite stopped, for there are many other
carriages on the road, all going in the same direction. Then
pa, growing impatient, orders black Pompey to drive out on
one side, whip up the horses, pass the others, and get ahead,
so as to escape from the clouds of white limestone dust, which
settles thick on the velvet collar of pa's blue cloth coat and in
the delicate pink marabou feathers of ma's bonnet: which Pompey can't do, for the faster he goes, the faster the others go,
making all the more dust; so that pa gets red in the face, and
jumps up in the seat, and looks ready to fight, and thrusts his
head out of the window and knocks off his hat; and ma looks
nervous, and black Pompey and yellow Cæsar both look white
with dust and fear.

A rural cavalcade indeed! Besides the carriages, buggies,

horsemen, and pedestrians, there are long droves of stock being
hurried on towards the town—hundreds of them. By the time
they come together in the town they will be many thousands.
For is not this the great stock-market of the West, and does not
the whole South look from its rich plantations and cities up to
Kentucky for bacon and mules? By-and-by our family carriage
does at last get to town, and is left out in the streets along with
many others to block up the passway according to custom.

The town is packed. It looks as though by some vast suction
system it had with one exercise of force drawn all the country
life into itself. The poor dumb creatures gathered in from the
peaceful fields, and crowded around the court-house, send forth,
each after its kind, a general outcry of horror and despair at
the tumult of the scene and the unimaginable mystery of their
own fate. They overflow into the by-streets, where they take
possession of the sidewalks, and debar entrance at private residences. No stock-pens wanted then; none wanted now. If a
town legislates against these stock sales on the streets and puts
up pens on its outskirts, straightway the stock is taken to some
other market, and the town is punished for its airs by a decline
in its trade.

As the day draws near noon, the tide of life is at the flood.
Mixed in with the tossing horns and nimble heels of the terrified, distressed, half-maddened beasts, are the people. Above
the level of these is the discordant choir of shrill-voiced auc-
tioneers on horseback. At the corners of the streets long-haired
—and long-eared—doctors in curious hats lecture to eager groups
on maladies and philanthropic cures. Every itinerant vendor
of notion and nostrum in the country-side is there; every
wandering Italian harper or musician of any kind, be he but
a sightless fiddler, who brings forth with poor unison of voice
and string the brief and too fickle ballads of the time, "Gentle
Annie," and "Sweet Alice, Ben Bolt." Strangely contrasted
with everything else in physical type and marks of civilization
are the mountaineers, who have come down to "the settle-

mints" driving herds of their lean, stunted cattle, or bringing, in slow-motion, ox-drawn "steamboat" wagons, maple-sugar, and baskets, and poles, and wild mountain fruit—faded wagons, faded beasts, faded clothes, faded faces, faded everything. A general day for buying and selling all over the State. What purchases at the dry-goods stores and groceries to keep all those negroes at home fat and comfortable and comely—cottons, and gay cottonades, and gorgeous turbans, and linseys of prismatic dyes, bags of Rio coffee and barrels of sugar, with many another pleasant thing! All which will not be taken home in the family carriage, but in the wagon which Scipio Africanus is driving in; Scipio, remember; for while the New-Englander has been naming his own flesh and blood Peleg and Hezekiah and Abednego, the Kentuckian has been giving even his negro slaves mighty and classic names, after his taste and fashion. But very mockingly and satirically do those victorious titles contrast with the condition of those that wear them. A surging populace, an in-town holiday for all rural folk, wholly unlike what may be seen elsewhere in this country. The politician will be sure of his audience to-day in the court-house yard; the seller will be sure of the purchaser; the idle man of meeting one still idler; friend of seeing distant friend; blushing Phyllis, come in to buy fresh ribbons, of being followed through the throng by anxious Corydon.

And what, amid this tumult of life and affairs—what of the justice of the peace, whose figure once towered up so finely? Alas! quite outgrown, pushed aside, and wellnigh forgotten. The very name of the day which once so sternly commemorated the exercise of his authority has wandered into another meaning. "County court day" no longer brings up in the mind the image of the central court-house and the judge on the bench. It is to be greatly feared his noble type is dying. The stain of venality has soiled his homespun ermine, and the trail of the office-seeker passed over his rough-hewn bench. So about this time the new constitution of the commonwealth comes in, to make the autocratic ancient justice over into the modern elec-

tive magistrate, and with the end of the half-century to close
a great chapter of wonderful county court days.

But what changes in Kentucky since 1850! How has it fared
with the day meantime? What development has it undergone?
What contrasts will it show?

Undoubtedly, as seen now, the day is not more interesting
by reason of the features it wears than for the sake of comparison with the others it has lost. A singular testimony to the
conservative habits of the Kentuckian, and to the stability of
his local institutions, is to be found in the fact that it should
have come through all this period of upheaval and downfall,
of shifting and drifting, and yet remained so much the same.
Indeed, it seems in nowise liable to lose its meaning of being
the great market and general business day as well as the great
social and general laziness day of the month and the State.
Perhaps one feature has taken larger prominence—the eager
canvassing of voters by local politicians and office-seekers for
weeks, sometimes for months, beforehand. Is it not known
that even circuit court will adjourn on this day so as to give
the clerk and the judge, the bar, the witnesses, an opportunity
to hear rival candidates address the assembled crowd? And yet
we shall discover differences. These people—these groups of twos
and threes and hundreds, lounging, sitting, squatting, taking
every imaginable posture that can secure bodily comfort—are
they in any vital sense new Kentuckians in the new South? If
you care to understand whether this be true, and what it may
mean if it is true, you shall not find a better occasion for doing
so than a contemporary county court day.

The Kentuckian nowadays does not come to county court to
pick a quarrel or to settle one. He *has* no quarrel. His fist has
reverted to its natural use and become a hand. Nor does he go
armed. Positively it is true that gentlemen in this State do not
now get satisfaction out of each other in the market-place, and
that on a modern county court day a three-cornered hat is
hardly to be seen. And yet you will go on defining a Kentuckian in terms of his grandfather, unaware that he has

changed faster than the family reputation. The fighting habit and the shooting habit were both more than satisfied during the Civil War.

Another old-time feature of the day has disappeared—the open use of the pioneer beverage. Merchants do not now set it out for their customers; in the country no longer is it the law of hospitality to offer it to a guest. To do so would commonly be regarded in the light of as great a liberty as to have omitted it once would have been considered an offence. The decanter is no longer found on the sideboard in the home; the barrel is not stored in the cellar.

Some features of the old Kentucky market-place have disappeared. The war and the prostration of the South destroyed that as a market for certain kinds of stock, the raising and sales of which have in consequence declined. Railways have touched the eastern parts of the State, and broken up the distant toilsome traffic with the steamboat wagons of the mountaineers. No longer is the day the general buying day for the circumjacent country as formerly, when the farmers, having great households of slaves, sent in their wagons and bought on twelve months' credit, knowing it would be twenty-four months' if they desired. The doctors, too, have nearly vanished from the street corners, though on the highway one may still happen upon the peddler with his pack, and in the midst of an eager throng still may meet the swaying, sightless old fiddler, singing to ears that never tire gay ditties in a cracked and melancholy tone.

Through all changes one feature has remained. It goes back to the most ancient days of local history. The Kentuckian *will* come to county court "to swap horses"; it is in the blood. In one small town may be seen fifty or a hundred countrymen assembled during the afternoon in a back street to engage in this delightful recreation. Each rides or leads his worst, most objectionable beast; of these, however fair-seeming, none is above suspicion. It is the potter's field, the lazar-house, the beggardom of horse-flesh. The stiff and aged bondsman of the glebe and plough looks out of one filmy eye upon the hopeless wreck of the fleet roadster, and the poor macerated carcass that in days gone by bore its thankless burden over the glistening turnpikes with the speed and softness of the wind has not the strength to return the contemptuous kick which is given him by a lungless, tailless rival. Prices range from nothing upward. Exchanges are made for a piece of tobacco or a watermelon to boot.

But always let us return from back streets and side thoughts to the central court-house square and the general assembly of the people. Go among them; they are not dangerous. Do not use fine words, at which they will prick up their ears uneasily; or delicate sentiments, which will make you less liked; or indulge in flights of thought, which they despise. Remember, here is the dress and the talk and the manners of the street, and fashion yourself accordingly. Be careful of your speech; men in Kentucky are human. If you can honestly praise them, do so. How they will glow and expand! Censure, and you will get the cold shoulder. For to them praise is friendship and censure enmity. They have wonderful solidarity. Sympathy will on occasion flow through them like an electric current, so that they will soften and melt, or be set on fire. There is a Kentucky sentiment, expending itself in complacent, mellow love of the land, the people, the institutions. You speak to them of the happiness of living in parts of the world where life has infinite variety, nobler general possibilities, greater gains, harder struggles; they say, "We are just as happy here." "It is easier to make a living in Kentucky than to keep from being run over in New York," said a young Kentuckian; and home he went.

If you attempt to deal with them in the business of the market-place, do not trick or cheat them. Above all things they hate and despise intrigue and deception. For one single act of dishonor a man will pay with life-long aversion and contempt. The rage it puts them in to be charged with lying themselves is the exact measure of the excitement with which they regard the lie in others. This is one of their idols—an idol of the market-place in the true meaning of the Baconian philosophy. The new Kentuckian has not lost an old-time trait of character: so high and delicate a sense of personal honor that to be told he lies is the same as saying he has ceased to be a gentleman. Along with good faith and fair dealing goes liberality. Not prodigality; they have changed all that. The fresh system of things has produced no more decided result than a different regard for material interests. You shall not again charge the Kentuckians with lacking either "the telescopic appreciation of distant gain," or the microscopic appreciation of present gain. The influence of money is active, and the illusion of wealth become a reality. Profits are now more likely to pass into accumulation and structure. There is more discussion of costs and values. Small economies are more dwelt upon in thought and conversation. Actually you shall find the people higgling with the dealer over prices. And yet how significant a fact is it in their life that the merchant does not, as a rule, give exact change over the counter! At least the cent has not yet been put under the microscope.

Perhaps you will not accept it as an evidence of progress that so many men will leave their business all over the country for an idle day once a month in town—nay, oftener than once a month; for many who are at county court in this place to-day will attend it in another county next Monday. But do not be deceived by the lazy appearance of the streets. There are fewer idlers than of old. You may think this quiet group of men who have taken possession of a buggy or a curb-stone are out upon a costly holiday. Draw near, and it is discovered that there is fresh, eager, intelligent talk of the newest agricultural implements and of scientific farming. In fact, the day is to the assembled farmers the seed-time of ideas, to be scattered in ready soil—an informal, unconscious meeting of grangers.

There seems to be a striking equality of stations and conditions. Having travelled through many towns, and seen these gatherings together of all classes, you will be pleased with the fair, attractive, average prosperity, and note the almost entire absence of paupers and beggars. Somehow misfortune and ill-fortune and old age save themselves here from the last hard necessity of asking alms on the highways. But the appearance of the people will easily lead you to a wrong inference as to social equality. They are much less democratic than they seem, and their dress and speech and manners in the market-place are not their best equipment. You shall meet with these in their homes. In their homes, too, social distinctions begin and are enforced, and men who find in the open square a common footing never associate elsewhere. But even among the best of the new Kentuckians will you hardly observe fidelity to the old social ideals, which adjudged that the very flower of birth and training must bloom in the bearing and deportment. With the crumbling and downfall of the old system fell also the structure of fine manners, which were at once its product and adornment.

V

A new figure has made its appearance in the Kentucky market-place, having set its face resolutely towards the immemorial court-house and this periodic gathering together of freemen. Beyond comparison the most significant new figure that has made its way thither and cast its shadow on the people and the ground. Writ all over with problems that not the wisest can read. Stalking out of an awful past into what uncertain future! Clothed in hanging rags, it may be, or a garb that is a mosaic of strenuous patches. Ah! Pompey, or Cæsar, or Cicero, of the days of slavery, where be thy family carriage, thy master and mistress, now?

He comes into the county court, this old African, because he is a colored Kentuckian and must honor the stable customs of the country. He does little buying or selling; he is not a politician; he has no debt to collect, and no legal business. Still, example is powerful and the negro imitative, so here he is at county court. It is one instance of the influence exerted over him by the institutions of the Kentuckian, so that he has a passion for fine stock, must build amphitheatres and hold fairs and attend races. Naturally, therefore, county court has become a great social day with his race. They stop work and come in from the country, or from the outskirts of the town, where they have congregated in little frame houses, and exhibit a quasi-activity in whatever of business and pleasure is going forward. In no other position of life does he exhibit his character and his condition more strikingly than here. Always comical, always tragical, light-hearted, sociable; his shackles stricken off, but wearing those of his own indolence, ignorance, and helplessness; the wandering Socrates of the streets, always dropping little shreds of observation on human affairs and bits of philosophy on human life; his memory working with last Sunday's sermon, and his hope with to-morrow's bread; citizen, with so much freedom and so little liberty—the negro forms one of the most conspicuous features of a county court day at the present time.

A wonderful, wonderful day this is that does thus always keep pace with civilization in the State, drawing all elements to itself, and portraying them to the interpreting eye. So that to paint the scenes of the county court days in the past is almost to write the history of the contemporary periods; and to do as much with one of the present hour is to depict the oldest influence that has survived and the newest that has been born in this local environment. To the future student of governmental and institutional history in this country, a study always interesting, always important, and always unique, will be county court day in Kentucky.

WILLIAM H. TOWNSEND

Not all of the court day trade on Cheapside was in farm produce and livestock. In his perceptive book about Lexington and central Kentucky, Lincoln and the Bluegrass *(Lexington, 1955), William H. Townsend (1890-   ) gives one of the most graphic accounts of the abuses of slavery in the sale of Eliza. A master's daughter, Eliza was brought under the auctioneer's hammer and was sold to Calvin Fairbank (1816-1898), a New England abolitionist, but not until the price had been run up to $1,485.00. Fairbank freed the girl, but it was only a short time until the New Englander himself was in the clutches of the law for his underground railway activities.*

The Sale of Eliza

THEN THERE came an afternoon in early May, 1843. Nearly two thousand people were assembled on Cheapside. The wealth and culture of the Bluegrass were there, as well as ladies and gentlemen from Cincinnati, Louisville, Frankfort, and as far south as New Orleans. Ordinarily a slave sale was an event that attracted only casual interest, usually attended by prospective purchasers and a few idle bystanders. But today a dense mass of humanity swarmed about the old, rickety auction block at the southwest corner of the courthouse yard, and the public square was filled to overflowing with men and women in fashionable attire.

Two persons stood on the block: one was the auctioneer in a long swallow-tailed coat, plaid vest, and calfskin boots, with a white beaver hat on the back of his head; the other was a beautiful young girl with dark lustrous eyes, straight black hair, and a rich olive complexion, only one sixty-fourth Negro.

She was white, yet a slave, the daughter of her master, about to be sold by his creditors to the highest and best bidder. Reared as a house servant in a home of wealth and culture, Eliza had acquired grace, poise, education, and other accomplishments most unusual in one of her station. Those who were selling her had taken no chances on her escape. For more than a week she had been confined in a filthy, crowded, vermin-infested slave pen with maimed and twisted pieces of humanity like William and Callie and Mose, and now she stood trembling and disheveled, staring with wide, frightened eyes into the up-turned faces of that curious throng.

With his hand clutching the girl's shrinking shoulder, the auctioneer addressed the crowd in businesslike tones. Here was a sprightly wench, such as never before had been offered at a public sale. She was skilled in all the household arts, dependable, trustworthy, and amiable in disposition. In the most insinuating tones he emphasized her exquisite physique and then called loudly for bids.

"How much am I offered for the wench?" he inquired in a harsh voice. The bidding started at two hundred fifty dollars. Rapidly it rose by twenty-fives and fifties to five hundred—seven hundred—a thousand dollars. When twelve hundred was reached only two bidders remained in the field: Calvin Fairbank, a young minister who had just recently come to town, and a short, thick-necked, beady-eyed Frenchman from New Orleans.

"How high are you going?" asked the Frenchman.

"Higher than you, Monsieur," replied Fairbank.

The bidding went on, but slower—more hesitant—smaller. The auctioneer raved and pleaded. "Fourteen hundred and fifty," said Fairbank cautiously. The Frenchman was silent. The hammer rose—wavered, lowered—rose again—then the flushed and perspiring auctioneer dropped his hammer and jerked Eliza's dress back from her white shoulders, exhibiting to the gaze of the crowd her superb neck and breast.

"Look here, gentlemen!" he shouted, "who is going to lose

such a chance as this? Here is a girl fit to be the mistress of a king!" A suppressed murmur of horror ran through the crowd. Women turned away and tried to leave. Exclamations of anger were heard on every side. But the man on the block, callous from experience, was not to be intimidated. He knew his rights: that under the law the weeping, cringing creature at his side was a chattel and nothing more.

"Fourteen sixty-five," ventured the Frenchman.

"Fourteen seventy-five," responded the preacher.

There was another frenzied appeal for bids, but none came, and it seemed that the contender from New Orleans was through. Sickened at the spectacle, the crowd was melting away when suddenly the auctioneer "twisted the victim's profile" to the dazed and incredulous audience and "lifting her skirts, laid bare her beautiful, symmetrical body from her feet to her waist."

"Ah, gentlemen," he exclaimed, slapping her naked thigh with a heavy hand, "who is going to be the winner of this prize?"

"Fourteen hundred and eighty," came the Frenchman's voice feebly through the tumult.

The man on the block lifted his gavel. "Are you all done? Once—twice—do I hear any more? Thr-e-e." The high bidder stood with a smile of triumph on his swarthy features. Eliza, knowing who the preacher was, turned an appealing, piteous face in his direction.

"Fourteen eighty-five," said Fairbank.

"Eighty-five, eighty-five—eighty-five; I'm going to sell this girl. Are you going to bid again?"

The Frenchman shook his head. With a resounding thud the hammer fell, and Eliza crumpled down on the block in a swoon.

"You've got her damned cheap, sir," said the auctioneer cheerily to Fairbank. "What are you going to do with her?"

"Free her," cried Fairbank, and a mighty shout went up from the dispersing crowd led, surprisingly, by the great proslavery advocate, Robert Wickliffe, in whose carriage Eliza and her new owner drove to the house of a friend while her "free papers" were being made out.

The sale of Eliza sorely taxed the allegiance of central Kentucky to its favorite institution and provoked wide discussion and comment. The emancipationists held it up as a hideous example of the barbarous slave code, while the opposition rather feebly contended that it was a most extraordinary incident, an extreme case never likely to occur again. And so the discussion went on for months until the approaching presidential campaign absorbed public attention.

ANONYMOUS

No ONE knows specifically who the author of this classic piece of backwoods humor was. It first appeared in the Spirit of the Times *in 1836. The locale of the story was Jessamine County, and the author signed himself "North Alabamian." Like so many of the magazine's authors, this one preferred to hide behind a pseudonym largely for the sake of humor itself. The quarter-race story has all the flavor of the day, and it was this kind of material that was to make the* Spirit of the Times *a famous journal of humor and sports from 1836 to 1860. The* Spirit *had a rebirth in 1836, after having been published from 1831 to 1833 as a colorless sports magazine. The quarter race was an early Kentucky institution which involved the great common people in duels of both wit and horseflesh. The flashy sport on horseracing of today would not especially like to claim descent from these informal main-street and old-field matches.*

The Mystery of Quarter-Racing

NOTHING would start against the Old Mare; and after more formal preparation in making weight and posting judges than is customary when there is a contest, *"the sateful old kritter"* went off crippling as if she was not fit to run for sour cider, and any thing could take the shine out of her that had the audacity to try it. The muster at the stand was slim, it having been understood up town, that as to sport to-day the races would prove a *water-haul.* I missed all that class of old and young gentlemen who annoy owners, trainers, and riders, particularly if they observe they are much engaged, with questions that should not be asked, and either can't or should not be answered. The business folks and men of gumption were generally on the *grit,* and much of the chaff certainly had been blown off.

A walk or gallop over is a slow affair; and without being in any way able to account for it, it seemed to be an extremely dry affair; for while the four mile was being done (*as the prigs have it*) I noticed many a centaur of a fellow force his skeary nag up to the opening in the little clapboard shanty, and shout out impatiently—"Colonel, let us have some of your *byled* corn—pour me out a buck load—there—never mind about the water, I drank a heap of it yesterday," and then wheel off to the crowd as if intent on something.

The race, like all things, had an end, and I had some idea, in imitation of Sardanapalus, "all in one day to see the race, then go home, eat, drink, and be merry, for all the rest was not worth a fillip," when I met Dan. He knows a little, finds out a little, and guesses the rest, and, of course, is prime authority. I inquired if the hunt was up. "Oh, no, just hold on a while, and there will be as bursting a quarter race as ever was read of, and I will give it 'em, so you can make expenses." I always make a hand when about, and thinking I might get a wrinkle by prying into the mystery of quarter-racing, I accordingly rode to the thickest of the crowd. A rough-hewn fellow, who either was, or pretended to be, drunk, was bantering to run his mare against any horse that had ploughed as much that season, his mare having, as he assured us, tended twenty-five acres in corn. Another chap sidled up to him, and offered to plough against him for as much liquor as the company could drink, or for who should have both nags—his horse had never run, as he did not follow it. Sorrel got mad, and offered to beat him in the cart, wagon, or plough, or he could beat him running one hundred miles, his weight on each, for five hundred dollars. Bay still disclaimed racing, but would run the quarter stretch, to amuse the company, for one hundred dollars. Sorrel took him up, provided Bay carried his present rider, and he would get somebody; Bay agreed, provided he would not get a lighter rider. It was closed at that, and two of Senator Benton's abomi-nations—$100 United States Bank Bills—were planked up. Bay inquired if they could stand another $50;—agreed to by Sorrel, who, observing Bay shell out a $100 note, said, there was no use of making change as his note was the same amount, and they might as well go the $100. This was promptly agreed to, and another one hundred dollars offered, and immediately cov-ered—there being now three hundred dollars a side. Now came a proposal to increase it three hundred dollars more; Bay said— "You oversize my pile, but if I can borrow the money, I'll ac-commodate you," and immediately slipped off to consult his banker. Dan now whispered, *"Spread yourself on the Bay."* Thinking I should run in while I was hot, I observed aloud—I should admire to bet some gentleman ten dollars on the bay. A Mr. Wash, or as he was familiarly called, Big Wash, snapped me up like a duck does a June-bug, by taking the bill out of my hand, and observing that either of us could hold the stakes, put it in his pocket. Finding this so easily done, I pushed off to consult my friend Crump, the most knowing man about short races I ever knew, and one who can see as far into a mill-stone as the man that pecks it. I met him with the man that made the race on the bay, coming to get a peep at the sorrel. As soon as he laid eyes on her he exclaimed—

"Why, Dave, you made a pretty pick up of it; I'm afraid our *cake is all dough*—that's old Grapevine, and I told you point blank to walk around her, but you're like a member of the Kentucky legislature, who admitted that if he had a failing it was being a *leetle* too brave."

"How could I know Grapevine?" replied Dave, doggedly; "and you told me you could beat her, any how."

"Yes," said Crump, "I think I can; but I didn't come a hundred and fifty miles to run them kind of races—Old Tompkins has brought her here, and I like him for a *sucker!*"

"Well," says Dave, "maybe I can get off with the race if you think you'll be licked."

"No," said Crump, "when I go a catting, I go a catting; its mighty mixed up, and there's no telling who's constable until the election is over; it will be like the old bitch and the rabbit, nip and tuck every jump, and sometimes the bitch a *leetle* ahead."

Old Tompkins, who had not appeared during the making of the race, now came round, and seeing the bay, said—"Popcorn, by G—d." He now came forward, and addressed the other party: "Boys," said he, "its no use to run the thing into the ground. If a man goes in for betting, I say let him go his load, but we have no ambition against you, so draw the bet to one hundred dollars; that is enough for a little tacky race like this, just make for amusement."—Carried by acclamation.

Now the judges were selected: a *good* judge does not mean exactly the same thing here as on the bench, though some of the same kind may be found there—it means one who is obstinate in going for his own friends. It did not seem to be considered courteous to object to the selections on either side, perhaps from consciousness of vulnerability. But one of the nominees for the ermine was a hickory over any body's persimmon in the way of ugliness. He was said to be the undisputed possessor of the celebrated jack-knife; his likeness had been moulded on dog-irons to frighten children from going too near the fire, and his face ached perpetually; but his eyes! his eyes! He was said to have caught a turkey-buzzard by the neck, the bird being deceived, and thinking he was looking another way; and several of the crowd said he was so cross-eyed he could *look at his own head!* It was objected to him that he could not keep his eyes on the score, as he did not see *straight,* and it was leaving the race to the accident of which of his optics obtained the true bearing when the horses were coming out. The objections were finally overruled, the crooked party contending that Nature had designed him for a quarter judge, as he could station one eye to watch when the foremost horse's toe struck the score, and could note the track of the horse that followed, at the same moment, with the other eye.

The riders now attracted my attention. It is customary, I believe, to call such "a feather," but they seemed to me about the size of a big Christmas turkey gobbler, without feathers; and I was highly delighted with the precocity of the youths— they could swear with as much energy as men of six-feet, and they used fourth-proof oaths with a volubility that would bother a congressional reporter.

There now arose a dispute as to whether they should run to or from the stand, it being a part of the mile track, and there being some supposed advantage to one of the horses, or the other, according as this might be arranged. It was determined by a toss-up at last, to run to the stand. After another toss for choice of tracks, and another for the word, the horses walked off towards the head of the stretch. Now it was "Hurra, my Popcorn—I believe in you—come it strong, lumber—go it with a looseness—root little pig, or die." And, "Oh! my Grapevine! tear the hind sights off him!—you'll lay him out cold as a wagon-tire—roll your bones—go it, you cripples!" &c., &c., &c.

Beginning to doubt, from all I heard, whether my friend Dave had been regularly appointed almanac-maker for this year, I hedged a five, and staked it with a young man that was next to me, riding a remarkable wall-eyed horse, and some time after staked another five dollars, with a person I had noticed assisting about the bar, and would be able to recognize again. I now flattered myself on my situation—I had all the pleasurable excitement of wagering, and nothing at risk.

Each side of the track was lined with eager faces, necks elongated, and chins projected, a posture very conducive to health in a bilious climate, as it facilitates the operation of emetics. I was deafened with loud cries of "Clear the track!" "Stand back!" "Get off the fence!" "The riders are mounted!" "They are coming!" "Now they are off!"—but still they came not. Without intending it, I found myself, and indeed most of the crowd, moving up towards the start, and after every failure, or false alarm, I would move a few yards. I overheard a fellow telling with great glee—"Well, I guess I warmed the wax in the ears of that fellow with the narrow brimmed white hat; he had an elegant watch that he offered to bet against a good riding-horse. You know my seventeen year old horse that I always call the bay colt; I proposed to stake him against the watch, and the fellow agreed to it without ever looking in his mouth; if he had, he would have seen teeth as long as ten-penny nails. It is easy fooling any of them New York collectors—they ain't cute: the watch is a bang-up lever, and he says if he was GOING TO TRAVEL he would not be without it for any consideration. He made me promise if I won it to let him have it back at one hundred dollars in case he went into Georgia this fall. It is staked in the hands of the Squire there;— Squire, show it to this here entire stranger." The Squire produced a splendid specimen of the tin manufacture; I pronounced it valuable, but thought it most prudent not to mention for what purpose.

Alarms that the horses were coming continued, and I gradually reached the starting place: I then found that Crump, who was to turn Popcorn, had won the word—that is, he was to ask "are you ready?" and if answered "yes!" it was to be a race. Popcorn jumped about like a pea on a griddle, and fret-

ted greatly—he was all over in a lather of sweat. He was managed very judiciously, and every attempt was made to soothe
him and keep him cool, though he evidently was somewhat
exhausted. All this time Grapevine was led about as cool as a
cucumber, an awkward-looking *striker* of old Thompson's holding her by the cheek of the bridle, with instructions, I presume, *not to let loose in any case,* as he managed adroitly to be
turning round whenever Popcorn put the question.

Old Tompkins had been sitting doubled up sideways, on his
sleepy-looking old horse—it now being near dark—rode slowly
off a short distance, and hitched his horse: he deliberately took
off his coat, folded it carefully, and laid it on a stump; his neck-
cloth was with equal care deposited on it, and then his weather-
beaten hat; he stroked down the few remaining hairs on his
caput, and came and took the mare from his striker. Crump
was anxious for a start, as his horse was worsted by delay; and
as soon as he saw Grapevine in motion to please her turner,
Old Tompkins swung her off ahead, shouting triumphantly,
"Go! d—n you!" and away she went with an *ungovernable.*
Crump wheeled his horse round before reaching the poles, and
opened on Old Tompkins—"That's no way; if you mean to
run, let us run, and quit fooling; you should say 'Yes!' if you
mean it to be a race, and then I would have turned loose, had
my nag been tail forward; it was no use for me to let go, as it
would have been no race any how until you give the word."

Old Tompkins looked as if the boat had left him, or like
the fellow that was fighting, and discovered that he had been
biting his own thumb. He paused a moment, and without
trying to raise a squabble, (an unusual thing,) he broke down
the track to his mare, slacked her girths, and led her back,
soothing and trying to quiet her. She was somewhat blown by
the run, as the little imp on her was not strong enough to take
her up soon. They were now so good and so good, and he proposed they should lead up and take a fair start. "Oh!" said
Crump, "I thought that would bring you to your milk, so lead
up." By this time you could see a horse twenty yards off, but

you could not be positive as to his colour. It was proposed to call in candles. The horses were led up, and got off the first trial. "Ready?" "Yes!"—and a fairer start was never made. Away they went in a hurry,

"Glimmering through the gloam."

All hands made for the winning post. Here I heard—"Mare's race!"—"No! she crossed over the horse's path!"—"The boy with the shirt rode foul!"—"The horse was ahead when he passed me!" After much squabbling, it was admitted by both parties that the nag came out on the left-hand side of the track was ahead; but they were about equally divided as to whether the horse or the mare came through on the left-hand side. The judges of the start agree to give it in as even. When they came down, it appeared that one of the outcome judges got angry, and had gone an hour ago. My friend that looked so many ways for Sunday, after a very ominous silence, and waiting until frequently appealed to, gave the race to the horse by ten inches. This brought a yell from the crowd, winners and losers, that beat any thing yet; a dozen of men were produced, who were ready to swear that gimlet-eye was a hundred yards off, drinking stiff cock-tail broth, and that he was at the far side of it when the horses came out, and consequently must have judged the result through two pine planks an inch thick; others swore he did not know when the race was won, and was not at the post for five minutes after. Babel was a quiet retired place compared with the little assemblage at this time: some bets were given up, occasional symptoms of a fight appeared, a general examination was going to be assured the knife was in the pocket, and those hard to open were opened and slipped up the sleeve; the crowd clustered together like a bee-swarm. This continued until about nine o'clock, when Crump, finding he could not get the stakes, comprised the matter, and announced that by agreement it was a drawn race. This was received with a yell louder, if possible, than any former one; every one seemed glad of it, and there was a unanimous ad-

journment to the bar. Though tired and weary, I confess that
I (for no earthly reason that I can give but the force of example) was inclined to join them, when I was accosted by a
person with whom I had bet, and had staked in the hands of
the young man riding the wall-eyed horse. "Well," said he,
"shell out my five dollars that I put up with that friend of
yours—as I can't find *him*." I protested that I did not know
the young man at all, and stated that he had my stake also. He
replied that I need not try to feed him on *soft corn* that way,
and called on several persons to prove that I selected the stakeholder, and we were seen together, and we must be acquainted,
as we were both *furreigners* from the cut of our coats. He
began to talk hostile, and was, as they brag in the timber districts, twenty foot in the clear, without limb, knot, windshake,
or woodpecker hole. To appease him, I agreed, if the stakeholder could not be found, to be responsible for his stake. He
very industriously made proclamation for the young man with
the wall-eyed horse, and being informed that he had *done gone*
three hours ago, he claimed of me, and I had to shell out.

Feeling somewhat worsted by this transaction, I concluded
I would look up my other bets. Mr. Wash I did not see, and
concluded he had retired; I found the stakeholder that assisted
about the bar, and claimed my five dollars on the draw race;
to my surprise I learned he had given up the stakes. Having
been previously irritated, I made some severe remarks, to all
of which he replied in perfect good temper, and assured me he
was the most punctilious person in the world about such matters, and that it was his invariable rule never to give up stakes
except by the direction of some of the judges, and called up
proof of his having declined delivering the stakes until he and
the claimant went to old screw-eye; and he decided I had lost.
This seemed to put the matter out of dispute so far as he was
concerned, but thinking I would make an appeal to my opponent, I inquired if he knew him. He satisfied me, by assur-
ing me he did not *know him from a side of sole leather*.

I left the course, and on returning next morning, I looked

out for Mr. Wash; I discovered him drinking, and offering large bets; he saw me plainly, but affected a perfect forgetfulness, and did not recognise me. After waiting some time, and finding he would not address me, I approached him, and requested an opportunity of speaking to him apart. Mr. Wash instantly accompanied me, and began telling me he had got in a scrape, and had never in his life been in such a fix. Perceiving what he was at, I concluded to take the whip-hand of him, and observed—"Mr. Wash, if you design to intimate by your preliminary remarks that you cannot return to me my own money, staked in your hands, I must say I consider such conduct extremely ungentlemanly." Upon this he whipped out a spring-back dirk knife, nine inches in the blade, and whetted to cut a hair, stepped off, picked up a piece of cedar, and commenced whittling. "Now, stranger," says he, "I would not advise any man to try to run over me, for I ask no man any odds further than civility; I consider myself as honest a man as any in Harris county, Kentucky; but I'll tell you, stranger, exactly how it happened: you see, when you offered to bet on the sorrel, I was out of soap, but it was too good a chance to let slip, as I was dead sure Popcorn would win; and if he had won, you know, of course it made no difference to you whether I had a stake or not. Well, it was none of my business to hunt you up, so I went to town last night to the confectionary, [a whisky shop in a log pen fourteen feet square,] and I thought I'd make a rise on chuck-a-luck, but you *perhaps* never saw such a run of luck; everywhere I touched was pizen, and I came out of the *leetle end* of the horn; but I'll tell you what, I'm a man that always stands up to my fodder, rack or no rack; so, as you don't want the money, I'll negotiate to suit you exactly; I'll give you my *dubisary*: I don't know that I can pay it this year, unless the *crap* of hemp turns out well; but if I can't this year, I will next year probably; and I'll tell you exactly my principle —if a man waits with me like a gentleman, I'm sure to pay him when I'm ready; but if he tries to bear down on me and make me pay whether or no, you see it is his own look out, and he'll see sights before he gets his money." My respect for Mr. Wash's dirk-knife, together with my perceiving there was nothing else to be had, induced me to express my entire satisfaction with Mr. Wash's *dubisary*, hoping at the same time that at least *enough* of hemp would grow that year. He proposed that I should let him have five dollars more for the stake, but on my declining, he said, "Well, there is no harm in mentioning it." He went to the bar, borrowed pen and ink, and presently returned with a splendid specimen of caligraphy to the following effect:-

State of Kentucky
Jessamine County.

Due Dempsey, the just and lawful sum of ten dollars, for value received, payable on the twenty-sixth day of December, 1836 or 1837, or any time after that I am able to discharge the same. As witness my hand and seal, this 30th day of May, 1836.

GEORGE WASHINGTON BRIGGS  SEAL

I wish you would try Wall street with this paper, as I wish to cash it; but I'll run a mile before I wait for a quarter race again.

ANONYMOUS

*L*EXINGTON *(1850-1875) was a "big name" horse. He gave Kentucky's reputation as a breeding and racing center an enormous boost. In grueling tests of speed and endurance in the Lower South, the Bluegrass horse proved himself a master of the track. Although not the first great thoroughbred, Lex-*

ington was the first Bluegrass horse to attract so much attention from the press. When he was finally retired to a Woodford County farm, his name was just as famous as that of the city for whom he was named. Sporting periodicals, the national newspapers, and sporting books have kept Lexington's memory green. So long as men discuss the history of racing in Kentucky, they will revive the memory of the famous colt and of his triumphs in the South.

This anonymous account of Lexington's record-setting four miles on April 2, 1855, at the New Orleans track appeared in the Spirit of the Times. Running against time, Lexington was permitted to have a horse accompany him each mile, although in the opinion of the reporter, the animal racing with the champion in the first and fourth quarters was of no aid.

The Fastest Time Made

THE MOST brilliant event in the sporting annals of the American turf, giving, as it has, the palm to the renowned Lexington, came off yesterday, over the Metairie Course, and its result greatly surpassed the most ardent hopes and enthusiastic expectations of the friends of the winner, and the lovers of turf sports.

The day was the loveliest of the whole season. As the hour appointed for the great contest approached, the town was all astir with excitement incident to the occasion. Vehicles of all sorts were in requisition, and our beautiful level shell roads were filled with them from the last paving-stone to the gates of the course. The displays in equitation during that busy part of the day, which may be defined as "going to the races," were almost as amusing and exciting as the greater event, for witnessing which so many thousand were intent.

The judges selected for the occasion were Gen. Stephen M. Westmore for the Virginia gentleman, Arnold Harris, Esq.,

for Mr. Ten Broeck, and John G. Cocks, Esq., the President of
the Metairie Jockey Club, as umpire. The timers were Hon.
Duncan F. Kenner, Capt. Wm. J. Minor and Stephen B. El-
liott, Esq.

It being the first event of the season, there was the usual
bustle at the gates, the distribution of the members' badges
and the strangers' badges, the admission to the different stands,
and, from the character of the event, an unusual rush of carriages, cabs, buggies, wagons, saddle horses and foot passengers;
and by three o'clock the course presented a most brilliant appearance. There were representatives of every section of the
country and almost every State in the Union, and among them
we were happy to see a goodly show of the fairer portion of
creation.

The field inside the course presented a most animated appearance, and the feeling in favor of the gallant Lexington was
general and decided; and as the predestined hero of the day
appeared upon the course, in company with his stable companions who were to be partners for a time in his trials, his
feelings and his fame—his bold, reaching and elastic step, his
unequalled condition, and his fearless, defiant look—conscious
of superiority and of victory—gave strength to his backers that
all was as it should be.

Of the temerity of his backers and owner, Mr. Richard Ten
Broeck, in standing before the world bidding defiance to all
the previous performances ever marked by a horse, we have before spoken as our feelings dictated, and his extraordinary self
reliance, based upon well directed judgment and sound sense,
cannot fail to place him in the estimation of true sportsmen as
the leader of the host. He knew he had an animal of unflinch-
ing game, coupled with lightning speed, and bravely did his
gallant ally respond to his call.

The betting was large. Lexington's appearance made him a
favorite, and before starting it was firm at $100 to $75 against
time and but few takers. The greater portion of the betting

had been done in town, and there were but few left who dared
to brave the lion in his lair. The conflicting opinions which
had been generally expressed in regard to the terms of the
match, and its mode of performance, caused a very general excitement, each party in turn expressing his views as to the right
of the points discussed, namely—that of allowing horses to start
with Lexington, to urge him to an increased speed, and the
propriety of giving the horse a running start. The judges,
however, ended the matter by deciding that he could do both.
The decision gave very general satisfaction.

Gilpatrick, upon Lexington, now prepared for action, and
as he started up the stretch on his proud courser, to do that
which no other horse had ever attempted, the man and horse
formed a beautiful and perfect picture. He turned him around
just below the draw gates, and as he reached the judges' stand,
when the drum tapped, he was at the pace it was intended he
should run. To our mind he was run too fast the first mile,
which he accomplished in 1:47¼, the first half mile in 0:53.
Upon reaching the stand it was intimated to him to go slower,
which he did.

Joe Blackburn was started behind him at the beginning of
the first mile, but the respectful distance he kept in his rear
must certainly have done him an injury rather than a benefit,
for at no time was he near enough for Lexington to hear the
sound of his hoofs.

The pace in the second mile visibly decreased; Arrow, who
was started before its commencement, waiting about thirty
yards behind Lexington. In the third mile Arrow closed the
gap, and Lexington, hearing him, was a little more anxious,
and slightly increased his pace. Upon entering the fourth mile
Arrow was stopped, and Joe Blackburn went at him again, but
as in the first instance, he was "like chips in porridge"—of no
benefit. Lexington darted off in earnest, running the last mile
in 1:48¾. He reached the head of the front stretch in 6:55,
running its entire length in 24¾ seconds. The whole time of

the four miles was 7:19¾, carrying 103 pounds, Gilpatrick being three pounds over weight. That the course was in admirable condition we need not assert, but that we have seen it in better order for safety and for time, we think we may assert. The writer of this was not present when Lexington and Lecomte met last spring, and can therefore make no comparison, but agrees with "A Young Turfman" that the extreme hardness of the track might prevent a horse from fully extending himself, which must have been the case with Lexington yesterday. He lost his left fore plate, and half the right one; and Gilpatrick at the drawgate in the last mile had no little difficulty in keeping him on his course, Lexington making violent efforts to swerve to the right where it was soft and heavy.

With regard to the time, not a doubt can be entertained, the official being slower than any other. Outside, by many experienced timers, it was made in 7:19¼.

The excitement attending the progress of this remarkable race cannot be described. It was intense throughout; and to those who had no opportunity of taking note of time, Lexington's deceptive fox like gait could not have given them hopes of success. The joyousness and hilarity everywhere visible, which followed the announcement that Lexington was the victor, showed the feeling of the vast majority of the vast assemblage.

It must be a source of the highest gratification to the rider of Lexington that he guided him through his perilous journey successfully, despite the prophecies and hopes of defeat that attended him. In this connection we may fearlessly assert that through a long career of usefulness and success of more than twenty years upon the turf, the name of Gilbert W. Patrick, better known as Gilpatrick, the rider, has never been tainted with even the breath of suspicion, and that the bright escutcheon of his name remains untarnished; and as this is perhaps his last appearance in public, it is the writers hearty wish that he may live to enjoy an uninterrupted flow of worldly comfort, and that when death calls him to answer that to which all living must respond, he may be full of years and honor. The names of Gilpatrick and Lexington are inseparably connected with the greatest achievement upon the American turf.

That this great race will go down to generations yet unborn as the fastest time made, is the honest conviction of the writer.

BASIL DUKE

IN LATER years Morgan's men were most sensitive about charges of horse stealing made against them by their Kentucky neighbors. The Bluegrass country saw the raiders dash across it, emptying stables as they went. More than one famous stallion found himself under the saddle of a hard-riding cavalryman who depended upon his mount to gallop him beyond danger. Basil W. Duke (1838-1916) explained horse pressing in his book, History of Morgan's Cavalry *(Cincinnati, 1867). He acknowledged the fact that his command stole horses or traded with owners of better horses on their own terms.*

Morgan's horsethieves, said Duke, were honorable men when compared with their Yankee counterparts. They never killed horses, they left a horse for every one they took, and every exchange was made in the presence of a commissioned officer. When Morgan was killed at Greenville, Tennessee, he had horses that were worth fabulous amounts of money. His success as a cavalry commander more often than not depended upon the quality of horses which his men rode.

The Art of "Horse-Pressing"

ONE SPECIAL cause of the degeneracy of the Southern cavalry, in the latter part of the war, was the great scarcity of horses and the great difficulty of obtaining forage within the Confederate lines, and consequently, of keeping the horses which we had in good condition. Morgan's men had the reputation, and not unjustly, of procuring horses with great facility and economy. Adepts as we were, in the art of "horse-pressing," there was this fact nevertheless to be said in favor of the system which we adopted: while making very free with the horse-flesh of the country into which we would raid, there was never any wanton waste of the article. We did not kill our tired stock, as did the Federal commanders on their "raids," when we got fresh ones. The men of our command were not permitted to impress horses in a friendly country. It is true that horses were sometimes stolen from people who were most devoted to our cause, and who lived within our lines, but such thefts did not often occur, and the perpetrators were severely punished. The witty editors of Yankee-land would doubtless have explained our rebuke of this practice, by an application of the old saying that "there is honor among thieves," which would have been very just and apposite. The difference between our thieves and those on the other side was, that the latter were entirely destitute of every sort of honor. General Morgan took fresh horses to enable his command to make the tremendous marches which ensured so much of his success, and to prevent his men from falling into the hands of the enemy, but he hedged around the practice with limitations which somewhat protected the citizen. He required that, in every instance where a man desired to exchange his tired horse for a fresh one, he should have his horse inspected by his company commander, who should certify to the condition of the horse and the necessity of the exchange. If the company commander certified that his horse was unfit for service, the man obtained from his regimental commander permission to obtain a fresh one, which had also, before it was valid, to be approved by the brigade commander. Whenever it was practicable, the exchange was required to be made in the presence of a commissioned officer, and, in every case, a horse, if the soldier had it, was ordered to be left in the place of the one impressed. When a man was without a horse, altogether, his company commander could impress one for him. No doubt, this seems to the unmilitary reader, only systematic robbery—but is not *that* going on all the time, all over the world? Is it not, too, a great comfort to the citizen, to know that (when he is robbed), there are laws and the "proper papers" for it!

When men or officers were detected with led horses, they were punished, and the horses were taken away from them, unless they could prove that they were entitled to them. Morgan's men were habitually styled "horse-thieves" by their enemies, and they did not disclaim the title—I should like to see a statistical report showing the number of horses stolen in Kentucky by the respective belligerents—we would lose some laurels. The Confederate Government could not, and did not attempt to supply the cavalry of its armies with horses. The cavalry soldier furnished his own horse, and (if he lost him), had to make the best shift he could for another. The cavalryman was not subjected to the rigid discipline of the infantryman, for the reason that he was harder to catch. It is more difficult to regulate six legs than two. For the very reason that it was outside of the pale of regular discipline and the highest military civilization, it was more necessary to give to the cavalry officers who practically understood that sort of service, as well as were men of controlling character. Such men could make of the cavalryman, a soldier—with an inferior officer or one who was awkward at cavalry business over him, he became an Ishmael.

JOHN JAMES AUDUBON

*JOHN JAMES AUDUBON (1785-1851) was a master fron-
tiersman. He saw Kentucky in its most primitive conditions.
He appreciated its wilderness paradise, and he understood the
backwoodsmen who invaded it. In many respects Audubon's
description of Kentucky beginnings is a more precise picture
of what actually happened than is the famous frontier essay by
Frederick Jackson Turner. He was able to record on paper the
anxieties, hopes, and accomplishments of a people on the move
westward. Like all observers of the contemporary frontier
scene, Audubon viewed his subject through the lenses of reverence. He was not so reverent, however, that he could not
appraise humanity's whims and foibles.*

*Some of Audubon's observations border on the tall tale. His
description of marksmanship is comparable to the boasts of
Davy Crockett and Mike Fink. The gun, like the axe, was a
tremendously important instrument of pioneering. It was a
source of protection, of food supply, and of sport. A good
marksman in the pioneer period was as much a hero as a robber
baron was a century later. This essay, published in the first
volume of* Ornithological Biography *(Philadelphia, 1831) and
later included under the title* Delineations of American Scenery and Character *(New York, 1926), is a classic of frontier
literature.*

The Management of the Rifle

WE HAVE individuals in Kentucky, that even there are considered wonderful adepts in the management of the rifle. To
drive a nail is a common feat, not more thought of by the Kentuckians than to cut off a wild turkey's head, at a distance of
a hundred yards. Others will *bark* off squirrels one after an-

other, until satisfied with the number procured. Some, less intent on destroying game, may be seen under night *snuffing a candle* at the distance of fifty yards, off-hand, without extinguishing it. I have been told that some have proved so expert and cool, as to make choice of the eye of a foe at a wonderful distance, boasting beforehand of the sureness of their piece, which has afterwards been fully proved when the enemy's head has been examined!

Having resided some years in Kentucky, and having more than once been witness of rifle sport, I will present you with the results of my observation, leaving you to judge how far rifle-shooting is understood in that State.

Several individuals who conceive themselves expert in the management of the gun, are often seen to meet for the purpose of displaying their skill, and betting a trifling sum, put up a target, in the centre of which a common-sized nail is hammered for about two-thirds its length. The marksmen make choice of what they consider a proper distance, which may be forty paces. Each man cleans the interior of his tube, which is called *wiping* it, places a ball in the palm of his hand, pouring as much powder from his horn upon it as will cover it. This quantity is supposed to be sufficient for any distance within a hundred yards. A shot which comes very close to the nail is considered as that of an indifferent marksman; the bending of the nail is, of course, somewhat better; but nothing less than hitting it right on the head is satisfactory. Well, kind reader, one out of three shots generally hits the nail, and should the shooters amount to half a dozen, two nails are frequently needed before each can have a shot. Those who drive the nail have a further trial amongst themselves, and the two best shots of these generally settle the affair, when all the sportsmen adjourn to some house, and spend an hour or two in friendly intercourse, appointing, before they part, a day for another trial. This is technically termed *Driving the Nail*.

Barking off squirrels is delightful sport, and in my opinion requires a greater degree of accuracy than any other. I first witnessed this manner of procuring squirrels whilst near the town of Frankfort. The performer was the celebrated DANIEL BOON. We walked out together, and followed the rocky margins of the Kentucky River, until we reached a piece of flat land thickly covered with black walnuts, oaks and hickories. As the general mast was a good one that year, squirrels were seen gambolling on every tree around us. My companion, a stout, hale, and athletic man, dressed in a homespun hunting-shirt, bare-legged and moccasoned, carried a long and heavy rifle, which, as he was loading it, he said had proved efficient in all his former undertakings, and which he hoped would not fail on this occasion, as he felt proud to show me his skill. The gun was wiped, the powder measured, the ball patched with six-hundred-thread linen, and the charge sent home with a hickory rod. We moved not a step from the place, for the squirrels were so numerous that it was unnecessary to go after them. BOON pointed to one of these animals which had observed us, and was crouched on a branch about fifty paces distant, and bade me mark well the spot where the ball should hit. He raised his piece gradually, until the *bead* (that being the name given by the Kentuckians to the *sight*) of the barrel was brought to a line with the spot which he intended to hit. The whip-like report resounded through the woods and along the hills in repeated echoes. Judge of my surprise, when I perceived that the ball had hit the piece of the bark immediately beneath the squirrel, and shivered it into splinters, the concussion produced by which had killed the animal, and sent it whirling through the air, as if it had been blown up by the explosion of a powder magazine. BOON kept up his firing, and before many hours had elapsed, we had procured as many squirrels as we wished; for you must know, that to load a rifle requires only a moment, and that if it is wiped once after each shot, it will do duty for hours. Since that first interview with our veteran BOON, I have seen many other individuals perform the same feat.

The *snuffing of a candle* with a ball, I first had an opportunity of seeing near the banks of Green River, not far from a large pigeon-roost, to which I had previously made a visit. I heard many reports of guns during the early part of a dark night, and knowing them to be those of rifles, I went towards the spot to ascertain the cause. On reaching the place, I was welcomed by a dozen of tall stout men, who told me they were exercising, for the purpose of enabling them to shoot under night at the reflected light from the eyes of a deer or wolf, by torch-light, of which I shall give you an account somewhere else. A fire was blazing near, the smoke of which rose curling among the thick foliage of the trees. At a distance which rendered it scarcely distinguishable, stood a burning candle, as if intended for an offering to the goddess of night, but which in reality was only fifty yards from the spot on which we all stood. One man was within a few yards of it, to watch the effects of the shots, as well as to light the candle should it chance to go out, or to replace it should the shot cut it across. Each marksman shot in his turn. Some never hit either the snuff or the candle, and were congratulated with a loud laugh; while others actually snuffed the candle without putting it out, and were recompensed for their dexterity by numerous hurrahs. One of them, who was particularly expert, was very fortunate, and snuffed the candle three times out of seven, whilst all the other shots either put out the candle, or cut it immediately under the light.

Of the feats performed by the Kentuckians with the rifle, I could say more than might be expedient on the present occasion. In every thinly peopled portion of the State, it is rare to meet one without a gun of that description, as well as a tomahawk. By way of recreation they often cut off a piece of the bark of a tree, make a target of it, using a little powder wetted with water or saliva for the bull's eye, and shoot into the mark all the balls they have about them, picking them out of the wood again.

After what I have said, you may easily imagine with what ease a Kentuckian procures game, or dispatches an enemy, more especially when I tell you that every one in the State is accustomed to handle the rifle from the time when he is first able to shoulder it until near the close of his career. That murderous weapon is the means of procuring them subsistence during all their wild and extensive rambles, and is the source of their principal sports and pleasures.

GEORGE DENNISON PRENTICE

*I*N *1830 the Whigs imported George Dennison Prentice (1802-1870) from New England to write a campaign biography of Henry Clay. He was prevailed upon to remain in Kentucky to edit the new Whig paper, the Louisville* Daily Journal, *which he did until his retirement in 1868, when the* Journal *was merged with the* Courier. *While he was in Kentucky gathering material for his book, Prentice wrote a series of letters to his old newspaper, the* New England Weekly Review, *describing the life of the natives.*

In Frankfort on election day, the Yankee editor observed a rough-and-tumble combat with no holds barred. His uncomplimentary comments on the "total depravity" of the Kentuckians was used against him by his arch rival, the Louisville Advertiser, *but Prentice weathered the storm and eventually drove the* Advertiser *off the streets.*

A Trial of Strength

DEAR SIRS: I have just witnessed a strange thing—a Kentucky election—and am disposed to give you an account of it. An election in Kentucky lasts three days, and during that period whisky and apple toddy flow through our cities and villages like the Euphrates through ancient Babylon. I must do Lexington the justice to say that matters were conducted here with tolerable propriety; but in Frankfort, a place which I had the curiosity to visit on the last day of the election, Jacksonism and drunkenness stalked triumphant—"an unclean pair of lubberly giants." A number of runners, each with a whisky bottle poking its long neck from his pocket, were busily employed bribing voters, and each party kept half a dozen bullies under pay, genuine specimens of Kentucky alligatorism, to flog every poor fellow who should attempt to vote illegally. A half a hundred of mortar would scarcely fill up the chinks of the skulls that were broken on that occasion. I barely escaped myself. One of the runners came up to me, and slapping me on the shoulder with his right hand, and a whisky bottle with his left, asked me if I was a voter. "No," said I. "Ah, never mind," quoth the fellow, pulling a corn cob out of the neck of the bottle, and shaking it up to the best advantage, "jest take a swig at the cretur and toss in a vote for old Hickory's boys—I'll fight for you, damme!" Here was a temptation, to be sure; but after looking alternately at the bottle and the bullies who were standing ready with their sledge-hammer fists to knock down all interlopers, my fears prevailed and I lost my whisky. Shortly after this I witnessed a fight that would have done honor to Mendoza and Big Ben. A great ruffian-looking scoundrel, with arms like a pair of cables knotted at the ends, and a round black head that looked like a forty-pound cannon shot, swaggered up to the polls and threw in his bit of paper, and was walking off in triumph. "Stop, friend," exclaimed one of the Salt River Roarers, stepping deliberately up to him, "are you a voter?" "Yes, by——," replied he of the Bullet Head. "That's a lie," rejoined the Roarer, "and you must just prepare yourself to go home an old man, for I'll be damned if I don't knock you into the middle of your ninety-ninth year." "Ay, ay," replied the other, "come on, then; I'll ride you to hell, whipped up with the sea sarpint!" They had now reached an open space, and the Salt River bully, shaking his fist a moment by way of a feint, dropped his chin suddenly upon his bosom and pitched headforemost toward the stomach of his antagonist with the whole force of his gigantic frame. Bullet Head, however, was on his guard, and, dodging aside with the quickness of lightning to avoid the shock, gave the assailant a blow that sent him staggering against a whisky table, where he fell to the ground amid the crash of bottles, mugs, and tumblers. Nothing daunted by this temporary discomfiture, the bully gathered himself up, and with a single muttered curse renewed his place in front of his foe. Several blows were now given on both sides with tremendous effect, and in a few moments the Salt River boy, watching his opportunity, repeated the maneuver in which he had first been foiled. This time he was successful. His head was planted directly in his antagonist's stomach, who fell backward with such force that I had no expectation of his ever rising again. "Is the scoundrel done for?" inquired the temporary victor, walking up and looking down on his prostrate foe. Bullet Head spoke not, but with the bound of a wildcat leaped to his feet and grappled with his enemy. It was a trial of strength, and the combatants tugged and strained and foamed at the mouth, and twined like serpents around each other's bodies, till at length the strength of the Bullet Head prevailed and his opponent lay struggling beneath him. "Gouge him!" "Gouge him!" exclaimed a dozen voices, and the topmost combatant seized his victim by the hair and was preparing to follow the advice that was thus shouted in his ear, when the prostrate man, roused by desperation and exerting a strength that seemed superhuman, caught his assailant by the throat with a grasp like that of fate. For a few moments the struggle seemed to cease, and then the face of the throttled man turned black, his tongue fell out of his mouth, and he rolled to the ground as senseless as a dead man. I turned away a confirmed believer in the doctrine of total depravity.

THOMAS D. CLARK

COCKFIGHTING in the Bluegrass has a history dating back to the marking of the first landlines. In earlier days men fought their roosters on streets and crossroads. Society, however, developed refinements which frowned upon wanton letting of blood, and the sport had to seek cover. Today no noisy sports page proclaims the frequent matches, and no radio announcer details their results. Even the jargon of the ring and the gaff is unknown to large numbers of Bluegrass citizens. The sport would not thrive under the shadow of the front page or the questioning of the grand jury.

It is hard for law-enforcing officers to find the cockpits, and local society is too busy with its own gaffing to interfere. Nevertheless the sport of cockfighting thrives. Its patrons always seem to get to the right place at the right time, and that gamecock and hen darting under the cover of a tobacco barn have done little to affect the egg and broiler market. It hardly goes without saying that the account printed here, from The Kentucky *(New York, 1942), was not dredged from yellowing historical documents which might give a historian a feeling of vicarious presence.*

The Sign of the Cockpit

THERE is an old pastime in the Bluegrass which has been practiced from the time the first settlement was made. Cooped up in many of the panniers which rocked back and forth from the sides of pack horses were gamecocks and hens. Old Virginia bloodstock was being brought across the mountains to entertain the Kentuckians in their moments of relaxation from the fight against the raw frontier environment. Since "cocking" is a bloody business, it made a ready appeal to the vigorous frontiersman. Likewise its gory aspects have caused it to be under a ban from certain elements in the Bluegrass. Its written history in the Kentucky River valley is exceedingly spotted. Once and awhile a traveler referred to it or a sporting magazine carried an article in the abstract about this sport. Frequently there were articles about cocking in the *Turf Register,* but these were written about procedure in breeding and training rather than as descriptive of the contemporary state of the art. Always, it seems, cocking has been an illicit consort of horse breeding and racing. In 1845 the sport was well developed in Bluegrass Kentucky. William Porter included a note in his miscellaneous column in the *Spirit of the Times.* He wrote: "Yesterday, and today were 'some' at Memphis, Tennessee. Shy and Means of Kentucky and Colonel Abingdon, of Tennessee, were each to show twenty-one cocks [a main], and $100 on each fight. If 'General Jim' heels for Old Kentuck, I should like to back him for a small smile."

Today there are many cockfighters in Bluegrass Kentucky. They do not shout their identity from housetops, but within the clan this fact is well known. In the winter and early spring, the sport goes on with a boom. Down a lonesome tree-lined country lane, a highway signal lamp burns in a farm gateway. This is the sign of the cockpit, and in the community, perhaps at the top of the nearest hill, a yellow light flickers dimly through the chinked cracks of an innocent-appearing tobacco barn. The visitor pulls his automobile up in line with the others parked in a semicircle. A group of men speaking in subdued tones stands about the door. Just inside the vestibule a ticket salesman asks a dollar for admission to the pit. Once inside the door, the visitor sees before him a strange row of latticework cages extending almost up to the ceiling across one end of the barn. In a hasty glance, these clumsily constructed enclosures have somewhat an Oriental appearance. From deep

in the block of cages comes a lusty crow from a long-legged
cock who is ready for the fight before him. In front of the coops
are tables and racks where the cocks are prepared for the pit.
A sweating man works away vigorously with a sharp pocket-
knife, fitting collars to the stubby shanks of a rooster. Another
holds the bird's feet in position to receive the gaffs. These are
long slender steel instruments with needle-sharp points. The
collars of the shanks are thrust down tightly over the collars of
the muted natural spurs and are tied on with leather thongs.
A few minutes later the cock will be placed in the ring to cut,
hack, and pick at an opponent until one or both of them are
dead. One of the cocks jumps up; a leg flashes past his opponent; the gaff goes home; and his victim is "rattled." A bead
of telltale blood bubbles on the end of the injured cock's beak,
and the referee shouts "handle your birds" to the managers.
The injured cock is gathered up in the handler's arms. The
handler places the bird's head in his mouth and draws off the
strangling ooze of blood. Next he bites the comb and blows
on its back. Again the cocks are in the ring to fight until one
or the other is dead or victorious.

Around the ring, loud jovial betters shout "two on the red,"
"five on the black," or banter with robust badinage, reflecting
upon the fighting capacities of the combatants in the ring. A
wave, a nod, a wink, raised fingers make and accept bets. There
is no centralized betting organization. A bet is a gentleman's
obligation, and the loser is obligated to hunt up the winner
and pay off.

Two cocks are released in the ring, and a wave of excitement
runs through the crowd. Enthusiastic cockers crowd up to the
ringside and talk in knowing professional lingo about the fight
in process. Back in the crowd docile farm women nurse babes
at breast and watch every hack and pick made by the bloodthirsty gamecocks. A bird is down; his wings and legs give one
ghastly shudder and then quiver to a dead stop. He is dead;
a gaff has touched a vital spot. But before the opposing cock

can claim the victory, he has to hack or pick at the dead bird once within twenty minutes or the fight is a draw.

Cockfighting has given rise to a strange lingo. A "dunghill" fowl is a coward who flies the pit and runs from a fight. His doom is sealed because his owner wrings his neck in disgust. A "huckster" is a sharp chicken trader, dealing usually in mongrel stock. Then there are the descriptive fighting qualities of cocks. They are "game," "close hitters," "bloody heelers," "ready fighters" with "good mouths," and are "quick to come to point." For months before a cock is pitted in combat he goes through an intricate series of maneuvers. He is "flirted," or tossed into the air, to develop his wings. He is held by his thighs and "fluttered" to strengthen his legs and wings. Before a fight the cocks are "dried out" by careful rationing of water; and when the season is over they are "put on the walks" to run wild in natural surroundings. Under a year of age, cocks are stags. They are in the height of fighting form if they live to be three; and at four they are ready for retirement. Cocks are fought in "hacks" or in single fights, in "mains" of fifteen to twenty-one cocks of one owner pitted against a similar number of another. They are fought in tournaments and derbies on terms agreed to between owners.

Cockfighting is sometimes called the poor man's sport in the Bluegrass, but actually many of its most ardent patrons are wealthy people. The clan is tightlipped where the sport is in danger of being prohibited. It is quite possible that hundreds of people have lived long lives in the Bluegrass without ever having heard of the cockpits in the region or having seen a cockfight. Yet along a country road a game cock flies across the road ahead of a speeding automobile, and a flock of timid hens take cover from the approaching machine under the tall grass in the ditch. Sometimes it has occurred that an enthusiastic cocker's family has not even known of his interest. An old-time fighter in the Bluegrass stood with one foot on the side of the ring and laughed heartily at the mess his wife got into with their preacher. She had cooked one of his gamecocks for dinner, but it had been rubbed with oil of peppermint, and the meat was ruined. It struck the old-timer as high comedy to see the preacher being offered gamecock for dinner.

This silent sport, hidden away behind the beckoning highway signal flare and the chinked walls of a tobacco barn with its improvised amphitheater about the pits, goes on with vigorous support. To stir up the Humane Society and the women's clubs would be bad business. Yet the Bluegrass Kentuckian of today has not undergone a tremendous change from the day when the cantankerous English travelers in the region spent much of their time reading the vigorous announcements of sport-to-be from the handbills tacked to tavern walls.

J. SOULE SMITH

SUCH erudite sources of Kentucky and Virginia lore as the editorial offices of the Louisville Courier-Journal *and the Richmond* Times-Dispatch *have come to sharp disagreement over how to make a mint julep. Unhappily, the* Courier-Journal *editors hoisted themselves on their own petard in the argument by introducing some foreign ingredients. They might have saved themselves from such horrendous embarrassment by turning through the files of the Lexington* Herald. *There the famous Lexington lawyer-journalist, J. Soule Smith (1848-1904), treated the subject of julep making with the same assurance and tenderness that James Lane Allen treated the Bluegrass itself. He settled once and for all the "mint crushing" argument: "Like a woman's heart, it gives it sweetest aroma when bruised."*

Zenith of Man's Pleasure

BUT IN the Blue Grass land there is a softer sentiment—a gentler soul. There where the wind makes waves of the wheat and scents itself with the aroma of new-mown hay, there is no contest with the world outside. On summer days when, from his throne, the great sun dictates his commands, one may look forth across broad acres where the long grass falls and rises as the winds may blow it. He can see the billowy slopes far off, each heaving as the zephyrs touch it with caressing hand. Sigh of the earth with never a sob, the wind comes to the Blue Grass. A sweet sigh, a loving one; a tender sigh, a lover's touch, she gives the favored land. And the moon smiles at her caressing and the sun gives benediction to the lovers. Nature and earth are one—married by the wind and sun and whispering leaflets on the happy tree.

Then comes the zenith of man's pleasure. Then comes the julep—the mint julep. Who has not tasted one has lived in vain. The honey of Hymettus brought no such solace to the soul; the nectar of the Gods is tame beside it. It is the very dream of drinks, the vision of sweet quaffings. The Bourbon and the mint are lovers. In the same land they live, on the same food are fostered. The mint dips its infant leaf into the same stream that makes the Bourbon what it is. The corn grows in the level lands through which small streams meander. By the brookside the mint grows. As the little wavelets pass, they glide up to kiss the feet of the growing mint, the mint bends to salute them. Gracious and kind it is, living only for the sake of others. The crushing of it only makes its sweetness more apparent. Like a woman's heart, it gives its sweetest aroma when bruised. Among the first to greet the spring, it comes. Beside the gurgling brooks that make music in the pastures it lives and thrives. When the Blue Grass begins to shoot its gentle sprays toward the sun, mint comes, and its sweetest soul drinks at the crystal brook. It is virgin then. But soon it must be married to Old Bourbon. His great heart, his warmth of temperament, and that affinity which no one understands, demands the wedding. How shall it be? Take from the cold spring some water, pure as angels are; mix with it sugar till it seems like oil. Then take a glass and crush your mint within it with a spoon—crush it around the borders of the glass and leave no place untouched. Then throw the mint away—it is a sacrifice. Fill with cracked ice the glass; pour in the quantity of Bourbon which you want. It trickles slowly through the ice. Let it have time to cool, then pour your sugared water over it. No spoon is needed, no stirring is allowed—just let it stand a moment. Then around the brim place sprigs of mint, so that the one who drinks may find a taste and odor at one draught.

When it is made, sip it slowly. August suns are shining, the breath of the south wind is upon you. It is fragrant, cold and sweet—it is seductive. No maiden's kiss is tenderer or more refreshing; no maiden's touch could be more passionate. Sip it and dream—you cannot dream amiss. Sip it and dream, it is a dream itself. No other land can give so sweet a solace for your cares; no other liquor soothes you so in melancholy days. Sip it and say there is no solace for the soul, no tonic for the body like Old Bourbon whiskey.

HENRY WATTERSON

*I*N *1918 the spirit of Carry Nation (1846-1911) triumphed, although Henry Watterson (1840-1921) had buried this misguided Bluegrass champion of prohibition with a few well-chosen editorial words seven years earlier. Now editor emeritus, Marse Henry interrupted his Miami vacation to send a "Temperance Lecture" to the Louisville* Courier-Journal, *which published it on February 9, 1919. This essay was later included in* The Editorials of Henry Watterson *(New York, 1923).*

Bourbon whisky was a major product of the Bluegrass, and Watterson spoke for the distilleries of central Kentucky as well as for the Louisville breweries when he wrote with prophetic vision a vivid prediction in American social history.

The Bottom of the Glass

I SHOULD not like to take the hand of a prohibitionist, if I knew him to be a prohibitionist. I should not like it because in the event that he be not a fool outright who could nowise have my respect or interest, or concern me, he must be sterile of mind and heart as well as a traitor to the institutions of his country.

The Constitution of the United States assures to each citizen the right to life, liberty and the pursuit of happiness. These are essential to freedom, to a free country and to free men. In the exercise of his rights the individual man must not tread upon, or put in jeopardy, the rights of his fellow-man. Nor within this limitation must he allow his own to be ignored or abridged.

The case against prohibition other than that it is a canting hypocrisy devised by rogues for the cheating of dupes, where it is not the broken reed of feminine hope, or a weak delusion of zealots, because in point of fact it does not prohibit, may be thus summarized:

First—It is the entering wedge to a sumptuary fanaticism which will not stop with the attempt at the denial of drink, but, given its bent and license, will set up a tyrannous supervision over every affair of private life and personal conduct, substituting, for self-determination, the will and rule of conventicle.

Second—It affects to establish virtue by law, substituting for the sense and sway of conscience the public acts and ordinances of assembly, thus making a political issue of religion and morality and removing it from the accountability of the minds and hearts of men.

Third—It is an assault upon the essential reason of our republican being, and the establishment of the spy-system, not to say the reinvestment of the star-chamber and the inquisition.

The quotation I have made from the oracle of Omaha reads like an editorial of say ten years ago out of a certain ribald sheet of Louisville. Recently the New York *World* has taken up the same cry. I am afraid that my good brothers Hitchcock and Cobb arrive upon the scene too late, that they reach the stable and propose to lock the door when the horse is gone, that, in point of fact, the Bolsheviki of prohibition have swooped down alike upon Hell-fer-Sartin and Yuba Dam, as well as upon New York and Nebraska, and that there is equally no balm in Gilead, nor sugar in the bottom of the glass.

The moderate use of drink has brought as much happiness into the world as its immoderate use has brought wretchedness. Even in America there is not percapita in any community one sot to a hundred moderate drinkers. Both in England and in the United States drunkenness has steadily abated under the ministrations of an intelligent morality.

In the European beer-brewing and wine-making countries drunkenness of the kind common to us is unknown. The throngs that gather in the public gardens are a sight to see. They are perpetually crowded. Noblemen and workmen touch elbows. Women and children come and go. Disorder is unknown. Cheese and sausage are the food staples. This has been going on day in and day out for hundreds of years, and furnishes a complete answer to the dogma of the American prohibitionists "that we can no more conduct the liquor business without producing drunkards than we can run rattlesnake ranches without raising poison."

One might as well say that we cannot run banks without raising embezzlers; or railways without encountering accidents; or cucumbers and cabbage without the risk of cholera morbus, the thief, the wreck, the bellyache, like the drunkard, being the exception. Shall we have no more fiscal institutions, no more lines of transportation, no more truck gardens and no more cakes and ale? Perish the thought, for what has been and is in Europe can be in America or anywhere else where the rule of sanity is observed.

We pretend to think we are a free people and we agree that the world is too much governed. Yet nowhere is individual liberty so assaulted as in the United States. Thoughtful Americans must see that there are worse evils than the drink evil; evils more subversive of the character of a nation, because more general and pervasive, less obvious and less reachable. The drunkard is usually in evidence. He may be dealt with. It is otherwise with the varying forms of personal and political corruption. Virtue is self-resistance to vice, not enforced obedience to drastic regulation, morality itself being relative. That may be moral in one country which is immoral in another country.

The "common good," about which we hear so much, like the "general welfare" clause of the Constitution, has been worked to death. The "common good" is the veriest abstraction. It is nowhere the same. It has its variants. Who is to decide what is the "common good"? Time was when the church, through its close corporation of ruling prelates, alone decided. The "common good" was their belief, or pretended belief, in prescribed religious dogma. The "common good" embraced certain customs, manners and clothing decreed by canon law as orthodox. The penalties assessed against the delinquent varied from hanging to burning, from the rack to the thumbscrew. They were applied by whichever church party found itself in the ascendant.

After centuries of strenuous trial in the effort to make men good by force of arms and tortures, both a costly and a ghastly failure, the self-ordained agents of God sowing the world in blood and flame, were sent to the rear and the doctrine of toleration—the bedrock of all freedom, of all enlightenment, of all good government—was established measurably throughout Christendom, but absolutely, as the founders thought, in the United States.

This the prohibitionists would set aside and nullify. To do so they fly in the face of Heaven itself. Treading the cloisters of the past in Europe, or traveling the thoroughfares of the present at home, I know but one torch to light the way, and that is the Spirit of the Man of Galilee, whose teaching from first to last was at war with force, appealing to the better nature and the reason of man, not his brutal passions and combative parts.

I might as well rail at God for bringing sin and disease and death into the world as seek to encompass them by sumptuary legislation. Men may be made hypocrites by law, but never saints. Religious truth has been rather obscured and retarded than accelerated by theologic controversy.

Repressive agencies culminate in reactions. Radical puritanism in England was succeeded by the debaucheries of the Restoration; and prohibition laws in the United States have not only not diminished drunkenness, but they have brought in their train scandals and evils quite as hurtful to the community at large as drink has brought to that limited section of the community given over to the excessive use of intoxicants; that is, contempt for law, evasions of law, extortion and adulteration, the corruption alike of the officials and the drink, lawful and needful revenues extinguished in favor of lawless indulgences; the fanatical preacher and the grafting politician uniting to work the spy system each for his own ends, but against the mass and body of society.

I am being constantly asked how long I think prohibition will last. If it be not accompanied by the stimulation of the drug habit, as in Turkey, where alone among the nations it has made a permanent lodgment, the reaction will come with the knowledge that in the cities it cannot be enforced. The constitutional inhibition may never be rescinded. But, like the fifteenth amendment in the Southern States, it will become inoperative. "It will be just as easy," says an old Mississippi friend of mine, "to get a drink as to keep a nigger from voting."

THOMAS D. CLARK

THE RECIPES of the old burgoomasters may be jealously guarded secrets, but one thing is certain: it takes a strong constitution to stomach the famous concoction of meat, vegetables, and seasonings. Furthermore, there is no such thing as a little burgoo; the experts claim that only by cooking in huge quantities can the delicacy of such proportions as 1,800 pounds of potatoes to ½ pound of curry powder be maintained. A more practical recipe for the modern kitchen is included in this brief sketch of the history of burgoo in central Kentucky by Thomas D. Clark (1903-   ), in The Kentucky *(New York, 1942).*

An Air of Mystery

IN THE very beginning of the white man's history in the Kentucky River valley some ingenious soul created a political dish which remains even yet a unique American food. Some dabbler in history has said that this famous stew was first concocted by John Hunt Morgan's men. Long before Morgan was born they were serving burgoo at political gatherings under the shade of huge oaks around Maxwell Springs. An earlier Kentuckian, writing to a friend in the East, invited him to come to Kentucky where he would give him a cup of hot burgoo and a glass of raw whisky. Perhaps the Easterner did not understand what outlandish concoction it was that he was to get in his cup. His dictionary could not tell him what it was. It originated back in the days when hunters counted up their day's kill in the thousands of squirrels, and when pigeons flew through the woods in veritable clouds, and bear, deer, buffalo, and hundreds of turkeys were available. The idea came from Virginia, where Brunswick stew was popular. Vegetables of all kinds were boiled along with the game meats, and the whole mass was highly seasoned with spices. This was a fine temptation with which to attract a crowd. Persons having houses to build, logs to roll, or politicians desiring to get a crowd to their speakings could depend upon the offer of a burgoo dinner to do the trick.

The old recipes have been forgotten because of the disappearance of game. Modern counterparts are still popular at race tracks, political speakings, conventions, and picnics. An all-day political rally without burgoo and barbecue would be about as exciting as a wedding without the bride. Several burgoo kings have placed imaginary crowns upon their brows, and have gone forth with an assortment of battered iron pots, pans, and tattered recipes to make and serve their special concoction. "King Gus" Jaubert became the famous postwar burgoomaster. He had a secret recipe, much of which he never revealed. For more than forty years Gus Jaubert prepared burgoo for the Kentucky meetings. His glorious triumph, however, came in 1895 when he prepared the famous food for 200,000 delegates to the Grand Army of the Republic reunion in Louisville. This Gargantuan meeting required 15,000 gallons of King Gus's delectable brew, along with 45 beeves, 383 sheep, and 544 barbecued pigs.

An earlier burgoomaker along the Kentucky River has left a recipe which has great possibilities of expansion. Based upon the proportions of six persons he used six squirrels, six birds, one and one-half gallons of water, one teacup of pearl barley, one quart of tomatoes, one quart of corn, one quart of oysters, one pint of cream, one-quarter pound of butter, two table-spoonsful of flour, and seasoned to taste with salt.

The modern pretender to the crown, Colonel J. T. Looney, has an elephantine recipe which requires 800 pounds of beef, 200 pounds of fowl, 168 gallons of tomatoes, 36 gallons of corn, 350 pounds of cabbage, 6 bushels of onions, 24 gallons of carrots, 1,800 pounds of potatoes, 2 pounds of red pepper, ½ pound of black pepper, 20 pounds of salt, 8 ounces of angostura, 1 pint of Worcestershire, ½ pound of curry powder, 3 quarts of tomato catsup, and 2 quarts of sherry. All this food is cooked over a slow fire for twenty-two hours. Burgoo cookers guard their secrets with a great deal of care. They tell you with an air of mystery that "this ain't all we use, we put in a few other little things, but that's a secret." They admit, however, that the greatest secret of all "is putting burgoo together." As to how good it is depends upon personal taste. Usually it is a tossup as to which has the greater kick in it, the cup of burgoo or the glass of raw whisky. Thus far no student of political affairs in Kentucky has investigated the direct results of burgoo and barbecue upon voting behavior at the polls. If Kentucky politics is "the damnedest," as Judge James H. Mulligan says in his famous poem "In Kentucky," then many of the sins are traceable historically to a languishing electorate gorged on burgoo and raw whisky.

ALLAN TROUT

*I*T IS *nip and tuck between Kentucky bourbon and Kentucky ham for possession of the throne of fame. Kentuckians feel sorry for Virginians because of their lack of discrimination* *in aged hog meat. They disdain to discuss the subject with anybody else, but when they must seek information and advice, inspiration, and philosophy on the matter, they turn to the king of the ridge runners, Allan Trout (1903-   ) of the Louisville Courier-Journal. On September 4, 1947, this distinguished barnyard scientist in Frankfort answered a question of paramount importance for a reader of his irrefutable column, "Greetings."*

Trout is a defender of a kind of Kentucky faith and tradition. He realizes the relativities of the simple things of life. The informalities of rural Kentucky life have their metes and bounds —even their rigid proprieties. Bottled ham gravy not only would be a gustatory anachronism, but a porcine sacrilege that would justify a skipper infestation of every smokehouse in the state.

Abundant Life

AT HAND is a valued inquiry from J. T. Wellman, of Louisville,

"Ham gravy is mighty good on cornbread or hot biscuits," Mr. Wellman writes. "Why not have it bottled for sale to gravy lovers?"

Thank you, Mr. Wellman. Your proposition to bottle ham gravy moves me to exclaim with Browning: "Ah, but a man's reach should exceed his grasp, or what's a heaven for?"

Man, sir, has hankered after food in combination ever since the Lord promised Moses to deliver the children of Israel into a land flowing with milk and honey. That promise from heaven has been succeeded by such terrestial combinations as bread and butter, peanuts and popcorn, jowl and greens, peaches and cream, and catfish and cornbread.

But the greatest of these is ham and gravy. The most nourishing liquid in this world is the gravy that fried ham gives up. It is made by pouring a little cold water into the hot skillet after the ham has been forked out onto the platter. You stir until the mixture stops sizzling, then pour it into a gravy bowl.

There is abundant life in ham gravy. It will put hair on the hairless chest of a man, or bloom into the pale cheeks of a woman. Breast-fed babies whose mothers eat ham gravy are destined to develop sturdy bodies and sound minds. Biscuits sopped in ham gravy will satisfy the gnawing appetite of a growing boy quicker than any combination of the patented foods we hear praised by radio announcers.

Now these combinations of complementary foods were not dictated by the palate alone. The law of supply also guided man to make his combinations appropriate. For example, where there is bread you usually find enough butter to spread on it. God knows there is as much popcorn as there are peanuts. The jowl in a bowl of greens will last about as long as the greens. Where there is cream, peaches are to be had. And I never heard of a mess of catfish ruined by the absence of enough meal to make cornbread.

But ham and gravy is a lopsided combination. The gravy always gives out before the ham. Nine times out of ten, the platter will be half full of ham when the last drop of gravy has been soaked up by the bread on some eager diner's plate. I have seen a bowl of gravy emptied on the first round, but with enough ham left for the second table.

That, sir, is why we cannot bottle ham gravy to sell to gravy lovers. A surplus of ham gravy cannot be attained.

JOE H. PALMER

JOE H. PALMER (1904-1952) brought to the readers of his racing column in the New York Herald Tribune *a wealth of miscellaneous information. Under a Lexington dateline he wrote one day this intriguing account of alcoholic jelly and of Mrs. Palmer's treasured* Blue Grass Cook Book. *With typical Kentucky aptitude for seeing the practical application of experimental undertakings, Palmer saw in "This Hellish Jell," as he entitled this particular column, a reputation-saving device for overbibulous ladies. This essay was later included in* This Was Racing *(New York, 1953).*

Jelly on Her Biscuit

MANY PEOPLE who want to learn about horses go at it the wrong way. They go to Cornell, where the animal husbandry department is considered very good. The proper thing to do is to sit in one of the four chairs which occupy the corner between the grill room and the elevators at the Lafayette Hotel here, say from 9 to 12 in the morning and in the early evening, and listen. After that you can go to Cornell and fill in the gaps, and you will know things the rest of the graduating class have not been taught.

It is not always certain that these things will be about horses. This department, in search of a refresher course (since the weather was too chilly to bathe in Elkhorn Creek), took up occupancy in one of these chairs next to one occupied by a Mr. George Krehbiel, who has bred and raced horses with fair success but is mainly concerned with picking winners at $4.60 for readers of "The Detroit News" and in betting on losing 20-to-1 shots.

"Stay put a minute," said Mr. Krehbiel. "I've got something for you."

He dashed off and returned presently with a small package, very heavy for its size. It was, said the printing on the top, "Old Forester Jell." The contents, it stated further, were "sugar, water, whiskey, citrus pectin and citric acid." It was, in other words, jellied whiskey, or whiskied jelly, as you care to put it. You eat it on things.

At this point I became convinced for the twenty-second time that I had no business sense, a matter which will come as no surprise to my friends.

I had discovered, or rather rediscovered, the idea behind this at least five years before, and if it had been put to commercial use I could have had enough money to get into really serious trouble.

We were having some people in to dinner and the companion of my joys and sorrows, observing that the meal was fairly heavy, was casting about for a light dessert. The casting was being done in the "Blue Grass Cook Book," a volume which deserves a column in itself. This particular copy had lost its covers, some of its pages and parts of the others, and ordinarily was kept tied up with a string.

It contained items like how to make soap, this being some time before social leaders could make money advertising that they washed their faces, but my pet in it was the recipe for bitters. "Take one and a half gallons of fine old whiskey," it began. At publication time, this wasn't much, for Kentucky then had a law that keepers of toll gates, who evidently had a habit of holding up their customers, could not charge more than twelve and a half cents for a pint of whiskey. At the moment, a man making bitters would be in for something like $35 before he got to the second ingredient.

The recipe extracted, this time, was for wine jelly. You take unflavored gelatin and dissolve it in water and put in a bit of lemon juice. Then, in this instance, a bottle of Madeira was dumped in, the whole business put in a mold and then in the refrigerator. I pointed out that this would not jell, because of the alcohol involved.

I should have had more respect for history. It jelled. When it was served, it looked like one of those quivery things which give children extra energy to break windows and to pull the kitty's tail. Our guests took a look at it, and you could see the thought forming in their minds, "Jello, by all the saints." But they bit it, for politeness, and then matters took a turn for the better.

The reasoning was that if wine would jell, anything would, and the idea was kicked around a bit until a neighbor with more initiative came in with a small blob of green material and said, "You've been talking about it. Now eat it." It was a stinger, though the wrong crème de menthe was used, and it was jellied. I ate it. Hell broke out.

A stinger, as I suppose you know, is made of brandy and white crème de menthe. If you order one at a bar, it will be made in a proportion of two to one and the bartender will use the cheapest brandy in the house. But if you know this worthy and can persuade him to change the proportion to six to one and use good brandy, the result is often remarkable. If you get one after dinner, you will sip at it for twenty minutes. But if it's jellied and you eat it with a spoon, it goes down in two. The detonation is more immediate, and will convince the most skeptical.

A warning should be added. If you try to jell a stinger, it will go into the refrigerator looking as sparkling as an autumn morning, and it will come out looking like something scraped from the bottom of the Missouri River. That's what the citric acid is doing in the Old Forester Jell. A dash of lemon juice and it stays clear.

This has also been tried with a Martini, which was introduced into the dining room at Jamaica. By actual count, eight people had a spoon in it, and it was pronounced remarkable if not prodigious. "Handy to take on a picnic," one man said.

You can see the multifold advantages of this. A lady traveling alone on a train, for instance, is sometimes sensitive about ordering a couple of slugs before breakfast fearing that a false, or even worse, a true, impression may be given to the passers-by.

But if she were just eating jelly on her biscuit nobody would pay any particular attention, and she could be stiff as a mink by Philadelphia.

It's a small corner, but you learn in it.

BOOK FIVE

The Treadmill
of Life

$\mathcal{R}$ELIGION has been one of the themes of Kentucky life. From the days when pioneers first knelt in prayer at Boonesboro to the present, religion has played a central role. The Craig brothers marching through the wilderness with a traveling congregation at their heels, that lone wanderer Francis Asbury, John Taylor, and Father David Rice, all were pioneers writing the first chapter of a long and colorful history.

By the turn of the century Kentuckians were sure of their land and homes. The Indians were gone, the woods were disappearing, and already the state was living under its second constitution. The time had come for a release of emotions. In western Kentucky in Logan County, the Magee brothers and others had set free a storm of emotionalism in 1800. A year later the same thing occurred in the Bluegrass at Cane Ridge. At no time in American frontier history had so many people come together. There was an outpouring of feeling which approached the proportions of a great tempest.

Fortunately there were eyewitnesses to the Cane Ridge meeting. William Burke remembered preaching from the trunk of a fallen tree. James B. Finley, later to become a famous

Ohio Valley preacher, fled the disturbing scene only to be stricken at the Blue Licks. By strange coincidence the Shakers arrived on the scene just as the meeting was in progress, and Richard McNemar gave his version of this historical moment. To the modern reader in a somewhat more sophisticated society the Cane Ridge affair with its emotional jerking and babbling is a strange phenomenon. Nevertheless, it was the beginning of a long tradition of camp-meeting revivalism in America.

While self-sacrificing ministers rode from cabin to cabin, other faithful servants were running the errands of humanity. Dr. Samuel Brown, Virginia immigrant, brought to the border a scientific knowledge of medicine. Smallpox was a scourge in the Bluegrass, and Dr. Brown carried across the mountains a combative virus which would halt the black slaughter. But Dr. Brown was in advance of the Kentucky legislature in his medical knowledge, and that great scientific body attempted to brake the wheels of medical progress. Possibly Dr. Richard Carter of Versailles concocted formulas that were more within the legislators' realm of knowledge and liking. This Bluegrass scientist brewed medical potions in prodigious quantities. He was ready and willing to treat the physically and emotionally ill. His remedies were good for everything from sciatica to disappointment in love.

There was that dark moment in Kentucky history when citizens of the Bluegrass were willing to resort even to Dr. Carter's nauseating potions. Water-borne Asiatic cholera spread in Lexington in epidemic proportions. The dead lay unburied, the doctors were unable to cope with the scourge, and what had been a fair land had become almost overnight a vale of tears.

After his minister and his physician, the Kentuckian in trouble turned to his lawyer. Quick-tempered Bluegrass gentlemen, even in more recent times, have been equally quick on the trigger or with the knife, and for their rashness they have had to answer to a jury of their peers. Jereboam Beauchamp, a murderer for the mixed motives of politics and a woman's honor, unsuccessfully faced trial in Frankfort, and so provided material for a whole series of novels based on the "Kentucky tragedy," from William Gilmore Simms to Robert Penn Warren. Charles Wickliffe's trial had a different outcome, but he was provided with a brace of defense lawyers, Henry Clay and J. J. Crittenden, who were without parallel in the Bluegrass.

The Civil War confronted the Bluegrass Kentuckian with his greatest decision. He could seek no help from his minister, his physician, or his lawyer; the decision was his alone to make. Some Kentuckians believed that they could maintain an armed neutrality between the warring sections, but before their eyes families split in their support and the young men of the state aligned themselves in opposing armed camps. Joseph Hergesheimer and John Fox, Jr., portrayed with sympathetic accuracy the personal strife caused by the outbreak of the Civil War. And three years after the close of the conflict, Henry Watterson saw how the essential values of Kentuckians had been submerged to satisfy the avarice of the conquerors.

Modern politics, too, has been marked with violence, and none more far reaching than the unsolved assassination of William Goebel, who was about to seize the governor's chair in spite of an adverse election return.

It may be a sign of reformation that in recent times flying lead has been on the side of law and order in central Kentucky. Given another place or another time, there is no doubt that a routine lynching would have occurred when a Negro was arrested for the rape-murder of a white child. That he was executed by due legal process was the outcome of the Second Battle of Lexington, when six white men were slain in order to save the life of a condemned murderer.

There are those occasions, rare indeed, when the situation is too much for the Kentuckian. Then he is likely to resolve the matter in the style of Henry Watterson: "To Hell with the Hohenzollerns and the Hapsburgs!"

JAMES B. FINLEY

POSSIBLY the greatest emotional upheaval on the early American frontier was the great Cane Ridge Revival of 1801. Hundreds of persons flocked to the little meetinghouse in Bourbon County to observe the strange experiences and were themselves overcome. The Reverend James B. Finley (1781-1856), a Methodist minister who dated his conversion from Cane Ridge, was one of those skeptics who felt the power of the overwrought emotions. More than forty years later, in his Autobiography *(Cincinnati, 1853), he recalled the awe-inspiring meeting.*

Awful beyond Description

ON THE way I said to my companions, "Now, if I fall it must be by physical power and not by singing and praying;" and as I prided myself upon my manhood and courage, I had no fear of being overcome by any nervous excitability, or being frightened into religion. We arrived upon the ground, and here a scene presented itself to my mind not only novel and unaccountable, but awful beyond description. A vast crowd, supposed by some to have amounted to twenty-five thousand, was collected together. The noise was like the roar of Niagara. The vast sea of human beings seemed to be agitated as if by a storm. I counted seven ministers, all preaching at one time, some on stumps, others in wagons, and one—the Rev. William Burke, now of Cincinnati—was standing on a tree which had, in falling, lodged against another. Some of the people were singing, others praying, some crying for mercy in the most piteous accents, while others were shouting most vociferously. While witnessing these scenes a peculiarly-strange sensation, such as I had never felt before, came over me. My heart beat tumultously, my knees trembled, my lip quivered, and I felt as though I must fall to the ground. A strange supernatural power seemed to pervade the entire mass of mind there collected. I became so weak and powerless that I found it necessary to sit down. Soon after I left and went into the woods, and there I strove to rally and man up my courage. I tried to philosophize in regard to these wonderful exhibitions, resolving them into mere sympathetic excitement—a kind of religious enthusiasm, inspired by songs and eloquent harangues. My pride was wounded, for I had supposed that my mental and physical strength and vigor could most successfully resist these influences.

After some time I returned to the scene of excitement, the waves of which, if possible, had risen still higher. The same awfulness of feeling came over me. I stepped up on a log, where I could have a better view of the surging sea of humanity. The scene that then presented itself to my mind was indescribable. At one time I saw at least five hundred swept down in a moment, as if a battery of a thousand guns had been opened upon them, and then immediately followed shrieks and shouts that rent the very heavens. My hair rose up on my head, my whole frame trembled, the blood ran cold in my veins, and I fled for the woods a second time, and wished I had staied at home. While I remained here my feelings became intense and insupportable. A sense of suffocation and blindness seemed to come over me, and I thought I was going to die. There being a tavern about half a mile off, I concluded to go and get some brandy, and see if it would not strengthen my nerves. When I arrived there I was disgusted with the sight that met my eyes. Here I saw about one hundred men engaged in drunken revelry, playing cards, trading horses, quarreling, and fighting. After some time I got to the bar, and took a dram and left, feeling that I was as near hell as I wished to be, either in this or the world to come. The brandy had no effect in allaying my feelings, but, if any thing, made me worse. Night at length came on, and I was afraid to see any of my companions. I cautiously avoided them, fearing lest they should discover something the matter with me. In this state I wandered about from place to place, in and around the encampment. At times it seemed as if all the sins I had ever committed in my life were vividly brought up in array before my terrified imagination, and under their awful pressure I felt as if I must die if I did not get relief. . . .

My heart was so proud and hard that I would not have fallen to the ground for the whole state of Kentucky. I felt that such an event would have been an everlasting disgrace, and put a final quietus on my boasted manhood and courage. At night I went to a barn in the neighborhood, and creeping under the hay, spent a most dismal night. I resolved, in the morning, to start for home, for I felt that I was a ruined man. Finding one of the friends who came over with me, I said: "Captain, let us be off; I will stay no longer." He assented, and getting our horses we started for home. We said but little on the way, though many a deep, long-drawn sigh told the emotions of my heart. When we arrived at the Blue Lick Knobs, I broke the silence which reigned mutually between us. Like long-pent-up waters, seeking for an avenue in the rock, the fountains of my soul were broken up, and I exclaimed: "Captain, if you and I don't stop our wickedness the devil will get us both." Then came from my streaming eyes the bitter tears, and I could scarcely refrain from screaming aloud. This startled and alarmed my companion, and he commenced weeping too. Night approaching, we put up near Mayslick, the whole of which was spent by me in weeping and promising God, if he would spare me till morning I would pray and try to mend my life and abandon my wicked courses.

WILLIAM BURKE

ONE OF the preachers Finley heard at Cane Ridge was the Reverend William Burke (1770-1853), who had been invited by the sponsoring Presbyterians to speak and then denied the opportunity because of his Methodist connection. Burke described the scene before him that Sunday morning in 1801 at Cane Ridge, and Finley printed it in his compilation of Sketches of Western Methodism *(Cincinnati, 1854).*

Shouts of Triumph

ON SUNDAY morning, when I came on the ground, I was met by my friends, to know if I was going to preach for them on that day. I told them I had not been invited; if I was, I should certainly do so. The morning passed off, but no invitation. Between ten and eleven I found a convenient place on the body of a fallen tree, about fifteen feet from the ground, where I fixed my stand in the open sun, with an umbrella affixed to a long pole and held over my head by brother Hugh Barnes. I commenced reading a hymn with an audible voice, and by the time we concluded singing and praying we had around us, standing on their feet, by fair calculation ten thousand people. I gave out my text in the following words: "For we must all stand before the judgment-seat of Christ;" and before I concluded my voice was not to be heard for the groans of the distressed and the shouts of triumph. Hundreds fell prostrate to the ground, and the work continued on that spot till Wednesday afternoon. It was estimated by some that not less than five hundred were at one time lying on the ground in the deepest agonies of distress, and every few minutes rising in shouts of triumph. Toward the evening I pitched the only tent on the ground. Having been accustomed to travel the wilderness, I soon had a tent constructed out of poles and papaw bushes. Here I remained Sunday night, and Monday and Monday night; and during that time there was not a single moment's cessation, but the work went on, and old and young, men, women, and children, were converted to God. It was estimated that on Sunday and Sunday night there were twenty thousand people on the ground. They had come far and near from all parts of Kentucky; some from Tennessee, and from north of the Ohio river; so that tidings of Cane Ridge meeting was carried to almost every corner of the country, and the holy fire spread in all directions.

RICHARD McNEMAR

A THIRD participant in the Cane Ridge Revival was Richard McNemar (1779-1839), an excommunicated Presbyterian who found in the "exercises" at the camp meeting an easy transition to Shakerism. A few years later he wrote The Kentucky Revival *(Cincinnati, 1807) to demonstrate the genuineness of the conversions that took place during that emotional storm. Cane Ridge was a significant movement in American religious history.*

Perfect Harmony

No one, who has not been an eye witness, can possibly paint in their imagination the striking solemnity of those occasions, on which the thousands of Kentuckians were convened in one vast assembly, under the auspicious influence of the above faith. How striking to see hundreds who never saw each other in the

face before, moving uniformly into action, without any pre-
concerted plan, and each, without intruding upon another,
taking that part assigned him by a conscious feeling, and in
this manner, dividing into bands over a large extent of ground,
interspersed with tents and waggons: some uniting their voices
in the most melodious songs; others in solemn and affecting
accents of prayer: some lamenting with streaming eyes their
lost situation, or that of a wicked world; others lying apparently
in the cold embraces of death: some instructing the ignorant,
directing the doubtful, and urging them in the day of God's
visitation, to make sure work for eternity: others, from some
eminence, sounding the general trump of a free salvation, and
warning sinners to fly from the wrath to come:—the surrounding forest at the same time, vocal with the cries of the distressed, sometimes to the distance of half a mile or a mile in
circumference.

How persons, so different in their education, manners and
natural dispositions, without any visible commander, could
enter upon such a scene, and continue in it for days and nights
in perfect harmony, has been one of the greatest wonders that
ever the world beheld; and was no doubt included in the visions
of that man, who, falling into a trance with his eyes open,
cried out—"*How goodly are thy tents, O Jacob! and thy taber-
nacles, O Israel! as the vallies are they spread forth, as gardens
by the rivers side; as the trees of lign-aloes, which the Lord
hath planted.*" . . .

Some things have lately taken place among us, which I think
more extraordinary than any I have seen or heard, since the
apostolic age. The case of Rachel Martin, was truly miraculous. I suppose you have heard of it. This extraordinary case
is illustrated by the following extract from another hand.—
"Last Saturday exceeded by far any thing I ever saw before.
Rachel Martin was struck the Thursday night after you left
this: She never eat nor spoke for nine days and nights. I was
there when she rose and spoke: her countenance was as it
were, refined [i.e. transfigured.] She told me she was free from

the world all that time: She says the work will increase." . . .

The like wonders have not been seen, except the KENTUCKY REVIVAL last summer, since the Apostle's days. I suppose the exercises of our congregation this last winter, surpassed any thing ever seen or heard of. I sometimes think it would have been well, if they had been kept in and never told.

It is certain, the natural man receiveth not the things of the spirit of God, for they are foolishness to him; hence Christ instructed his disciples not to cast pearls before swine; for the same cause, so little has been published abroad concerning the deep things of God, made manifest among the people called *New-Lights;* and for the same reason, these things can be but slightly touched at present.

That the power was supernatural by which such multitudes were struck down, required no arguments to prove; and had they never risen again, there might have been some reason for charging it to the devil: but who has power to kill and make alive again? could any one with the rationality of a man, suppose that any thing short of the power of God, could suspend the functions of animal life for an hour, a day, or a week, and again restore them with additional brightness?—Is nature wont to assume such apparent changes, as for tens and fifties, moved at the same time by the same instinct, to forget the use of every limb, and prostrate fall, no matter where, and yawn, and gasp, and expire in a cold sweat? This belongs not to nature, and as little does it belong to nature to exempt her sons from wounds and bruises, broken limbs, and aching heads, in case of such repeated and dangerous falls as were common among the *New-Lights.* And least of all, could nature's power extend to their resurrection, after an hour, a week, or nine days trance. Who wants a miracle to arouse his faith, and fix it on the sacred truths recorded in the scriptures; let him recognise the camp-meeting, let him find the man, or woman, whose immortal part for hours and days traversed the regions of eternity, while the breathless body lay as a spectacle of terror to surrounding friends. The learned expositor of scripture, and the one whom he opprobriously terms an infidel, are equally baffled with the falling exercise; the one upon his hypothesis, that there never was such a thing as a miracle in the days of the apostles; and the other, that there never was to be any such thing after. All their experiments and researches were in vain, to reduce this operation to some natural cause. Their feeling the pulse, changing the situation of the person, applying smelling bottles, bathing with camphire or cold water, letting of blood, &c. could never make half the discovery in the case that those made who came with their barrels of whisky to retail out to the multitude. By such it was abundantly proved, that the readiest way to keep clear of this extraordinary exercise, was to drown the soul in debauchery and vice. Many circumstances, beating and confounding to the wisdom of man, attended the exercises mentioned, which for the sake of brevity have to be omitted. And yet however extraordinary these things were, they were not considered by the people as the most evidential of a work of the true spirit: something much greater was commonly expected to succeed their resurrection, of greater importance than any thing that went before. The word of exhortation is ranked among the apostolic gifts, and as such it was considered by the *New-Lights*. This gift was generally expected on the occasion of rising from the before mentioned trance, and such expectations were very commonly answered. The exhortations delivered on those occasions by all ranks and colors, but especially by small children, were so evidential of a divine power, so searching to the conscience, so wounding to the sinner, that the most obstinate unbelievers have fallen down, like those of old, and confessed that God was in them of a truth.

It required a spirit more incredulous, than that which has commonly been called infidelity, to deny a supernatural agency in the case of such pathetic and powerful addresses from little children—not only unlearned, but also of the most bashful and unpopular cast of mind. Such little ones, of eight or ten years old, raised upon the shoulders or held up in the arms of some one, in the midst of vast multitudes, would speak in a manner so marvellous and astonishing, that persons of the most rugged passions would dissolve into tears; and professors of the foremost rank, confess that hitherto they had been total strangers to that heavenly sense and feeling, which distinguishes a child of God. So deep were the effects of truth, delivered in the simple language of a child, of which the following may serve as a short specimen.

"O the sweetness of redeeming love! O if sinners knew the sweetness of redeeming love, they would all come to the overflowing fountain!" The general gift of exhortation was to search out the state of the sinner, convict him of sin, and warn him to fly from it; and they often came so pointed, even to naming out the person, and publicly arraigning him for specific crimes, that often evil spirits, whose work is to cover iniquity, and conceal it, were stirred up to great fury; and those possessed with them, would come forth in a great rage, threatning and blaspheming against the author of the revival, and bold as Goliah, challenge his armies to a rencounter. ·Could nature, without bloodshed and slaughter, overcome beings so fierce? Or must it not be something supernatural? To see a bold Kentuckian (undaunted by the horrors of war) turn pale and tremble at the reproof of a weak woman, a little boy, or a mean African; to see him sink down in deep remorse, roll and toss, and gnash his teeth, till black in the face; intreat the prayers of those he came to devour, and through their fervent intercessions and kind instructions, obtain deliverance, and return in the possession of the meek and gentle spirit which he set out to oppose:—who would say the change was not supernatural and miraculous? Such exorcisms, or casting out of evil spirits, are justly ranked among the wonders which attended the *New-Light*: Nor could the man once delivered from the *Legion,* go home with greater joy to tell his friends what great things Jesus has done for him, than many returned from these encamping grounds, to announce to their former companions, their happy change.

WILLIAM LITTELL

LEGISLATORS have seldom in American history demonstrated an intelligible understanding of any kind of science. Those of 1798 in Kentucky were no exceptions. Dr. Samuel Brown (1769-1830) had transported cowpox virus over the mountains and had begun a campaign of vaccination which was to save hundreds of thousands of lives in Kentucky. Because his patients developed light cases of cowpox, the statesmen in Frankfort jumped to the conclusion that the Lexington doctor was spreading smallpox. They passed on January 30 a law, recorded in The Statute Law of Kentucky, *vol. II (Frankfort, 1811), by William Littell (1768-1824), which is today a footnote to folly.*

The Said Distemper

BE IT ENACTED *by the General Assembly,* That if any person or persons whatsoever, shall wilfully or designedly presume to import or bring into this commonwealth, from any country or place whatever, the small-pox, or any variolous or infectious matter of the said distemper, with a purpose to inoculate any person or persons whatsoever, or by any means to propagate the said distemper within this commonwealth, he or she so offending shall forfeit and pay the sum of one thousand pounds for every offence so committed; one moiety thereof shall be to the informer, and the other moiety to the use of the poor of the county where the offence shall be committed, to be recovered with costs, by action of debt, bill, plaint or information, in any court of record within this commonwealth.

And forasmuch as the inoculation for the small-pox, may, under peculiar circumstances, be not only a prudent but necessary means of securing those who are unavoidably exposed to the dangers of taking the distemper in the natural way, and for this reason it is judged proper to tolerate it under reasonable restrictions and regulations. . . .

Any person having first obtained in writing (to be attested by two magistrates,) the consent of a majority of the house-keepers residing within three miles, and not separated by a river, creek or marsh a quarter of a mile wide, and conforming to the following rules and regulations, may inoculate or be inoculated for the small-pox, either in his or her own house, or at any other place. No patient in the small-pox shall remove from the house where he or she shall have the distemper, or shall go abroad into the company of any person who hath not before had the small-pox, or been inoculated, or go into any public road, where travellers usually pass, without retiring out of the same, or giving notice upon the approach of any passenger, until such patient hath recovered from the distemper, and hath been so well cleansed in his or her person and clothes, as to be perfectly free from infection, under the penalty of forty shillings for every offence, to be recovered, if committed by a married woman, from her husband; if an infant, from the parent or guardian; and if a servant or slave, from the master or mistress.

RICHARD CARTER

WHILE *Transylvania University's famous medical faculty engaged in numerous professional rows, or combated diseases with the most modern drugs known to them, Dr. Richard Carter (1786-?) of neighboring Versailles felt fewer scientific inhibitions in his campaign against both diseases and disappointment in love. His famous book,* Valuable Vegetable Medical Prescriptions *(Frankfort, 1815), may not have modern medical significance, but a copy now sells for enough to pay a sizable portion of the expenses of an extended stay in a modern hospital. Dr. Carter was a prodigious compounder, and his remedies were never scanty ones.*

Morning, Noon, and Night

RECEIPT the 22nd: Fill a twenty gallon kettle with sliced elecampane roots, and boil them well in water, pour off the sirop and fill the kettle with water again, and boil the same roots the second time, pour off the sirop as before, then clean your kettle and strain all your sirop through a flannel cloth, into it, and boil it down to about eight gallons and a half, then strain it into your barrel. Then get green comphry slice fine and fill a ten gallon pot with it, and boil it down in the same way, until you have about six gallons of sirop, then strain it and add it to the same barrel. Then boil half a bushel of angelica roots well to a gallon of sirop, strain it and add it to the barrel. Then fill a twenty gallon pot full of life-everlasting, boil it well in the same way, down to two gallons, and add that to the barrel after you strain it well. Then boil thirty gallons of spikenard roots in the same way, down to six gallons of sirop, strain it and add it to the barrel. Then boil ten gallons of the roots and tops of ground ivy well, strain the sirop in a tub. Then boil five gallons of white plaintain leaves well, and strain the sirop in the tub with the other. Then boil the same quantity of heart leaves in the same way and strain the sirop in the same tub. Then put the whole of the contents of the tub in a vessel and boil it down to two gallons and add it to the barrel. Then fill a ten gallon pot full of the bark of the roots of yellow poplar, and boil it down and strain it, and then reduce it to two gallons, and strain it in the barrel. Then fill a five gallon pot with mullen roots and boil and strain it as the rest were done and then strain it in the barrel, when it is reduced to half a gallon. This makes in all twenty-eight gallons, to which you must add five gallons and a half of good clean honey, a quart of good Madeira wine, a pound of pulverised columbo, a pint of the elixir of vitriol, and ten gallons of good apple cider (after boiling it down to five.) Then let it work well and settle, and if it is too sharp or strong for the patient, you may add more honey. There will be agreeable to this arrangement about forty gallons, about thirty of which, is pure medicine. The dose may be varied as necessity requires, from half a table spoonful to a table spoonful, and in most cases should be given morning, noon and night, and in pulminary complaints, coughs, &c. a tea spoonful of linseed oil, sweet oil, or dog's oil should be added to each dose; but if the patient's stomach will not bear it, fresh butter warmed, and neither washed nor salted will make a very good substitute. This medicine is wonderfully efficacious in all cases of consumptions, phthisics, hooping cough, measles, a cough proceeding from the last stage of a fever, and cough proceeding from the dropsey. The patient should not make use of any salted hog meat, sweet milk, cider nor spirits, but may be permitted to use fresh shoat, beef, chickens, squirrels, mutton, panado, rice, butter-milk, and a little water and wine.

Receipt the 23rd: Get thirty gallons of good strong apple cider, and put three table spoonfuls of ground black mustard seed, and handful of beat horse radish roots to every quart, and three pound of salt petre to the thirty gallons. Fill a ten gallon pot full of dried elecampane roots, and boil them well in water, strain the sirop, and boil the same roots the second time in the same way, strain the two sirops together, and boil it down to four gallons, and add it to the cider, then add a gallon of parsley roots, and let it stand about ten days and it is fit for use, and may be given in doses from the contents of half a table spoonful to a table spoonful, which may be given three times per day, and in severe chronic complaints, may be increased to two table spoonfuls three times per day. The diet of the patient should be light and cooling, and consequently he or she should abstain from the use of sweet milk, strong coffee, and rusty bacon, and keep out of wet, damp or night air, but breathe freely in the open morning air. This medicine and regimen is good in cases of sciatic gouts, rheumatisms, palsies, ague, apoplexies, convulsive fits, gravel, dropsies, &c.

Receipt the 41st: Fill a twenty-five gallon still with elecampane roots and water, distill it and preserve the proceeds, then fill the still with spikenard roots and water, and still it in the same way, and in like manner preserve this, then fill the still with horehound, and treat it likewise, then run off two still fulls of ground ivy in the same way, after which clean the still, and put back all the liquid that has been extracted from all those herbs and roots above mentioned, and add five gallons of good whiskey, run it off as you would in making whiskey and save it as long as there appears to be any strength in it. Then put it in a cag, and to every gallon add half a gallon of honey, a table spoonful of refined nitre, a table spoonful of dried pulverised Indian turnip, and a pint of middling strong lie made of the ashes of dry cow dung.

Then get a peck of pollepody, a peck of cinquefril, and a peck of white plantain; put these into a pot and boil them well in water, strain it, add three gallons of cider to it, boil it down to three gallons, and to every gallon of this add a quart of the above sirop. This medicine may either be taken in a little wine and water, or new milk. We give from half a table-spoonful, to a wine glass full, three times per day, during which the patient must not eat any thing high seasoned, strong nor sweet, and he should be very careful that he does not take cold or even heat his blood. It is best to commence with small doses at first, and increase the dose as the patient's strength increases. This medicine is not at all dangerous unless you give too much for the patient's strength. If this medicine causes the patient to sweat, produces a soreness in the breast, or increases the cough, you may know that it is too strong, and consequently it must be weakened with honey until those symptoms abate. This is good to break any fever, and is excellent in the last stages of the consumption, phthisic, and the cold plague. If the cough is very hard add to every dose a tea spoonful of sweet or linseed oil.

The herbs and roots that you are herein directed to distill, will not produce as well in the heat of summer, as they will in the spring or fall, so by these directions, you may know how to regulate it so as to get all the strength and should not run it too far.

C. W. SHORT

No GREATER scourge ever beset Kentucky than the blighting cholera epidemic of 1833. People in Lexington and the surrounding country died in droves. It seemed that God had deserted humanity in this part of Kentucky. The Lexington doctors were called upon to treat a disease of which they had no knowledge. Some of them turned to the use of calomel in mountainous doses, while others resorted to the witchery of bleeding. Even the doctors fell victims to cholera along with their patients. On June 18, in a moment of impenetrable gloom, Dr. C. W. Short (1794-1863) wrote a letter to the Frankfort Commonwealth *describing the plight of the population of Lexington and warning that Frankfort might be next.*

That Awful Scourge

You MAY probably have heard before this that we have been visited by that awful scourge of the human race—the cholera. It is but too true, that it has proved more malignant, fatal and indiscriminate in the selection of its victims in Lexington than in any other town in the union—perhaps of the world. We rested in supposed security, relying too much on the high and elevated situation of the place, its far inland position, general healthfulness and total exemption from all the common causes of disease. But as if to mock the calculations of man, and set at utter defiance all reasonings on the subject of the origin, propagation, prevention or cure, this most anomalous and strange disease has at last laid hands upon us, with a violence that more than compensated for its delay. For two weeks past our town has been one scene of sickness, death and burial for in that time not less than 350 of our inhabitants have been swept away, and they, too, by no means from the ranks which more commonly supply its victims, but from the most respectable, sober and useful citizens. That is so emphatically true that I have not heard of the death of one solitary drunkard! Three of our physicians, out of about twelve practitioners, have fallen its victims and most of the remainder have been overcome by the prostrating influence of the poison, together with their own ceaseless exertions. I have been confined to my bed and the house for the last four days, and several of my family have had attacks; as yet, however, my house has been spared a mortal visitation; but my near neighbor, Mr. Gratz, has buried ten members of his family.

I have viewed this pestilence at a distance with horror; I have watched its approach towards us with fearful apprehension; I have endeavored to study its inscrutable character, and to be prepared, with some degree of confidence, to enter upon the conflict with it, but I must confess that its horrors have surpassed my most horrific conceptions, and its mortality has baffled the best concerted and most boldly executed practice.

Within the last two days there has been a material abatement in the number of cases and I have heard of no new one this morning. Whether this is but a respite for the destroying angel who is whetting his scythe for the harvest, or whether he is about to take his flight to some other devoted place, God in his omniscience only knows. May it never be my lot to view the ghostly lineaments of his face again.

But yesterday the city was the Eden of the Western World; there was an union of all the comforts of life, of all its elegancies; a people hospitable in their homes, accomplished in their manners. That spot seemed, of all other in this favored land, more exempt from the visitation of disease and those sad occurrences which interrupt the enjoyment of life. Look at her today! Gloom and sorrow and mourning in every habitation. Instead of being a Goshen, with lights in each dwelling, the sound of gladness is unheard, for the voice of grief has penetrated every house. The population of that city is usually a little more than 6000. There, as in Maysville, at the approach of the cholera the people fled to the country, reducing the number by more than one-third. Some of the most enterprising and interesting of both sexes have been swept away, for in that place the disease made no distinction—the bond, the free, youth and age, male and female, have alike fallen before it. At length it has ceased and its departure is certain. Years will roll away before the memory of this visitation is forgotten. The infant settlement of Lexington was dismayed by the disastrous battle of the Blue Licks; but under that calamity they were buoyed up by a reliance upon their manhood. The cholera brought with it more terror than hordes of savages, for it came on the viewless couriers of the air and bade defiance to human strength. There is truth in the answer that the citizens did not believe that the cholera could come there. Hence the premonitory symptoms had been neglected and the tempting fruits of the season had been heavily used. Add to this, too, the panic which seized upon the people and moved along in conjunction with the pestilence, arrayed in his livery and equally as potent to destroy. In Frankfort we cannot be too vigilant.

Fear not! But trust in Providence wherever thou may'st be.

ROBERT PENN WARREN

THE TRIAL in Frankfort of Jereboam Beauchamp (? -1826) for the murder of Colonel Solomon P. Sharpe (1787-1825) created as much excitement as any trial in the Bluegrass. Although the trial lawyers were not so brilliant as in many a case, the political tensions were tremendous. The Court of Appeals had dared nullify an act of the legislature to bring relief to the state banks which had crashed as the result of the panic of 1819. Immediately the Jacksonian leaders in Kentucky began a movement to reorganize the court—Beauchamp belonged to this faction; Sharpe, to the Old Court group—and the state was seriously divided into the opposing camps. Besides the political aspects, the Beauchamp-Sharpe affair also involved the honor of a woman, and these two elements have made the Kentucky tragedy a popular theme for novelists. The latest of these, Robert Penn Warren (1905-   ), revived the theme in his popular novel, World Enough and Time *(New York, 1950). He explored in perceptive detail this story, making Beauchamp a gallant man who defended a woman's honor by the Kentucky code.*

Lie for Lie

THE TRIAL began on June 6, 1826.

It was a brilliant, sweltering morning, unseasonably hot, and the courtroom was jammed, and the crowd—a restless, uncertain crowd streaked with violence and guffawing humor like fresh butchered bear meat with gristle and sweet fat—spilled out into the yard and into the street, waiting.

At ten o'clock the clerk said, "Jeremiah Beaumont, hold up your hand!" . . .

"Jeremiah Beaumont," the clerk began again, "I will read you the charge."

Then he read: "The Grand Jurors of the Commonwealth of Kentucky, empaneled in the County of Franklin . . . in the name and by the authority of the Commonwealth of Kentucky, upon their oaths do present . . ."

Jeremiah says that he listened intently, but that the words came to him strangely as though the tale they recited had no meaning for him, and could never have:

". . . and two inches below the breast bone one mortal wound of the breadth of one and one half inches and of the depth of five, of which said mortal wound so given as aforesaid . . . and so the Grand Jurors upon their oaths aforesaid, do say that the aforesaid Jeremiah Beaumont in manner and form aforesaid, feloniously and of his malice aforethought, did strike, thrust, stab, kill, and murder the said Cassius Fort . . ."

And all this against the peace and dignity of the Commonwealth of Kentucky, it said. It was signed: Nathan Gregg, Attorney for the Commonwealth.

Nathan Gregg, very clean, scrubbed, handsome, razored and pomaded, sat there rolling an unlighted cigar in his fingers and staring at the floor, studying justice.

The clerk finished, looked up, and demanded: "What say you—are you guilty or not guilty?"

Jeremiah replied: "Not guilty."

The clerk demanded: "How will you be tried?"

Jeremiah replied: "By God and by my country."

And the clerk: "God send you a happy deliverance!"

"Amen," Jeremiah said clearly, and straightened his waistcoat. It was a buff-colored waistcoat ornamented with little tufts of black wool and pewter buttons. . . .

The first two days passed in the selection of jurors. On the third day the long procession of witnesses began, the barman at Mackey's Tavern, where Jeremiah had first applied upon his arrival in Frankfort, the barman from the Weisiger House, and some man who had been talking with the barman—or claimed to have been—when Jeremiah came. They all testified stoutly that Jeremiah had worn a handkerchief on his brow, a handkerchief with a cross-barred design, and the Weisiger barman was so far carried away by his zeal that he described Jeremiah as "a fellow looking like he was all worked up to devilment and murder, with his eyeballs rolling but him trying to be sly all the same and wanting a room secret and private." At this point Mr. Madison protested the opinion, and his objection was sustained.

The drift was clear: Jeremiah had been seen wearing a cross-barred handkerchief, and a cross-barred handkerchief had been found at the Saunders door, hacked, and bloodstained. And so the trial began with a lie, a lie to be compounded.

"A lie," Hawgood said, leaning to Jeremiah, "another few lies like that and there will be no case. We can handle the handkerchief." And he smiled sourly to himself.

Jeremiah smiled, too, but inwardly. Yes, they could handle the handkerchief.

Then Caleb Jessup was called and sworn. . . .

Jessup's testimony was what Jeremiah had expected. He swore that Jeremiah when he arrived had worn on his brow a cross-barred handkerchief, dirty with smoke and sweat. That he had been very insistent to get a private room. That late he had gone out of the house as quietly as possible, but the stairs had creaked. It had been some time after midnight, for the watch had just cried. (*Oh, the liar, the liar,* Jeremiah had exclaimed bitterly to himself, for the stairs had not creaked and at that hour he had been far from the house. He had been far from the house and could prove it. He could prove the lie on Jessup. He could get a witness—why, at midnight or near he had been talking to Mr. Allenby's old colored man in the alley—he could prove it! And his heart froze: yes, he could prove it, and if he proved it, he would prove that he had stood in the alley by the Saunders door.)

Jessup was going on: That Mrs. Jessup had heard the stairs, too. That next morning Jeremiah had gone white and shaken like a girl when they named the murder to him, and couldn't eat his breakfast, though "it was a good mess of vittles and fit fer any honest man," and that Mrs. Jessup had had her feelings hurt for the slight. That when he, Jessup, reached the Saunders house he found a cross-barred handkerchief lying in the bushes near the door and that started his suspicion so that he returned to his own house to question the stranger.

("The handkerchief," Mr. Madison whispered, "the handkerchief—he has sworn it. We have him there!")

That the stranger had said he had finished his business in Frankfort and had received his land patents, when everybody knew now there were no patents at the office. That he, Jessup, had not detained the stranger, not wanting to suspect anybody wrongly and without good advice, but that he had ferreted out his name and place. That he, Caleb Jessup, always undertook to do his duty, like when he was sheriff, and that his heart was full of grief for Colonel Fort, for Colonel Fort was his brother-in-law, and like a brother to him, God bless him.

Mr. Madison rose for the cross-examination. The hush fell on the room. Mr. Madison stood solidly in the space before the witness, for the moment not noticing him, looking back over the crowd, out the windows where the late afternoon light now slanted in, out the windows at the sky, as though he had been alone.

Then he turned to Jessup, almost with surprise, or as though recollecting an unpleasant duty.

"At what spot did you find the handkerchief?" he asked quietly.

"Right on the south side that biggest lilac bush near the Saunders door on the back side the walk."

"At what hour did you find it?"

"Not before a quarter past seven, and not later than seven-thirty."

"How do you know?"

"It was seven o'clock when I left my house to come walking over. I seen the clock just before I left."

"If the defendant is convicted will you claim a share of the reward?"

Nathan Gregg was up, livid with rage. "I object!" he cried.

"Objection sustained," Judge Cooper said.

Mr. Madison bowed to the Judge. Then turned to Jessup: "Your heart is full of grief for Colonel Fort?"

"Grief!" Jessup began, "Why Cass was like a brother—he . . ."

"I object!" Nathan Gregg screamed.

"Objection sustained."

Mr. Madison bowed again, murmuring, but murmuring quite distinctly, "I beg your pardon—I was not sure I had heard the witness aright, on the point of his love."

Then he stood, waiting, while the laughter and the catcalls flared over the room like a grass fire in August, and the Judge's gavel punished the desk to splinters, and Jessup's face exuded oil like a chunk of tallow in the sun.

When the silence had returned, Mr. Madison flicked one glance over Jessup, from head to heel, a glance like a flick of spittle from the side of the mouth—so Jeremiah describes it— and strolled to his seat.

There was no re-direct examination.

Mrs. Jessup was the last witness of the day. She had been sitting there all those hours, waiting to say what she knew she would have to say, sweating in her good black dress—it had been a *good* dress once, even if it was too tight for her now and popped the seams, even if there were stains like oil on the black, even if her hands were raw and hangnailed and red against the black.

She rose, and with an incongruous rustle of the silk, moved across the open space, footing the boards timorously like bad ice, stealing a glace from face to face—the faces of strangers, of enemies, where wrath or contempt might suddenly flash forth. But she did not look at Jeremiah.

She gave her testimony in a dead, flat voice that carried only a few feet. Yes, that man had worn a barred handkerchief on his head. Yes, he had gone out of the house just after midnight. Yes, she had known the hour, she had heard the watch cry. Yes, she had heard him come in later. Yes, at breakfast he was queer-like when he heard the news. And after he had gone she had started to set his room aright and on the hearth, in the ashes, she had found what was left of a dark green, almost black, silk scarf or handkerchief. It must have got put out before it burned, for some water had been thrown on the coals. Maybe because the slop jar was full. She had to admit it was full. Anyway, the scarf or whatever it was had a knot in one corner and toward the other end of what was left was a hole cut out nice and neat about the size of your eye. She hadn't thought anything about it then, but had thrown it back. But later her husband, Mr. Jessup, he told her how the murderer wore a mask or something on his face, so she said how she had found this, and he got excited and she ran upstairs and grubbed in the ashes and found it. But she must have flung it on some hot coals in the corner where the water didn't get, because it had now smoldered some more and part was gone. But she had saved the rest.

At this Nathan Gregg produced the remnant of Jeremiah's green silk handkerchief, wrapped up in a piece of paper, the handkerchief he had worn on his brow on the ride to Frankfort and later had flung into the fire. Now Nathan Gregg gave it to the jury. The men passed it from hand to hand. All the while, Mrs. Jessup stared devotedly at the floor. She had never taken her eyes from the floor during her testimony.

On the cross-examination, Mr. Madison focussed his attention on the matter of the hole in the handkerchief. He produced a paper and requested that Mrs. Jessup draw the size and shape as true as she could of what she had originally found. Then the hole in its proper location. Was she sure that her sketch was about right? Would she swear it?

She answered yes, in a voice not above a whisper.

(Jeremiah leaned to Hawgood. "She is lying," he said. "You

can tell she is lying. That blackguard of a husband made her lie." Hawgood nodded.)

Had the very corner of the unconsumed part of the handkerchief shown the twist and pressure of a knot?

She answered yes to that. And the jurymen inspected the corner.

Mr. Madison picked up the sketch, and with the edge of his own handkerchief measured the distance from the corner to the indicated hole. He moved across to stand beside Jeremiah. He stood there a moment, while the room went dead quiet.

Then, in the quiet, he leaned, placed the corner of his handkerchief at the back of Jeremiah's neck, and brought the border forward toward the left eye. His thumb marking the distance to the hole according to Mrs. Jessup's sketch struck Jeremiah's head just at the forward edge of the ear.

"Look, gentlemen," Mr. Madison said, very softly. "I beg you, look. A strange eye-hole it would have been, gentlemen, to fall here. Perhaps it was an ear-hole. Though, of course, a trifle too small for this apparatus." He touched Jeremiah's ear.

The jurymen were leaning and staring, shuffling and snickering.

"Come," Mr. Madison invited, "won't one of you make the experiment?"

So the foreman came, measured from the chart on Mr. Madison's handkerchief, and applied it to Jeremiah's head.

Mr. Madison returned to Mrs. Jessup. When he spoke he had the constrained, patient air of someone dealing with a child, or an invalid. "My dear madame," he said, "my dear madame, you have seen where the hole . . ."

"Oh, I don't draw so good," she wailed. "I don't draw so good . . . I drawed the best I could but . . ."

"My dear madame," Mr. Madison repeated, more soothing than ever, "I am sure that you drew it very well. I am sure it was very true. Why, a lady who makes the nice calculations of sewing and household tasks would have an eye trained true and . . ."

"Oh, I drawed it the best I could!" she wailed, her head drooped on her chest, her shoulders shaking.

"Now, madame, now, madame," he murmured over and over, waiting for the fit to pass.

It was over at last, and he leaned at her: "Just one more question, and I apologize to impose upon your sensibilities. But just one more. You said that the hole had been cut out?"

She nodded, not trusting her voice.

"The handkerchief is very dark," he said, "a very dark green. Could it not have been burned out by contact with a coal, and you might not have noticed the char at the edge, for the fabric is so dark in color? For you did not look too carefully then, did you madame? For there was no reason to look carefully then? To you then it was just a rag on a hearth?"

She did not reply.

"Might it not have been burned?" Mr. Madison asked again, in his enormous patience.

Mrs. Jessup flung up her head as at a sudden stab of pain, and showed her fearful, tortured, gray face, and fixed her gaze on him.

Then Jessup coughed. He coughed twice. She looked at him. Then flung her wild, despairing gaze over the room. Suddenly she fixed on Jeremiah's face. . . .

Mr. Madison recalled her to the question. He asked again if the hole might not have been burned.

Jessup coughed.

She swung to face Mr. Madison.

"No!" she cried despairingly, twisting her weight in the chair, clenching her raw hands on the black silk, "no—it was cut—the hole was cut!"

Mr. Madison waited, while her head sank again to her chest, and her gaze fixed on the floor.

Then he said: "Thank you. That is all."

She tottered to her seat. And as she sat there, shapeless and sunk and heavy in the black, Jessup kept staring at her, gnawing his nether lip like a chunk of gristle to get the juice.

Jeremiah meditated that he did not envy her that coming evening in the privacy of her chamber.

The following day John Saunders took the stand to give his account of the night of the murder.

Then Mrs. Fort was called.

Jeremiah had not known that she was in the room. She had not been present on previous days, and this morning he had not noticed the gaunt figure in black, with the black veil, which Nathan Gregg now escorted like a queen to the stand. . . .

She was telling how when she had entered the hall, after hearing a noise, she had seen the assassin seize her husband by the wrist.

Then Nathan Gregg: "Did you see the assassin's face?"

She hesitated a long moment. Then she looked, for the first time, at Jeremiah. She peered at him, as though from shadow, ambush, or cranny, all her face sharpening at him. . . .

She peered at him, and he was sure that she was going to say, yes, she had seen the face of the assassin, and that was the face. And her finger, stiff and dry as bone, would point at him.

She would tell that lie. That was the lie the world would tell. She would say it.

But she did not say it. "No," she said, "I did not see—the murderer's face."

That was a trick, it was bound to be a trick, she was telling the truth to trick him.

"But I heard his voice," she said.

But not my voice, Jeremiah thought, *for my voice was disguised.*

"I heard his voice," she was repeating, "and I would know it anywhere, it rings so in my ears."

"Have you heard that voice since?" Nathan Gregg asked.

"Yes," she said.

"Will you please relate the circumstances?"

So she said that one day in May she had come with her brother, Mr. Saunders, to the Marton house, and Mr. Marton had conducted them to the door of the prisoner's room, which was ajar of a purpose, for all had been arranged. She had heard three men speaking within, and had picked out the prisoner's voice immediately. All had been arranged for the test. Mr. Marton had asked two gentlemen to call on the prison at a certain hour and talk with him. She had wanted this, though for a long time she had not believed the prisoner guilty, but that voice had been ringing in her ears, and she had known it.

He knew she was lying. She could not have known his true voice that night.

Then, looking at her, he knew that she was not lying. If what she said was a lie, it was a lie that she believed. It was her truth.

Ah, that is the thing to fear, he thought, *not the lie the world tells as a lie, but the lie the world holds as its truth.*

He was afraid. For the first time.

In the cross-examination, Hawgood concentrated on one issue, that of the voice.

Had she known what men were in the room with the prisoner?

No.

Did she now know?

Yes.

Who were they?

They were Mr. Sims Motlow and Mr. Amos K. Puckett, citizens of Frankfort.

Was she acquainted with either of the gentlemen?

With both.

How long had she known them?

She had seen Mr. Motlow around ever since he came to Frankfort, perhaps ten or twelve years. She had known Mr. Puckett for three years, more or less.

How well did she know Mr. Motlow?

She had a speaking acquaintance.

Ah, a speaking acquaintance?

Yes.

Did she have a speaking acquaintance with Mr. Puckett?

No.

Had she ever heard him speak?

Yes, but she had not known his name at the time. He had come to her brother's house and asked for him. Later her brother had told her the name.

How long ago?

Perhaps five or six months.

Who had chosen the men to go talk with the prisoner?

Her brother.

Might she not have remembered their voices and guessed that the third voice was that of the prisoner?

No. No. That would have been impossible. The voice rang in her ears.

Jeremiah was covertly watching the jury during the cross-examination. He was sure that they were impressed by Hawgood's attack. How could they fail to be impressed? But when he looked back at Mrs. Fort, he found nothing but certitude in her face. She was sure of her lie.

On what day of the month had she gone to the Marton house? Hawgood was asking.

She had gone on May 17, she said.

On May 17, Jeremiah thought. And: *Why, that was the day before they came to take me to the jail.*

So that was it. Mrs. Fort's identification had been strong enough to make Nathan Gregg sure that he could convict. But why had not Mrs. Fort identified the voice sooner? It had been ringing in her ears, she said. Why had she waited?

Jeremiah did not have the answer. But we have it. She had not done so because she feared that to accuse Jeremiah Beaumont would be to define his motive as revenge for Fort's seduction of Rachel Jordan, would be to cast her, Mrs. Fort, in the role of the unloved wife. She could not bear that thought.

But now she had changed her mind. Or circumstances had changed. Jeremiah sensed some change in the drift of things. Behind all the words and the waiting, some force was operating that he could not identify.

The words went on. . . .

All lies, all lies! Jeremiah thought. Then knew that it was not all lies. It was lies and truth, and lies told for truth and lies told for gain or vengeance, all twisted together. . . .

It was late in the seventh day of the trial. The sun struck in long, leveling rays across the heads of the crowd in the room. Judge Cooper lolled massively back, like a gorged bear, easy in the somnolent last wash of the afternoon. But his eyes blinked brightly under the shaggy brows.

But Nathan Gregg called one more witness. It was Carlos Bumps, his pig's eyes confident and cunning in his great slick face, a kind of animal grace in his movement despite the excess flesh and slovenly posture.

After the usual preliminaries, the prosecutor asked that he tell his tale in his own way.

"Me and two of the boys on the patrol," he began, "we was on Washington Street that night and it was gettin late, long past curfew, and we seen two nigger gals coming down the street. But bout the time they come close, two men what was drunk, like you could tell, come round the corner and seen them gals. One of them fellers grabbed a gal, but she squealed that kind of nigger-gal squeal and jerked back, and she and that-air other gal, they run up the street. Them boys with me— they was Ike Serle and Tom Postum—they started to talk and joke with them drunk fellers, but I was standing back some and seen another feller come along . . ."

Then Nathan Gregg interrupted: "Can you identify that man?"

"Yeah," Bumps said, "yeah, I shore can."

"Who was it?"

Bumps rolled his head easy on his shoulders, letting his

glance slide along the row of faces. Then it stopped, and without even turning his body, lifted his left hand and jerked the
thumb contemptuously over the left shoulder. "Him," he said,
"that-air Beaumont."

"What time was this?"

"Late. I know, fer eleven o'clock had done been called."

Nathan Gregg flashed his quick look of triumph over the
jury, then turned again to Bumps. "And now, Mr. Bumps," he
said, "at what hour did you go to the house of John Saunders?"

"That's sort of gettin ahead," Bumps said, and lolled back
easy and squinted at Gregg. "I seen something else, long afore."

"Well?" Gregg demanded, irritation flickering in his tone.

Mr. Madison was leaning toward Hawgood, whispering.
"Look, look," he whispered, "that blackguard is making a fool
of Gregg, he has deceived him, somehow."

And Hawgood, intent on Bumps, nodded.

"Yeah," Bumps was saying. And then with the faintest shade
of insolence: "Don't you want me to be tellin *all* I seen?"

"Yes," Gregg said. "Yes, of course. Tell it!" And Gregg
stiffened in his fine clothes.

"Yeah," Bumps said, "I seen that-air Beaumont come past,
his collar up and his hat pulled down, but it warn't that cold.
And he stopped of a sudden, just afore he got to the corner."

Bumps paused, shifted easily in his chair like a man relaxing
for pleasure, and waited for a second, to relish the silence all
around.

"Yeah," he said, "he stopped. Then he went over to the
door, and stood clost like he was knockin soft—but I couldn't
hear nuthin—and the door opened up, and it was dark inside.
The door opened up quick, like somebody was waitin in the
dark . . ."

Mr. Madison spoke sharply: "I object! The comments are
not relevant."

And Judge Cooper: "Objection sustained!"

Bumps looked up at the judge with easy innocence. "I'm

shore sorry, Judge," he said plaintively, "I was just aimin to tell the truth."

"Then that-air Beaumont," Bumps was continuing, "he slipped easy in the door, in the dark, and the door shut."

Bumps paused again, and shifted luxuriously in his chair. The chair creaked in the stillness.

"It was the third door off the corner," Bumps said. "Yeah," he repeated, "the third door." Then he sat up straight in his chair. "It is the door of the office what belongs"—he pointed— "to him."

His finger was pointing like a pistol at the heart of Sugg Lancaster.

It might have been a pistol, for Sugg Lancaster's face was white and sick with fear.

Mr. Madison leaned across Jeremiah to Hawgood. "My God," he whispered harshly, "I see it all. It's a trick to pin it on the New Court, to make the murder a conspiracy, to . . ."

And Bumps had eased back in his chair now and was saying ". . . and that-air Beaumont muster gone to git the lay of the land, to find out how the house was, and Colonel Fort's room and . . ."

Madison was up. "I object! The witness is . . ."

"Objection sustained!" Judge Cooper said.

And all the while Gregg stood there, stiff and stunned, swallowing hard.

"I see, I see it all," Mr. Madison was whispering, "it's a . . ."

And Jeremiah saw it too. It was a plot, brilliant and simple, to tie him and Lancaster together in the same package. Whatever had pointed to the guilt of one now pointed to the guilt of both. The argument would be simple. Lancaster by his own admission had known Jeremiah. Lancaster, close to the inner circle of New Court, had played on Jeremiah's prejudices and made of him a willing instrument. He had spied out the house for him. He had given him the last information and instructions. And Lancaster and Jeremiah would hang together.

Jeremiah now saw it all. Bumps and Jessup had everything.
They had a stronger case than the single case against Jeremiah.
They had cut Lancaster out of any share of the reward. They
had drawn Mrs. Fort and Saunders into their plan by making
Fort's death appear the result of a New Court conspiracy. That
had flattered Mrs. Fort's vanity and soothed her fears of being
named the unloved wife, and so she had been willing to identify
Jeremiah's voice.

Had Gregg been party to the project? Clearly not, Jeremiah
decided. Gregg's shock and Bumps' insolent relish had been
too real. It would have been easy for Jessup and Bumps to
point out to John Saunders that Gregg was, after all, New
Court in sympathy and would naturally prefer to treat the
crime as one of personal vengeance and not partisan fury. So
they would keep their secret and spring it on Gregg in court.
Then he would be forced to follow that line. If he wanted a
conviction. And Gregg wanted a conviction above all.

We can accept Jeremiah's guess. It accounts for all the facts.

Gregg had rallied and was continuing with the direct examination of his witness. Bumps was telling all the dreary and
predictable lies, the handkerchief at the Saunders door, the
boot pattern, the dirk, how Jeremiah had stolen both dirk and
handkerchief to destroy the evidence.

Mr. Madison's cross-examination was cool, savage and protracted. To take one section of the transcript:

Mr. M.: Where did you first notice the loss of the dirk?

B.: At Mr. Smart's house.

Mr. M.: You have testified that Mr. Beaumont had stolen
it from you?

B.: Yeah, he done it.

Mr. M.: How do you know?

B.: Well, a man just knows.

Mr. M.: How? Did you see him? Did you feel him? Did
you smell him?

B.: I just knowed.

Mr. M.: Are you sure, Mr. Bumps that you did not lose the dirk? After you had found that it would not cut the handkerchief, after you remembered that the wound in the victim was made by an edged weapon, after . . .

Objection.

Objection sustained.

Mr. M.: Well, Mr. Bumps, let us accept, for the purpose of discussion, that you did know by your mystic intuition that Mr. Beaumont had stolen your precious and incriminatory dirk. You say that you knew the fact at Smart's house?

B.: Yeah.

Mr. M.: When did you notice the loss of the handkerchief?

B.: At Bardstown, in the tavern.

Mr. M.: You have testified here that Mr. Beaumont had stolen it from you.

B.: Yeah.

Mr. M.: In the Bardstown tavern, when you discovered the loss, did you not first accuse Mr. Crawford of having lost it?

B.: Now look here, I ain't gonna be . . .

Mr. M.: You will answer the question. And may I remind you of the law of perjury?

Objection.

Objection sustained.

Mr. M.: Did you accuse Mr. Crawford of having lost it?

B.: Yea, but it was afore I knowed that . . .

Mr. M.: You have answered the question. You have admitted that you first accused Mr. Crawford of having lost the handkerchief.

B.: But you ain't sayin I . . .

Mr. M.: When Mr. Beaumont insisted that hunt be made for the handkerchief, you opposed such a plan?

B.: I didn't oppose nuthin. I just knowed that that-air Beaumont had stole it.

Mr. M.: How did you know it?

B.: I just knowed it.

Mr. M.: Like you *just knowed* he had stolen the dirk?

B.: Yeah.

Mr. M.: You were the custodian, Mr. Bumps, of two very important pieces of evidence. According to your account, you discovered that a dangerous and subtle fellow had stolen one piece of evidence, and then the next day you allowed him to steal the second. Don't you feel that you were a—a trifle—careless, Mr. Bumps?

Objection.

Objection sustained.

Tumult in the court.

It was a sad day for Bumps. Nothing could protect him— the objections of Gregg, his arrogance, his powerful hulk or the great hands that worked and knotted emptily in his lap with the knuckles glistening with sweat. Nothing could protect him against that cold, grinding savagery.

It was a torture and an exhibition. Jeremiah knew that it was an exhibition. He suddenly knew that Mr. Madison had long since finished with Bumps for all practical purposes. He was staging an exhibition. For whose benefit?

And then Jeremiah knew. It was for the benefit of Mr. Crawford. For Crawford's turn was to come, and now he could watch what might be in store for him. Oh, it didn't matter about Bumps, he would squirm and sweat and then it would be over. But it would matter for Crawford, to be ashamed before men, to be proved a liar, a dupe, and a fool, to be proved the companion of louts and knaves, to suffer the barbs and ironies of a gentleman like Mr. Madison, high-fronted, correct and severe in his black, confident in rank and power.

And Crawford knew, too. You could know that he knew, for he sat there streaked white in the face, gnawing his ragged mustache, staring with the fascination of horror at Bumps, his brother in abomination, the index of his last ruin. He had had land and servants—not much land and not many servants, but enough, enough. He had held his head up, and men like

Mr. Madison had acknowledged his grave bow. But now he was stuck in a stinking harness shop in a back street, and all that was left him was his black coat and his honor, and in an hour, a day, Mr. Madison would flay his honor from him, and that poor, threadbare black could never huddle him warm against the chill of disgrace.

So Crawford came to the stand, with the gaze of Jessup and Bumps, on one side, fixed upon him, and on the other, the gaze of Mr. Madison. So he could lift his eyes to neither side. At first, after the oath, he looked at the floor, and then, out of some last strength or desperation to escape, out of the window, over the heads of the people, into the glittering sky.

His tale was halting and confused. Gregg fretted and fumed under his professional calm, as Crawford blurred the answers to his questions. Yes, Bumps had tested the boot of Beaumont against the pattern. Had it fit? Yes, but in a manner of speaking. Had it fit? A man might say so if he made due allowance. Allowance for what? Well, the pattern wasn't drawed too well. Who drew the pattern? He himself had drawn the pattern. Had he known that the pattern wasn't drawn well. He had drawed the best he knew. How had he known it wasn't drawn well? Bumps had said it woggled, but for himself, he didn't know. Did woggling mean a mere wavering of outline? You might say so. Aside from the wavering of outline, the pattern had fit the boot? Yes—yes, if a man made due allowance and wanted to say so in a manner of speaking and—

Hawgood leaned to Mr. Madison and whispered, "Poor Gregg, he is breaking down his own witness for us."

Mr. Madison nodded, and studying Crawford, whispered back: "I never saw a more unwilling liar. If we nurse him, he may tell the truth in the end."

"Yes," said Hawgood, "and have his throat cut in an alley. Look at Bumps!"

Jeremiah looked at Bumps. Bumps was leaning forward, and baleful cunning glinted in the pig's eyes. "Yes," Jeremiah said, "there's murder there." He laughed. "And why shouldn't there be murder? With every word Crawford utters, Bumps loses a dollar."

And so it went on for the whole dreary tale. Crawford gave and took back, took back and gave. As Jeremiah puts it, he "spoke in riddles and shadow, gagged on *yes* and retched at *no*, and sought to conceal himself in the dusk of circumstance." And all the while Gregg suffered and fumed to fetch him out into the light.

"I'll fetch him out," Mr. Madison whispered grimly.

"He'll come to one bait," Jeremiah replied.

"What?"

"Your implicit belief in his honor."

Mr. Madison snorted. "Honor!" he whispered, "honor—that poor boggler!"

"Yes, honor," Jeremiah said. "For he will come to the lure of your belief that he will speak the truth."

"He will be afraid," Madison said.

"Yes," Jeremiah said, and studied Crawford again, "but he might risk it."

"And die for it," Mr. Madison said.

Hawgood, with his gaze fixed curiously on Crawford said, "Yes, yes, and die for it." Then he added, still looking at Crawford: "But men have died for truth before."

In the early afternoon, the dreary tale was over. And Mr. Madison took the witness. He took him with a massive courtesy and profound respect. He wished to compliment the witness, he said, on the love for the public good and attachment to justice that had inspired him last December "to leave the press of business and his thriving affairs" (at this the witness visibly straightened and looked about with a pitiful air of pride and vindication) and seek to "bring an assassin to book." Mr. Madison appreciated, he said, the difficulty of setting forth with perfect certainty small events of the past. And he more deeply appreciated the scruples exhibited by the witness in refusing to commit himself to statements on which he could not be perfectly clear before God and man.

At this point Nathan Gregg was on his feet, objecting.

But Mr. Madison interrupted him, "Am I to understand, sir," he demanded of the prosecutor, "that you do not share my belief in the scruples of the witness?"

Judge Cooper's gavel came down. "Will you proceed to business and question the witness," he ordered.

Mr. Madison bowed.

Crawford's answers were still larded with *disremembers* and *manners of speaking,* with evasions and confusions, but question by question he moved in an imperceptible drift, like a chip on the tide of Mr. Madison's certainty. He eddied and shifted, but the tide was sure. He looked into Mr. Madison's face and found there his strength, the illusion of strength. To Crawford, as Jeremiah says, Mr. Madison was a staff for the hand and the shadow of a rock.

The result, substantially, was that the pattern had not fitted the boot, that the dirk had torn rather than cut the handkerchief; that Bumps had lost the dirk and refused to search for it; that Bumps had lost the handkerchief, accused Crawford of having done so, and opposed any search; that the pattern produced at the Court of Inquiry might not have been the original pattern of the track under the Saunders' window, for he could not remember any identifying mark.

Then it was over, and as Crawford rose to go back to his seat, he found the eyes of Bumps and Jessup upon his. His knees gave and his hands trembled.

It was the end of the day.

"He may save his soul yet," Hawgood said.

"Wait till tomorrow," Mr. Madison replied. "They have not finished with him."

They had not finished with him. For the next morning, Crawford, sick in the face, sat for the re-direct examination by Gregg. Crawford remembered better now. He remembered that there had been a mark on the original pattern, a curious whorl in the paper, and that same whorl appeared in the pattern used at the Court of Inquiry. Many things came back to mind now. And he said them in his sick voice and never lifted his eyes from the floor.

"He lies, and all know it," Madison said savagely.

That seemed true—that all knew Crawford lied. And all knew that the trial was good as over and Jeremiah would walk out free. All seemed to know it except Gregg. Why didn't Gregg know it?

Then Jeremiah remembered: Gregg was depending on Marlowe and Marlowe's lie. Jeremiah remembered that with wicked glee, thinking how Marlowe would come on the appointed day to confound him. Then, with a stab of fear, he remembered one more thing: he, Jeremiah Beaumont, was also depending on Marlowe and Marlowe's lie. *Well, lie for lie,* he thought grimly, and the fear was gone. He knew which lie Marlowe would tell.

CALVIN COLTON

*B*LUEGRASS *politics was serious business in the first half of the nineteenth century. Opponents naturally assumed that they might become involved in personally unpleasant situations, and some even assumed there might be great violence. The Wickliffe-Benning tragedy was just such an incident. This affair stirred central Kentucky to fever heat. As exciting as the facts of the case were, the arguments produced by the defense counsel were more so. Few persons in Kentucky history have had two abler criminal lawyers defending them than did Charles Wickliffe (1807-1829). The contest in the courtroom was not between the Commonwealth's Attorney and the de-*

*fense, but rather it was a contest of arguments between the
defensive attorneys. Kentucky's legal giants, Henry Clay (1777-
1852) and John Jordan Crittenden (1787-1863) were before the
public in a display of talents extraordinary. In* The Life and
Times of Henry Clay *(New York, 1845), Calvin Colton gave the
background of the trial and a synopsis of the defense arguments,
together with a reconstruction of Clay's peroration that won
Wickliffe's acquittal.*

Prisoner on This Blessed Day

IN THE case of the commonwealth of Kentucky against Charles
Wickliffe, for killing Mr. Benning, editor of the Kentucky
Gazette, in Lexington, tried in 1829, Mr. Clay and the Hon.
J. J. Crittenden were counsel for the defendant. The case arose
from the following facts: Robert Wickliffe, Esq., the father
of Charles, had been running for the legislature against John
M. M'Calla, both of Lexington, during which time the latter
had published in the *Gazette* an article defamatory of his opponent, over the signature of *"Dentatus,"* which Charles proposed to resent for his father, but, being a minor by a few days,
his father forbade it. As soon, however, as he came to his majority, he called on the editor, Mr. Benning, and demanded
the author of *"Dentatus."* Mr. Benning asked time to consult
the author, which was granted. M'Calla, naturally preferring
that Benning should be exposed, rather than himself, told him,
that he was not obliged to give up the author, that he might
fall back on the privileges of an editor, and treat the demand
with contempt. He advised Benning, however, to arm himself
against the interview. Accordingly, when young Wickliffe
called, Benning declined giving the author, advised Wickliffe
to be content, and endeavored to intimidate him by saying,
that, if he knew the author, he would be the last man he would
wish to see. Whereupon an altercation ensued, and Benning

flourished his cane over the head of Wickliffe in a menacing manner, when the latter drew a pistol, and shot him. At this moment, Benning was darting into an adjoining room, as Wickliffe supposed, to seize a musket standing in the corner, which Wickliffe had seen. When some persons rushed in to interfere, Wickliffe was standing with another pistol in his hand, waiting for his opponent, and said: "Keep back. Let him come with his gun." But Benning had fallen from the first shot, and soon after died.

The defence set up was *excusable homicide*. Mr. Crittenden preceded, adduced the law and precedents, and made an able and eloquent defence, which the intelligent spectators supposed had exhausted the argument, so as to leave nothing for Mr. Clay. To their surprise, however, they saw Mr. Clay, when he rose, entering a new field. After a brief exordium, alluding to the facts, that it was a long time since he had been so engaged, and that nothing but the peculiar interest of the case, and his regard for the family of this unfortunate young man, would have induced him to appear on the occasion, he left behind him the entire field of argument, which had been so thoroughly explored by his colleague, and planted himself on the *natural right of self-preservation*—a right, he said, vested by the Creator in all animated being, on earth, in the air, in the waters—which was given to the first of our race, which all his posterity inherit, and which will abide to the last generation; and as a consequence of this right, that, whenever a man had just cause to believe that his life was in jeopardy, he was justified in slaying his antagonist, though it should afterward appear, that the danger was not real.

It can not be denied, that imagination was set to work in an argument of this kind; but it was imagination hovering over the nucleus of a sound principle, and lighting on a foundation as firm as the base of the hills. It was tasking this faculty of the human mind, given for use, with one of its legitimate functions—enticing and prompting it, in an appropriate exigency, to dive deeper than the organized forms of society, to rise higher, and to expatiate over a wider field, still keeping company with a principle, which every man finds in his own breast, as an ineradicable law of his being, and which he feels, knows to be right—*that he may defend his own life against impending violence.*

There was another point, on which Mr. Clay touched before the jury, constituting rather an appeal, than an argument, which, it has been represented, was overwhelming in its effect. It will be seen, however, in view of the whole case, as made by the evidence, that it was not only legitimate, but natural, and extremely forcible. It was the 4th of July, the natal day of American freedom, when Mr. Clay made this defence, and when the case was delivered over to the jury. The main point, which Mr. Clay urged, as already seen, was the *right of self-defence;* and it was made on the *evidence.* Here, then, according to the testimony, was a young man, who, most unfortunately, had killed an antagonist, to prevent being himself killed, which he supposed was the intention of his adversary, in his starting to seize a murderous weapon. This was precisely the principle, on which the Declaration of American Independence was founded. From the 4th of July, 1776, this anniversary had been a national jubilee—the joyous occasion of patriotic recollections—the day for every American to be glad in. The sun was bright, and everywhere throughout the bounds of this happy Union, except in Lexington, a nation of freemen were celebrating the achievements of their forefathers, who rose in *self-defence,* not to *kill,* but to assert a nation's rights, the rights of man. *Here was a* CASE: For asserting these rights, this young man was in court, a prisoner—a prisoner on this blessed day—surrounded and filled with the gloom of anxiety, his parents and friends anxious, all anxious, whether, on this birthday of a nation's freedom—freedom, acquired at the peril of the honor, the fortune, and *lives* of a whole people—whether he, the prisoner at the bar, who had only done the same thing, for the same object, should have a verdict of acquittal from a jury of freemen; whether he should go out, to smile and rejoice, under this smiling and rejoicing day, or whether he should be led, still a prisoner, and *condemned,* from this court to the jail, and from the jail to the penitentiary? "In his veins, too, runs the blood of all the Howards." His mother was a Howard, one of the best families in Kentucky.

The jury were absent but a few minutes, and by one o'clock young Wickliffe was free!

Mr. Clay spoke two hours and a half, and it has been represented by those who heard him, that he rose *above* himself, went *beyond* himself, astonished the court, the jury, the audience, and filled all with amazement.

Some of the graver passages of this effort of Mr. Clay, recited from memory to the author, by one who was present, and though doubtless imperfect, were certainly very striking, and not unworthy of the distinguished advocate. It is to be regretted, that such a labor of genius, prompted by the best, and addressed to the best feelings, should have been for ever lost, except in its immediate effect. One of the more humorous, sarcastic, ironical passages, the author is tempted to give, represented as follows: "Who is this redoubtable *'Dentatus?'* One would suppose, from the answer given to the just demand of my unfortunate client, that he were a Hercules in prowess, and a Cæsar in valor. Who is *'Dentatus?'* "—the manner and intonations of Mr. Clay, in putting this question, first in one way, and then in another, with unutterable significance, are represented to have been withering, annihilating. "Dentatus" himself was present, but, before the answer came out—the pause was as terrible as the question—"Dentatus" had vanished!—"Who is 'Dentatus?' Why, gentlemen of the jury"—here Mr. Clay drew himself down from his erect posture, till half bent, reducing himself to the smallest possible dimensions, looking like a dwarf, bringing his palms together, and with a voice as diminutive as he himself seemed to be, coming out from lips planted in the focus of an indiscribably ironical countenance— "why, gentlemen, *it is nobody but little Johnny M'Calla!*" A gentleman of some prominence in Lexington, since that time a member of Congress, but then a youth, is represented to have said, that, during the pendency of this question, "Who is 'Dentatus?' " recollecting, that he had written something against the father of young Wickliffe, begun to suspect himself, dodged behind another person, in fear of the eye and finger of Mr. Clay, and muttered to himself, "I am not 'Dentatus,' but, if he says so, I am a dead man." When, however, to his great relief, *"Little Johnny"* dropped from the lips of Mr. Clay, he breathed freely again, was proud of his acquittal, rose and stretched his neck to see *"Little Johnny"*—for whom all other eyes were also searching—"heard the floor crack" where he had seen "Little Johnny" but a moment before, and lo! "Little Johnny" was invisible!

Charles Wickliffe was killed in a duel, some time after his acquittal, by George J. Trotter, who succeeded the unfortunate Benning as editor of the *Gazette,* and Trotter has since been an inmate of the insane hospital!

JOSEPH HERGESHEIMER

As A BORDER state, Kentucky was caught midway in the crisis between the North and the South. The state had sent emigrants to both sections, and its economic interests were with both regions. Peace and national harmony was the only course between the sections which would serve the best interest of Kentucky. Joseph Hergesheimer (1880-1954), in The Limestone Tree *(New York, 1931), deals with a Kentucky in travail. Mixing fictitious names with those of real persons he develops a story of a Kentucky caught in the opening moments of a fratricidal war which the state's leaders tried so hard to prevent.*

The Right Age for Neutrality

ON THE third anniversary of the death of her husband, Manoah Abel, Susan Abel put on a white dress. She was preparing for the evening—it was an excessively hot day at the end of July—and the cool white India muslin was an enormous relief after the quantities of black clothes she had worn. The change, so soon after Manoah's death, must, she realized, cause a great deal of comment in Frankfort; all the women of her husband's numerous family and connections would resent it; but they would keep the comments, the resentment, to themselves; she would never hear them. That was partly because of her character—Susan did not encourage the familiarity of advice; and part because she was not a Kentuckian. She had been Susan Cutts, from New York City; Manoah met her in Washington, where, at that time, her father was a United States Senator. If she had been a Kentuckian, she knew, in all probability, she would never have laid aside the marks of a deepest mourning. Kentucky women were like that—they owned an indissoluble attachment, at once sentimental and passionate, for the men they married. Indeed, it was the custom to refer to the women who survived their marriages as the relicts of the masculine deceased.

A faint smile appeared for a moment on Susan Abel's face. A maid was on her knees, at Susan's back, settling her skirt; a second slave stood patiently with details of Susan's dress: a Chinese silver paper fan on a carved ebony stick, a minute square of Binche lace and a black enamelled vinaigrette. Yes, she told herself, the Kentucky women made miraculous wives; but, then, the men of Kentucky were equally splendid husbands. Manoah, as a husband, had been almost faultless; he was both tender and considerate, invariably patient with her, and decided. There had been nothing negative about Manoah

Abel. Quite the reverse. He was so positive that, more often than not, she had been concerned about the possibilities of his temper and acts. He had killed one man, Jarrot Bensalem; and, in spite of his asserted hatred of any violence, she had felt that provocation might easily produce other victims. She watched with a painful intensity for this trait—rather it was a tradition—in their son Elisha.

Susan Abel moved over to a long mirror; she did not trust negroes with even so slight an affair as a skirt. She had married Manoah in 1831, and they had gone directly to Frankfort; it was now 1861; and after thirty years she still disliked black servants. The truth was, she recognized, that she didn't do well with them. She was too stiff, too formal, too particular. It was necessary, she had discovered, to treat negroes with a direct interest and affection, and both, in that quarter, were impossible for her. Frankfort, compared with New York, was very simple and informal. Kentucky had been extremely generous, amiable with her; yet, now, she considered that her life here had not been a complete success. Its main engagement, her marriage, was extremely happy; at the same time she had never felt entirely at home.

In addition, her money created a difficulty in a society where money had very little reality. It wasn't, in Frankfort, regarded as an overwhelming fact; its power and influence were not obvious: the opportunities it created simply made a barrier between her and more narrowly limited individuals. The simplicity of Manoah's air where her great richness was concerned had been remarkable—he had regarded it with the honest and unaffected pleasure of a child. Her daughter Delia, who had married Robert Folkes and lived in Philadelphia, owned little of her father's simple charm. Delia, privately, was elaborate and cold. She had, Susan Abel thought, all the hard and unattractive qualities of the Cutts family. I used to be like that, she told herself, leaving the mirror. Her marriage, to the degree that she was capable of change, had changed her. A difficulty, however, existed all through her relationship with Manoah—she could never cure the impression that he was, at heart, actually childlike. Most women, she knew, enormously admired that quality in men they loved. Well, she didn't. There her hardness was apparent. She had, in consequence, felt slightly superior to Manoah. She didn't want to be superior to him; she wasn't, she told herself countless times; but that attitude—always, thank God, successfully concealed—remained faintly to harass her.

It came to this, generally, that people in the North were, perhaps fundamentally, different from the people of the South. The South was sustained by another tradition, local to itself. Provincial, Susan considered. It thought, she continued, with its heart; but then there was more than a chance, no better than the other, that in the North feeling was confined to the head. That, just now, was a very important realization, with a war beginning between the Union and the Confederacy. It was especially valuable, she thought, to Kentucky. Kentucky, lying between the two warring sections, owned the qualities, the necessities, of both; and, at any price, it must remain neutral. Her marriage to Manoah Abel was an example of what she meant—Elisha Cutts Abel, the result of that, belonged both to the North and South. She found Elisha waiting for her in the little drawingroom below.

"Mother!" he exclaimed; "it's simply marvelous to see you in white again. What a surprise. If I had known it nothing could have taken me out. I told Mason Hazel I would go to Greenland for supper." She studied him with a sharp repressed anxiety. Elisha was not—anyone could see that—strong. He was too thin. His cheeks were too hollow. He had pale hair, carefully brushed on a shapely head, the gray-blue eyes of his father, and a sensitive, colorless mouth. At the same time his voice, like his convictions, was strong; he had, his mother insisted, an unconquerable spirit. "I am glad you are going to the Hazels," she told him. "It's splendid for you to be with a lot of young people. I must have them here very soon. I think we are both too serious."

A quick shadow, a darkening frown, gathered on his features. "We can't help that," he pointed out. "It's a dreadfully serious time. John Hazel and Callam, and he's only sixteen, have joined Captain Morgan's company. With Mason that makes all three of them in the Lexington Rifles. Belvard Sash belongs to the Union Home Guards, and Wickliffe, his brother, is going right in the Confederate army. That puts me in a pretty poor light, with half my family for state's rights and the other half enlisted against them." She answered quickly and severely. "It does nothing of the kind. You are exactly right. Mr. Crittenden told you what he thought. Even Mr. John Breckenridge agreed with him. Kentucky will be neutral, Elisha; you will be far more useful if you stay neutral too. I detest all this enlisting and talk about arming Kentucky. You must not be carried away by it." He said, "I wonder if you are right? If that will be possible? I can't tell, mother, am I full of my own ideas or yours. You see, I am nearly twenty-four, and they ought to be my own." That, Susan informed him, must depend upon his comprehension. "If you are intelligent, if your ideas are your own, you won't help to create a war by going into it. You won't listen to the wild talk of people who have nothing to lose. The majority is always like that. Either you are superior or you are not. It is easier not to be. To go with the mob. There are difficulties connected with superiority, it is never popular, but I prefer it to the other. I especially prefer it for you. You will answer your doubts, you see, by what you do. Your actions will show how independent you are." The expression of troubled questioning, she observed, did not leave him.

"I suppose you are right," he half-heartedly agreed. "That doesn't make it easier for me when all the rest have ideas that are worth fighting for. I don't know anyone my age who is neutral. It isn't the right age for neutrality. I can tell you this—I haven't a particle of sympathy with the South. I'm for the Union. Father taught me that. He was always for it. He said Kentucky must never desert it. If I am neutral it will be to help the United States. Keep them together. Mother, I warn you, if Kentucky does uphold the Union I will support it with a Lincoln gun."

Her conversation with Elisha put Susan in a bad humor; she had, with Elisha gone, dinner alone, and through it she preserved a rigid demeanor. She drank neither sherry nor Madeira but, contrary to the local feminine habit, took brandy with her coffee. Susan was sixty years old; an age, she asserted, when she could with entire propriety drink what she pleased. Lately, she realized, she had been annoyed a number of times by Elisha. That was a new aspect of their relationship; he had not, until the present, been stubborn or contradictory. He had been willing to listen to her. He still, actually, listened to her, but now it was with reservations. He continually advanced opinions different from hers. She wanted him to have a mind of his own, in short to be a man, but she knew what was best for him. There was a great difference between the vigor of his spirit and the capability of his body, and she had to keep one from exhausting, breaking down, the other. It was, for example, absurd for Elisha even to consider being a soldier. He could not endure the hardships of a military life and campaigns. Elisha took cold at the slightest provocation, and there were other minor complications—his skin was too sensitive to bear the touch of wool. All his underclothes were especially made in New York of a fine cotton. In winter his greatcoat was deep with fur. He could only eat especial things, especially prepared. No, Elisha should never become a soldier.

That painful necessity would not arrive, Susan reassured herself, walking in the garden. The sky was densely purple with stars like a thin silver dust. The heat, she thought, had increased. The gate on Wilkinson Street clicked, and she could see the vague approaching form of a man. It was James Harlan. "I am glad you are here," she said at once, crisply; "I'm in what you might call a state of mind; you are always a relief." He begged her not to be too certain of that. "Are you alone for the evening?" he asked. "Yes," she replied, "I am. Until Elisha returns from Greenland. I should think at midnight." Harlan was glad of that. "James Speed is here from Louisville," he explained; "there is a gentleman with him we would both like you to meet. To listen to, Susan. It is Lieutenant William Nelson."

"Mr. Harlan," she replied, "Bull Nelson is the last man I want to see here. I am surprised. You ought to know how I feel about him." She could see that Harlan was smiling at her. "Dear Susan," he asserted, "you have made yourself so important to us, to the cause of Kentucky, that it is your duty to see him. The truth is we have something of the greatest importance to discuss. If you will allow me I'll fetch James Speed and Nelson." James Harlan's insistence, Susan realized, had increased her feeling of annoyance. She met the three men in her most formal drawingroom and at once conceived a marked dislike for William Nelson. He was a big robust man with a bright colored face and dense curling black hair; a man full of physical vigor and assertiveness. His manners were well enough.

"This is a privilege," he told Susan, with a bow. James Speed and Harlan were silent. "I asked Judge Harlan to bring me here," Nelson proceeded directly. "That, really, is why Speed and myself are in Frankfort. For the purpose of seeing you." Susan Abel said remotely, "Sit down, Mr. Nelson." She took a place on the small sofa under James Sash's portrait. "Mrs. Abel," Nelson proceeded, "you know, of course, all about what we now call the Lincoln guns. You know how I persuaded Mr. Lincoln to let us have five thousand muskets for the loyal men of Kentucky. You will remember they were shipped to Cincinnati and that I forwarded some to Jeffersonville, across the river from Louisville. Well, as you know too, they were at last delivered to the right men among us. The Home Guards in the different counties got them. Mrs. Abel, we said if the Home Guards were at least as well armed as Simon Buckner's State Guard we could make sure the rebels wouldn't force Kentucky into the Confederacy. We could keep

Kentucky neutral. A lot of people believed that, some believe
it still. They think the state can and ought to stay neutral.
That," he said gravely, "is now impossible."

"What does that mean?" Susan Abel demanded sharply. "I
don't understand you. Mr. Nelson, why is it impossible for
Kentucky to stay neutral?"

"For three reasons," Nelson concisely replied; "the first is
the fact that neutrality does not and never can exist. Neither
side wants it. Kentucky has a safe majority for the Union. At
the same time there is a strong state rights sentiment. Men
are for you or against you but they are not neutral. When the
State Legislature, in May, declared for that it was actually a
Union measure. When it refused to call a sovereign convention, and refer the position of the state to the people, that was
a Union measure. The legislature, frankly, was afraid to risk
so much. The Union leaders needed time. They knew that
when the Kentucky people deliberated it would be to act
sensibly."

"You make it sound like a legislature of women," Susan
commented.

He ignored that. "The second reason is physical," William
Nelson asserted. "We have seven hundred miles of unprotected
border, and three Union states, on the North, but on the
South there is one Confederate state, Tennessee, and only one
important passageway into Kentucky. We are cut off, in other
words, from the South; we are a continuous land, except for
the Ohio river, with the North. Mrs. Abel, we are not a cotton
state; negroes are unimportant to us; what Georgia and Ala-
bama want would be fatal here. There are some of us who
think the Union can't be held together without Kentucky. If
that is so it would be fatal to hesitate."

"None of that is new or very moving," Susan replied. "We
all realize Kentucky borders on the Ohio and that there are
mountains in Tennessee. Please remember that I have given
a large amount of money to help organize, and even arm, the

Home Guards. When I did that I was assured it would be used to keep Kentucky out of the war. That promise, Judge Harlan will recall it, was made to me in this room. Now you say it was impossible. My money must be spent for a purpose I abhor."

"What Mrs. Abel says is true," James Harlan confessed. "I wish I could contradict it. I can't. Events have proved too much for us. The Southern sentiment especially. That in itself forced us to give up all hope of remaining neutral." It had been vain from the first, James Speed added. "Perhaps there will be neutrality in heaven; Nelson is right, there is none, worth the name, on earth. Walker, the Confederate Secretary of State, wrote Magoffin for troops as early as April. The same month Blanton Duncan advertised in the *Louisville Journal* he was enlisting men for the South. We all know what Taylor's purpose was in Kentucky. My brother, Joshua, who is close to the President, told me that Mr. Lincoln admitted our need of Kentucky."

"How can it matter what Mr. Lincoln admits?" Susan asked contemptuously: "if I have any sympathy with the South it is because of Mr. Lincoln. He is too grotesque! Fortunately he isn't important. We must have him, I suppose, for four years, and then he can be forgotten."

"The third reason," William Nelson went on, "is more difficult to explain. The Kentucky mind, Mrs. Abel, is instinctively loyal. The attachments of a Kentuckian are firm. We are not a cunning people. It is possible we could be called slow-minded. I am not certain that is a bad quality. It is not bad where the stability of a country is concerned. Such people are, at bottom, practical; the history of the state has been a record of practical difficulties: commerce and currency and the soil. The South is different. It is chimerical. No, the South would not suit us. We belong by nature and situation and spirit to the Union." He convinced Susan of nothing. "You must not expect me to support you in any of this," she told Harlan. "I

won't help to drag Kentucky into a war that will divide families and set brothers to killing each other. I am sorry I gave
a dollar for the Lincoln guns." James Harlan rose and bowed
profoundly. "Forgive us," he begged her; "this is all most
unbecoming to your charm."

Susan Abel, naturally, said nothing to Elisha about the visit
of Judge Harlan with Speed and Lieutenant Nelson. She had
breakfast with him late of the following morning, in a small
half-open paved space back of the diningroom. The house had
been built by James Sash, early in the century; he had attached
a conservatory to the diningroom; but Susan, when she moved
with Manoah to Frankfort, had changed it into a pleasant and
informal place for breakfast. She gathered it had been very
vigorous at Greenland. "Wickliffe Sash all but had a fight with
Belvard," Elisha told her. "You wouldn't have guessed they
were brothers. Wickliffe is the only one in his family who is
for the South. He enlisted in Saunders Bruce's company, at
Lexington, last week. He told Belvard that no one who was
anything would be a black Republican. Not in Kentucky. He
said only storekeepers and men from the mountains were. It
didn't matter, Wickliffe said, what they did or thought. They
were not gentlemen."

"Didn't Wickliffe think his brother Belvard was a gentleman?" Susan asked. He ignored that. "Wickliffe said the
Southern cause was beautiful," Elisha continued; "but there
wasn't any nobility at all in the North. They just wanted to
steal our niggers. You couldn't love the North, he said, but
you had to love the South." His mother wanted to know what
he had replied. "It was hard," Elisha admitted. "Most of what
I could say seemed so cold. After Wickliffe. It was no good
bringing up the Constitution again. I did explain how hard
we had tried to make a country, and fought against nearly
everybody to do it, and how frightful it would be for it all to
go to nothing. The Hazels agreed with Wickliffe of course.
Mason said he wouldn't allow anyone to come into his garden

and take a flower let alone his negroes. I don't know why—
and it's exactly what I said—but all the arguments for the South
are so much handsomer than any of ours."

"Emotion appears handsomer than reason," Susan Abel carefully explained. "It isn't really. Only the most superior people
understand and appreciate reason. It's nonsense to say that all
the highly-bred men of Kentucky are for states rights and the
rest are storekeepers. Mr. Crittenden is for the Union, and
so is Mr. Guthrie. Judge Nicholas is Union, and Doctor Breckenridge and Judge Harlan and Mr. Todd and Garrett Davis
and George Robertson. They were every one friends of your
father's. General Combs is a Union supporter, and Mr. Bris-
tow is and Charles Marshall. That is why Kentucky must stay
out of the war. Elisha, we'd be so badly injured we would
never recover. Never." He spoke doubtfully. "I don't know
if I told you, mother, Camp Dick Robinson is going to be offi-
cially opened the day after election, and I want to be there.
Everybody will. All the Sashes, of course, and the News. Even
the Hazels and people who are against it."

Susan Abel was silent; she was, seemingly, intent upon her
coffee cup. In reality she was thinking as rapidly as possible:
Camp Dick Robinson was the Union station for recruits William Nelson had established on the Danville pike south of Lexington. She did not want Elisha to grow familiar with it; she
wanted to keep him as far removed as possible from the military
spirit it must create; but, obviously, she could not forbid him
to go there. After all, as Elisha had pointed out, he was twenty-
three years old. "I am certain it will be stupid," she said;
"there won't really be a camp, with soldiers and drilling, for
weeks yet; but if the family is going, and you'd like to, I'll go
with you." It seemed to Susan that a faint disappointment settled over Elisha; and that increased the annoyance with him
that had possessed her for the last few days. She barely restrained an angry comment. "It will be very nice," he said,
rising. "Will you excuse me. I have to ride into Frankfort."

Susan wondered, alone, about her whole attitude toward Elisha. Her demands, where he was concerned, were very rigid. Possessive. But, she repeated, she wanted him to have a right sort of life, full of the things she knew were good for him. There was more than a chance, with his father's uncritical blood in him, that he might make a serious and perhaps fatal error of choice. She must prevent that. Elisha had no interest in girls; none in marriage; until now Susan had been privately glad of that. Perhaps it was a mistake. If she could select a girl suitable for Elisha, a girl at once well-born and simple and modest, she might be a help with him. Together they could, without doubt, manage Elisha.

He wasn't, Susan Abel realized, easy to manage. There was Cutts blood in him as well as his father's. She was driving with him to the camp established on Dick Robinson's farm; it was the middle of morning; the sky was overcast, threatening rain, and the heat had mitigated. The Danville pike was filled with carriages and wagons all moving toward the encampment. Susan saw most of her familiar world. The camp itself, exactly as she had predicted, was the reverse of impressive. There was no military organization, no officers formal in smart uniforms, no stirring music. A company of men from Tennessee was actually in rags. William Nelson, accompanied by Thomas Bramlette and a Mr. Landrum, came up to her at once. She presented Elisha to Lieutenant Nelson and was carefully polite. "You see," Nelson said pleasantly, "we are still practical instead of imposing."

Susan was appropriately gracious. "Our tents," he continued, "are the maple trees, and our guns are sticks. We hope to change that." James Harlan, mounted on an informal stand, spoke. He had dismissed, Susan realized, all pretense of neutrality. A nondescript collection of recruits stood facing him, and back of that the carriages and wagons, the countryside, were banked. "Men of Kentucky," Judge Harlan said, "and those of you who have come from Tennessee, we welcome you here to earth of the United States. You stand on soil of the Union. This, today, is an especial part of the glorious state of Kentucky. Today it is especial, an enlisting place for men who believe in the Union, but tomorrow I hope it will be no more than part of the soil of a whole loyal state. Anything else is unthinkable."

Gabriel Sash was standing beside Susan Abel's carriage, and he said, "That is plain enough. If it goes on like this we'll have Simon Buckner and the State Guard shooting us down." Not, she returned, without some show of justice. "I am opposed to all of it, Gabriel," she reasserted. "If you want to keep out of war stay away from powder. It was a mistake, I see now, to arm the Home Guards. Let General Buckner march his companies into the Southern army. That wouldn't hurt us. Not really. Kentucky can take care of itself." He replied, "I am afraid it is too late. Now that we have a Union legislature. The states rights party only carried one district in the west." Elisha asked what that would mean. His mother answered for Gabriel Sash. "If there are enough hotheaded fools, like those around us, it will mean war. One part of you, Elisha, will turn on the other." Mr. Crittenden was speaking.

"I have consistently tried to avert the possibility of a strife too terrible for words. Kentucky, of olden time, has been inured to battle, but Kentuckians have never fought among themselves. History has indicated what the horrors of that fratricidal war must be. Courageous men, honorable and bitter in principle, arrayed in the panoply of Bellona. Desolated mothers. Our silver streams, in that event, would run crimson, a lurid glare bathe Kentucky in the tints of hell. But there are worse things than living streams of blood. There is One, the greatest of all, who willingly gave His blood to purify men. If Kentucky, in her noble turn, is forced to emulate Him—," Susan Abel turned to her son. "I am sorry," she said; "I am quite faint. Do you mind very much taking me home." There was nothing, naturally, that could furnish him with an objection. When they were free of the camp Elisha gazed at her curiously. "Do you know," he said at last, "that is absolutely the first time I ever heard you were faint. It ought to worry me a lot." She touched his hand affectionately, and sat back with closed eyes.

JOHN FOX, JR.

*L*ONG *before Joseph Hergesheimer saw in Kentucky's plight as a neutral state the material for a novel, John Fox, Jr. (1862-1919) wrote what is possibly his best book,* The Little Shepherd of Kingdom Come *(New York, 1903). The author's most vital concern was with the divergency of social and political reactions between the Bluegrass and the mountains. Chad Buford was an emotional witness to the fratricidal war. He stood by and saw brothers choose sides, and then he himself had to make the decision which cut him off from his relatives and friends in the Bluegrass.*

The Low Sound of Sobbing

THROUGHOUT that summer Chad fought his fight, daily swaying this way and that—fought it in secret until the phantom of neutrality faded and gave place to the grim spectre of war— until with each hand Kentucky drew a sword and made ready to plunge both into her own stout heart. When Sumter fell, she shook her head resolutely to both North and South. Crittenden, in the name of Union lovers and the dead Clay, pleaded with the State to take no part in the fratricidal crime. From the mothers, wives, sisters and daughters of thirty-one counties came piteously the same appeal. Neutrality, to be held inviolate, was the answer to the cry from both the North and the South; but armed neutrality, said Kentucky. The State had not the moral right to secede; the Nation, no constitutional right to coerce: if both the North and the South left their paths of duty and fought—let both keep their battles from her soil. Straightway State Guards went into camp and Home Guards were held in reserve, but there was not a fool in the Commonwealth who did not know that, in sympathy, the State Guards were already for the Confederacy and the Home Guards for the Union cause. This was in May.

In June, Federals were enlisting across the Ohio; Confederates, just over the border of Dixie which begins in Tennessee. Within a month Stonewall Jackson sat on his horse, after Bull Run, watching the routed Yankees, praying for fresh men that he might go on and take the Capitol, and, from the Federal dream of a sixty-days' riot, the North woke with a gasp. A week or two later, Camp Dick Robinson squatted down on the edge of the Bluegrass, the first violation of the State's neutrality, and beckoned with both hands for Yankee recruits. Soon an order went round to disarm the State Guards, and on that very day the State Guards made ready for Dixie. On that day the crisis came at the Deans', and on that day Chad Buford made up his mind. When the Major and Miss Lucy went to bed that night, he slipped out of the house and walked through the yard and across the pike, following the little creek half unconsciously toward the Deans', until he could see the light in Margaret's window, and there he climbed the worm fence and sat leaning his head against one of the forked stakes with his hat in his lap. He would probably not see her again. He would send her word next morning to ask that he might, and he feared what the result of that word would be. Several times his longing eyes saw her shadow pass the curtain, and when her light was out, he closed his eyes and sat motionless—how long he hardly knew;

but, when he sprang down, he was stiffened from the midnight chill and his unchanged posture. He went back to his room then, and wrote Margaret a letter and tore it up and went to bed. There was little sleep for him that night, and when the glimmer of morning brightened at his window, he rose listlessly, dipped his hot head in a bowl of water and stole out to the barn. His little mare whinnied a welcome as he opened the barn door. He patted her on the neck.

"Good-by, little girl," he said. He started to call her by name and stopped. Margaret had named the beautiful creature "Dixie." The servants were stirring.

"Good-mawnin', Mars Chad," said each, and with each he shook hands, saying simply that he was going away that morning. Only old Tom asked him a question.

"Foh Gawd, Mars Chad," said the old fellow, "old Mars Buford can't git along widout you. You gwine to come back soon?"

"I don't know, Uncle Tom," said Chad, sadly.

"Whar you gwine, Mars Chad?"

"Into the army."

"De ahmy?" The old man smiled. "You gwine to fight de Yankees?"

"I'm going to fight *with* the Yankees."

The old driver looked as though he could not have heard aright.

"You foolin' this ole nigger, Mars Chad, ain't you?"

Chad shook his head, and the old man straightened himself a bit.

"I'se sorry to heah it, suh," he said, with dignity, and he turned to his work.

Miss Lucy was not feeling well that morning and did not come down to breakfast. The boy was so pale and haggard that the Major looked at him anxiously.

"What's the matter with you, Chad? Are you sick?"

"I didn't sleep very well last night, Major."

The Major chuckled. "I reckon you ain't gettin' enough

sleep these days. I reckon I wouldn't either, if I were in your place."

Chad did not answer. After breakfast he sat with the Major on the porch in the fresh, sunny air. The Major smoked his pipe, taking the stem out of his mouth now and then to shout some order as a servant passed under his eye.

"What's the news, Chad?"

"Mr. Crittenden is back."

"What did old Lincoln say?"

"That Camp Dick Robinson was formed for Kentuckians by Kentuckians, and he did not believe that it was the wish of the State that it should be removed."

"Well, by ——! after his promise. What did Davis say?"

"That if Kentucky opened the Northern door for invasion, she must not close the Southern door to entrance for defence."

"And dead right he is," growled the Major with satisfaction.

"Governor Magoffin asked Ohio and Indiana to join in an effort for a peace conference," Chad added.

"Well?"

"Both governors refused."

"I tell you, boy, the hour has come."

The hour had come.

"I'm going away this morning, Major."

The Major did not even turn his head.

"I thought this was coming," he said quietly. Chad's face grew even paler, and he steeled his heart for the revelation.

"I've already spoken to Lieutenant Hunt," the Major went on. "He expects to be a captain, and he says that, maybe, he can make you a lieutenant. You can take that boy Brutus as a body servant." He brought his fist down on the railing of the porch. "God, but I'd give the rest of my life to be ten years younger than I am now."

"Major. I'm *going into the Union army.*"

The Major's pipe almost dropped from between his lips. Catching the arms of his chair with both hands, he turned heavily and with dazed wonder, as though the boy had struck

him with his fist from behind, and, without a word, stared hard
into Chad's tortured face. The keen old eye had not long to
look before it saw the truth, and then, silently, the old man
turned back. His hands trembled on the chair, and he slowly
thrust them into his pockets, breathing hard through his nose.
The boy expected an outbreak, but none came. A bee buzzed
above them. A yellow butterfly zigzagged by. Blackbirds chat-
tered in the firs. The screech of a peacock shrilled across the
yard, and a ploughman's singing wailed across the fields:

> Trouble, O Lawd!
> Nothin' but trouble in de lan' of Canaan.

The boy knew he had given his old friend a mortal hurt.

"Don't, Major," he pleaded. "You don't know how I have
fought against this. I tried to be on your side. I thought I was.
I joined the Rifles. I found first that I couldn't fight *with* the
South, and—then—I—found that I had to fight *for* the North.
It almost kills me when I think of all you have done—"

The Major waved his hand imperiously. He was not the man
to hear his favors recounted, much less refer to them himself.
He straightened and got up from his chair. His manner had
grown formal, stately, coldly courteous.

"I cannot understand, but you are old enough, sir, to know
your own mind. You should have prepared me for this. You
will excuse me a moment." Chad rose and the Major walked
toward the door, his step not very steady, and his shoulders a
bit shrunken—his back, somehow, looked suddenly old.

"Brutus!" he called sharply to a black boy who was training
rosebushes in the yard. "Saddle Mr. Chad's horse." Then,
without looking again at Chad, he turned into his office, and
Chad, standing where he was, with a breaking heart, could
hear, through the open window, the rustling of papers and the
scratching of a pen.

In a few minutes he heard the Major rise and he turned to
meet him. The old man held a roll of bills in one hand and
a paper in the other.

"Here is the balance due you on our last trade," he said, quietly. "The mare is yours—Dixie," he added, grimly. "The old mare is in foal. I will keep her and send you your due when the time comes. We are quite even," he went on in a level tone of business. "Indeed, what you have done about the place more than exceeds any expense that you have ever caused me. If anything, I am still in your debt."

"I can't take it," said Chad, choking back a sob.

"You will have to take it," the Major broke in, curtly, "unless—" the Major held back the bitter speech that was on his lips and Chad understood. The old man did not want to feel under any obligations to him.

"I would offer you Brutus, as was my intention, except that I know you would not take him—" again he added, grimly, "and Brutus would run away from you."

"No, Major," said Chad, sadly, "I would not take Brutus," and he stepped down one step of the porch backward.

"I tried to tell you, Major, but you wouldn't listen. I don't wonder, for I couldn't explain to you what I couldn't understand myself. I—" the boy choked and tears filled his eyes. He was afraid to hold out his hand.

"Good-by, Major," he said, brokenly.

"Good-by, sir," answered the Major, with a stiff bow, but the old man's lip shook and he turned abruptly within.

Chad did not trust himself to look back, but, as he rode through the pasture to the pike gate, his ears heard, never to forget, the chatter of the blackbirds, the noises around the barn, the cry of the peacock, and the wailing of the ploughman:

> Trouble, O Lawd!
> Nothin' but trouble—

At the gate the little mare turned her head toward town and started away in the easy swinging lope for which she was famous. From a cornfield Jerome Conners, the overseer, watched horse and rider for a while, and then his lips were lifted over his protruding teeth in one of his ghastly, infrequent smiles.

Chad Buford was out of his way at last. At the Deans' gate, Snowball was just going in on Margaret's pony and Chad pulled up.

"Where's Mr. Dan, Snowball?—and Mr. Harry?"

"Mars Dan he gwine to de wah—an' I'se gwine wid him."

"Is Mr. Harry going, too?" Snowball hesitated. He did not like to gossip about family matters, but it was a friend of the family who was questioning him.

"Yessuh! But Mammy says Mars Harry's teched in de haid. He gwine to fight wid de po' white trash."

"Is Miss Margaret at home?"

"Yessuh."

Chad had his note to Margaret, unsealed. He little felt like seeing her now, but he had just as well have it all over at once. He took it out and looked it over once more—irresolute.

"I'm going away to join the Union army, Margaret. May I come to tell you good-by? If not, God bless you always.

CHAD."

"Take this to Miss Margaret, Snowball, and bring me an answer here as soon as you can."

"Yessuh."

The black boy was not gone long. Chad saw him go up the steps, and in a few moments he reappeared and galloped back.

"Ole Mistis say dey ain't no answer."

"Thank you, Snowball." Chad pitched him a coin and loped on toward Lexington with his head bent, his hands folded on the pommel, and the reins flapping loosely. Within one mile of Lexington he turned into a cross-road and set his face toward the mountains.

An hour later, the General and Harry and Dan stood on the big portico. Inside, the mother and Margaret were weeping in each other's arms. Two negro boys were each leading a saddled horse from the stable, while Snowball was blubbering at the corner of the house. At the last moment Dan had decided to leave him behind. If Harry could have no servant, Dan, too, would have none. Dan was crying without shame. Harry's face was as white and stern as his father's. As the horses drew near the General stretched out the sabre in his hand to Dan.

"This should belong to you, Harry."

"It is yours to give, father," said Harry, gently.

"It shall never be drawn against my roof and your mother."

The boy was silent.

"You are going far North?" asked the General, more gently. "You will not fight on Kentucky soil?"

"You taught me that the first duty of a soldier is obedience. I must go where I'm ordered."

"God grant that you two may never meet."

"Father!" It was a cry of horror from both the lads.

The horses were waiting at the stiles. The General took Dan in his arms and the boy broke away and ran down the steps, weeping.

"Father," said Harry, with trembling lips, "I hope you won't be too hard on me. Perhaps the day will come when you won't be so ashamed of me. I hope you and mother will forgive me. I *can't* do otherwise than I *must*. Will you shake hands with me, father?"

"Yes, my son. God be with you both."

And then, as he watched the boys ride side by side to the gate, he added:

"I could kill my own brother with my own hand for this."

He saw them stop a moment at the gate; saw them clasp hands and turn opposite ways—one with his face set for Tennessee, the other making for the Ohio. Dan waved his cap in a last sad good-by. Harry rode over the hill without turning his head. The General stood rigid, with his hands clasped behind his back, staring across the gray fields between them. Through the window came the low sound of sobbing.

HENRY WATTERSON

O*N DECEMBER 25, 1868, Henry Watterson (1840-1921) had been editor of the Louisville* Courier-Journal *just a month and a half. He had, nevertheless, spent three years watching the South being brought under the domination of the radical Republican party. He saw the shape of the error which was growing in the nation. Instead of restoring the Union and erasing old hatreds, the radicals were opening deep new wounds and further irritating the old sores.*

Dipping into pioneer Kentucky history, Marse Henry found a theme for his Christmas-day editorial for the young Courier-Journal. *He spoke from the vantage point of freedom in the borderland, yet from a region where sympathy for the South had become intense. He was able to name the miscreants who were perpetrating the reconstruction blunder upon the South, and to view their despotism with a keen sense of its future meaning.*

These Noble Sentiments

A LITTLE after mid-day on the 25th of December, 1778, a group of ten or a dozen pioneers in buckskin knee-breeches and linsey-woolsey hunting-shirts gathered around a log heap in front of a cabin, which, from a high cliff, overlooked the frozen bed and snowy banks of the Kentucky River. It was very bleak and cold. The sun had not shone out since the second day of the month. The streams were everywhere choked with ice. The very springs were inaccessible, and game was scarce and powder scarcer still. Foremost among the little knot of woodsmen were Daniel Boone and James Harrod; and they had met, as they declared, to offer up their prayers to God on behalf of the "brave men and patriots" who were "fighting the battles of freedom beyond the mountains." They knelt down and ¡ rayed accordingly; they sang a hymn; they adopted what they called a resolution; and then, having affirmed devotion to the cause of the colonies against the Crown, they dispersed, each going his several ways, but all inspired by the same good purpose and free-born spirit.

In those days there were negro slaves in Massachusetts. There were none in Kentucky. But the laws of commerce and of climate had their way. The Massachusetts slaveholders found that negro labor was not profitable among them. They, therefore, sold their slaves into the South and invested the money in that which was profitable. No one blames them. They did what they thought was best and what they had undoubted right to do. The times were not so "civilized" nor so "progressive" as they have since become. Doubtless if Massachusetts had the matter to reconsider and go over again, she would free all of her slaves, vote each family a homestead, build for each a snug cottage and, having comfortably stowed the poor dears away in cosy homes, kindle for each a blazing fire, put a kettle on it and thrust into the kettle a Christmas turkey, amid whose steaming odors the songs of Whittier and of freedom would ascend to heaven!

Time sped on. There was a deal of trouble for many and many a year; and wars with the savages; and wars with Britain; and wars with Mexico, and tariff wars and what not. But the country went on growing and prospering until it was so big and prosperous that it forgot its early vows and its early struggles and its early lessons. More's the pity! It forgot them all, and it fell together by the ears and no man can say that it did not demonstrate to the full its boasted fighting capacity. Somebody, however, had to get the better of the shindy; and the muscle and the numbers were with the North, and the North came out winner. It won not only the practical item which it contended for, but in the scuffle it got several trifles which it had not at first expected; so that, the arms of the combatants

being laid aside, the spectacle that was presented to the world
was curious to see—slavery gone; secession abandoned; the
Union in condition for immediate restoration; and peace hovering, like a goddess crowned with olive-leaves, about the
threshold of every home in the land.

We do not propose to review what followed. Kentucky was
not one of the seceding States. She stood true to the principles
which were enunciated in those memorable resolutions at
which it is common to hear men sneer. Whatever may be said
of those resolutions, they embody a just and true spirit, and
mean nothing which is base, or sordid, or narrow, or slavish,
or mean. Kentucky's head was with the Union and her heart
was with the South; for it is the nature of a generous and
manly people to sympathize with the weak in its struggles with
the strong. The war closed. Kentucky alone of the free States
that were left in the Union was true to herself and to the professions with which the war was begun. She proscribed no one.
She gave welcome to all. Today she is prosperous, peaceful,
happy. The laws are better enforced in Kentucky than in
Indiana. There is less crime in Kentucky than in Ohio. Tennessee is poor. Missouri is poor. Both are the victims of des-
potic power running roughshod over the liberties and disre-
garding the private rights of the people. In Kentucky there is
no partisan militia. In Kentucky there are no franchise laws.
In Kentucky there are no threats of confiscation. Public opinion is the only arbiter of public questions, and every man is
allowed to hold office who obtains votes enough. As in Massachusetts, public opinion is very much one way. There the people
are Republicans for the most part; vote the Republican ticket;
decline to vote for Democratic candidates or Democratic measures and are, we dare say, conscientious. Here it is exactly
reversed. We are, for the most part, Democrats; we vote the
Democratic ticket; we decline to vote for Republican candidates
and measures; we are perfectly honest and think we have a
right, as free citizens of a free republic, to decide for ourselves.

For so doing and so thinking we are denounced as traitors to our country and a despotism is sought to be placed over us by those who claim that we ought to be forced to vote for Republican candidates and Republican measures, and who declare that if we do not, we are guilty of rebellion and should be punished therefor.

This was not the spirit of Boone and his companions, who prayed God to bless Massachusetts on Christmas day, 1778. It was not the spirit of the Kentuckians who fought the battles of the country from King's Mountain to the City of Mexico. It is a new-born spirit; the spirit of rapine and war, not of liberty and peace. That the people of Kentucky should regard it with detestation is reasonable and natural. That they should cling the more tenaciously to their original fastening as the pressure from without becomes more violent is also reasonable and natural. But they are not intolerant nor inhospitable, but kind, generous, peaceful, enterprising, progressive; faithful to the past; liberal with the present; hopeful of the future. The snows of nearly a hundred years have come and gone since the Christmas of 1778. Many a change has come also over the land. The canebrakes are all gone. The old pioneers are all gone. Their graves are deep-sunken under the ploughshare, and are hid beneath the clover blooms. But the hardy manhood; the warm, impulsive love of freedom; the honest hatred of persecution; the keen sympathy with the weak and suffering, all these noble sentiments that honored the lives of the fathers remain and are illustrated by the children in the unanimity with which they resist the despotism set up over their brothers of the South. Remove this despotism, and we may divide on a thousand issues; but as long as it continues we are one in opposing it as unnecessary, tyrannical, and cruel.

HUGHES, SCHAEFER, AND WILLIAMS

In SOME respects post-bellum Kentucky history can be divided into two distinct periods. The date of the division can be pinpointed on January 30, 1900, when William Goebel (1856-1900) was shot. This incident also marked a changing phase in Kentucky politics. Historians have written many pages on the Goebel tragedy, and the subject is still good for an extended and heated conversation. No one knows precisely who killed the Covington politician, although experts of all sorts have named the murderer and the courts sent two men to the penitentiary for the crime.

The reasons for Goebel's murder are known. These are involved in a long era of failure in the process of democratic government in Kentucky, during which interests of all sorts had enjoyed a relatively free hand in self-service from the state government. As yet one of the best background sources for this important incident is that written by three newspapermen, Robert E. Hughes, Frederick W. Schaefer, and Eustace L. Williams, That Kentucky Campaign *(Cincinnati, 1900).*

Awful Deed of Wrath

"Goebel has been assassinated!"

Never did news travel so fast over Kentucky as did this brief, sharp announcement on the morning of January 30, [1900] that told in a flash that the strain had been broken with a crime.

The bare mention of the fact conveyed almost a picture to one's imagination—Goebel, within hand's reach of his prize; composed, wary and steeled to act relentlessly at the proper moment—some one with his brain on fire—the shot!

The whole country had been keyed up to the news of the awful deed of wrath by the fascination that attends the play of a master hand in delivering a master stroke. The fight of Senator Goebel to win the governorship had seemed decisive and effective in almost every step of its progress before the legislature. Poised upon the parapet of the besieged citadel of his opponent, he had seemed prepared to cry with the next clock-work move of a mystic destiny—not sooner, not later— "I have it!"

"Who fired the shot?" That was the first question the news brought out.

If possible, the curiosity about this was as instant as the shock produced by the fact of the shooting.

"No one knows!" Nor did any one know a month after— nor two months after that.

No one was certain that he saw the shot fired. There were several shots heard, but Senator Goebel dropped down beside the fountain in the wide statehouse yard, picked off from somewhere by a marksman with true aim. The assassin fired from the executive building, said some one. Several persons were out and about when the shot was fired. One was only a few steps from him. Senator Goebel was seen to fall and quiver, while groans of agony broke from his lately sphinx-like lips; but no one was sure that he could point to the source of the bullets that rattled against the bricks of the walk that led up to the frowning front of the ancient capitol.

Everywhere there was discussion of the deed.

"Somebody got him!"

"Yes, they say he can't live!"

"Likely to be trouble."

"Yes; lot's of desperate people on both sides up at Frankfort. Soldiers called out."

"Bet somebody gets Taylor."

"Maybe."

"How will it end?"

The legislature was already in session. The house was plodding away at some minor matters, the minority on edge for the next move that might be forced on the contests. The senate was droning, nothing doing, Senator Goebel, to whom the majority looked for its command, being late.

In at one of the gates of the almost deserted square hurried three men, one somewhat in advance of the other two. That was Warden Eph Lillard of the penitentiary. The others were Senator Goebel and his close champion, Jack Chinn. As they proceeded up the walk Lillard forged ahead and Chinn dropped behind slightly, being something of a heavyweight and winded by his walk from the hotel. He was the most immediate witness of the wounding of his leader, and told it in these words:

"As I could not walk rapidly, Goebel fell back with me, while Lillard walked about 30 yards ahead of us through the yard toward the state building. No conversation occurred between us, so far as I can remember. I was on Goebel's right, and he was about two feet ahead of me when the first shot was fired. The fountain is in the center of the pavement, about 60 feet in front of the broad steps of the state building. When we were about half way between the fountain and the steps I heard the report of a rifle.

"At almost the same instant Goebel bent double, groaned harshly, clutched at his right side, fell to his knees. I said:

" 'My God! Goebel, they have killed you,' but was a little too far away to catch him.

" 'I guess they have,' he said as he was falling.

"He fell to his right and then forward, rolling over on his back. I think his right knee struck the pavement first. He raised in a moment as if to get up on his elbow, when I said:

" 'Lie still, Goebel, or they might shoot you again.'

"The first shot struck Goebel and it was fired from one of the upper floors of the executive building, just east of the general assembly building, to which we were going.

"The first shot was followed in quick succession by four others, and I heard the bullets hum by me and over the body of Goebel. I am of the opinion that the second shot was fired from a side window, while the first was fired from a front window. It is my impression that they were rifle shots.

"I looked for the shots, trying to locate exactly where they came from. Everybody seemed to keep away except Eph Lillard and Representative Owen Cochran. I called out: 'Won't somebody come and help carry Goebel away?' when the crowd rushed up.

"Mr. Lillard was almost in the door ahead of us when the shooting occurred. He turned and came running to Goebel's side, while Owen Cochran came up at the same time. These men and others picked him up and started with him to the hotel.

"I thought they had killed Goebel instantly when he fell. The blow seemed to stun him and his eyes were set. I thought he was gone."

JOE JORDAN

*L*YNCHING *was one of the South's greatest tragedies. By 1900 this practice had reached proportions of anarchy in some parts of the region. Law enforcement frequently was exercised by irresponsible and fiendish mobs who ignored established courts and meted out justice in their own barbarous ways. Few of these mobs met with any real resistance from elected officers, and still fewer of them were ever identified and brought into court for trial.*

Kentucky generally escaped the bloodletting which occurred in the Lower South. In 1920, however, Petrie Kimbrough (1889-1920), alias Will Lockett, a Negro, murdered a ten-year-old white girl at South Elkhorn in Fayette County. News of this tragedy spread like wildfire. A mob was formed to take the Negro away from the sheriff, but it was thwarted when Lockett was hustled off to Frankfort penitentiary. When he was brought to trial in Lexington, the town was crowded with highly excited persons who expressed a determination to lynch the boy. There was said to be mobsters from the Lower South who had come to show the local boys how to hold a good lynching. In this frantic moment of excitement the governor appealed to the United States Army for aid. The First Division of regular troops was sent to Lexington, and in a short time order was restored. Veteran soldiers with machine guns were not cowardly southern sheriffs, and rowdy lynchers were not anxious to receive hot blasts of lead. Justice was done in the courtroom. In his essay, "Lynchers Don't Like Lead," in the Atlantic Monthly *for February, 1946, Joe Jordan (1901-   ), then city editor of the Lexington* Leader, *described this interesting case where for the first time a lynching bee was headed off by the use of troops.*

The Folly of a Few

TWENTY-SIX years ago, on February 9, 1920, a mob at Lexington, Kentucky, bent upon lynching a Negro who was on trial for murdering a white child, charged the Fayette County courthouse. The members of the mob, all white men, were fired upon and repulsed by white soldiers and white civil officers. Six men were killed and fifty or more were wounded. Of the hundreds of newspapers throughout the United States which hastened to praise Fayette County officials for their somewhat astonishing stand against mob violence, many pointed out, as did the *Brooklyn Eagle* in a typical comment, that the Lexington incident marked "the first time south of Mason and Dixon's line that any mob of this sort had actually met the volley fire of soldiers."

At the time, a number of the writers of editorials indicated a cautious belief and hope that the "Second Battle of Lexington" might mark a turning point in the method of dealing with mobs. It now appears that they were right. In 1919, mobs had lynched eighty-three persons in the United States. That figure has not been approached since the Lexington mob was dealt with so vigorously. In 1944, there were only two lynchings in the entire country. To avoid the danger of selecting by chance two unusual years, it is safer to consider five-year averages. In the five years preceding 1920, mobs had lynched an average of sixty-one victims a year; in the five years preceding 1945, lynchings averaged fewer than four a year.

A decisive encounter between determined officers and a determined mob was bound to occur sometime. It occurred at Lexington, that February day in 1920, because the mob picked the wrong town for a lynching party. Fayette County had not seen a lynching in fifty years. It didn't see one then, and it hasn't seen one since. Thousands of outsiders flocked to Lexington on the day of the trial, and some Alabamians who arrived the day before, disclosed to reporters that they had made the long trip to have a part in the expected lynching. They misjudged the temper and underestimated the courage of the county officials, who had issued plain warnings that anyone attempting to take the prisoner from them would be killed.

Will Lockett, the Negro who was to be tried, had killed a ten-year-old white girl at South Elkhorn, in the southern section of Fayette County. It was a revolting crime. The child had been seized when she was walking to a country school less than 400 yards from her home. She had been dragged into a cornfield and there her skull had been crushed by repeated savage blows with a large rock. Her body, half hidden under a fodder shock, had been found after she failed to appear at school.

Lockett, a World War I veteran who still was wearing his Army uniform, had left a country store in the neighborhood shortly before the crime was committed, and was suspected immediately. He was found six hours later, six miles away. A doctor and two other civilians who captured him took him to

Lexington hurriedly, for they feared a mob would form and they wanted to get him into the hands of the law.

At Lexington police headquarters, Lockett confessed promptly. He was removed to the county jail, but almost at once the officers decided it would be safer to take him to the state penitentiary at Frankfort. When he was led out of the jail, a crowd already was beginning to form in the street, but it was not large enough to menace the officers who had him in charge, and within an hour he was behind the walls of the Frankfort prison.

As news of the crime spread, the crowd in front of the jail increased, and by dark it numbered several hundred. Its members refused to accept the jailer's statement that Lockett had been taken to Frankfort. There is a traditional procedure in such cases, and it was followed. The jailer consented to admit a committee to search the jail and inspect the prisoners. The committee, which included a farmer by whom Lockett had been employed, looked into the faces of all the frightened Negroes in the jail and went out to assure the crowd that Lockett was not there.

Of course, there have been many similar cases in which the wrong man has been identified and dragged out, but the Negroes in the Lexington jail were lucky that night. The mob then went to police headquarters, where a similar search was permitted. Convinced that Lockett had been taken to Frankfort, the mob's leaders attempted to charter interurban electric cars for the trip to the state capital, but traction-company officials refused to accommodate them, and approximately three hundred men set out in automobiles.

The late Edwin P. Morrow, then Governor of Kentucky, was informed by telephone that the mob was on its way to Frankfort. He acted with characteristic vigor. One hundred special deputies, armed with shotguns and rifles, were sent to the penitentiary to reinforce the regular guards there. Governor Morrow took charge at the prison gate.

Meanwhile Sheriff Bain Moore of Franklin County had taken

a force of men to the outskirts of Frankfort, on the Lexington
Pike. He stopped the first cars in the caravan from Lexington,
had them turned crosswise of the road to establish a blockade,
and warned the mob members that they would meet certain
death if they attempted to remove the prisoner from the penitentiary. Most of the men turned back. A few who got past
the sheriff's barricade were arrested on Governor Morrow's
order when they appeared at the prison gate.

The crime was committed and Lockett was arrested on
Wednesday, February 4. A Fayette County grand jury indicted
Lockett the next day on a murder charge, and his trial was set
for the following Monday, only five days after the slaying.

Everybody realized that a serious situation could develop
when Lockett was returned to Lexington for the trial. Circuit
Judge Charles Kerr and County Judge Frank A. Bullock—in
Kentucky the county judge is the administrative head of the
county government—conferred with other county officials, with
Mayor Thomas C. Bradley of Lexington, and with Governor
Morrow. It was decided that there would be no running away
from the issue by postponing the trial to a secret date or ordering a change of venue. Governor Morrow promised a company
of state troops from Campbell County, in northern Kentucky.

It was admitted that the public did not have so much respect for "Home Guards" as for the Regular Army soldiers,
and the officials looked longingly toward Camp Taylor, less
than a hundred miles away, where the crack First Division
Regulars, veterans of World War I, were stationed. The Governor could not obtain Federal troops, however, without cer-
tifying that a state of lawlessness existed with which the state
authority was unable to cope.

In the interval between Lockett's arrest and his trial, the
Lexington newspapers pleaded for peace and order. Negro
organizations adopted resolutions "condemning the horrible
outrage" and demanding that the guilty member of their race
"be punished promptly and adequately." A group of South
Elkhorn residents met Saturday afternoon at the courthouse

and issued an appeal by T. L. Hardman, brother of the slain girl, which was carried in both Lexington newspapers Sunday morning.

"As a brother of Geneva Hardman, who was murdered by Will Lockett, and as a representative of her family," he said, "I request all of our friends and all those who sympathize with us not to indulge in any violence or create any disturbance when he is brought here for trial. The authorities have acted promptly, the man is under arrest, he has been indicted promptly and his trial fixed for Monday. I feel sure that a prompt and speedy trial will take place and that any jury impaneled will find him guilty and punish him adequately for the horrible crime he has committed. . . . I would hate to see the life of any other person endangered as the result of violence by reason of conflict over a brute like this, and I therefore urge all citizens, for the good name of the county and in the interest of law and order, to do nothing to interfere with the orderly processes of the law."

In an editorial headed, "Let the Law Take Its Course," the *Lexington Leader* commented: "If this bereaved brother can assume such an attitude at this time, certainly those who sympathize so deeply with him can afford to await calmly the verdict of the jury. . . . The people of Fayette County can afford to let the law take its course in this case. They cannot afford to incur the just criticism of the people of the nation which would follow a resort to mob rule." The *Lexington Herald* advanced similar arguments. Sunday morning the congregation of the South Elkhorn Christian Church, composed entirely of neighbors of the murdered child, adopted a resolution calling for orderly administration of the law. Every effort was being made to prepare the public for the crisis expected on Monday.

These appeals appeared to have had the desired effect in Fayette County itself. In a news story the day before the trial, the *Herald* reported: "Indignation on the part of the citizens last night turned into determination that the law should take its course." The *Leader* found that "the mob spirit, which was prevalent immediately after the atrocity was committed, has died down and has been replaced by a willingness to let the law take its course." The *Leader* added, however, that there had been "reports that other counties would send delegations here to 'get' Lockett."

Both newspapers repeatedly assured the public that there could be but one outcome of the trial—speedy conviction and a death sentence. Said a *Leader* news story: "It is anticipated that if Lockett is sentenced to be electrocuted, as it is generally believed he will be, the same military protection will be given him while he is on his way to the penitentiary where the electrocution will take place. . . . It is thought the trial will be a speedy one. After the jury is chosen, the actual trial ought to be over in a very short time." Thus it was hoped to make clear to the public that the issue was not whether Lockett would be punished, but whether the punishment would be carried out lawfully or by a mob.

Adjutant General J. M. Deweese, who was to be in charge of the state troops, issued a brief, forceful warning: "The responsibility for any bloodshed at this trial will rest on those who disregard their duty as citizens and attempt to take the law out of the hands of the constituted authorities." Fayette County Sheriff J. Waller Rodes, who had hurried home from a business trip to Texas to take charge of the county's defense measures, said, "Under no circumstances will the prisoner be taken away from the guards."

At one o'clock Monday morning, the day of the trial, police began stretching steel cables in the empty streets, to keep spectators at a distance from the courthouse. The lines were no more than boundary markers, since it would be easy enough to slip through them. At 3:45 A.M., a special train arrived from Frankfort, bringing Sheriff Rodes, General Deweese, the prisoner, and the state troops. The train stopped before it reached Union Station, and the soldiers marched two blocks with their prisoner and entered the courthouse without incident.

By seven o'clock, a crowd had begun to form on Main Street,

in front of the courthouse. It grew rapidly. The trial had been set for nine o'clock. When that hour approached, there were immense crowds on the Main Street and Short Street sides of the building, but officers kept everyone outside the cables except officials, prospective jurors, newsmen, and just enough spectators to fill the courtroom.

The approach to the main entrance of the courthouse is by broad flights of stone steps which lead to the second floor. All ground-floor entrances had been barred. The first flight of front steps ends at a level landing which runs off to the right and left to connect with walks from Upper Street and Cheapside, at an elevation higher than the Main Street sidewalk and the front lawn. Soldiers were stationed behind the stone parapet around the front of this landing. A machine gun had been set up on the landing. At the top of the highest flight of steps, just inside the wide front doors, were more soldiers with rifles and deputies with shotguns. Soldiers also had been stationed in various offices in the building, at open windows commanding the steps.

The defense setup appeared to be adequate. Men attempting to reach the front doors would have to get through the cable barrier (which would not be difficult, but would separate them from the crowd), then cross a bare, level space approaching the steps, and mount the steps in the face of fire from the protected soldiers, who had been posted in positions that would enable them to sweep the steps with rifle and machine-gun fire. That it would be the height of folly to attempt to storm such a position, any man of judgment could see—but mobs are not made up of men of judgment.

The crowd that surrounded the courthouse square was estimated by some observers to number 8,000 to 10,000. Such guesses usually are high. A conservative estimate would be 5,000 to 6,000. Of these, comparatively few were there with any serious idea of attempting to take the prisoner out of the courthouse. Most of them had come out of curiosity, half hoping, perhaps, that they would see fighting. University of

Kentucky students (I was one of them) had left the campus in droves, flocking to the downtown district to share in the excitement, in spite of repeated warnings for all peaceful citizens to stay out of the danger zone. The authorities had pointed out that spectators would be in as much danger as participants if a battle developed. Many lookers-on were in a nervously jovial mood, exchanging jokes about how fast they would run if shooting started.

Presently people began to point out a man with a coil of rope over his left shoulder. He pushed his way forward to the cable, at a point directly in front of the steps. In addition to the ones who appeared to be in his party, other grim-faced men began sifting through the crowd and gathering around him. The merely curious spectators who happened to be in that vicinity dropped back and were replaced by additional angry, cursing men who "meant business."

Thus the nucleus of the mob was formed. It appeared to be unplanned, this concentration. Naturally, the ones who actually considered rushing the courthouse would gather at the spot from which the charge would have to start, and as they got together and bolstered one another's courage, perhaps no one of them wanted to appear cowardly before his fellows and so they all persuaded themselves that the thing could be done, that the civil officers and soldiers would not dare shoot white men to protect a Negro murderer.

The courthouse clock struck nine times. Everybody realized that if anything was to be done, it would have to be done soon. The threats and cursing became louder up near the barrier, while those in the background ceased their joking, suddenly aware that the situation might turn dangerous after all.

Inside the courthouse, as we were to learn later from the newspapers, the trial started promptly. Judge Kerr was on the bench. Every seat in the courtroom was filled, but no one was allowed to stand in the spectators' section, behind the rail. In front of the rail, in the space reserved for jurors, attorneys, and court officials, a few men were standing, among them County

Judge Bullock. Lockett sat at the defense table, surrounded
by four deputies. The bailiff rapped for order, pounding his
gavel on a desk across which he had laid an automatic shotgun.

As had been predicted, the trial proceeded with a minimum
of delay. A jury was selected quickly. The only question asked
each prospective juror was whether he had any conscientious
scruples against the death penalty. The court had appointed
two leading members of the bar as defense counsel, George R.
Hunt and Colonel Samuel M. Wilson. Mr. Hunt filed a de-
murrer to the indictment, explaining that he was doing it "as
a matter of form," but that the indictment appeared to be
properly drawn.

Asked whether he wished to plead guilty or not guilty, Lockett mumbled a reply inaudible to the spectators. "Defendant
pleads guilty, your Honor," the clerk announced.

Only one witness testified, a man who established the fact
of the child's death and told of finding her with a heavy stone
on her face. The defendant did not take the stand. Colonel
Wilson read Lockett's honorable discharge from the Army,
which stated that his character was "very good," and then read
a statement in which the defendant asked for a life sentence.
"I know I do not deserve mercy," it said, "but I am sorry I
committed the crime and I would give anything if the little
girl could be brought back to life."

Colonel John R. Allen, Commonwealth's Attorney, made a
brief prosecution argument to the jury. "In all the history of
crime in the United States," he said, "there has been none to
equal this in cruelty. In the name of the law, and of the little
girl who was murdered, I ask you to act quickly, and suggest
that you return a verdict without leaving the jury box."

While this was taking place in the courtroom, the crowd in
the street became more restive. A deputy sheriff engaged in a
brief fist fight with a man who had crawled under the cable
barrier, and the man was dragged away by two policemen. A
newsreel cameraman had been admitted to a cleared space on
the lawn and had set up his camera near the equestrian statue

of Confederate General John Hunt Morgan. He had taken pictures of the soldiers and the crowd, but apparently he wanted something showing action or emotion. "Shake your fists and yell!" he called out to the nearest spectators. They obligingly did so.

The people who shook their fists and yelled to please the cameraman were just outside the cable barrier, but they were a hundred foot or so east of the nucleus of the real mob. Their action, however, was like a spark in the highly charged atmosphere. It was answered by a roar from the mob—a savage, bestial roar. I was not to hear anything like it again until the radio carried to America the roars with which a Nazi mob responded to an impassioned harangue by Hitler on the eve of Munich.

Men in the forefront of the mob hoisted the cables and went under them quickly, as if the shouts had been a signal. The man with the rope was among the leaders.

General Deweese had taken a stand in an open space at the approach to the first flight of steps. His men had orders not to shoot unless he fired his revolver twice into the air. As the leaders of the charge approached the General, he backed about twenty steps, pistol in hand. When they reached him, he grappled with two of them, and struck one over the head with the pistol. The others surged around him and in a moment had mounted the first flight of steps and reached the landing. They bowled over a machine gunner and kicked his gun aside.

Deweese fired the two signal shots, and a withering volley was discharged. Men piled up on the steps, some wounded, others dropping to escape the bullets. A dozen or more who had passed the landing before the firing began rushed on up the remaining steps to the front doors, but turned back and ran when the soldiers and deputies who had been stationed inside the doors surged out with rifles and shotguns pointed at them.

The one burst of firing, which lasted only a few seconds, had halted the mob, and the soldiers held their fire. Some witnesses

estimated that as many as fifty shots had been fired by members
of the mob at the defenders of the courthouse; others denied it.
That there was some firing from the mob was certain, for three
policemen and one soldier were wounded, and today there
are still chipped places where bullets struck the stone front of
the courthouse.

All the merely curious spectators—except the ones who had
been hit—broke and ran as soon as the firing started. The
action-seeking cameraman, lugging his camera, tripod and all,
sped past many of them before they reached Limestone Street,
a block east. (For some strange reason, almost everyone ran
east, even those who had been standing west of the steps.) The
number of spectators hit never was determined accurately.
Some of the soldiers said later that they had fired over the
heads of the mob leaders who were mounting the steps. Their
bullets went into the crowd or shattered store windows across
the street. At least one man was fatally injured, who had been
standing backed up against a store front on the opposite side
of Main Street. A woman clerk inside a store was struck in the
ankle by a bullet.

Of those who had fallen on the steps, the uninjured and
slightly injured crawled away, and the others were carried
away. One man was taken to a doctor's office near-by and died
there within a few minutes. Four others died at hospitals before midnight. The sixth victim died several days later.

Twenty-one wounded persons were treated at hospitals. The
newspapers said "scores" were treated at drugstores for less
serious injuries, such as being peppered by nearly spent buck-
shot or being knocked down and trampled. Fearing prosecution, several members of the mob who were shot were reported
to have been taken home by friends. Avoiding hospitals, they
were treated by their physicians, and no reports were made.
That as many as fifty were wounded appears to be a conservative estimate.

In the courtroom, Colonel Allen was making the closing
statement to the jury when the crowd's roar was heard, followed

by firing. "It's started!" several spectators shouted, leaping to their feet. Deputies pointed pistols and commanded them to sit down. The trial proceeded.

The jurors quickly reached the expected verdict—death. Lockett was called around and Judge Kerr stood to pronounce sentence. At that moment an excited man ran into the court-room and shouted, "Judge, you better let 'em have the nigger! They're going to tear the courthouse down if you don't!"

Again the deputies pointed their pistols and Colonel Allen— not an honorary but a military colonel, to whom it would be no new experience to be under fire—calmly counseled the crowd in the courtroom to remain seated. Judge Kerr as calmly proceeded with the sentencing, specifying that Lockett should die March 11 in the electric chair at Eddyville Penitentiary and concluding, "May the God of All Mercy have mercy on your soul."

Down in the street, as soon as the first shock was over and the mob members grasped the unbelievable fact that the officers and soldiers actually had fired upon them, had wounded many, and probably had killed a number of them, a cry for vengeance went up. Now they wanted not the prisoner alone, but the men who had stood up against them. Crowds broke for the pawnshops, seeking weapons. Several farsighted pawnbrokers had had their places locked all day, the doors barred and the windows shuttered.

Two shops were open. Joe Rosenberg later reported to police that "forty or fifty" pistols had been taken from his shop; Harry Skuller said he had been robbed of "fifty or sixty" weapons. Boxes of cartridges were picked up along with the pistols. (Later, the two pawnbrokers wasted money on news-paper advertisements appealing for the return of their prop-erty. Not a single one of the "borrowed" weapons ever was recovered.)

The shooting had cleared out all the idlers, and the surly crowd that milled around in front of the courthouse was now composed exclusively of those who "meant business." As the news spread, more and more armed men arrived and the situation, to all appearances, was worse than it had been before the shooting. There were reports that dynamite had been sent for, that the courthouse would be blown up, that a special train loaded with mountaineers from eastern Kentucky was on the way to Lexington.

Unknown to the mob was the fact that Governor Morrow had decided he now could certify truthfully to Federal authorities that there existed a state of lawlessness with which the state authority was unable to cope. The First Division Regulars had entrained at Camp Taylor and were on their way to Lexington.

The shooting had begun at 9:28 A.M. Then came the raids on pawnshops and the arrival of reinforcements for the mob. During the succeeding hours, one of the *Leader's* numerous extra editions related, "The courthouse was besieged by increasing numbers of armed men, who displayed an increasingly threatening attitude." By General Deweese's order, Judge Kerr, Judge Bullock, and other county officials remained inside the building, for by that time they were as much the objects of the mob's wrath as the prisoner himself. Lockett sat in a prisoners' lockup adjacent to the courtroom, handcuffed, with his head bowed. He had taken little apparent interest in the trial, and barely had raised his head when he heard the firing outside the building.

As the day wore on, tension increased minute by minute and the besieging force steadily grew larger, but the leaders of the mob bided their time. There were reports that they were waiting for dynamite, that they were waiting for reinforcements, that they were waiting for darkness so they could shoot out the street lights and overwhelm the defenders of the building. The strain was beginning to tell on the "Home Guards," many of whom were teen-age boys whose previous military experience had been confined to drilling one night a week in a National Guard armory. They looked frightened.

Finally, at 3:20 P.M., the special train from Camp Taylor steamed through the yards and stopped at Mill and Water Streets, only two blocks from the courthouse, but out of sight of the mob. Out of the coaches poured streams of battle-hardened veterans, who quickly fell in and marched north on Mill Street with bayonets fixed. Leading them was a color guard bearing the United States flag, a banner which in the sixties often had been carried into Lexington to the accompaniment of despairing groans from the town's leading citizens.

Lexington during the War Between the States had been a Confederate stronghold in a border state. It had been captured and recaptured, and had lived alternately under the United States and Confederate States flags. Now it was being occupied again, but there were no groans that day from the leading citizens as the Regulars executed a smart turn into Main Street and bore down upon the mob, with the Stars and Stripes at the head of the column. Indeed, one of the beleaguered county officials peering out of the courthouse windows—a man who, like most of us Kentuckians, had been taught from childhood to take pride in being an Unreconstructed Rebel—laughingly admitted later that he had been somewhat astonished to hear himself shouting, "That's the prettiest flag I ever saw!"

The soldiers moved steadily east on Main Street and swept the mob before them. No shots were fired from either side. Here and there an occasional inflamed individual attempted to put up an argument and was cracked over the head with a rifle butt; now and then a sullen straggler was hurried along by a light prick with a bayonet point. But for the most part the men who had been so bloodthirsty instantly lost interest in fighting and took to their heels. Magically, within five minutes, all streets approaching the courthouse had been cleared. Khaki-clad sharpshooters looked over the eaves of all structures in sight of the county building.

Never did a city submit more happily to invading forces

than Lexington surrendered that day to the United States troops. Martial law was declared, and the citizens marveled at the efficiency with which the soldiers took charge. Twelve patrols were organized and assigned headquarters. As darkness approached, soldiers began patrolling Negro districts, the tobacco-warehouse district,—which had been threatened because the sheriff and several other county officeholders were interested financially in the warehouses,—and the Union Station, to guard against the expected arrival of the mountaineers, which never came to pass.

Another place that needed guarding was the ROTC Armory at the University of Kentucky, which contained hundreds of rifles and thousands of rounds of ammunition. Twice during the day, members of the mob had made unsuccessful attempts to enter it. Directly across Limestone Street from the campus was a fire-department station, which an Army captain selected as convenient headquarters for his patrol. To his request that the station be kept open all night, a surly fire-department captain replied that he intended to lock up the lower floor and retire with his men to the dormitory above. The fireman was arrested and hustled off to jail. The military was in charge, and before long that fact was impressed upon all citizens, whether or not they sympathized with the mob.

The next day Brigadier General Francis C. Marshall, commanding the U. S. troops, summarized Monday's events in a terse statement: "This community has set fine example against Bolshevism and lawlessness and has killed several of its own citizens in upholding law and order."

"Folly's Harvest of Sorrow" was the heading over a *Leader* editorial the day after the riot. It said in part: "The folly of a few men, maddened for the moment by a spirit of revenge, seeking the life of a miserable creature at the very instant condemned to die for his crime, compelled the servants of the law to fire upon a mob in Lexington Monday morning. The majesty of the law was upheld, but at frightful cost."

The *Herald* expressed sympathy for the families of the victims, but added that "there is pride that the law was protected, that the officers of the law observed their solemn oath both to execute and to defend the law." It said the affair proved two facts: that the guilty would be punished surely and swiftly, and that "he who attempts to violate the law goes to meet death."

Jere Reagan, Chief of Police, commented: "There can be no question as to the absolute necessity of firing. Those who forced their way through the lines meant business. I am sorry innocent persons have been killed, but enough warning had been given."

Further evidence that General Marshall was the law in Fayette County was given Thursday, when he directed Judge Kerr to summon a special grand jury to investigate the law violations that had occurred Monday, and to indict the guilty persons. The jury commissioners selected what was recognized immediately as a "hand-picked" grand jury, composed of citizens who would not hesitate to indict the mob members. A week later, this jury was discharged, since it appeared that any indictments the body voted probably would be thrown out of court because the names of the jurors had not been drawn by chance from the jury wheel in the usual manner.

A new jury was drawn from the wheel. It heard witnesses and reported that the members of the mob were "mostly from other counties than Fayette, who were there for the avowed purpose of rescuing the prisoner from the authorities." It called the bloody riot "an unfortunate affair," and concluded that it would be unwise to return indictments, since the subsequent trials "would only tend to aggravate an already tense situation."

"Here we find a new principle injected into the processes of the law," the *Leader* declared in a bitter editorial. "Officers of the law, instead of seeking to punish the guilty and acquit the innocent, must first determine whether the trials of men presumably guilty of serious crimes and misdemeanors would disturb the public mind and 'tend to aggravate bitter feelings in the state.' " There the matter rested.

Lockett had been taken out of Lexington Tuesday night, under the protection of 400 soldiers. No attempt was made to sneak the prisoner out of town. The soldiers openly marched through the streets with him to the Union Station. Thirty-two officers and 472 soldiers remained in Lexington to maintain order. This force was reduced gradually until, on February 22, thirteen days after the riot, General Marshall proclaimed an end to martial rule, "law and order having been restored."

Lockett died in the electric chair at Eddyville Penitentiary on March 11, in the presence of nineteen Fayette County witnesses, including two brothers of his victim. Three days before the execution, he confessed the slaying of four women, one in Indiana, one in Illinois, and two in Kentucky, all by choking. Thus the child he killed in Fayette County had been his fifth victim.

The Kentucky General Assembly, which was in session in Frankfort when the Lexington riot occurred, enacted a law changing the penalty for rape from death in the electric chair to public hanging in the county in which the crime had been committed. Presumably the theory was that the mob lust for vengeance would be appeased by a convenient outdoor hanging which all could witness. A number of revolting exhibitions were staged under this law. The type of persons attracted to such events enjoyed themselves so thoroughly and behaved so atrociously that the law was repealed. Any effort to appease the mob spirit probably was unnecessary, anyway; the Second Battle of Lexington appeared to have dampened Kentuckians' ardor for lynching parties.

HENRY WATTERSON

BLUEGRASS Kentuckians, noted for their generosity and tolerance, at times were driven to the end of their rope. When all else had failed, they minced no words in directing the object of their distaste. Henry Watterson (1840-1921), in one of his shortest editorials for the Louisville Courier-Journal, *on September 3, 1914, let go a blast at the Hohenzollerns and Hapsburgs that was almost as explosive as the tragic shot at Sarajevo. Herman Ridder (1851-1915), editor of the New York* Staats-Zeitung, *shared in the volley for his apologist stand on Germany. This editorial was republished many times—and soundly denounced for its profanity by various church papers—in those troubled autumn days when Europe caught on fire with World War I.*

To Hell

Herman Ridder flings Japan at us. Then he adduces Russia. What does he think now of Turkey? How can he reconcile the Kaiser's ostentatious appeal to the Children of Christ and his pretentious partnership with God—"Meinself und Gott"—with his calling the hordes of Mahomet to his aid? Will not this unite all Christendom against the unholy combine? May Heaven protect the Vaterland from contamination and give the German people a chance! To Hell with the Hohenzollerns and the Hapsburgs!

ABOUT THE EDITOR

For a quarter of a century Thomas D. Clark, a native of Mississippi, has been associated with the University of Kentucky department of history, which he now heads. During that time he has become an outstanding historian of the South, the frontier, and Kentucky, and has gained a reputation which has led to his election to the presidency of the Southern Historical Association (1947) and of the Mississippi Valley Historical Association (1956-1957).

A graduate of the University of Mississippi, Mr. Clark holds an M.A. degree from the University of Kentucky and a Ph.D. degree from Duke University. He is the author or editor of many books and articles, including the standard textbook of Kentucky history. For four years (1948-1952) he was managing editor of the *Journal of Southern History*. To the people of the state, however, he is best known as a colorful speaker and an indefatigable collector of Kentuckiana. Samples of his informal style, distinguished by apt, picturesque figures of speech, have, at the insistence of the publishers, been included in this book.

ABOUT THE BOOK

Bluegrass Cavalcade was composed and printed in the University of Kentucky printing plant. It is set in Linotype Baskerville, with headings in Ludlow Eusebius and ATF Garamond. The book is printed on Warren's Olde Style antique wove paper and bound, by the Von Hoffmann Press of St. Louis, in Columbia's Bradford buckram cloth.

www.ingramcontent.com/pod-product-compliance
Lightning Source LLC
Chambersburg PA
CBHW030934020726
47498CB00001B/236